THE LONG HITCH HOME

THE LONG
HITCH HOME

Jamie Maslin

Skyhorse Publishing

Skyhorse Publishing books may be purchased in bulk at special discounts for sales promotion, corporate gifts, fund-raising, or educational purposes. Special editions can also be created to specifications. For details, contact the Special Sales Department, Skyhorse Publishing, 307 West 36th Street, 11th Floor, New York, NY 10018 or info@skyhorsepublishing.com.

Skyhorse® and Skyhorse Publishing® are registered trademarks of Skyhorse Publishing, Inc.®, a Delaware corporation.

Visit our website at www.skyhorsepublishing.com.

10 9 8 7 6 5 4 3 2 1

Library of Congress Cataloging-in-Publication Data is available on file.

Print ISBN: 978-1-62087-831-6
Ebook ISBN: 978-1-63220-033-4

Cover designer: Anthony Morais
Cover photo credit: Thinkstock

Printed in the United States of America

for
Emily

ACKNOWLEDGEMENTS

There are many people who deserve a special mention for their help during the creation of this book. I wish to express my gratitude to all of the many wonderful and varied people (over eight hundred) who so kindly gave me a ride during my long hitch home; to Danilo Gärtner, Owen Coomber, Wim Vanderstok, Ethan Martin, Wolfgang Glowacki, Jessica Nilsson, Manon Margain and Etienne Margain for providing many of the beautiful photographs used to illustrate this book. As always a special thank you must go out to Lucas Hunt: agent, gentleman, poet, friend; for his encouragement during the writing process and staggering patience in waiting for delivery of a long overdue manuscript. Above all, I must thank my amazing wife Emily, for her belief in me and my writing, and for paying my share of the rent during this long, drawn-out creative process.

In the interests of protecting anonymity, certain names and minor details have been strategically altered in the text.

There's a voice that keeps on calling me
Down the road, that's where I'll always be.
Every stop I make, I make a new friend
Can't stay for long, just turn around and I'm gone again.
Maybe tomorrow, I'll want to settle down,
Until tomorrow, I'll just keep moving on.

—The Littlest Hobo

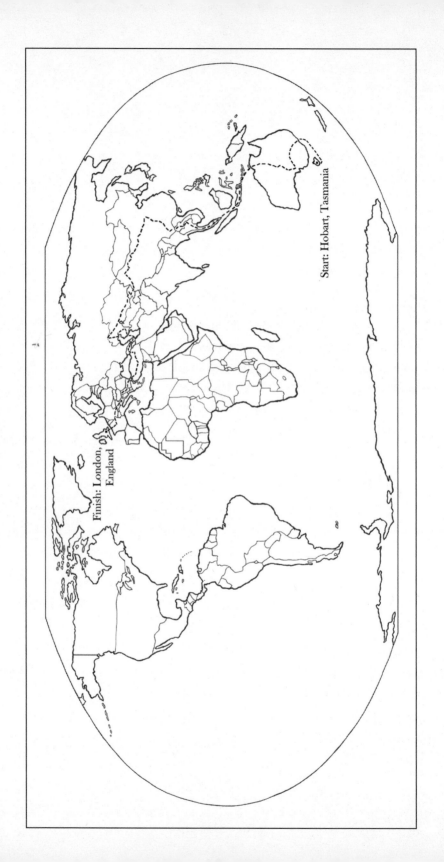

Start: Hobart, Tasmania

Finish: London, England

CONTENTS

PROLOGUE

The shrill of a military ambulance siren jolted me from my slumber as if I'd been punched squarely in the face. In an instant we were all on high alert, jumping from our seats inside the dank Red Cross field hospital, hastily preparing for the vehicle's arrival.

"Go! Go! Go!" yelled someone outside.

Grabbing my helmet I ran down the aisle between two rows of steel-framed beds and collided with a petite nurse fixing a bandage around a soldier's bloodied head, knocking her to her knees. There was no time for apologies. I powered through, running past battered soldiers and a barely human-looking corpse that had been dumped unceremoniously near an ammunition box. My heart pounded in my chest. I hoped I wouldn't be the one who made a critical error this time.

Forcing my way through the tent's heavy fabric, I stepped into a torrent tearing apart the earth, creating ankle-high pools of muddy slop. Within moments the obese droplets had soaked me through. The rain fell with an unnatural intensity, the likes of which I had never experienced before. I shivered.

Seconds later the ambulance skidded to a halt, slewing sideways and throwing a vile spray in its wake. Two medics reached it first. Wrenching open its rear doors with a critical urgency, they hauled out a stretcher holding a motionless form.

A primal wailing came from inside the vehicle.

I reached the ambulance and stuck my head in.

Three bloodied casualties remained. The nearest cried out, clutching what looked like a bullet wound to the abdomen. He would have to walk. Supporting him as best I could we hobbled inside the tent, just in time to see a fellow medic pretending to have sex with the corpse.

We burst out laughing.

"Cut!" shouted the director.

It was my third day on set as an extra, a job I was doing not out of love for the silver screen but for some quick hard cash while I was working out what to do with my life. Today I had been given the part of a Second World War medic. The day before it was a U.S. Marine, the week before that a British P.O.W.

All was not going well.

This particular scene, shot in the clearing of a pine forest in southern England, was battering us into submission. It had taken most of the morning and countless retakes. By now all involved were soaking from the rain machine suspended from a crane above the set, and were more than ready for a hot drink and a bacon sandwich. It would be a long time coming.

"Do you know how much it costs every time one of you fucks this up?" yelled Rupert, an Assistant Director.

He was fresh out of school—an expensive one—and rumor had it only got the job through family connections. He was the least-liked person on set, and competition was running high for that accolade.

"Move over to the ambulance and stay put until I tell you!" he yelled at the extras in the tent. He accompanied his demand by giving those within arm's reach a slight push as they went past.

Could he be any more condescending?

Yes.

"Chop, chop. Quick as you can, I don't have all day!" he added.

But then he manhandled the wrong person.

A big, muscled, no-nonsense ex-army corporal—a real one just playing the part of a medic on set—spun around and eye-balled Rupert with real venom.

"Don't touch me, boy!" he asserted in an uncompromising military tone that superseded Rupert's tenuous authority. "Why do you touch people as they walk past? Are we incapable of reaching a point fifty feet away without you physically guiding us in the line of travel, or do you just have a thing about feeling up strangers?!"

My heart warmed to him immediately.

Rupert went white. The threat of real violence was in the air.

He might have had a fancy-sounding job title, but in reality Rupert was the lowliest of the multiple Assistant Directors on set, being a so-called third AD, one step up from the starting job in film—a production assistant or "runner"—and so was hardly in a position to sack the guy.

Rupert stared at the ground, squirmed uncomfortably, then backed down.

"Sorry," was all he could muster in a meek voice.

I never saw him touch another extra.

It was another couple of hours before we got the scene right and made it back to the expansive catering tent. The place was heaving with a couple hundred extras: Nazis, U.S. Marines, Red Cross Nurses and Medics, all lounging at long tables looking bored. The majority had spent the morning here, waiting to be called for their particular scene. Not surprisingly, the best food had already been devoured, leaving us with the vegetarian option for lunch—lukewarm bean-based casserole.

I headed for a table containing a couple of "U.S. Marines" with whom I'd worked the previous day: Chris, a big Greek personal trainer in normal life, who had a strange obsession—or, more likely, complex—with critiquing the size of other men's biceps, as well as an odd pride in his almost total covering of gorilla-like body hair, and Russell, a full-time extra and total movie nerd who had been in just about every major feature film shot in the U.K. over the last decade.

"Guess who you've just missed?" asked Russell as I sat down.

"Job done! Job done!" said Chris suggestively with a smile, impersonating the legendary oddball on set, who supposedly concluded all his sentences this way. I had yet to meet him.

"Is he here today?" I asked, intrigued at the prospect of meeting the man who had been the talk of the set the day before and had acquired the nickname, Captain Black—so called for his resemblance to the fictional nemesis of Captain Scarlet in the hit 1960s Supermarionation, *Captain Scarlet and the Mysterons*.

"The good Captain's been giving it the large portion all morning. He's really starting to put people's backs up. Lost track of all the shit he claims to have done," said Chris, who began to count on his hand, "Dance instructor on Harry Potter; personal stunt coordinator for Tommy Lee Jones; former stockbroker; 7th Dan Aikido black belt; archery instructor on Robin Hood, tactical weapons specialist; ex-Special Forces but currently in the military police."

" . . . who of course give him time off to be an extra," chipped in Russell, rolling his eyes.

"And he's only twenty-four! The guy's completely delusional. If he'd done half of what he claims, he sure as hell wouldn't be scraping by doing slightly above minimum wage background work," concluded Chris before adding, "Got very puny arms too."

Slightly above minimum wage or not, I wished I were getting more of it. The hourly rate wasn't so good, but the real money was from all the additional things you got paid for: having your hair cut, getting wet on set, changing costume, receiving your lunch late. The list went on. I'd been booked for a few more random days this month but some of those on set had got weeks of solid work, and a decent slab of cash. I had a couple of other part-time jobs as well, setting up stages for pop and rock concerts, and gardening for a friend's landscaping firm. None of it was big money, but if I wanted to go traveling, especially on the epic overland trip I had in mind, I needed all I could get.

I told the others of my plan to head abroad.

"You're not going to write about your travels again are you?" asked Chris with a wry smile.

"I might."

"Are you sure that's a good idea?"

"Can't see why not."

"It's just, I read an online review of one of your books the other night."

"Oh?"

"Yes, it said, 'The author sounds like a bit of a tool.'"

"Sounds accurate enough," I laughed.

"How's your last one selling?" asked Russell.

"I'm working as an extra. I think that tells you everything you need to know."

Indeed it did. The trade was littered with artists, writers, musicians, and other creative types who hadn't quite made it, at least to the degree of earning a living from their chosen craft. I'd had over forty jobs since leaving school, ranging from factory cleaning to investment banking, from sales to laboring, nearly all had been stop-gaps while I attempted to make a go of something else I was working on in my spare time—which, until recently, had never taken off. With the publication of my first book—a travel memoir on Iran[1] —the year before, I had naively assumed I would be waving goodbye to such an exasperating working life, and that I could finally become a full-time travel writer. If I ever wanted this to happen, then one thing was certain—I needed to start selling more books.

Whether writing about my travels or not, adventure and exploration are, and always will be, essentials in my life. For me, they are like breathing— they keep me alive. Their promise nurtures my spirit when stuck in awful dead-end jobs, and while actually traveling the experience renews me afresh, letting the real me emerge, not the shadow of my true self I frequently feel when trapped in tedious, low-paid employment. So often between trips a sort of sleeping sickness descends upon me, a stagnation of spirit borne out of the monotony of making ends meet by any means. And my home town, London, was exacerbating the problem. True, it is a wonderful and varied capital city, and there is much in Samuel Johnson's old adage that to be bored of London is to be bored of life, but it does also depend on what sort of life. If stuck in London with little money, it can quickly grind you down, with dejection and alienation soon setting in. Most of my good friends had now departed, and were scattered across the country and globe, leaving me wondering why I still remained. It had become a rut. With no car, and rarely having any disposable income, I was nearly always stuck there on weekends, most of which my girlfriend worked, leaving me alone and poor in one of the world's most expensive cities. So I would wander, trying my best to wring every last drop of interest from its free museums, architecture, and parks that, by now, I had visited and gazed upon all too often, and which seemed to have their color slowly leaching from them. I needed to shake off the gray and get the sparkle back, to wake from my emotional slumber and live life to the fullest again; to swap monotony for rapture through action, doing, and being. I needed to get out of London; to make good my escape, and the further away the better.

And I knew of a powerful and time-tested method of escape: hitchhiking.

If there is one form of travel that awakens the real me, it is setting off on an adventure by way of a stranger's car. Hitchhiking is the travel equivalent of a jolt from a defibrillator, an in-at-the-deep-end shock to the system that within moments of climbing into a random vehicle leaves me reborn as if a different person. On the road you are blessed with the company of such varied characters who drift freely in and out of your life, giving you the opportunity to become acquainted with people from backgrounds who, outside of the hitch, you might never meet. You never know who is going to pick you up, how long you'll travel with them, and what opportunities will come your way. I ached for new experience, and knew that through hitchhiking it was guaranteed. I needed to gaze upon new landscapes and buildings, to experience new cultures, to meet new people, to taste new foods, but most of all to feel alive again—I needed to journey once more, for within the hitch was life itself.

My plan was simple, to hitchhike home from just about the furthest point it was possible to go to from England—the southernmost tip of Australia, the island of Tasmania, where my girlfriend's family came from and we had arranged to spend Christmas together. To make it back from Tasmania would encompass roughly 18,000 miles through nineteen countries: Australia, Indonesia, Malaysia, Thailand, Laos, China, Kyrgyzstan, Kazakhstan, Azerbaijan, Georgia, Turkey, Bulgaria, Serbia, Croatia, Slovenia, Austria, Germany, France, and finally England. It would take me past wonders man-made and natural, through the changing of four seasons, and across huge environmental extremes of barren desert, tropical forest, towering frozen mountains, and verdant temperate pasture. I anticipated the journey taking between 3-6 months, for which I had around three thousand U.S. dollars to cover food, accommodation, visas and contingencies. It would be a tight budget and a trip like none I had completed before.

I couldn't wait to begin.

CHAPTER ONE
A Devil of a Place

The island of Tasmania, or "Tassie," as it is affectionately known to Australians, is a special place. The southern most Australian state, if you keep going south from Tasmania the next landmass you'll hit is the frozen continent of Antarctica. It is the twenty-sixth largest island in the world, roughly the size of the Republic of Ireland but with a population of just over half a million, fifty percent of whom live in Tasmania's capital, Hobart, the second oldest city in Australia. This leaves vast swathes of the island empty wilderness. Towering forests, craggy wind-swept mountains, thundering waterfalls and elegant sweeping beaches abound. Unlike the dry heart of the Australian mainland, Tasmania's climate is temperate. It has cold winters and highly variable summers in which you can experience four seasons in a single day. It is home to some of Australia's best-preserved historic architecture and convict sites (the island was founded as a penal colony), the world's tallest hardwood trees—the colossal Swamp Gums (Eucalyptus regnans) which can reach heights of 330 feet—and one of my favorite animals, the Tasmanian devil. This rowdy, muscular, dog-sized mammal is the largest carnivorous marsupial on the planet with the most powerful bite of any mammal relative to body mass.

After a delightful Christmas with Emily and her family in Hobart—a charming historic waterfront city, whose skyline is dominated by the dramatic four thousand foot peak of Mt. Wellington—it wasn't long before my mind turned to the Australian mainland and my imminent long hitch home. The only exceptions that I was prepared to make to my rule of *nothing but hitching* back to England, were when I was in a city—where it is next to impossible to hitchhike—or on seafaring sections of the trip. Under those circumstances I would pay for a ferry to the next landmass, or a local bus to get me to the city's outskirts. Other than that, I'd thumb a ride the entire way. A ferry left Tasmania from the northern town of Devonport for the mainland city of Melbourne, but I wondered if I could begin my journey in more style than that.

Every year one of the world's most difficult yacht races, *The Sydney to Hobart*, sets off, as its name suggests, from Australia's most populous and renowned city, Sydney, for Hobart, 630 nautical miles away across the treacherous waters of the Bass Strait. It begins the day after Christmas with most competitors arriving in time to enjoy the New Year celebrations in Tasmania—although many fly back immediately after arriving to celebrate in Sydney instead. With more competitors sailing to Tassie than back to Sydney, I decided to try to hitch a ride on one of the sparsely-crewed yachts heading to the mainland after the race.

The alarm clock rang in the bedroom I was sharing with Emily at her family home, heralding the New Year with a ghastly electronic shriek, rousing me as if I'd been prodded awake by needles. I groaned, hit the snooze button, and closed my sluggish hangover-heavy eyes. In what seemed like seconds it was tormenting me again. I turned it off. Could I really be bothered to get up and traipse around the marina first thing in the morning? If I wanted a yacht though, I had to get cracking. Looking over at Emily, whose curly locks spilled over the downy pillows, I snuggled in for a final departing hug, her warmth and beauty tempting me to stay.

Minutes later I was driving away from the forested slopes of Mt. Wellington, down through empty tree-lined streets, past Victorian and Georgian properties dripping in character, towards the city center's waterfront heart,

Sullivan's Cove—the landing site used by the British when founding the city in 1804. Located here is the main marina, Constitution Dock, where a flotilla of racing yachts was berthed, their gently swaying masts visible from afar. I left the car by a small park and began strolling toward them past a cobblestoned area of former Georgian sandstone warehouses, once used to store grain, whale oil and wool, now converted into galleries, cafés, craft shops, pubs, and restaurants. From the marina itself ran multiple piers where row upon row of racing yachts were berthed. These ranged in size, modernity and value, reflecting the different racing divisions—and wallet size of the owners. It was a beautiful sunny morning, making for a dazzling display of light on the water's surface. Skipping across the marina was a cooling salty breeze, creating a symphony of pinging sounds from the yachts' taught halyard lines that blew against the hollow aluminum masts along which they ran. Accompanying this were the lonely cries of gulls overhead, the fluttering of official race flags, and the faint lapping chop of the ocean against the yachts' brilliant white hulls.

As I gazed at the myriad vessels, an agitated excitement enveloped me; a euphoric realization that this could be it: if I found a place on a yacht then my hitchhiking adventure would begin. Once more I would enter that sacred realm where I feel most complete—being on the move. Already the torpidity of London was fading from my spirit. But logically speaking I didn't feel too optimistic of getting a ride. After all, the place was awash with world-class yachtsmen, whereas I had practically no experience, having done but a basic sailing course some eight years earlier and next to no sailing since. There was no shortage of yachts to ask though. It was a numbers game, I figured. If I asked enough people, then I'd be in with a chance.

Despite it being New Year's Day, a surprising number of people were up and about, tinkering with their yachts, displaying no sign of being worse for wear from a heavy session the night before. Strolling down the pier I approached a man on the first yacht to my left.

"Excuse me," I said, with a buoyant smile, "I don't suppose you're looking for crew for the return leg to Sydney?"

"No, we're from Tassie. We're not sailing back."

I thanked him and moved on to the next yacht where a bronze-skinned, white-haired man in his sixties was pottering about on board a sleek medium-sized yacht.

I greeted the yachty, and asked if he was looking for crew to sail back to Sydney.

He looked me up and down.

"Yes."

Bloody hell. I hadn't been expecting a positive response from the second vessel I approached. His matter-of-fact reply left me stumped, and I paused, tongue-tied for a second, struggling for a coherent response. He came to my assistance.

"Have you sailed before, and more importantly do you get seasick?"

I proceeded to exaggerate my previous experience and assured him that I didn't get seasick. This was untrue. On the first day of my sailing course I'd spent a good while throwing up over the side. I wouldn't be letting that inconvenient truth throw a wrench in the works. After all, my sickness hadn't lasted more than a couple of hours, so I hoped I'd be okay this time. I'd need to be. It was a four to five day sail to Sydney and we could be in for some exceptionally rough seas. The previous Monday had seen winds of fifty knots hammering the yachts as they made their way to Hobart. The going had been so rough that even veteran wave rider and seven-time world surfing champion Layne Beachley, who was crewing on board a one hundred foot supermaxi, came down with such severe seasickness that she was confined to her bunk from the first day of the race until the last. I hoped I wasn't asking for more than I could handle.

"We leave in an hour and a half from the Sandy Bay Yacht Club after the winners' presentation. Can you make it there in time?" asked my potential skipper.

I hadn't been expecting this either, having assumed that no one would actually set sail today. I figured most people would head back some time after New Year's Day, giving me plenty of time to pack and say goodbye to Emily, whom I wouldn't be seeing now for several months. But I wasn't about to turn down what seemed like a tremendous stroke of luck, so I gave a resounding, "Yes."

After the briefest of introductions—his name was Tony, and the yacht's, named in honor of his wife, *Eleni*—I bade my new skipper goodbye for now and turned on my heels to make a hasty trip back to get packed and say my farewells.

Tony called out after me.

"If you're not there in time we'll leave without you."

My heart pounded in my chest as I ran to the car. In my excitement I fumbled with the door lock, dropping the keys on the sidewalk. I struggled to find the right one and then had similar panic-induced difficulties with the ignition. I floored it all the way back to Emily's, the car's tires letting out a screech on the hot asphalt as they came to an abrupt stop outside her home. I was in a real hurry, but instead of rushing inside, I sat still for several seconds, let my heart settle and gathered my thoughts. An excited smile crept across my face—I was about to sail over six hundred nautical miles across a stretch of notoriously difficult ocean and start my hitchhike back to England.

The good times were about to begin!

Emily was still curled up asleep when I arrived, wrapped in the fluffy duvet which she had rearranged so that it was around her head like a huge shawl, leaving only the round of her face visible. I smiled at her tenderly, then gently rocked my sleeping beauty to consciousness, her big blue eyes looking up at me through the sea of covers.

"I've got good news and bad news, darling."

She guessed. "You leave today."

"In about," I checked my watch, "an hour and fifteen minutes."

In what is without doubt the quickest and least thought-out packing I've ever done for such a vast trip, I threw everything I had taken with me to Australia into my backpack, stuffing it down with brute force. There was far more than I needed, or had intended to take on the journey back, having planned for Emily to carry superfluous items on the plane with her. There was no time for this now. It all had to come, essential or not. I'd work out what could be offloaded later. After a brief, though fond, farewell to Emily's family, we jumped back in the car and headed for the yacht club in nearby Sandy Bay.

The place was packed in readiness for the official winners' presentation. The competitors were all seated at a patio area outside the main clubhouse with views across the marina, where a small purpose-made stage had been erected for the event.

Taking a seat behind some media cameramen covering the action, we settled in with a cooling drink to watch the proceedings, sheltering beneath a parasol from the now-roasting sun. It was only when Tony was presented with an award—a wooden plaque with a cross-section of a yacht—that I realized he'd won his race division. Photos followed of him and his winning crew posing with the trophy.

When proceedings came to a close, we approached Tony, who introduced us to the crew. Other than Tony, only one of the racers, Albert, a twenty-one year-old engineering student from Sydney, was returning to the mainland on the yacht. The rest of the original crew were flying. The new team that I'd be joining consisted of Steve, a burly and bearded sea dog in his forties from Brisbane, and Jessica, a blonde Swedish girl in her thirties, currently living in Tasmania.

Minutes later I was being shown onto my floating home for the next few days by Albert, while Emily waited on the pier. She looked upset. After stowing my backpack down below I went up to console her.

"Don't worry Ems, I'll be home before you know it."

There was no time to chat, and so with some tender parting words and a warm last embrace, we said goodbye.

CHAPTER TWO
Departing in Style

The sail out of Hobart takes you through the vast sheltered estuary of the Derwent River, which gradually widens past oyster-clad rocky coves, sandy beaches and picturesque penguin-populated islands, on its way to the cold treacherous waters of the Tasman Sea beyond.

Less than twenty minutes sailing and already Hobart was disappearing from sight, with the towering summit of Mt. Wellington now my final visual reminder of the city. Steve passed around a huge container of sunscreen while Tony, currently manning the yacht's huge blue helm wheel, gave us the low-down on the coming day's routine.

"We'll be sailing in rotating shifts of three hours; Albert and Steve on one, Jessica and Jamie on another, with me fluctuating between the two as necessary. You'll either do a single night shift from midnight until 3 a.m., or a double from 9 p.m. until midnight, and then 3 a.m. until 6 a.m."

This meant we'd be getting no more than three hours sleep at a time. I was still pretty tired from last night's session on the sauce and this morning's early start, so hoped I'd get the single shift.

"Jessica and Jamie are on the double tonight."

Shit.

Before reaching the Tasman Sea we put on waterproof jackets, and Tony handed around seasickness tablets in readiness for the bumpy ride to come. It was just as well. When we rounded the final headland and hit open ocean, conditions changed dramatically. Huge dark swells appeared from nowhere, lunging the yacht up and down. No longer sheltered from the wind, the sails took the strain, with the yacht heeling to one side.

"Pull in the main sheet," shouted Tony.

To capitalize on its propelling effect we hardened up the main sail further, hauling on its chunky line, then locking it in place on a tighter angle to sail closer to the wind. Explosions of water erupted against the hull as we sliced into oncoming freight train waves, covering us with spray as the wind lashed our faces.

To our immediate left, rising vertically from the ocean floor were the beginnings of some of the most striking coastline in all Australia—the fortress-like cliffs of the Tasman Peninsula, some reaching a thousand feet. Many of the ominous gray rock formations that make up the cliffs resemble chimneys, and have acquired appropriate monikers: organ pipes, fluted cliffs, totem poles. The waves smashed against their unyielding bases, creating bursts of brilliant white.

Further up the coast the towering cliffs flanked the entrance to a bay that led to an infamous former penal colony, Port Arthur. For the convicts transported here from Britain, glimpsing the forbidding surroundings of their final destination for the first time must have been terrifying. They were sent to the end of the world from which they knew return would be all but impossible.[2]

By late afternoon Jessica took a turn for the worse and was sick over the side of the yacht. Despite feeling sorry for her, I couldn't help but be pleasantly surprised with my own lack of sickness so far. It was to prove short-lived.

In the interests of staying alert and awake on my first night shift, I decided to heed Tony's advice and get my head down for a couple of hours before it commenced, and so shuffled into one of two narrow sleeping sections at the stern of the yacht. With a low roof just above the bed, it was a tight fit, although not uncomfortable, and came complete with a thin mattress enclosed by a netted section that prevented you from falling out due to the yacht's steep angle and frequent bumps.

In what seemed like minutes, but was actually a hiatus of a couple of hours, I felt someone tugging at my foot.

"You're on in ten minutes," said Albert, who clambered back on deck.

Crawling out of my little den, I stood as best I could in the cabin, holding onto the railing of the stairs to steady myself as the yacht lurched violently back and forth. Putting on the waterproof jacket, pants, boots, and gloves that Tony had supplied me with took the best part of ten minutes to achieve. I knew from experience that the longer you spent below deck in an upright position the more likely you were to get seasick, and so from now on I decided to sleep fully clothed in my waterproofs. By the time I emerged into the cool evening air and clipped my chunky safety harness to a big metal ring on deck I was feeling queasy. With my arrival, Steve and Albert headed below to sleep. Jessica was already on deck and looked like she was feeling better after grabbing some sleep in one of the other bunks. She sat perched on the elevated side of the yacht, angled out of the water by the wind's force on the sails. I clambered up to join her while Tony manned the helm.

Being summertime it was still light, although by now there was a low golden sun. I stared at the glowing cliffs in an attempt to take my mind off feeling nauseated. The thing was, I didn't want to admit to myself that I was downright seasick. The moment I did, I knew there would be no return. But with the churning seas showing no signs of abating, and having no option to lie down, it didn't seem likely the feeling would subside. As day slipped to night and true darkness enveloped our world, I began to feel progressively worse, the turbulent motion building inside of me until I could take no more. In an act of defeat, I stumbled to the other side of the yacht closest to the water and began retching into the sea. I continued until my stomach had nothing left to give. An overriding desire to lie down saturated my consciousness. The first opportunity was hours away, and if conditions got no better, I had at least four more days of this to go. Not that I was wholly downcast. A colorless image of the tedium of my existence in London flashed before me—I might be feeling sick now but at least I was feeling something.

The second shift of the night followed a similar pattern to the first with the sickness only departing when, exhausted, I finally crawled into bed at its end.

I awoke the next morning for my 9 a.m. shift to far calmer seas and a stronger constitution. Sticking my head up on deck, I was greeted by a gentle and renewing breeze playing its way across the idyllic surroundings of one of Tasmania's most iconic and photographed locations, Wineglass Bay. This stunning bay curved, as its name suggests, into the graceful arc of a wine glass, and was framed behind by undulating green hills, thick with bushland and dotted with the occasional rugged boulder. Along the shore stretched the whitest sands, lapped by waters the color of unblemished turquoise. It was the most idyllic spot to have woken to, and the perfect place to stop off for breakfast.

"Who wants a cup of tea?" asked Jessica to all on deck, before heading down to get the kettle going on the yacht's nifty little stove. We had a leisurely breakfast of small individual boxes of cereal, eaten direct from the packet, which we poured milk into to save on washing up. The sailing was pretty easy going for most of the day, with much calmer waters than the one before, and it wasn't long before the final rocky headland of Tasmania was disappearing behind us and we were sailing into the "paddock" of the Bass Strait—a notorious open stretch of water separating Tasmania from mainland Australia. Despite its reputation, we were lucky and encountered propitious weather, so much so that we hoisted the yacht's huge billowing yellow spinnaker sail—apparently an uncommon thing to do because of the high winds endemic in the area.

For the rest of the day we saw no land or other vessels, bestowing a liberating feeling of the desolate, as if the outside world had ceased to exist, accompanied only by a jellyfish drifting idly by, or a sea-bird gliding overhead.

When night arrived, Jessica and I took it in turns handling the helm across the expanse of darkness. We were treated to some of the most magnificent stars I've ever seen, a layered drape of dazzling complexity and awe, whose intensity seemed to burn holes in the cold charcoal-black atmosphere. Every so often the glorious silver arrow of a shooting star would streak across the firmament, its tail lingering for a split second in the wake of the matter disintegrating into flashes at its head. And my spirit would soar.

Jessica and I chatted for most of our nocturnal shift, and even discovered we'd both taken salsa lessons—something Emily had cajoled me into of late—from the same person, "Super Mario, the million moves man," but on different sides of the planet. Jessica was extremely keen on salsa and even ran her own dance parties in Hobart. Literature was another common ground of interest, with Jessica considering writing a book, a fiction of some sort, although sadly she hadn't worked out much beyond this. It was an enjoyable shift, made all the more so by knowing that it was, for us at least, the only one of the night, and when it came to an end we would sleep until dawn.

By early morning the landmass of the world's largest island, and the only island that is also a continent, was apparent, not by sight but by smell. I'm not suggesting that mainland Australians stink—although there are probably plenty of Tasmanians who would subscribe to this—but rather that the distinct aroma of bushland and forest drifted across the water a good hour before the continent itself came into view, appearing on the horizon amid a vivid sunrise of orange and angry pink.

It wasn't long before a lone seventy-five foot high, square sandstone tower, topped with battlements, appeared among distant bushland, standing proudly above red cliffs at the entrance to Twofold Bay.

"That's Boyd's Tower," announced Tony.

The tower had been built by a Scottish entrepreneur, Benjamin Boyd, in 1847 as a lighthouse, but ended up being used as a lookout by local whalers to spot their prey. It was now part of the Ben Boyd National Park, at the entrance of which it stood. Just up from the tower was a pulp mill of colossal proportions, complete with several mountainous hills of reddish wood chips, the likely source of the scent that had alerted us to land when miles out at sea.

A pleasant day of sailing commenced, followed by a night shift of epic proportions. Jessica, Tony, and I were treated to marine phosphorescence the likes of which I had no idea existed, its sublime arrival coinciding with the appearance of a pod of dolphins playing about next to the yacht. It was as if I'd taken some super strong LSD, such was the intensity of the colors radiating from the water. One moment the dolphins were up close, exploding out of the sea beside us, throwing psychedelic-colored water into the air and sounding off their characteristic clicks and whistles, the next they had darted off, and the ocean was silent again, leaving us scanning for their return.

"Over there!" one of us would shout on spotting an illuminated wake, and the party would start over again. It lasted for about ten minutes before the dolphins departed for good, leaving me on a natural high for the rest of the night.

"I've seen phosphorescence like that once before in Thailand," said Tony, in the calm considered manner of an experienced mariner, something I took to be rather telling. Tony was in his sixties and had sailed most of his life, so if he'd only seen phosphorescence of such brightness once previously, then I was very lucky to have scored such a sight on my first major sailing trip.

All things considered, it was a pretty uneventful trip back to Sydney from here on in. We moored up in the marina of the exclusive Castlecrag area five days after setting off, having covered 630 nautical miles.

CHAPTER THREE

A Meth to My Madness

"Where you bloody going?" asked a tired-looking and wrinkled middle-aged woman through the open passenger window of a powerful-looking Holden Commodore sedan. Behind the wheel sat an equally aged man wearing a baseball cap and a pair of shades. We were on the western outskirts of Sydney—a location I had arrived at early in the morning after scoring a ride from Tony.

"I'm heading west, trying to get to Port Augusta," I told them.

"We can take you to Dubbo," said the driver, revealing the most horrendous set of worn down black-and-yellow-stained teeth I'd ever seen.

I had no idea where Dubbo was, so I began to make inquiries and handed over my map to the woman, holding up three cars on the thin strip of truck stop exit road behind us.

They began blasting their horns.

With no further ado the woman leaned out of the car window to face those waiting behind.

"Oh, fuck off with yous!" she yelled, accompanying this with the middle finger.

She turned to me and calmly pointed out where Dubbo was. It was to the west. I got in.

Tires screeched and we were off.

A bony hand thrust into the back.

"I'm Bindi."

We shook.

"I'm Jamie, nice to meet you."

"Robbo," announced the driver, reaching around with his palm down and elbow up for a handshake in the manner of a gangster holding a gun—taking his eyes off the road for an uncomfortably long period in the process.

"We're not a couple by the way," he said, gesturing to Bindi, as if this was important information to state upfront.

"Nah, been mates for years," replied Bindi. "Be too weird to root now!"

They both laughed.

I hoped Robbo wasn't clarifying for my sake in case I fancied a crack at her.

"You'd be a bloody pommy, wouldn't you, Jamie?" asked Bindi.

I answered in the affirmative, that I was indeed an Englishman—"pommy" being Australian slang for their English betters.

Robbo, it soon became clear, drove like a lunatic, weaving his way in and out of traffic at far too high a speed on the Great Western Highway that led from Sydney towards the Blue Mountains, a region of spectacular forested gorges, roughly thirty miles west of the city. As we approached the Blue Mountains, houses became more sparse and the landscape gradually changed, until we were twisting our way down craggy hillside roads cut into the cliff, eventually giving way to pastures and rolling hills dappled with gently swaying eucalyptus trees.

"If there weren't so many fucking cunts on the road we'd be flying along!" exclaimed Robbo.

He could have fooled me.

Despite Robbo and Bindi's penchant for profanity, they were super friendly to me, offering cigarettes, sodas, and candies my way and taking genuine interest in my trip. With a bit of prompting they began to tell me about themselves. Both were Koori Aboriginals, which came as something of a surprise to me as neither was particularly dark skinned. (The Koori are the original inhabitants of land that now encompasses the states of New South Wales and Victoria.)

I asked them some generalities about the Koori as well as other Aboriginal people.

"The Murri Aboriginals from Queensland are a bit uppity, think they're better than us," said Robbo.

"And you've got to be careful of them ones from the Northern Territory," added Bindi. "They've got powers. Can point a bone at you or sing you back."

Pointing a bone, Bindi explained, was the Northern Territory Aboriginals' way of placing a curse on someone; singing you back, a method of magically enchanting the subject of their affection to return to them, willing or not.

Robbo put on a CD of Koori country music, by Roger Knox.

"He's known as the black Elvis and the Koori king of country," said Robbo. "Listen to the words."

These featured the chorus lyrics, "The brown skin baby, they take him away." This, I knew, was a reference to the so called "stolen generation" of Aboriginals, a racist government policy based on theories from the eugenics movement, whereby Aboriginal children—usually with a degree of mixed blood—were forcibly stolen from their parents and placed in Christian missions where their culture and language was banned, in a quest to "civilize" and have the color "bred out of them." Roughly 100,000 children[3]—equating to as many as 1 in 10 of all Aboriginal children[4]— were kidnapped from their parents, causing untold misery and suffering. The practice also saw stolen children shipped off as bonded labor to ranches or white middle-class homes as servants. Many were lied to and told their family had died; others, as documented in an official inquiry of 1997, were physically and sexually abused.[5] Astonishingly, the policy ran from 1910 right up until 1971.[6] Such was the social upheaval and trauma caused, that huge numbers of Aboriginal children turned to alcohol, drugs, and violence, which resulted for many in a premature death. Even now, the life expectancy of Aboriginal Australians is lower than the rest of the world's other 90 indigenous peoples.[7] Sadly, Bindi's own family bore this out. She was forty-seven years old but told me she had seen five of her fifteen siblings die. When we drove past a roadside cemetery she leaned out of the car and shouted, "Hello sis!"

"When I die I'm gonna have my Maltese dog buried at my feet," she said, adding, "Don't worry, he's already dead. Had the poor bugger cremated."

"Came pretty close to copping it myself recently too," continued Bindi. "Hubby was driving with me in the passenger seat when we got hit head-on by a truck with bull-bars. Broke my wrists, had my spleen patched, broke my right hip, collar bone, lost eight teeth and broke my right leg. Hubby died four times over, broke his jaw, cheekbones, and his head swelled to the size of a beach-ball. Family only knew him from his tattoos."

Bindi showed me, with a touch of pride, some of her scars.

"Tell him about the surgeons," said Robbo, with a giggle.

"Oh, yeah," laughed Bindi. "After my hubby came round from his operation, to check he was with it they said to him, 'Davo, can you tell me who the Prime Minister is?' He says, 'How the fucking hell should I know!'"

After about two hours on the road we arrived in the small town of Bathurst, the oldest inland settlement in Australia and the site of the country's first significant gold discovery, which led in the 1850s to a frenzied gold rush. Gold was discovered here by an English jack-of-all-trades, Edward Hargreaves, whose first foray into gold mining came with an unsuccessful attempt to strike it rich in the gold fields of California. Despite two fruitless years of panning in the U.S., his trip there was not in vain. Having noted a remarkable similarity between the geography of California and areas he had previously seen in Australia, he decided to try his luck Down Under. His hunch paid off, and it wasn't long before he found payable amounts of gold at Summer Hill Creek, just outside Bathurst. News spread like wildfire, and within a month of his discovery the area was descended upon by a thousand prospectors panning in streams, lifting up rocks and cracking open boulders.

Soon gold was found all over the place and in massive quantities, especially in the neighboring state of Victoria, setting off a gold rush of such epic proportions that within just a year of Hargreaves' discovery, over half the male population of Victoria were searching for it. Towns and cities suffered severe and rapid depopulation as fortune seekers abandoned their jobs and families, and rushed to the gold fields in search of riches. Such was the manic stampede that in under ten years six hundred thousand new migrants flocked to Australia, a country which, until the discovery of gold, it had been nearly impossible to encourage anyone to settle in.

The ramifications of this were huge, for it effectively saw the end of Australia being used as a vast dumping ground for Britain's undesirables. To be sent there in chains before gold's discovery had meant an effective life sentence no matter how short the prison term since few could ever hope to raise the funds to return to Britain. But now, with prisoners having the prospect of discovering riches beyond their wildest dreams on completion of their sentence, getting transported to Australia became an opportunity. And so a fatal blow was dealt to Australia as a prison continent, and slowly a country began to emerge instead.

We drove through the area now, one of its few notable features observable from the road was a sprawling red-brick prison complex—in which you could see prisoners exercising inside through the perimeter security fence.

"Wouldn't fancy being in there," I casually remarked to Bindi, just making conversation.

"Nah, did eight months myself for shoplifting," she responded in the same manner.

This was interesting.

In no way do I mean to justify Bindi's light-fingered tendencies, but it is a fact that Aborigines are imprisoned in Australia today at five times the rate that South Africa imprisoned blacks during its universally acknowledged ultra-racist apartheid era.[8] And for the state of Western Australia it climbs to eight times the apartheid rate.[9] I wondered if this had played a part in her sentence.

Conversation flowed between us about law and order, prison and the police, leading Robbo to tell me about a friend of his who had been robbed at gun point. When interviewed by the police the officer had asked him, "Can you tell me what sort of gun it was?" To which he answered: "The type that puts great big fucking holes in you!"

It wasn't long before we rocked up in the town of Orange, known, ironically, as "The Apple City," due to the district's prominence as a center for apple growing. Named after the Prince of Orange, not the fruit, the town's elevation and climate prevents the growing of oranges, or as Robbo put it to me, "You piss ice cubes here in winter."

"D'you wanna Macca's, Jamie?" asked Bindi (Macca's being Australian slang for McDonald's) as we pulled into the parking lot of said restaurant.

"I'll get us a Happy Meal each," insisted Robbo.

Having intended, like many trips before, to fast on my first day on the road in order to get into the proper mindset for the rigors of the journey ahead, I initially tried to politely decline.

Robbo overruled me.

"Don't worry about it, mate," he said, "I help so many people out I'm thinking of joining the fucking priesthood!"

It sure would have made for some interesting sermons.

Robbo went in by himself, coming out minutes later with a Happy Meal apiece and a fistful of straws.

"D'you mind if I keep the toy for my grandkids?" asked Robbo, as he handed me a meal.

Wow. He looked aged, in a worn kind of way, but not old enough to be a granddad.

I thanked him for the meal and handed over the toy, a plastic alien figure.

"Jamie, have you got a pair of scissors?" he asked.

"I've got a knife, will that do?"

Robbo nodded his agreement. I dug around my backpack and retrieved my Swedish "Mora" bushcraft knife. Using a cigarette packet as a makeshift cutting block, Robbo proceeded to delicately slice through one of his many straws, doing so at an angle to create a stumpy shovel-like implement at one end.

"What's it for?" I asked.

"Smoking meth," he answered matter of factly, as if this was the most normal thing in the world. I realized now why his and Bindi's teeth were so horrendous—they both had "meth mouth," a side effect of crystal meth addiction, which causes addicts to clench their jaw and grind their teeth, while the drug dries out the mouth and accelerates tooth decay.

Ten minutes outside town and we came to a stop on a deserted stretch of road. Out came a small folded-up piece of what looked like greaseproof paper from the car's glove compartment. Inside was the methamphetamine—crystal meth. Bindi was first up. Using the purpose-made straw shovel, she scooped up a serving of meth and placed it in the middle of a piece of aluminum foil, about four inches square. Robbo held a cigarette lighter beneath this while Bindi sucked through the straw, taking a deep drag of the wispy vapor spiraling off the foil. She held it back, then, with a palpable "huh," exhaled, filling the car with fumes. Robbo followed suit afterwards then offered the straw my way.

"You fancy one, Jamie?"

"I'm okay, thanks," I replied, having never really been one for drugs.

"It's alright, we've got extras. We sell a bit in Dubbo, that's why we made the trip to Sydney," replied Robbo, as if surely the reason for my refusal must be polite concern for his dwindling supplies, as opposed to not wanting to become an addict.

I declined again, laughing inwardly to myself at the rapid change in my situation since this morning. Hours earlier I was hanging out with a millionaire, sailing about on his spectacular yacht, and now, here I was with a couple of small time drug dealers, passively smoking crystal meth in the back of their car.

I loved hitchhiking.

I stood by the side of a quiet and peaceful length of road, surrounded by an expanse of dry-looking flat fields peppered with gum trees, and bade farewell to Bindi and Robbo.

"Don't forgot to call me tonight if you can't get a lift," said Robbo, having offered me a sofa to crash on at his place moments earlier.

With a big dusty wheel-spin, they pulled off back in the direction of Dubbo, having gone out of their way to drop me on the other side of town on the road heading west. Their lift had covered roughly 250 miles and lasted over four hours, and by now it was early afternoon, and a hot one at that.

Vehicles were a bit thin on the ground but soon enough an SUV pulled up with two beefy guys about my age inside, who drove me to a spot opposite a tiny regional airport a few minutes up the road.

"Don't camp past Cobar on the road tonight," advised the driver, on hearing I intended to throw my tent down for accommodation. "Could be Aboriginal land and they might not be too friendly."

Soon I was moving again, driving through the small rural town of Narromine with a dark-skinned Aboriginal couple in their middle years, Thomas and Irene. As we headed west in their large saloon they insisted I help myself to pieces of their recently purchased pepperoni pizza, and swigs from a big bottle of coke.

"I used to work all over here in the cotton fields," said Thomas, as he drove through vast agricultural areas of endless dry fields.

"Have you traveled much around the country?" I asked.

"Never left the state."

Being something of an outdoor/survival enthusiast and amateur botanist, I was keen to learn something of Australia's wild edible flora, known colloquially as "bushtucker." I asked Thomas if he retained any of his ancestors' traditional knowledge in this area.

"Nah, white man fucked me!" he replied, flashing a smile my way.

They dropped me in the tiny village of Nevertire, just down the road from a huge grain-handling facility. I waited across the road from a tin-roofed pub, opposite a railway track and some scrub bushland beyond. By now it was late afternoon and although still hot, the sting had gone from the sun.

Would I make it to the outback town of Cobar by nightfall? It was possible, but far from guaranteed. After about thirty minutes of smiling with a thumb raised at the occasional passing motorist, the majority of whom drove farming pickups, a people-carrier pulled over. Inside was what I first took to be a family of Aboriginals.

"Where are you going, mate?" asked the male driver in an unidentifiable accent that was definitely not Australian, despite his efforts to embellish the question with a local colloquialism at the end.

As luck would have it they were heading all the way to Cobar. I clambered in.

"Where are you from?" I asked as we pulled off.

"Papua New Guinea," said the driver, introducing himself as Pakap.

The rest of the family were: his wife, Jennly; their three high school-aged daughters, Sandra, Joyleen, and Gaile; and their seven-year-old son, Fraser.

Pakap was a geologist and had recently moved to Australia with his family to work in the mining industry, a sector that was currently booming due to increased exports to China, causing the overall Australian economy to boom also and the price of everyday goods to hit the roof.

"How are you finding school here?" I asked his oldest daughter.

She hesitated, before answering, "It is good."

Pakap elaborated for her. "She thinks Australian children are badly behaved. In Papua New Guinea you don't answer the teacher back."

Having at one stage considered going through Papua New Guinea—located just beyond Australia's northeastern tip—I knew a bit about the country, and so Pakap and I chatted for a while about the place, in particular the astonishing array of different languages there. These number over eight hundred, making it by far the most linguistically varied country in the world.

"When I hear Aboriginals speak on television, I sometimes think I recognize some of their words," said Pakap.

Not more than ten minutes into the journey, Pakap queried where I was staying tonight.

"Hello, hello," I thought. I'd already been offered a place to crash by two lifts today, was he about to make it a third? I sure hoped so. Cobar was my final destination, so if not, then it was my dependable old tent and the dusty side of the road for me.

On hearing of my far from salubrious sleeping plans he turned to Jennly, speaking briefly to her in his native tongue. They culminated the dialogue with a shared nod of the head.

This was looking promising.

"You are welcome to stay with us. I'm afraid it won't be Aussie food tonight, but a combination of Aussie and Papua New Guinea."

That was fine by me. Not long on the road and the landscape became less agricultural, far more what I would consider the proper outback—a rather loose term in Australia usually reserved for the wilder areas beyond the farming or "bush" lands. My assessment seemed accurate when the sign for the next remote settlement, Nyngan, announced proudly, "Welcome to Nyngan and the great outback."

Make no mistake, the outback is one hardy place, with Nyngan being the perfect example of the wild environmental extremes possible within it. In 1990 a horrendous flash flood tore the town apart, seeing to the evacuation of the entire population. Severe flash floods also occurred the year before and continued to plague the town four times over the next decade and yet, just eighty miles down the road in Cobar, not a drizzle of rain was recorded for a full five years during this period.

Darkness had fallen by the time we pulled into the remote town of Cobar, where Pakap wanted to show me one of the area's local mines.

Driving in the dark through unlit back roads, with the occasional kangaroo bouncing into the full beam of our headlights, we made our way uphill, eventually arriving at a scenic lookout on top of Fort Bourke Hill. Stepping out of the car into a dark and hot night, humming with a low background symphony of insects, I really felt like I had arrived in the outback. I was 430 miles from where I started this morning, and the surroundings couldn't have been more different. Making our way past a couple of nearby satellite dishes and huge concrete water tanks, we came to a small metal shed perched high above a precipice—open fronted on one side to get in, but with a big protective cage on the other to prevent falling out. Down below was the mine. My eyes took a while to adjust to the light, before the cavernous size of the gaping expanse below me became apparent. Hewn into the rocky earth were massive terraces leading down, like a giant's staircase, to the base of this enormous chasm.

Suddenly the sound of an approaching truck reverberated across the landscape, its headlamps appearing on the mine's distant lip, revealing an unseen gravelly track snaking its way towards the belly of the mine.

"What do they mine here?" I asked.

"Gold," replied Pakap. "Got other local mines excavating copper, zinc, silver and lead. The copper mine north of town produces nearly a million tons of ore a year and is the second deepest in Australia, goes down nearly one and a half kilometers."

"Wow," I replied. That sure sounded like a long way to me.

"Gets very hot down there. One of the biggest mining costs is air conditioning."

I gazed towards an opening cut into the wall at the bottom of the mine that the truck had disappeared into.

"Are there many people working in there now?

"They never stop; mining goes on twenty-four hours a day, seven days a week."

Pakap went on to explain that one of the reasons mining was so profitable in Australia was that unlike undeveloped countries with similar resources, Australia already had all the modern infrastructure needed to exploit it in place, especially transport. After all, it's not much use having huge deposits in the back of beyond if there's no functioning road or rail system that allows you to get the stuff out of there.

On arrival back at Pakap's house we retired to the garden with a condensation-dripping bottle of ice cold beer while the rest of the family busied themselves preparing the evening meal. As Pakap and I sat nursing our beers beneath a fig tree amid sweltering heat, I asked him about the differences in lifestyle and culture between Papua New Guinea and Australia.

"In tribal Papua New Guinea we don't have the same concept of poverty. If you lose your job in the town or city you would not be destitute, you'd just move back to your tribe who would look after you and give you a row of land to plant vegetables and another row for something else. And we would never put our father or mother into a care home like in Australia. This is very alien to us. In Papua New Guinea, if someone does not have children we say, 'How sad they do not have someone to look after them when they are old.'"

Pakap went on to explain that in tribal Papua New Guinea the concept of individualism didn't exist in the same way either.

"If someone does something wrong in Australia or urban parts of Papua New Guinea, then it is the individual who is held responsible, but in tribal Papua New Guinea, if someone does something wrong to another tribe, then it is their whole tribe that is responsible. Just as it is my responsibility now to help my tribe financially. This will be a hard concept for my son to understand."

Pakap also said that very few marriages broke up in Papua New Guinea, and that if they did then all wedding presents, such as livestock, had to be returned.

After three beers a piece, little Fraser came out for a chat. He was very well behaved and when, after talking for a while, Pakap decided it was time for him to go in again, Pakap simply said, "That is enough." To this, Fraser dutifully nodded and went inside without a protest. Moments later the food was ready.

Laid out buffet-style on a big table was an assortment of chicken drumsticks, chunks of beef, roast potatoes, salads, a big bowl of communal gravy, and a mountain of assorted vegetables.

"In Papua New Guinea we eat a lot of vegetables," said Pakap.

We sat and ate together on the sitting room floor while the rest of the family waited in the kitchen. So much for fasting on my first day on the road; I couldn't have been better fed. When we'd eaten our fill, Pakap and

I finished off with a couple more cold ones in the garden, and when it was finally time to crash, I did so on a super comfy bed in the sitting room, kindly set up for me by Jennly.

As my first proper day on the road drew to a close, it was with a warm feeling of satisfaction, a deep sense of comfort borne out of the altruism and acceptance that had been shown to me by the people who had drifted into my life today. The family's hospitality was touching, as was that of my other rides so far, from whom I had been given food, drink, offers of accommodation, cigarettes, even chemical stimulants. And that was all to the good. But it was the gift of temporary companionship that struck me the most. The kindness I'd experienced was so unlike the impersonal toils of my existence in the big city madness of London. On the road it's easy to cast that madness aside, to connect instead to a simple shared humanity, to emerge once more complete and real.

CHAPTER FOUR

I'm Not Racist But . . .

T hink Texas is big? Forget it. The state of Western Australia is over three and a half times the size. What about Europe? Well, if you exclude the chunk of Russia within Europe's borders then every other European nation would collectively fit into Australia. And here's the thing, you'd still have 667,657 square miles to play with—that's leftovers just shy of five extra Germanies.[10] Ponder that for a moment, if you will.

In fact, if you ignore Alaska and Hawaii, then the mighty United States, at 3,081,029 square miles, is, give or take, the same size as Australia, at 2,973,952 square miles. Australia is, to put it bluntly, one bastard big country. But that's only part of the story; with a population of just 22 million people, nearly all of whom reside in major urban centers dotted around its perimeter coastline, Australia is also staggeringly empty. The majority of the continent is virtually deserted.

I couldn't quite believe how small a dent over 430 miles of hitching the day before had made into it. In Britain it would equate to two thirds of the country's entire length, but here it was trivial.

I should have known better. Ten years earlier I had hitchhiked across Australia in the other direction, starting in Perth on the west coast, heading east over the mighty Nullarbor Plain to Port Augusta, and finally ending north in Darwin. My memory of how oversized the country was had faded. Such large sections of the journey had been along virtually identical, single-lane roads that cut a straight-as-an-arrow course across so flat and similar a landscape that it was difficult to distinguish one section from the other; and more so in retrospect. The Nullarbor Plain was a case in point. A two day drive in a straight line over hundreds of miles showcased nothing but super-flat shadeless red desert with the occasional smattering of low lying rock, scrubby spinifex, and bluebush.

I had been on the road for the last three hours waiting for a ride.

Pakap had dropped me just outside Cobar on a long thin road that stretched to the horizon. Earlier in the morning he had shown me the same touching hospitality as the previous night, serving up a delicious home-cooked farewell breakfast of fried eggs on toast, washed down with strong and aromatic dark black coffee. I hoped for the same sort of luck today, but it had yet to materialize.

Despite being mid-morning the temperature was already baking hot, with a mirage visible on the empty asphalt ahead. There was no breeze to lighten the stifling air and it was only going to get hotter. On either side of the road, and into the distance, was quintessential Australia: scorched red earth, gum trees, and scattered brush. To stop myself from overheating I waited in the dappled shade of a gum. Eventually a huge articulated truck appeared in the distance, but before it got anywhere near me it came to a halt next to a picnic rest-area a couple of minutes walk away. A male driver clambered down the ladder-like stairs leading from his cab to sit at the table. This was an opportunity I couldn't miss. And so, with the intention of asking for a ride face to face, I began the hike back towards him.

He looked up from his sandwich and briefly stared my way as I approached and must have known exactly what I was going to ask. After all, why else would I be out here on the side of the road with a dirty great backpack?

"Morning," I said, in my most cheerful upbeat tone, eliciting from the trucker a reluctant, almost imperceptible, nod of the head, followed by a cagey, "G'day."

I came straight out with it and asked him for a ride.

"Sorry, mate. Not allowed to pick up hitchhikers for insurance reasons. If we do, it's instant dismissal."

"No worries," I replied nonchalantly, as if it was neither here nor there to me whether I was stuck on the side of the road for another three hours. "So where you heading?" I asked, sitting down at the table with the ulterior motive of building a bit of rapport first, before asking him to bend the rules and give me a ride. We chatted about nothing in particular for a few minutes before he asked me, out of the blue, and with sinister emphasis, "Have you met any of our blacks here yet?"

Oh great, I thought, here comes that all too familiar Australian—a racist.

"Got a lift from a delightful Aboriginal couple yesterday out of Narromine," I replied. "Insisted on giving me some of their pizza and coke."

He looked at me in disbelief, as if something didn't compute.

"You must have been very lucky. Most of them aren't like that."

He commenced a bigoted diatribe, prefaced, of course, with the classic, "I'm not racist, but . . . " in which I was informed: "They're not the same as your black fellas in England," "We call them coons here," and "They're very lazy people," among other kangaroo shit.

A truck drove past in the opposite direction carrying goats.

"They'll be eaten by the filthy Arabs," he said. "People hunt the feral goats and ship them off to the Middle East."

He moved on to that other conversational favorite of xenophobic Australians—how you can barely move in the country now for all the hordes of illegal immigrants overrunning the place.

"D'you know there's even a KFC in Sydney where you can't get bacon on your food in case it upsets the fucking Muslims?"

He left no doubt as to what he'd like done to those of Islamic faith.

"Was speaking to a couple of the boys back from Afghanistan, said if the mussies don't take their hands out of their pockets when they tell them to, then they just shoot 'em."

It continued in predictable tabloid fashion.

"All the hard working tax payers of this country are being screwed by the immigrants. The dirty bludgers even have the right to appeal to the high court now."

"Are you not allowed to appeal to the high court, then?" I asked.

"Err, well, yeah, I guess, in theory," he responded. "But it would be very difficult to do."

The crazy thing about all this to me, was not so much that this stranger held such views, but that he deemed it perfectly acceptable to launch into them with an unknown visitor to the country. I was no longer interested in a lift with him, so in an attempt to divert the conversation for a few minutes while I made the most of sitting down, I asked him about the dangers of driving his truck, which had giant, super-chunky bull bars on the front that looked big enough to tackle an elephant, and a warning sign that announced "EXPLOSIVES."

"Roos are the biggest problem at night. If you hit a roo, the bars will normally throw it off to the side, but if it goes underneath it can cause you a bit of trouble. You'll most likely be stuck on the road next morning fixing up the damage."

What he said next was astonishing.

"If you hit an Aboriginal you don't stop."

At first I thought it was a sick joke.

"It's happened to me twice now. Once when a guy pushed a woman into my path. Second one was just wandering about on the road."

He was serious.

Incredulous, I asked him why on earth he hadn't stopped.

"Oh, it's not a problem, you just drive on to the next town and report it there. Hit one on the way down from Darwin and reported it in Alice Springs. Cop asked, 'Where you heading?' told him 'Perth.' He said, 'Have a good journey.' That was it."

As I struggled to get my mind around this, the throaty sound of an approaching four-wheel-drive cut through my considerable bewilderment, jolting me back to the task at hand. I jumped up and sprinted from the picnic area to the side of the road and stuck out a thumb. A beefy old-style Ford SUV with huge off-road tires approached at high speed. To my delight the driver hit the brakes and came to a dramatic lurching stop just beyond my position. I ran over.

A big muscular guy in his thirties with a cheerful, rugged face and a broad smile sat behind the wheel.

"I'm going as far as Broken Hill," he announced.

Broken Hill was a full day's drive westward. This was superb news.

Running back to the picnic table, I grabbed my backpack and, without so much as a "good bye" to the trucker, headed for the rear of the SUV. Inside was a mattress, two surfboards, multiple fishing rods and assorted camping supplies. I threw in my pack. Moments later I was perched inside the front, high above the road. The engine gave a guttural growl, I was thrown back in the seat from acceleration and we were off, heading into the barren outback proper.

My new traveling companion was Zedediah—"Zed" for short—an itinerant miner from Coffs Harbour on the east coast, who worked a couple of weeks on, then had a week off, giving him plenty of time to surf, fish and enjoy the considerable wage he earned from mining. We hit it off immediately, and in no time Zed was telling me about himself.

"I had all manner of boring menial jobs scraping by before getting into mining. Worked in factories, cleaned dishes, you name it."

Zed explained that breaking into the mining industry was no mean feat; it was, apparently, a bit of a closed business, difficult to get a foot in the door unless you had a family member or close friend already working there, but once you did, the money was serious.

"After all the years of terrible pay, I almost feel guilty when I look at my pay packet at the end of the month."

With a bit of subtle prying, I asked him how much he got.

"About two to three grand a week."

Not too shabby.

"I tried for years to get into mining with no luck, and then out of the blue a friend called me up and asked if I was still trying to get into it. He got me a job out in the middle of nowhere. I moved there immediately and have never looked back."

Zed and I plowed onwards together into a magnificent, visually seductive landscape, arresting in its eerily desolate and expansive beauty—a world bisected by the perfect seam of a uniform flat horizon: huge sky colliding abruptly in simple geometry with the unyielding elemental power of the earth, cleft so perfectly in two as to appear more a seascape than of land. The lower half comprising dry light-brown savannah; the upper half, penetrating, deep blue sky with sparse low-lying cumulus clouds. And all illuminated by the purest, brightest light that cast the clouds above a lustrous white and the grasses of the near roadside below a shimmering blonde.

As we drove deeper into the wilderness abyss we chatted away like old buddies.

I mentioned my earlier conversation with the racist trucker.

"It's a real shame," he said, shaking his head with genuine embarrassment. "There's a lot of racists here, almost to the point where it's socially acceptable."

After nearly three hours on the road, we approached the first outback town along our route, the remote dwelling of Wilcannia, home to about five hundred people, as well as what is perhaps Australia's most shameful statistic: the average life expectancy for an Aboriginal in Wilcannia is just thirty-seven years. And this in a country ranked as the richest place on earth by a Credit Suisse Global Wealth report. Just before reaching the village, we crossed an old wrought-iron vertical lift bridge with a welcome sight beneath it—a river.

"Fancy a swim, Jamie?"

Damn right, I did.

Driving into Wilcannia, it had the distinct feel of a ghost town, with no shortage of boarded up shop fronts and barely anyone on the streets. Suddenly the town's houses petered out and we came upon a dirt track, of sorts, leading through the bush. This was what Zed was after, and his four-wheel-drive monster made for. He hit the gas. The truck came into its own, tearing across the super bumpy landscape, its giant engine giving a throaty roar that mirrored our excitement as we lurched and jolted about in all directions towards the river. The chunky oversized tires locked up, bringing us to a dramatic skidding halt on a grassy bank covered with thin, curly leaves from multiple eucalyptus trees lining the river. Silty-colored water stretched a couple of hundred feet to the opposite bank, flowing at what looked an invigorating, if slightly daunting, pace for a swim. Kicking off our shoes, we threw on our bathers and approached the water.

"Keep an eye out for crocs," said Zed, scanning the river from left to right.

I laughed.

He wasn't going to get me with that one. I knew crocodiles weren't found this far south. Although, to be fair, there was probably no shortage of snakes, spiders, or other Aussie outback nasties within the vicinity that could despatch an unlucky Brit just as easily as a crocodile. After all, the world's ten most poisonous snakes are all Australian, as is the world's most poisonous arachnid, the funnel web spider; the world's most poisonous fish, the stonefish; the world's most poisonous tick, the paralysis tick; not to mention the most poisonous creature on earth, the box jellyfish. No other country has as many animals that can kill you, nor in so agonizing a manner.

I put this out of my mind and waded into the water with Zed. Squelchy mud wrapped around my toes as my feet sank into the warm sludge underfoot, creating satisfying explosions of cloudy sediment, diffusing the clarity of the clearer water near the bank. I gradually waded deeper. Having been so hot for so long, the water had an instantaneous cooling effect on my sizzling skin. I felt like a piece of heated steel being doused. Another few steps and the bank dropped away beyond our depth. I submerged my head, flipping back my hair like a shampoo commercial, bringing immediate clarity to my sun-weary mind. Zed and I swam leisurely for a couple of strokes before the current seized us, dragging us downstream with a surging force. Struggling, we paddled against the water, never pausing for a breather. One moment of rest equaled succumbing to the rush of thousands of gallons of water. With more than a mild struggle, we made it to the calmer water of the bank. After catching our breath we got back on the road. Five minutes out of town and we were on another long stretch of deserted asphalt, slicing its way through a parched and barren landscape of rusty-colored sand, mottled with low-lying, grayish-green brush.

Zed turned to me with a complete no-brainer.

"You wanna drive for a bit?"

We pulled over and swapped places. I'd never driven anything as powerful as the 5.8 liter V8 monster that I was about to take the reins of. Buckling up, I slowly turned the ignition key, tentatively giving her some revs. The beast beneath my feet growled like a restrained bull about to be let out of the cage at a rodeo. I had no intention of sparing the horses, so I held on tight and dropped the clutch. The acceleration was epic, launching me into my seat as we scorched off into the void ahead. With the windows down in place of air-conditioning, hot desert air blasted throughout the cab, letting us feel connected and part of the barren landscape across which we powered. I loved every minute of it, and with Zed's permission took his baby up to some serious speeds on the empty road, but no matter how hard I pushed her, she was always a giving mistress with plenty more waiting in the wings. A guy's vehicle to be sure.

An odd feature about hitching is that quick bonds are often formed. On the road complete strangers open up to you. Maybe it was the confined space of the cab, or possibly the open, expansive environment we drove through, but it seemed to encourage Zed and me to talk, and it wasn't long before he was telling me about some of the hardships of his youth.

"My life's really working out now and I feel happier than ever, but it wasn't always that way," he told me. "I was abused as a boy, and the depression led me to turn to alcohol, drugs, and pornography. Slit my wrists and even tried to hang myself."

He showed me a long, thick and painful-looking scar on his forearm.

"What happened to the person who abused you?" I asked, not really knowing if this was an appropriate thing to query, but justice and retribution was my first reaction.

"He's in prison," he stated flatly. "I got to give evidence against him recently, as did some other people he abused."

"How long did he get?"

"Eighteen years."

We talked of this for a while, with Zed going on to tell me how he'd kicked all his addictions and even helped counsel other victims of abuse.

"I'm at ease now and finally enjoying life," he told me with a contented smile.

Two hours of driving in a straight line, and by early evening we reached the mining town of Broken Hill, where Zed was starting work in the next couple of days. Known as the *Capital of the Outback*, Broken Hill is a delightful oasis of civilization amid the barren expanse of nothing surrounding it, being home to around 19,000 people. It's a long way from anywhere: the closest major city is Adelaide, 320 miles away. The town's other colloquialism, *The Silver City*, is a reference to the huge deposits of silver, lead and zinc found there in 1855 by boundary rider Charles Rasp, who made his discovery when out checking fences. Rasp secured his fortune soon after, and became one of the founding members of a syndicate that established what would later become Australia's greatest industrial powerhouse—mining company Broken Hill Proprietary Ltd. The town became a thriving mining center, which, at its peak in 1893, had sixteen mines and employed nearly 9,000 miners toiling away in cramped, roasting-hot underground shafts. Today things are different. Gone are the picks and shovels, with high explosives being the weapon of choice for getting at the precious ore within. Huge chasms the size of apartment blocks are blown clean out of the earth, then scooped up and spirited away by colossal trucks.

Two major mining companies operate in Broken Hill now, but their operations easily dwarf the efforts of the town's boom years. Such mechanical productivity has seen a big decline in Broken Hill's population, which has nearly halved since the 1950s. A good example that illustrates the scale of mining in Australia today, is when the country's largest mining company Broken Hill Propriety Ltd, merged with Billiton plc in 2001 (to become BHP Billiton), the world's biggest mining company was born that at the time of writing is the sixth largest listed company on the planet, in terms of market value,[11] with profits greater than the gross domestic product of ninety-three countries.[12]

I drove into the town along an attractive high street with multiple buildings possessing that classic outback feature, a double tiered veranda—providing shade for shop fronts along the sidewalk, and for the balconies of pubs and restaurants above. The town had a cheerful and relaxed feel about it, and retained a good helping of stunning old architecture, including a red-bricked post office with huge clock tower, and a grandiose town hall with lavish arched windows and intricate filigree work on its façade. Dominating much of the town to the south were several sprawling mullock mounds—giant man-made hills of leftover waste material from mining. Perched on top of one was a café.

I pulled up opposite a bronze statue of an Australian World War I soldier throwing a Mills Bomb (hand grenade). Zed and I got out to go in search of food, and after a brief perusal of what the place had to offer—which wasn't much, as almost everywhere was closed—we selected the local Democratic Club. Most clubs in Australia are a bit on the peculiar side, in that you don't actually need to be a member to use them. All we had to do was sign a big book at the door to get temporary membership, and we were welcomed inside its dated surroundings to enjoy its extensive café and bar. I went for a succulent roast chicken and veggies, while Zed got himself half a cow, in the form of a super thick and juicy-looking T-Bone steak.

"This one's on me," said Zed, as we approached the register.

I protested but it was no good.

"You can get me a drink instead," he offered by way of compromise. "I'll have a lemon, lime, and bitters."

As we tucked into our veritable feasts, Zed's cell phone went off. It was his boss, with good news for him but disappointing news for me. He had booked Zed into a local hotel for the night, scuppering our previously discussed plans of finding a local river to set up camp next to. It looked like I'd be roughing it alone, and there'd be no scenic riverside camping for me. It would have to be at a spot near the road, I couldn't be wasting the following morning traipsing back to one.

"I can drop you out of town if you like," suggested Zed.

This was a big help. The last thing I wanted to do was pay for a central campsite.

Zed's "out of town" turned out to be a good twenty miles past Broken Hill, by a lonely picnic shelter on the side of the road in the absolute middle of the desert. It was perfect. By the time we got there, the last of the remaining light was fleeing from a darkening restive sky.

"You sure you're gonna be alright out here?" asked Zed, looking around at the desolate and barren landscape that stretched in all directions.

"Yeah, no worries," I said, content that I had plenty of water and that come the morning the remoteness would pay dividends with any drivers that happened by.

After a fond farewell, I stepped out of the comfort and safety of the truck into the stark isolation of the windy outback, churning the surrounding sand into an airborne fury that lashed my face with such force as to be painful. A final wave and a toot of his horn, and Zed spun his four-wheel-drive beauty around and drove off into the distance. I stood motionless, watching through screwed up eyes as he disappeared from sight into the darkening abyss. Pensive contemplation at an end, I hastily set up camp, doing so on impossibly hard earth that felt like a cold slab of iron and bent several of my tent pegs in half. It was a relief to crawl inside, cloistered from the howling wind and sand that lashed against its taut nylon walls. Out came my inflatable "Therm-a-Rest" bedroll, a Christmas present from Emily, and minutes later I was lying down, drifting off into a contented sleep.

CHAPTER FIVE

Aussie Rules and British Tools

"I was sheep shearing with this Irish bloke up in New South Wales and on the way back to Broken Hill we spot this ewe with its head stuck in the fence. She looks at me, and me back at her with a twinkle in my eye. So I say to this Irish fella, 'shall we?' and he's like, 'okay.' So I go ahead and have my wicked way with the sheep, and when I'm finished I say to the Irish bloke 'your turn,' and he goes and sticks his head in the fence!"

I laughed.

"I'm not saying that it's true, but it's a sheep shearer's yarn," said my first ride of the morning, Brett, a rough-as-guts, happy go lucky, thirty-two-year-old sheep shearer who picked me up shortly after dawn in a sporty black sedan.

"Been pissed here many times, rolling rotten drunk!" said Brett, as we drove through the ramshackle hamlet of Cockburn that was home to only twenty-five souls and straddled the boundary of states New South Wales and South Australia.

"I know every publican in every town around here," said Brett, as we drove on into another seemingly endless barren void. "If you work like a horse you've got to drink like a horse. And shearing's the second hardest job in the world."

"What's the hardest?"

"They haven't worked it out yet!"

He picked up a vicious-looking set of spiked shearing combs from the dash board.

"Worst bit is when you jab it up your fingernail or cut yourself. My old man lost six pints of blood, his heart was pumping that fucking fast. The hardest of men just cry sheep shearing. It's the only job where you still take a sweat towel to work—gotta stop the stuff getting in your eyes!"

Brett handed the spikes to me for inspection.

"So what is it you do, Jamie?" he asked.

"I write books."

"Never read one in my life," he exclaimed proudly, before adding, so as not to offend me, "My misses reads them, like."

Brett was certainly a laugh a minute, and had no end of anecdotes to enliven the monotony of the flat outback scenery.

"We had this fucking fat Maori chick called Rangi who got a job out on the station, cooking for us shearers. Whale of a woman, eighteen stone of blubber she was. Come morning smoko, we went to the kitchen and there was no sign of her, so we had to make our own sangers. Lunchtime comes around and she's still nowhere to be seen, so we have to make that too. Everyone thought she'd quit. Only discovered where she was when one of the boys went to the dunny. It was a great big drop toilet, and stuck down there, right at the bottom, up to her shoulders in shit, was Rangi—who fell in after the seat collapsed under her fat arse. Lowered a rope in but she was too heavy, so we had to rip the bloody walls and roof off the thing. Threw a chain in on the bucket of a tractor and winched her out. Give her credit though, she was game alright. Showered off and started to cook. None of the boys were too keen to eat now though, so the boss goes in and tells her, 'Sorry, luv, but we're gonna have to let you go.' Some days it's better you just stay in bloody bed!"

Several stories later, and I asked Brett if he'd seen much of the country.

"I drove all around Australia once, and without a license too. Been done for drunk driving six times. Would have been jail time but it was in different states," he told me with a satisfied grin.

He was currently on a provisional license plate.

"You can get up to some great speeds on these roads. They used to do the Cannonball Run out here from Alice Springs to Darwin. Got banned after two Japanese crashed their Ferrari at over 300ks. Killed them and two officials."

I told Brett that when I got near Alice Springs I planned to visit Australia's most iconic natural wonder, Uluru (formally known as Ayers Rock), a giant sandstone monolith that changes color with the moods of the sun, and asked if he'd been there.

"Yeah, but I didn't go right up to it. Abbos charge you fifteen dollars, then spend it on piss and go and stab each other."

Since "Abbo" was the Australian equivalent of "nigger," I decided to hastily change the subject. I may not have liked his vernacular, but neither did I want to fall out with him over it and see my ride cut short. So I steered the conversation in a different direction, asking Brett if he had any good music on his MP3 player, which was currently plugged in but silent.

"Choose something for yourself," he offered.

I flicked through his collection and was surprised to see a large cache of England's cheesiest old crooner, Cliff Richard.

"I didn't have you down as much of a Cliff Richard man," I said to Brett with a smile, expecting to be told that Cliff had only wormed his nasty way onto his MP3 after the wholesale dumping of someone else's collection on his. After all, Cliff Richard is the sort of person your Grandma listens to.

"You're kidding. I fucking love Cliff!" he replied, in all sincerity.

A couple of hours drive and we arrived at a remote junction in the middle of nowhere. Brett was heading south, whereas I needed to head west for the small town of Peterborough. It should have taken about three hours to get here, but the way Brett nailed it, we shaved a full hour off the drive.

A short lift in a white SUV from a couple of butchers who skinned sheep for a living, and I made it to Peterborough—formerly Petersburg, but renamed due to anti-German feelings during World War I. Grabbing a meat pie and sauce for lunch—an Aussie favorite—I hiked to the other side of town, where a turning led towards my final destination of today, Port Augusta.

I threw down my pack on the dusty red earth beside the road, and surveyed my surroundings. To my right was the iron fence of a small home across the road; to my left, beyond an abandoned lot, was a cream-colored warehouse building that was part of a steam railway museum; and ahead, just up the road before it took a gentle curve to the left and disappeared from sight into farming lands, was a small rectangular reservoir.

There weren't many cars passing and those that did showed little interest in stopping. After about an hour in the blistering sun, a bare chested, heavily tattooed man from the house opposite called out to me.

"Be careful out here," he said. "Been a few hitchers come a cropper."

"I should be okay," I replied, trying to allay his concern, "I'll be camping near the road and I've got plenty of gear with me."

"No, I meant murdered," he stated. "There's some bad sorts around these parts. Have you seen the film *Wolf Creek?*"

I hadn't, and had no intention either. It was, I knew, loosely based on true events, where several backpackers were killed by a serial killer in the outback.

I told him I'd be careful.

A painfully slow three hours of waiting passed before I struck it lucky again, with another white SUV pulling up—a popular choice of color out here because of its heat reflecting qualities.

Two tough-looking guys sat up front, the driver of which looked as hard as they come with deep set eyes and a furrowed leathery face. After quickly establishing where they were going, I jumped in.

"I bet you're loving the cricket," said the driver as we pulled off—a reference to England having just beaten their Australian foes in the Ashes series.

"Always good to see you guys lose once in a while," I replied.

The driver introduced himself as Billy and the passenger as his son, Duke. Both worked in the steel trade in Whyalla, about 130 miles away.

"Got a good pommy friend from London, he was amazed at the scenery out here. He's an old fella but a real good cunt, can drink a pint of piss standing on his head," said Billy as we drove through a panorama made up increasingly of agricultural land. More "bush" now than outback.

If a particular journey is summed up by a particular topic of conversation, then this one was hunting, and Billy and Duke's love of it. Pigs, rabbits, goats, wombat, you name it, they were into shooting and trapping it.

"Got all the freezers stocked up with meat and fish at home," said Billy, who did most of the talking, with Duke only chipping in rather sheepishly now and again. It left me with the distinct impression that Duke was still in his old man's shadow, despite being in his late twenties or early thirties.

"Catch so much fish that we sell it to the local fish and chip shop," said Billy, before adding, "On the sly, like. If you get caught busting conservation quotas the cunts will throw the fucking book at you!"

"What would you get?" I asked.

"Big fine and you'll be looking at about a year inside."

Seemed fair enough to me.

The further we drove the lusher the scenery became. Up ahead, about five minutes drive in the distance, the dark form of a lone rain cloud drifted from left to right towards the center of the long straight road in front of us. As if on cue, upon it reaching the road the cloud burst open, relinquishing a long, slightly curved, trail of water in an otherwise blue sky. On either side was sunlight, illuminating the cloud and creating a picture-perfect contrast of light and dark.

We found ourselves passing through a twisting section of hillsides, where Billy pulled over so we could all take a leak. "See that, Jamie," said Duke, pointing with his free hand to a beautiful pink cockatoo in a nearby tree. "That's a galah."

"Do they make good eating?" I asked jokingly, since he and Billy seemed to hunt most everything else.

"They say the best way to cook a galah is in a billy can," replied Duke. "But you've got to weigh it down with a rock inside. After a couple of hours boiling, you carefully take the galah and the rock out, then you throw away the galah and eat the rock. If you're lucky, it doesn't taste of galah!"

Back on the road I mentioned my ambitious plan of reaching Uluru by tomorrow night.

"Used to call it Ayers Rock," said Billy in disgust, clearly disapproving of it now being officially recognized by its original Aboriginal name. I wasn't particularity surprised; earlier he'd referred to the Aboriginals as "coons" and "niggers."

"I thought Uluru was spectacular when I went there," piped up Duke.

"Nah, just a big rock in the desert," said Billy.

This seemed to be the way of it with Uluru. You either loved it or couldn't see what all the fuss was about. I wondered what I would make of it.

By late afternoon we finally arrived at Port Augusta, a city by Australian standards but a small town most everywhere else, having just 13,000 people. The place was cut in two, with half of it on the west side of a vast sloshing coastal inlet, the Spencer Gulf, and half of it on the east side. As we drove over a bridge spanning the surprisingly foamy water between the two, Billy asked me where I wanted to be dropped.

"Outside the city if possible, on the road to Alice Springs if you're passing it."

"No worries, we'll go by it on the way home."

As we approached the necessary junction on the outskirts of town, I thanked them for the ride and began scanning the area for a suitable spot to throw down my tent.

"If you want you could always come and stay at my place," said Billy out of the blue. "Get yourself a good night's sleep and I'd even give you a fish feed too."

The image of a full plate of fish and chips drifted into my consciousness. I'd only had a meat pie today so the thought of a good meal was mighty tempting, illegally caught or not.

I agreed.

We drove west past five huge old water tanks, covered from head to toe in murals and graffiti, then took a turn south towards Whyalla. Industrial infrastructure appeared on its outskirts, including a steel works and a huge landlocked war ship outside a maritime museum.

"That's the HMAS Whyalla," said Billy. "World War Two warship built locally."

We dropped Duke off first at his house, then Billy and I headed towards his place.

"That's where we sell our excess fish," said Billy as we passed a fish and chip shop around the corner from his bungalow, on a quiet suburban street.

He welcomed me into a surprisingly kitschy home and made a beeline for the fridge. Out came two cans of ice cold Cooper's lager.

"Cheers, Jamie," said Billy, raising the can in a welcoming toast.

Three dogs in the backyard spotted him through the kitchen window and went crazy. No sooner had Billy unlocked the back door and the dogs were near frothing at the mouth with excitement, jumping up on him and me—with a little too much enthusiasm for my liking.

"They're pig hunting dogs," said Billy proudly, play-wrestling with one in the process, before leading me out back into a huge metal shed. In here were several freezers, a speed boat with a humongous outboard engine, and multiple nasty-looking animal traps with horrible metal jaws—of the type an animal would have to gnaw its own limb off to escape from.

"This one's a dingo trap," said Billy, picking up the biggest of them all. "Gave one to my pommy friend as a sort of souvenir to take home to England, but the bloody customs wouldn't let him take it out the country."

After a quick look at the traps, boat, and mountainous freezer contents, which looked big enough to feed half the town, we adjourned inside to look at his gun collection. Or should I say, arsenal: bolt-action hunting rifles in a range of styles, huge double-barrel shotguns, sniper-like rifles with telescopic sites; you name it.

"Wanna have your picture taken with one?"

Why not, I thought, and posed in the backyard with a shotgun that looked capable of taking down an elephant.

"I used to have some lovely guns, Jamie, some beautiful semi-automatics, but that cunt in Tasmania ruined it for all of us," said Billy, referring to a massacre at Port Arthur where a lone gunman killed 35 people, after which semi-automatic weapons were banned.

It wasn't long before Billy was good to his word of earlier and cooked me up a delightful "fish feed," taken from a stockpile of fresh stuff in the fridge, which he fried in a homemade beer-batter and drizzled in juice from lemons taken from a small tree in the backyard. It was fantastic and there was far more than I could possibly finish.

Over our meal, Billy told me about his former work as an armed guard on security vans.

"My only regret was not getting raided, so I never got the chance to jump out, all guns blazing, and shoot the cunts."

Despite Billy's clear and appreciated hospitality to me, I can't say I particularly warmed to the bloke, despite my outward friendliness. He seemed an odd sort of person; a bit too obsessed with guns and killing for my liking, with what at times seemed the mentality of a fourteen year old.

"I would have loved to have gone to war!" he said to me when talking about Australia's involvement in the Vietnam War—a subject which, along with military history in general, he was eager to discuss.

He showed me a picture of his other son, Duke's brother, in military uniform.

"He had to pull out of going to Iraq after getting irritable bowel syndrome. Broke his fucking heart it did. He was so excited at the prospect of going to war. Before his diagnosis, Duke said to him, 'I want you to bring me back an ear.'"

My opinion of Duke took a nosedive. Despite my revulsion at his sick request for a war crime souvenir, I'm ashamed to say, that in the interests of keeping my free accommodation, I didn't articulate my disgust, but remained silent instead and went back to my fish and chips.

After eating we retired to the sitting room with a cup of milky tea, where Billy showed me some photos of himself in his twenties playing "Aussie Rules," or Australian Rules Football, a rough and tumble game where burly men in skimpy shorts and "wife beater" tank tops run about a field with an egg-shaped ball that they punch to each another instead of throw—in addition to doing plenty of punching of each other too.

"I referee it now but back in my day I was a force to be reckoned with," said Billy with a satisfied smirk. "You could say I *played the game*," he said. "I was up in front of the disciplinary board many a time."

We chatted of this for a while before Billy appalled me again. This time when talking of how hard he had found it when his sons left home.

"It was awful, like I lost my best mates who I would go trapping and fishing with," he said, starting off innocuously enough, before adding, "We still do it together but it's not like it was. Back in the day we'd be sitting around the house and one of them would turn to me in the evening and say 'Dad, d'you wanna go shoot cats at the dump?'"

"You shoot cats?" I asked incredulous, interrupting Billy's happy reminiscing of the good old days.

"Yeah, shooting cats is great fun, you'd love it!"

Billy was definitely a strange character, that's for sure. Later in the evening he surprised me again, this time when he spoke movingly about his father's battle with leukemia and how it had killed him, showing a sensitive side so very different to the macho gun nut of earlier. But then, not thirty minutes later, when again relating his passion for military history, he recalled a discussion he'd had with someone about the Japanese.

"Cunt tried telling me there was nothing wrong with the Japs now, so I said to him, 'The best thing about Hiroshima is that it's still causing leukemia there today!'"

I made my excuses and retired to bed shortly afterwards.

CHAPTER SIX
Indecent Proposal

The road to Alice Springs and I have history. In 2001 that long, straight, barren stretch of asphalt handed me my longest, hottest, and most demoralizing hitchhiking wait ever. At the time I'd been dropped roughly 100 miles outside of Port Augusta, after hitching there from Perth, in an area called Nurrungar where a lone roadhouse and a few scattered tin-roofed dwellings stood in an expanse of nothing. I'd camped there overnight and got out on the road at dawn the following morning, with hopes of making it to Alice Springs by nightfall, 650 miles away. But no plan survives contact with the enemy.

There were so few vehicles heading north that I ended up sitting by the shadeless roadside, squinting into the heat-haze, waiting for the shining reflection of a car or truck to appear on the horizon. It took so long before it reached me that I'd watch its gradual approach for several minutes, until I was within sight of the driver, at which point I'd get up and attempt to thumb him or her down, only to watch forlornly, time after time, as they drove on past. I waited eight hours in temperatures that climbed to 110 degrees Fahrenheit with no sun hat, shades or sunscreen, and with water that got so warm it was like sipping from a hot bath, until, finally, someone showed mercy upon me and stopped. By the time they did I was battered and delirious from the sun. To this day I have never tasted a beverage as sublimely satisfying as the frozen carton of iced coffee the driver gave me from his cooler, which turned from a solid block to a drinkable slush within minutes.

I hoped to God I didn't get stuck at the same spot today.

Getting out of Whyalla proved easy enough with Billy dropping me on the outskirts of town by a factory. Here two steel workers who had just finished their shift, gave me a lift to Port Augusta. On the way there I was asked again, "Have you met any of our black fellas?" and also warned of the dangers in the outback, with the film *Wolf Creek* getting another plug, and the notorious murder of a British man on the road out of Alice Springs to Darwin mentioned. Billy had been similarly vocal about this and described his own characteristic precautions.

"Whenever I travel on the road up to Darwin, I always keep a gun on the front seat with a full clip ready to go."

And so, with such fears, I perhaps shouldn't have been surprised by the response I got from the first person to stop for me on the road to Alice Springs; although, with hindsight, it was something of a surprise they stopped at all.

"You're not going to harm me, are you?" asked a startled-looking woman in her seventies, as she pulled up in a rust bucket of a car, making for the oddest introduction I've ever had from someone who's pulled over for me.

"No," I answered, "I'm British."

I have no idea why I said that. Although in a sense it held within it the overall message I wanted to convey—that I was a foreign visitor, here to take in the sights not dump her corpse in the trunk.

"Are you sure you're not going to harm me?" she asked again.

I reassured her as best I could.

She looked wary and on edge, like she wanted to help but had heard one too many horror stories.

"Oh, I don't know," she said, nervously clutching her hair.

I didn't want to see my lift slip away from me. And so, I decided it best to reassure her once more, and then to just open the door and get in before the old girl changed her mind.

"I promise I'm not going to harm you," I said, gently opening the front passenger door, constantly talking to her in soothing tones as I did so. I got in. There were several blister packs of medication in the passenger foot well. She gave me a hesitant nod and we were off.

"Say hello to Tiny?" she said, nervously.

"I'm sorry?"

She partially unwrapped a blue towel on her lap revealing the most scrawny little dog I've ever seen, with legs thinner than my fingers.

"You're not going to need to pee are you, Tiny?" she said to the little runt. "He might need to go," she concluded. "Would you like to hold him?"

Hell no. But before I had a chance to decline she reached over and dropped towel and animal on my lap. Both stank. Of mangy dog and urine. I recoiled at the stench.

"Are you afraid of him?" she asked, misreading my reaction.

"Err, yes," I said, in the hope she'd take him back. It didn't work.

"Oh, silly," she said, touching my forearm, "He's only little."

She introduced herself as Margaret, and then moments later was asking me again if I was going to harm her. This turned out to be a mildly disturbing repetitive feature of a generally strange and awkward ride. I'd talk to Margaret for a while, trying to engage her in conversation, and just when it looked like she'd settled into the idea of driving with a hitchhiker, she'd ask me again if I was going to harm her. The worry for me was that at some point her paranoia would get the better of her and she'd have a change of heart about picking me up, and would leave me in the middle of nowhere, which was exactly where we were. The next gas station was one hundred miles away.

Adding to the feeling of overall awkwardness was another, by now familiar, element to the ride, which reared its head once more when I mentioned my excitement at soon seeing Uluru.

"Aboriginals think it's *their* land now!" said Margaret, raising her voice to a near shriek, leaving no doubt as to what she made of that.

The ride eventually came to an end at my old hitching nemesis—the desolate outpost of Nurrungar. Here a fork in the road—the first proper turning we'd come across so far—led east towards the small town of Woomera, where Margaret was heading. I needed north so this was the end of the line.

As I watched Margaret's lone car disappear into the distance towards Woomera, I gazed out across the familiar flat landscape where I'd spent those torturous eight hours all those years ago, and wondered how I would fare this time. Like it or not, I was where I was, and felt a certain defiant attitude towards the area, a sort of "bring it on" mentality that was willing and able to take anything it could throw at me.

The last time I was out here, it had been with the express intention of hitching to Uluru. In fact, this had been the only reason I'd hitchhiked out of Perth in the first place. I had desperately wanted to visit the mysterious and iconic rock, whose color reflected the shifting mood of the sun, images of which I had been bombarded with from television, magazines, posters, and brochures for years. But things hadn't quite gone according to plan, and since then Uluru had been a thorn in my side, something that had riled me for the last decade. The plan back then had been to first reach Alice Springs—the nearest town to Uluru—and to then hitch on to Uluru itself. But by the time I arrived in Alice Springs I was in a dire financial situation, down to my last thirty Australian dollars. This hadn't been through poor management of my funds, but rather, from getting ripped off by a man whom I had briefly worked for, along with several other travelers, selling vending machines—only to find myself issued with wage checks that bounced.[13] Having no credit card, access to an overdraft, or return flight home, I traipsed around every bar, restaurant, shop, and office that I could find in Alice Springs, in a desperate search for work. None had any. I was left with a stark choice: either continue hitching north another 930 miles to the next substantial settlement, the city of Darwin, where I could almost certainly find work due to its size, or stick around in Alice Springs and become properly destitute. Having already hitchhiked 2,640 miles specifically to see Uluru, I was damned if I was going to leave without attempting to hitch the extra 290 miles out there to visit it first. However, try as I might I failed to get a ride, despite waiting nearly as long as I had at Nurrungar—racking up about seven hours on the side of the road at Alice Springs in insane temperatures, during which some hilarious joker threw a bag of half-eaten McDonald's at me from the window of his car. The next day I took my last throw of the dice in Alice

Springs, spending it in a fruitless search for work until the evening, when I reluctantly decided to try my luck hitchhiking north instead to Darwin. I promised myself though, that I would return after I'd found work and had the funds to get out to Uluru. And in the strictest sense, I was true to my word. I arrived in Darwin the next day and secured a job soon after; and I did indeed head back towards Uluru; it's just that at a decade later, this took longer than envisaged.

I found myself a suitable spot at Nurrungar and waited. And then waited some more. Today's vehicle count was low, temperature high, and the number of sand flies astronomical. The rapacious little buggers were all over me, swarming about my face, trying to get at my eyes and mouth. Unzipping the hidden mosquito netting of my sun hat, I pulled it down over my head. It worked a treat, providing an effective, if slightly odd, respite from their advances. Although they were prevented from getting through the netting, the flies were still crawling all over it and buzzing away, just centimeters from my face, at an instinctively uncomfortable proximity.

Nurrungar was an odd area to wait in. Somewhere out there in the desert, hidden from view from the roadside, was a one-time highly restricted military facility, run jointly during the cold war by the U.S. Air Force and Australian Department of Defence; an installation that leaked Australian Department of Defence documents reveal controlled satellites used to pin point targets for the U.S. bombing of Cambodia, a secret and illegal act which killed half a million people.[14]

After about forty minutes of waiting, a red van approached on the horizon. When it was close enough for its driver to actually see me, I pulled off my fly net. As the van gradually got nearer I could see a lone woman behind the wheel. Despite the lift from Margaret, I didn't hold out much hope of her stopping, especially since the next proper town, Coober Pedy, was 230 miles away, meaning she'd have to be willing to take me at least this far by herself. But to my delight, as she got closer, the van began to slow down, coming to a stop beside me.

"Come on, get in!" said an enthusiastic bob-haired girl in her early twenties, wearing a black tank top.

I thanked her and pulled open the sliding rear door, revealing a mattress and assorted camping supplies inside. I threw my backpack in and took a seat up front.

"I'm Mandy," said my new driving companion, reaching over to shake my hand, exposing a tattoo of a lizard on her wrist.

With introductions aside, I asked where she was heading.

"Broome," she replied. "Long drive, hey?"

At over 2,360 miles, it certainly was.

"What about you?"

"Darwin, but I'm going to stop off at Uluru first."

"It's your lucky day, me too."

This was sweet, joyous music to my ears. Not only had I managed to score a lift out of the dreaded Nurrungar in double-quick time, but it was going direct to the elusive Uluru that had thwarted me for so long, and, what's more, was heading north afterwards. I'd avoid having to hitch out of Alice Springs, and would practically make it to my final destination in Australia too, since, to get to Broome, Mandy would have to go within 200 miles of Darwin. In all, the ride would equate to roughly 1,720 miles through a hot and treacherous landscape that had got the better of me once before. But not this time. All I had to do was sit back and enjoy the ride.

Mandy was talkative, and told me much of her life in Adelaide where she was a horticulture student. She was currently on her holidays and heading to Broome to work at an oyster farm where you could get well-paid cash-in-hand work. She was partly heading there for the money, partly for the adventure, but mostly to get away from her boyfriend who, in her words, was "such a dick." When I asked why she was going out with him then, she replied, with a confused shake of the head, "I don't know."

The drive was an unsurprisingly desolate one along a sparsely used road, which had many dead kangaroos on its side, and even the occasional bloated corpse of a cow—most likely coming from Anna Creek, the world's largest cattle ranch located hereabouts, which at six million acres (the size of Belgium) is eight times as big as the world's second largest ranch, King's Ranch in Texas. Ranches in this part of the world are so ridiculously oversized to cope with the impotency of the land, which has to make do with an average rainfall of just eight inches a year—and sometimes no rain at all. For the ranchers of Anna Creek this works out at about three good years in every ten.

"If we find some fresh road kill we should cook it tonight," said Mandy as we passed another decomposing carcass. "My family's a bit feral like that."

Road kill was fine by me. I'd picked up a whole roe deer in the U.K. once, and even a hare; both were delicious. Mandy took things way beyond my concept of "food for free" however.

"When my mum and I were in Darwin we came across a house with some pet ducks in the garden, so we snuck in there and took one."

"You stole someone's pet?" I asked, dumbfounded.

"Yeah, was bloody tasty too!"

I didn't know quite what to make of that.

Three and a half hours of driving and we arrived at the next settlement, Coober Pedy, an outback town of roughly 2,000 people, billed as the opal mining capital of the world. Coober Pedy's surrounding terrain made for an interesting break from the flat monotony, consisting of thousands of distinctive pyramidal mounds scattered across the landscape—leftover debris from opal mining. This had occurred in the area since 1915, when a group of prospectors out hunting for gold stumbled instead upon copious quantities of opals. For the miners who set up in Coober Pedy, life was, and still is, hard. Temperatures can push 120 degrees Fahrenheit and the area suffers from an extreme lack of water. Nearby is the world's largest salt pan, Lake Eyre, covering 3,500 square miles, into which drains a fifth of Australia's water, but that doesn't mean you'll find much of the stuff there; it has only filled up four times since records began in 1885. Such an extreme scarcity of water saw the early residents limited to a meager two gallons a week. The town is so hot that miners who live year round in Coober Pedy do so in homes underground known as "dugouts," where the temperature is much cooler. This practice is reflected in Coober Pedy's name, which in the local Aboriginal language means "white man's burrow." There was even an underground Catholic church.

Back in the van we continued north until just before nightfall, when we pulled off the side of the road, set up camp and got a fire going. In a frying pan we cooked up sausages, eggs, and beans; a hearty fare which we settled down to with a strong cup of tea. When the crepuscular light finally slipped away and night descended on a clear desert sky, we were treated to a wondrous display of stars, millions of little diamonds scattered across a timeless, inky-black sky. Our campfire's faint light stretched out to the nearby bushes, illuminating them with an orange haloey glow. Beyond, everything was darkness.

Perhaps it was the soothing primeval crackle of the fire's dancing flames, or perhaps Mandy just needed someone to talk to, but soon she began to divulge her motivations for making the trip. She delved into the detail of what sounded like a highly dysfunctional relationship of several years, which, for whatever reason, she couldn't quite bring herself to terminate.

"There's no love in it. It's only sex now and the sort of sex we have doesn't involve love."

Perhaps I shouldn't have pried, but I guess I was curious as to what she meant. Mandy explained how she and her boyfriend took part in what I suppose you'd describe as extreme bondage or kinky sex, including ropes, restraints, and other paraphernalia.

Interesting.

"It was fun and exciting at first, but it's not love, is it?" she said, suddenly seeming really down, almost to the point of tears.

"Do you love him?" I asked.

"I don't even like him!" she replied. "He went to Thailand with his mates to fuck prostitutes, and didn't even pretend that he didn't when he got back."

I tried to counsel her as best I could, telling her that if she was unhappy in the "relationship" —a term I used very lightly—then she should end it.

"Yeah, I *should*," she replied sheepishly, which seemed to imply she realized such logic well enough, but still had no intention of actually following through with it.

I awoke shortly after dawn to a chorus of galahs heralding the beginnings of a fresh day. Unzipping the mosquito dome of my inner tent, I emerged to a crisp, crystal-clear morning with a huge blue sky, and immediately set about getting the fire going again.

As ember was nurtured into the flickering new life of a flame, I looked out across the desert's bright-red sands and ruminated on how alive I felt at this moment—largely because I was living within it, centered in the nexus of the here and now, not worrying for tomorrow, for I had no idea what tomorrow or today would bring. It was just the way I liked it. There is something about the open road, and the allure of the possibilities that come with it, that I find deeply satisfying. I can rationalize some of my motivations for traveling, for dropping everything safe and commonplace, and running off into the unknown, but there is a larger part of me that can't quite articulate the power of this elusive internal calling. It is an innate primal drive that I simply obey. For to deny it is to deny myself. I have read of geneticists who have identified what is colloquially known as the explorer or adventure gene, a mutation of gene DRD4, known as DRD4-7R, or 7R for short. Research has shown that 7R is tied to restlessness, curiosity, novelty seeking, and risk taking, making those who harbor the gene more likely to embrace exploration, movement and new ideas. I wondered if I possessed it. It is found more frequently in migratory cultures than in sedentary ones, and in one study among Kenya's cattle herding tribesman, the Ariaal, it was observed that those carrying 7R were healthier—in terms of being stronger and better fed—than those who didn't. However, among the Ariaal's settler cousins, those who carried 7R tended to be less well-nourished and successful. It seemed to ring true with my own life: flourishing on the move; stagnating when stationary.

When the fire was good and hot, Mandy joined me from the van, bringing with her the ingredients to make a classic Aussie bush food: damper bread.

To make a damper, or unleavened, bread, in its most elemental form, you simply mix flour and water into a dough, then cook it in the embers of a fire. Done this way there's no need for a pot or other utensils and, best of all, there's no washing-up afterwards. Dampers were first made by the Aboriginals using wild acacia seeds which they ground into a flour between rocks then added water to make a dough. They would then bury this in embers to cook. When the early explorers saw this they borrowed the concept, substituting their own flour for the acacia flour and adding other ingredients when they were available. Mandy chucked in some rosemary and onion in hers, while I threw in some salt and milk powder in mine. Other handy ingredients are baking soda and, best of all, warm beer—the heated yeast from which helps the bread rise.

We cooked them for about half an hour, then excavated the dampers with a long gnarled stick. They weren't much to look at as they emerged from the coals, having an overall coating of ash and a charred black outer crust, but as we cut into them a soft, moist, fluffy center was revealed, which was surprisingly tasty, especially when served with melted butter.

Breakfast completed, we struck camp and got back on the road, driving until mid-afternoon when we reached the Erldunda turning for Uluru, which now lay only 157 miles away to the west. I'd been past this spot on my previous lift out of Nurrungar, but back then had made the mistake of continuing north 123 miles to Alice Springs with the intention of finding employment. As we turned west now at Erldunda a triumphant smile crept across my face. Every mile from here on in was closer to a place I had hungered to visit for far too long.

We continued until we reached a roadhouse, outside which was a giant outback "road train." Road trains are long trucks, in which the tractor unit pulls not one, but four trailers, making for some tricky overtaking for other road users. We pulled in beyond the road train and stopped for gas. I filled her up while Mandy went inside the shop to pay, emerging with a slab of beers, which she immediately indulged in. There was about sixty miles to go so I offered to drive. She accepted.

"You want one?" offered Mandy, as she clambered into the back, reclining on the mattress with her stash.

I was tempted but declined. It wasn't just that I didn't fancy the prospect of a bit of literal drunk driving, but having only had a damper to eat today, I knew it would go straight to my head. To have finally made it out here almost bordered on a spiritual journey for me, and so as much as a beer would have gone down a treat, I wanted my first impression of Uluru to be a sober one. Eventually I caught sight of it. Jutting abruptly from the flat horizon to a height of over 1100 feet, emerged the unmistakable loaf-shape monolith of Uluru, standing proud and alone like an immortal orange beacon amid a hauntingly empty expanse of desert wilderness. My heart skipped. It was like a giant magnet and I a piece of iron drawn towards it. I was mesmerized by its size, beauty, and awe, and drove staring more at Uluru than the road, a feeling that intensified the closer I got. Currently a soft orange hue, the scattered clouds above cast this strange isolated mountain with its ruffled near-vertical walls into shifting dappled patterns of light and dark, highlighting random undulating grooves and the overall ripples of its surface.

By the time we arrived at the entrance to the Uluru Kata Tjuta National Park I was on a high. Purchasing a ticket for twenty-five dollars, I drove down to one of the main scenic lookouts, the Uluru Sunset Viewing Area, where several tourists had parked to take photos and soak in the grandeur of the view. I got out to do likewise. Mandy remained prostrate in the back drinking, but pulled open the van's sliding door so she could see Uluru at the same time. I left her to it and wandered off for a better look.

Uluru is no easy place to describe. Sure, you can talk about its physical shape, the history of the site, or go into details about its geology—and rest assured, dear reader, I will—but there is so much more to Uluru, something indefinable that is difficult to convey, especially if you want to avoid sounding like a New Age hippie. But sound like one I must, for an intangible quality exists there, a deep and powerful atmosphere that seeps into you. Gazing out at this sacred rock I could almost feel it calling to me, bypassing logic and connecting with my heart. It was hypnotic, transfixing me. If I broke my gaze to look elsewhere, the rock would pull me back again. The longer I stared at Uluru the more connected I felt to it and the wider landscape, an expansive feeling where I could almost sense the ageless rhythm of this giant desert heart beating too within my own.

I stood for the best part of forty minutes just watching, soaking in the atmosphere. I tried to imagine the majesty the first explorers must have felt on stumbling upon it, and could so easily understand why it was a sacred site to the Aboriginals. It was to me, too. And I think it would be for just about anyone with their blood still pumping. There is an old surfing saying: "If surfing doesn't make you feel alive then you are probably already dead." For me, the same could be said of Uluru. I headed back to the van, jumping in up front.

"Why don't we drive right up close to Uluru?" I suggested, turning around to face Mandy who was still reclining on the mattress.

"Why don't you come and join me in the back?" she replied.

Uh-oh. This could prove awkward.

"I don't think that's a good idea," I responded.

"Come on, don't be the fun police, Jamie," she said, slightly biting her bottom lip afterwards and fixing me with a suggestive lingering stare.

I tried changing the subject. "So what do you say, shall we drive up to Uluru?"

"We've got all day tomorrow for that. Come on, get into the back with me and let's have some fun. I'm so horny right now!"

"Mandy, I've got a girlfriend," I said, taken aback by her forwardness.

"You don't know what she's up to while you're away. Come on, why don't we get wild?"

"Mandy, please don't do this."

"Do you ever get wild, Jamie? Think of all the things we could do."

She reached up and undid a small bulldog clip used to fasten a curtain across the rear window. "I wonder what we could do with this," she said, looking at it with fake curiosity.

Why hadn't more things like this happened to me when I was single?

After all, Mandy was kind of attractive in a sort of "out there" crazy kind of way, but I had zero intention of ever cheating on Emily. And not just because of the betrayal it would have been of her; I could well do without the guilt as well. If I had been single then it would have been a different story. But I wasn't single and Mandy knew it, which riled me. As did the location she had chosen for her advances, which was now tainting my experience of Uluru. A minute earlier I was soaking in the sublime beauty of somewhere I considered a sacred site. But instead of savoring Uluru's serenity and atmosphere, I was now fending off the sexual advances of a kinky girl, carrying more than a little emotional baggage to boot.

I turned the ignition on and began to drive towards Uluru, focusing again on it, my head clearing in the process.

Mandy sulked in the back.

As the rock grew closer, the more magnificent it became. Skirting along its side, I found myself craning my neck upwards, my attention darting from the road to the visual treat towering above. From afar, Uluru almost appears smooth, but up close that all changes. In places the surface is like a frozen liquid, contorted into waves and hollows; in others it is speckled with deep pock marks and lined with furrowed fissures; others still are weathered into huge channels and gullies. It is far more varied in form than it appears in photographs and is awesome in every way.

I pulled up by a small parking lot at the beginning of a walking trail that circumnavigated Uluru. We both got out for a quick look and to touch the rock, but didn't have time to walk the track this evening; that would have to wait for the morning. The park closed soon, so I suggested to Mandy that we head back to the sunset viewing platform and watch as the rock slowly transformed from orange to red. She agreed.

We weren't long back at the lookout, when Mandy began to hit on me again. Now more than ever I just wanted to watch the sunset illuminating Uluru, but she kept persisting. Eventually she insisted that we head off to find a camping spot outside the National Park. This could have waited until after the sun had slipped away, but despite being reluctant to depart early, there wasn't much that I could do. It wasn't my vehicle so I had little choice in the matter, unless I said farewell to Mandy, which would mean waving goodbye to my lift towards Darwin too. I considered this option but was reluctant to lose a ride of 800 miles. It would also be a long walk out of the park if I couldn't get another ride this evening. Since I planned to be up before sunrise in the morning, I could do without the added exertion now. And so we headed off to try and find an unofficial campsite, with me driving and Mandy sitting up front. After much fruitless searching we happened upon an empty section of land that looked suitable enough, but just as I started to pull up Mandy reached over and began massaging my neck.

"Mandy, I've got a girlfriend!" I protested, coming to a halt and turning off the ignition.

"Ahh, what's the matter with you!" she nearly shouted back at me.

"Right that's it, I'm out of here," I said. "I can't be putting up with this shit for the next few days. Thanks for the lift, but this is at an end!"

She didn't take it well and began to cry.

"I don't know why I bother, you try and help someone out and then this is how they repay you," she whimpered.

"What are you on about? I appreciate the lift but you keep fucking hitting on me! What part of that don't you understand?!"

She wallowed in self pity and generally made no sense in a conversation that went round in circles until she finally agreed to drop me in the small service town of Yulara, situated about 11 miles from Uluru itself. By the time we arrived it was dark.

As Mandy drove off and disappeared into the night it was a relief to see her go.

CHAPTER SEVEN
A Town Like Alice

The first magical glimpse of Uluru by astonished European eyes was had in 1873 by William Christie Gosse, who happened upon the mighty monolith while leading an expedition to find a route from central Australia to the west coast. "This rock is certainly the most wonderful natural feature I have ever seen," wrote Gosse.

In many respects Gosse's historic discovery was only possible thanks to the astonishing prior achievements of Scottish explorer, John McDouall Stuart, whose expeditions first mapped a route through the desolate center of Australia, from which other explorers could then set off. The magnitude of Stuart's undertaking and achievements is difficult to overstate, for the terrain he crossed is some of the most inhospitable on the planet, and before him next to nothing was known about Australia's interior; no maps of it existed.

Stuart's expeditions broke the mold in both their planning and execution. His planning exemplified the bushcraft philosophy of the more you know, the less you carry. In contrast to other expeditions of the day, Stuart traveled extremely light. Just about everything he and his small party of men carried was essential to the trip. Although that might sound a rather self-evident way to plan for such an undertaking, it couldn't have been more different from the approach of Stuart's contemporaries, in particular his competition, Robert O'Hara Burke and William John Wills. Like Stuart, Burke and Wills were also attempting to travel the country from south to north, an achievement sought by the government of the day to establish a telegraph line.

Unlike Stuart's pack-light and travel-fast approach, Burke and Wills took the pack-ridiculously and end-up-dying-painfully approach. Items Burke and Wills's ill-fated expedition deemed of such essential importance as to take on a four thousand mile return hike across uncharted territory include: three-quarters of a ton of sugar, dandruff brushes, rockets, sixty pounds of curled horse hair, six tons of firewood, a heavy oak table with accompanying stools, a stationary cabinet, and that old imperative that no self-respecting expedition party would be seen without, a Chinese gong. But my favorite items on the Burke Wills manifest are, "Nipples, assorted 4 dozen," and "Kangaroo Thongs." Whether kangaroo thongs were thongs made *from* Kangaroo hide for the exclusive use of the explorers, or whether they were thongs made *for* kangaroos, perhaps to be slipped on said creature to spice up a lonely night in the outback, I couldn't tell you. There is, of course, another alternative, that they are something wholly innocuous of which I am unaware, but given my thus-gained knowledge of Australians, this seems unlikely.

Within a year of setting off, Burke and Wills's expedition—which consisted of twenty-seven camels, twenty-three horses, and nineteen men lugging between them some twenty tons of kit—was down to only two camels and three men. Just one man would successfully complete the expedition. Both Burke and Wills died in the desert. But they were hardly alone in meeting such a demise at the hands of the unforgiving outback or in their penchant for expeditionary over-packing. Perhaps the best example of the latter comes from Thomas Mitchell, a man who in 1830 explored over three thousand miles of parched Australian outback lugging with him a couple of wooden boats that never saw a lick of water. "Although the boats and their carriage had been of late a great hindrance to us" he wrote, undeterred by the experience, "I was very unwilling to abandon such useful appendages to an exploring party."

But back to the hero of our tale, John McDouall Stuart, who knew better, or, more accurately, learned better. Stuart devised his pack light and travel fast method after being attached to a failed expedition of 1844 led by Captain Charles Sturt, who saw fit to take along with him into the outback a flock of two hundred sheep, as well as six drays and, of course, a boat—he was convinced, like many of Australia's early explorers, that the country's interior would contain an inland sea. Having witnessed how not to do it, Stuart formulated his own approach. In addition to traveling light and fast, the other striking feature of his expeditions was that instead of plowing on along a desired route and hoping to find water on the way—as most other expeditions did—Stuart let the presence of water itself dictate his route of travel.

He became an absolute master of sourcing a drink from nature, and did so in super dry, merciless landscapes where others would have only found death. Stuart would rise early before the heat-haze of the day distorted vision, and from the highest point meticulously survey the landscape with a telescope, looking for the slightest hint of water. This might be a particularly vibrant-looking tree or bush, the presence of pigeons or finches, even animals such as kangaroos that sometimes dig for water. But it was his discovery after scaling a small hill one evening that Stuart credits to his eventual success in pushing north. Here, in the most inhospitable part of the continent where it might not rain for years, Stuart was confronted by the most improbable sight: a bizarre line of small hills with water bubbling out of their summits. These were mound springs, a permanent supply of ground water that rises to the surface under pressure. Most of the water feeding the mound springs of central Australia originates from the highlands in the northeast of the country, and travels westwards underground through aquifers at a rate of around three to ten feet a year, taking about two million years before it bubbles up again. This has led to their precious liquid being described as "fossil water." Because of its creeping speed through aquifers, the water holds within it high quantities of dissolved solids which over time have concentrated around the springs, forming the distinctive mounds for which they are named.

The mound springs proved of such strategic importance to Stuart that they eventually allowed him to break though the interior of the country and continue on to the tropics of the north, to finally reach the sea. His monumental achievement in surveying the center of the continent led, in 1872, to the completion of a telegraph line that ran nearly two thousand miles from Port Augusta in the south of Australia to Darwin in the north. Today this route is roughly followed by the single lane road I took north out of Port Augusta, named, in Stuart's honor, the Stuart Highway.

Stuart's achievements paved the way for future expeditions within the center that set off from the telegraph line, including William Christie Gosse's the year after the line's completion, which "discovered" Uluru—from a European point of view, of course, as the site had been used for at least ten thousand years by the local Aboriginal people. Gosse wrote of his discovery, "This rock appears more wonderful every time I look at it, and I may say it is a sight worth riding eighty-four miles of spinifex sandhills to see." He named the site Ayers Rock in honor of the chief secretary of South Australia, Sir Henry Ayers, a name that stuck until 2002 when it was officially given the dual name of Uluru / Ayers Rock.

I set off for Uluru long before sunrise, striking my camp at a large caravan park in Yulara a little after 4:30 a.m. When pitching up the night before, the park office had been closed, allowing me to slip in without paying the extortionate seventeen dollars a night fee—a smidge expensive, methinks, for a six foot square patch of grass. As such, I had every intention of slipping out again without paying, and did so over a low fence next to a road—just in case the entrance was manned at this time in the morning to check on the few vehicles likewise departing.

Hitching in the dark can be problematic, so I set off along a curving, mostly unlit, road on foot, heading towards the National Park in the not unlikely event that no one stopped for me. Luck though, must have been on my side, as not long into my hike a lone set of headlights appeared in the distance behind me. Soon the car to which they belonged began to slow, gradually taking its time to pull over in what seemed an assessment of whether I was a safe bet or not to pick up. It would have been clear where I was going; just about anyone up at this hour was off to do the same thing: watch Uluru from the sunrise viewing area.

My new lift was Didier, a vacationing Frenchman driving a rental car. Minutes later we entered the park together and pulled up at the viewing area's full parking lot. A good hundred people were already waiting here, hoping to see the dawn work its wonders on Uluru. Expectations for something spectacular were high, with all gathered having no doubt previously seen remarkable photos of Uluru cast a magnificent crimson by the rising sun. Alas, it wasn't to be. A cloudy horizon led to a subdued and subtle sunrise.

Didier and I set off for the rock itself.

The trail around Uluru starts at the same point as a climbing route up Uluru begins. Climbing the rock is a contentious issue. Although climbing is not banned outright by the traditional Aboriginal owners of Uluru—the Pitjantjatjara and the Yankunyjatjara, to whom the site was officially returned in 1985—they do strongly request that you don't climb. Uluru is a highly sacred site to them and they intensely object to tourists walking all over it, desecrating the surface. Unfortunately, people often go to the toilet up the top, polluting the water holes below, and I even met a girl on my first trip to Australia who boasted of having sex at the summit.

Culturally, the Aboriginals' objection to climbing Uluru lies in their traditional obligation to look after visitors' well-being, and their belief that if someone injures themselves or dies climbing—to date thirty-five people have lost their lives this way—then that person's soul is trapped in the area, somewhere it does not belong. This causes extreme sadness and mourning in their community. The route the climb sets off from is also of great spiritual significance to the local Aboriginals, as it follows the traditional route that their mythical ancestors, the wallaby men, are said to have followed on their arrival at Uluru.

I had no intention of climbing Uluru, but one of the most common arguments you hear to justify doing so is, "I respect the Aboriginals' beliefs, but they're not my beliefs." To me, that's a lame excuse. At its essence the debate is all rather simple. If I were a guest in someone's home and they politely asked me to refrain from doing something with or to a possession of theirs because they found it highly culturally offensive, then I would. Their house, their rules. And the same should apply to Uluru.

Didier and I set off together along the trail around Uluru, snaking our way around the side of the rock which was every bit as glorious as the day before. The walk was delightful and lent a whole new perspective to Uluru and its myriad features. We passed ancient rock paintings, natural watering holes, cliff formations in the shape of breaking waves, huge tiered bowls eroded into the rock's surface over millennia by giant waterfalls, caves, ceremonial sites, and plenty more besides. On nearing the end of the six mile circular trail, Didier leaned in and tenderly touched Uluru's surface.

"I'm agnostic and don't believe in spiritual things," he said. "But you can almost believe the rock has energy."

I knew what he meant.

We parted company soon after, with Didier heading to the nearby airport and me setting off for Uluru's sister site, Kata Tjuta, formerly known as the Olgas. Kata Tjuta is a series of spectacular dome-shaped rock formations that rise 1790 feet above the surrounding plains, making them, in places, 650 feet higher than Uluru. Despite sixteen miles separating the two sites, they are conjoined underground, being different protruding sections of the same vast curved layer of sandstone. Both are around 100 million years old and referred to by geologists as bornhardts. The presence of Uluru and Kata Tjuta towering above the plains is accounted for by them consisting of more resilient rock than their surroundings, which, over millions of years, have eroded away at a faster rate than the rock has. The individual fault lines and weaknesses of Uluru and Kata Tjuta have led to them wearing down in distinctly different ways, giving both a unique appearance and personality. To the Aboriginal owners of the land, these patterns of erosion are full of meaning. They tell the story of their concept of creation, in particular the actions and journeys of ancestral beings across the landscape, how these ancestral beings created the world and the marks they left on the landscape as they went. Others tell of the connection Aboriginal people have to the land, animals, plants, each other, and their ancestors.

Within minutes of waiting on the road I got myself a lift from a female Aboriginal tour guide called Mini. She wasn't going to Kata Tjuta but a settlement in its general direction, so offered to drop me at the turning for it. On the way I asked her about traditional Aboriginal methods of lighting fire.

"I can't tell you about it," she said. "It's a man's skill, so they're not my stories. We operate tours where you can learn the skills of the men on one tour, and the skills of the women on another."

The tours teaching women's skills apparently specialized in the gathering side of things, with attention paid to wild edible foods or "bushtucker."

"Is there much bushtucker around here?" I asked, looking out across the seemingly barren plains.

"Jamie, we're driving through a supermarket," replied Mini.

I would have liked to learn a bit of this, but we reached the junction a minute later.

My next ride was quick coming and arrived in the form of a vacationing Russian couple, Olgar and Valery. When Olgar pulled off, he did so on the wrong side of the road (Australians drive on the left) which luckily for him was empty. Valery yelled at him in Russian, eliciting a jolting moment of realization in which Olgar swerved back to the left-hand lane. Neither spoke much in the way of English so it was a quiet ride, in which I marveled at the rounded orange forms of Kata Tjuta growing larger as we approached.

Kata Tjuta consists of thirty-six rock domes, reflected in the Aboriginal meaning of its name, which translates as "many heads." The first European to see Kata Tjuta was Ernest Giles on his inaugural expedition, which set off in 1872. He reached Uluru soon after but was pipped at the post of being the first white man there, missing out on the accolade by a matter of days to William Christie Goose. But then, on the upside, he did furnish the world with an unsurpassable memoir passage detailing a rather novel meal he partook when half dead from starvation and dehydration, and practically blind from scurvy. His description sums up better than any other I know, the hardships suffered by Australia's early explorers and of the absolute unforgiving nature of the outback:

> I heard a faint squeak, and looking about I saw . . . a small dying wallaby . . . I pounced upon it and ate it, living, raw, dying—fur, skin, bones, skull, and all. The delicious taste of that creature I shall never forget. I only wished I had its mother and father to serve in the same way.

A large section of the hike around Kata Tjuta was closed today for safety reasons due to the searing temperatures, leaving only one area open to explore—"the windy gorge." After agreeing to meet Olgar and Valery back at their car in an hour, I struck off along the trail by myself. Rising up on either side of the thin stony track were huge rounded orange cliffs accentuated by a cloudless deep-blue sky. Just like Uluru, a peaceful and timeless atmosphere enveloped Kata Tjuta. I felt an odd sense of belonging here, as if I could stay put forever, simply contemplating these enigmatic rocks and their wide open, expansive surroundings.

The gorge lived up to its name, channeling the merest of breezes into a cooling draft and providing a welcome respite from today's temperatures, now over 100 degrees. On either side of the trail was a green belt of vegetation that roughly followed the route of a small trickling stream. I stopped off and dunked my head in the water. It was bliss. I remained with my head submerged for a good twenty seconds, as my temperature dropped and my hair yielded to the current. It was a short walk of around forty-five minutes, up and then back down the valley, and by the time I finished I was bone dry. I stayed in the area with Olgar and Valery for some time, just soaking in the atmosphere, until they decided to head on to Alice Springs, my next stop, roughly 270 miles away, offering me a ride along the way.

Several close calls occurred on the journey there when, once again, Olgar pulled out on the wrong side of the road following a refreshment break, but eventually we arrived in one piece. By now it was late afternoon, and raining hard. Olgar, Valery, and I said our goodbyes in the center of the town, where they dropped me so I could source somewhere to stay. My options were limited. The cheapest single room I could find was over a hundred dollars, so I had little choice but to opt for somewhere I normally avoid with a vengeance—a youth hostel.

I hate hostels. And in particular I hate dormitories. Maybe it's a throwback to the two year stretch I served in boarding school dormitories from the age of ten to twelve, but I find dorms, and hostels in general, thoroughly depressing. However, with nowhere near enough money to fork out for a single room, my only other option was to sleep rough, something I had previously done in Alice Springs. But with tonight's heavy rain this option seemed even less appealing, and since there was nowhere feasible in sight to throw my tent, a hostel it would have to be. So it was with a reluctant sigh of resignation and a deep intake of breath that I stepped inside the Alice Springs YHA to inquire about a bed for the night.

"Our cheapest is a sixteen share mixed dorm at twenty-four dollars a night," said the girl behind the counter.

I did some quick mental arithmetic. That was 384 dollars for every night they filled the room. I asked to see it. It wasn't like its state was going to sway my decision one way or the other, rather I was stalling the inevitable. I knew what it would look like and it faithfully matched my expectations—it was shit. Backpacks, clothing, wash bags, and assorted knick-knacks were strewn over nearly all the bunk beds, which were crammed, sardine-like, into a musty smelling room. The bathroom was down the hall. To make the best part of 400 dollars a night out of such a crappy room was disgraceful.

"How much did you say it was?" I asked again, despite knowing the price.

"Twenty-four dollars a night."

"Mmm," I responded, pretending to be only mildly pondering a stay.

The girl looked about, then spoke in the hushed tones of someone departing sensitive information. "I tell you what, if you don't tell anyone I'll give you the member's discount."

"How much is that?"

"Twenty-one-fifty."

I took it.

I left at first light after a restless night having been woken up by a streetlamp shining into the curtainless room. I made it to the outskirts of Alice Springs in double-quick time after a fortuitous bit of in-town hitching at some traffic lights, where a young Asian car salesman picked me up and dropped me outside his place of work: a Ford dealership on the edge of town. It was the perfect spot, just beyond lay the beginnings of the desert. I waited for about two hours before another car pulled up, this time driven by a young Polynesian girl, Sinaboana, who, from her actions, I can only conclude was new in the country. If cheerfulness and enthusiasm to help was all I needed to get to Darwin, then Sinaboana was just the ticket. Unfortunately, her concept of the realities of hitchhiking and what it actually entailed were limited.

I told her I was heading north. She told me to get in. We set off.

"How about that spot?" she said, gesturing to a shaded area on the side of the road after driving—and I kid you not—no more than 500 feet from where we started. I looked at her bamboozled; surely she was joking. She wasn't. When I explained that I was trying to reach Darwin, 930 miles away, it was her turn to look bamboozled. She was apologetic to a fault.

"I'm so sorry," she said, looking downcast. "I saw you from the other side of the road and felt sorry for you, so thought I'd turn around to help."

In soothing, if slightly confused tones, I told her it was okay. Moments later I was back on the roadside scratching my head in sheer bewilderment at the absurdity of the situation. She drove off back into town.

Thirty minutes passed and it looked like my luck had changed when a car with three Asian guys in pulled over. I grabbed my pack and headed towards it.

"Thanks guys," I said in an upbeat voice through the open front window, then asked them where they were going.

The driver looked back at me with an awkward smile. "Err, Darwin."

"Excellent, so am I."

"Hold on," piped up a lone disgruntled-looking guy in the back. "We don't have room."

There was loads of room.

"Then why did you stop?" I asked with a mixture of annoyance and confusion.

"I'm sorry," said the driver, who sounded like he meant it, then pulled off.

I was speechless, and stood open-mouthed staring as the car disappeared in exactly the direction I needed to go. It seemed to me that the driver had decided to give me a lift and was eager to do so, but during the small interval between him stopping and me reaching the car, he had been talked out of it by the other passengers.

Why did I always find hitching out of Alice Springs such a pain in the arse?

Another hour passed and while aimlessly glancing around I spotted some hitherto unnoticed text-like graffiti on the back of a nearby road sign. I ambled over for a gander. Scribbled haphazardly in different pens was an assortment of messages from past hitchhikers.

"Hitching for the fun of it . . . all the way from home town Toowoomba—Emily (that smelly kid), 18/2/01—OK!" "Patrick was here 12/04/99 (France)," "Jan Fanna 30/08/2002," "Miguel was here 12/02/03 (France)," "1st hour, Playa Czech," "Fred was here for 6 hours, remember to smile." "Were still waiting hours," "Us too it's so long 12/02/03 Julien Miguel (French)" "Valentin Rechand & Julie dest hitcca French represent."

After these was scribbled the message: "If U R here U are doing the right thing. Take your chances! Look for the adventure and U just might find what every body is looking for."

I corrected some grammar and moved on.

After somewhere in the region of four and a half hours in total, my wait finally came to an end when a white pickup truck towing a small enclosed trailer pulled up. Behind the wheel sat a guy of about forty, and this time, thankfully, there was no nonsense with him changing his mind or trying to drop me a minute's drive down the road.

My new companion was Mark, an army transport soldier driving from Tasmania to Darwin, where he was heading to relocate for work. To be on the move again and take the weight off my feet was bliss, and in no time we were deep into the country's rusty colored desert heartland, a colossal expanse of nothingness. We could have been on another planet.

Conversation filled the void, ebbing and flowing from subject to subject until Mark turned it, without prompting, to that favorite Australian conversation killer—at least with foreign visitors—asylum seekers.

"Some of them," he said, referring to asylum seekers trying to reach Australia by boat, "arrive with Gucci clothing and iPads. If you can afford 20,000 dollars to get here, then you're not a refugee!"

He was talking bollocks.

It was reminiscent of the media smears I'd witnessed against asylum seekers when in the country back in 2001. The canard in vogue at the time was that a group of despicable Iraqi asylum seekers who were trying to reach Australia by boat in order to bleed its welfare system dry, had thrown their own young children overboard into the perilous waters in a dastardly, sacrificial attempt at garnering the attention of the gallant Australian Navy, so as to "blackmail" them into taking them ashore. The Australian Prime Minister of the time described the asylum seekers', behavior as "against the natural instinct" and a senator labeled the Iraqis as "repulsive" and "unworthy of Australia." Others gleefully got stuck into those seeking the right of refuge, with the country's immigration minister claiming their actions were "clearly planned and premeditated [with] the intention of putting us under duress," and the leader of the opposition alleging that the asylum seekers carried out "an outrageous act."

None of it was true.

The asylum seekers had abandoned ship after the nearby Australian Navy opened fire across the leaking vessel's bows.[15] (It sank the next day.) And of course there were no children "thrown overboard"—confirmed by a senate inquiry into the affair, and admitted to by the chief of the Australian navy.[16] The whole charade had been used to defend the government's anti-refugee policies, which had recently come under fire following the government's refusal to allow a Norwegian freighter to land in the country after it had plucked 433 Afghan asylum seekers from a near-certain watery grave.[17] Instead of helping the traumatized men, women, and children, the Australian government ordered commandos to storm the Norwegian freighter[18] and for the Afghans to be sent to remote island detention facilities in the Pacific.[19]

Even today, years after the government and media's claims about asylum seekers deliberately throwing children into the water have been proven as false, you still hear people bandying them about. After all, it's so much easier to put a lie out there than to retract it. So I did my best to put this case to Mark, and tried to convince him that his Gucci and iPad claims were likewise bullshit. I proceeded in as diplomatic a manner as possible. After all, I'd had a long hot wait before he'd picked me up, so I didn't fancy seeing the lift terminated by him due to a difference of opinion. I mentioned a highly publicized case that had occurred just weeks earlier where a rickety wooden craft full of asylum seekers—the majority from Iran and Iraq—had been smashed to pieces against the rocky coastline of Australia's Christmas Island, killing fifty on board, including women and children.

"None of those struggling in the water for their lives or getting smashed lifeless against the rocks appeared to be decked out in the latest Gucci threads," I suggested.

He pondered this for a second.

"Yeah, you might be right, mate," he thoughtfully conceded.

After driving for about two hours we reached Barrow Creek, a tiny township with a permanent population of around ten people. We pulled up outside a red tin-roofed pub and popped inside for a cool drink. The interior was something else. Covering the walls, and just about every available surface both in front of and behind the bar, as well as on the bar itself, were impromptu adornments left by visitors from around the world: handwritten messages, bumper stickers, foreign bank notes, postcards, signed Aussie Rules footballs, baseball caps, photographs, flags, business cards, etc. The quirky tradition of leaving behind memorabilia was apparently inspired by an old sheep shearer's practice where, in order to ensure they had enough money for a drink the next time they happened by, itinerant shearers would write their name on a banknote and pin it to the wall.

Other curiosities inside the pub included a collection of antique leather bush hats and several lumps of what, at first glance, appeared to be strange bits of rock, but were—if the local nursing a cold beer at the bar was to be believed—fossilized animal excrement.

Not long after setting off again, when roughly eight miles north of Barrow Creek, we passed a notorious spot on the side of the road where, in 2001, British backpacker Peter Falconio was murdered. The case had gripped Australia, and was something that numerous people who gave me a lift, both on this and my prior hitchhiking journey through Australia, brought up to highlight the dangers in the outback.

Mr. Falconio and his British girlfriend Joanne Lees had been traveling the Stuart highway at night in their Volkswagen Kombi van, when they were tricked into stopping by the driver of a white pickup, who indicated there was a problem with the back of their van. Falconio pulled over, as did the driver of the pickup, who came to a halt behind the Kombi. Lees stayed in the vehicle while Falconio got out to investigate, at which point Lees heard what she initially assumed was their exhaust pipe backfiring. The next thing she knew, the stranger from the pickup was pointing a gun in her face and forcing her from the van. She was bound behind her back with linked cable ties, then gagged, and bundled into the pickup truck. Soon after her assailant briefly disappeared—thought to be so he could move Falconio's body—at which point Lees seized her opportunity, running into the dark and desolate landscape to hide among the spinifex bushes. She was quickly pursued by her abductor, who attempted to hunt her down with his dog and the use of a flashlight. Despite coming close enough that Lees could hear his footsteps, her pursuer failed to find her. After hours in hiding she emerged onto the highway and flagged down a "road train," by which stage she had managed to slip her bound hands back behind her legs and out over her feet. Falconio's body was never found.

It was an interesting case, to be sure, and one I'd had a somewhat loose encounter with—in the form of getting picked up by one of the original suspects on the same stretch of road in 2001 (the year of the murder), when hitching out of Alice Springs to Darwin. Back then a car had pulled over for me in the early evening, whose driver looked a carbon copy of a widely distributed police sketch of the man wanted for the murder. Now this may sound foolhardy, but I can't say the driver's uncanny similarity to the wanted poster put me off accepting the lift. I'd spent nearly the entire day prior to this failing to get a ride and was down to around twenty dollars, so I urgently needed to get to Darwin to find work, otherwise I'd be fully broke. And so, I figured I'd just have to deal with any potential shenanigans from the driver if and when they came.

Within five minutes of setting off on what was about to be a nine hundred mile overnight drive on a sparsely used road through a barren desert, the driver regaled me with an encounter he'd had at a local service station. As he was filling up, a staff member working the register had repeatedly looked his way with concern. When his tank was full the driver popped inside to use the bathroom and buy a drink, but as he was leaving several police cars came screeching to a stop in front of him, from which jumped a swarm of panicky-looking cops, all guns drawn and pointed in his direction—the staff member having tipped them off that a dead ringer for the widely circulated police sketch was currently buying gas.

"It all ended okay in the end," my lift back then had told me, turning to look me in the eye while displaying the faint indications of a suppressed smile. "Guess they must have *believed* my alibi."

He paused for a moment, letting the emphasis of his remark sink in.

"Ahhhhh!" he exclaimed with a laugh. "Just kidding, mate. It all checked out fine."

Oh, how very funny.

The next spot of significance that Mark and I passed was the tiny settlement of Wycliffe Well, billed as the UFO capital of Australia, an area where you could, supposedly, see something the Aborigines called the Min Min lights—mysterious balls of light said to appear in the sky and randomly hover about, before disappearing again. We passed straight through the place, which was little more than a solitary road house, only stopping some twenty miles further on, when we got to an area just off the side of the road known as Devil's Marbles, or Karlu Karlu in the local Aboriginal dialect.

I'd been here once before but only in the dead of night with my murder suspect friend, and for no more than five minutes. And so, as Mark and I now reached the site in the full glare of an intensely blazing sun, it was with a feeling of intrigue and excitement to finally see what the place was actually like.

It was magnificent.

Giant boulders, many smooth and near spherical in shape, ranging from the size of a car to larger than a house, were strewn across the desert landscape, piled into random heaps or perched in the most haphazard manner imaginable, balancing on tiny, delicate-looking bases. Some were cleft perfectly in two by the forces of nature, others eroded into elongated cigar-like forms, or giant soccer ball shapes, all were the color of tangerine.

We got out on our feet and had a good walk about, scrambling over the surface of a rock formation to reach a lookout where several "devil's marbles" perched. A wondrous view greeted us at the top, a panorama across a wide open landscape punctuated by random outbreaks of similar formations that stretched far off into the distance.

After a good exploration of the site, we headed down to read a noticeboard in a designated camping area, where we learned that the reserve covered nearly four and a half thousand acres, and was considered a sacred site to the Aboriginals, who believe that people from their creation period, the dreaming, still live in caves among the rocks. Part of a sign included a passage from a senior traditional owner:

They're real people like us. You can see them. A long time ago I went with my billycan down to the creek here to get some water. One of these secret people came out and started playing with me. I couldn't go away. My mother came and got me, saved me. After that we never camped at this place again, never. They're kind these secret people, but they can make you mad. They can change you into one of them. They can say, "Follow me," and you can't go back. It happened like that for my cousin. He disappeared. The old people made a big ceremony, singing the ground and the rocks to make them let my cousin come back. We've lost that song now. We've got no songs to bring children back.

Mark and I continued on the road until twilight, pulling off after spotting an old abandoned cattle shed in the distance, accessible on a bumpy red-sand track. Even before stepping from the comfort of Mark's truck, it was clear the area had an eerie atmosphere. It would have to do though, we needed to set up camp before dark and could use the shed to hide Mark's vehicle behind so our presence was undetectable from the road. We got out together to investigate the shed, both coming to an abrupt halt when no more than two steps inside it.

Bullet holes riddled the creaking tin walls and roofing, through which the remainder of the evening's faint twilight filtered, bestowing on the chilly interior the appearance of a murky nighttime sky with faintly glowing stars.

"This place feels spooky," stated Mark.

I concurred.

We pitched our tents outside and got a fire going. When nightfall arrived I cooked up another damper bread for supper, while Mark got stuck into some of his more convenient pre-packaged supplies. Not long after, we turned in for the night.

Suddenly, from out of nowhere, an almighty crash inside the shed jolted me awake to a panicked state of high alert.

"What was that!" exclaimed Mark from his adjacent tent.

We scrambled out of our little domes and ran to the shed.

Mark was first to reach it, shining his flashlight in before taking a tentative step inside. I joined him.

It was empty, filled with nothing but the same creepy atmosphere.

We headed out to check the surrounding area.

"Could have been a black fella out here," concluded Mark, scanning about the landscape with the beam of his flashlight, highlighting random bushes for a closer inspection.

I wasn't so sure. On several occasions I'd camped in areas where deer or other mammals had gone past my tent in the dead of night and startled me awake. In such a confused state they had sounded just like humans, but then after hastily unzipping my tent I had discovered they were anything but. Most likely a kangaroo had got inside the shed through one of the gaping openings in its walls, then bumped into something and departed before we arrived.

But I wasn't taking any chances. I'd heard too many horror stories of serial killers in the outback for that. And so, although I didn't sleep with one eye open, I made sure my camping knife was close to hand.

CHAPTER EIGHT
Darwin Dilemma

Suddenly a cloud burst overhead, setting off a battle between raindrop and wiper for the vacant territory of the windshield. Uzi-like rapid-fire liquid bullets peppered the cool glass surface, as the wipers frantically swatted back and forth in a valiant attempt to halt the rain's advance and re-establish visibility. The wipers gained but fleeting advantage, only to be inundated a millisecond later by a deluge of kamikaze-like reinforcements. It was a close fought fight, and one that broke out increasingly often the further we went north.

It had taken us another day and a half of solid driving, including a night stop at a campsite in the town of Katherine, to get within striking distance of our final destination, Australia's northern most coastal city, Darwin. We had stopped off at some thermal springs and a beautiful gorge along the way, and by now the parched desert landscape had faded out, replaced instead by a lush tropical savannah woodland, which was, if anything, suffering from too much water. This is often the way of it in Australia. One extreme or the other. At this very moment, three quarters of the eastern state of Queensland was declared a disaster zone due to horrendous flooding. Its capital city, Brisbane, had seen over thirty suburbs submerged and thousands forced from their homes. The State's premier described the reconstruction task as being of "post-war proportions."

Mark and I finally pulled into Darwin around lunchtime, and said our goodbyes in the city's uninspiring modern center. Darwin was just how I remembered it. A dump.

Stepping out of Mark's vehicle, one of the first things I saw was a huge black pickup truck drive past with a big window sticker in the shape of the Australian map, within which was written: "FUCK OFF WE'RE FULL!"

Australia may be many things, but full it ain't.

My priorities today were simple: find a boat out of here.

After a reluctant check-in at a local backpackers' hostel, I took a quick shower, had a shave, and generally spruced myself up by means of a shirt and dress pants, in readiness to visit one of the city's two yacht clubs. I wanted to make inquires at the Darwin Sailing Club to find out if anyone was planning a trip across the Timor Sea any time soon, and to post a flyer on their noticeboard asking for crew work in the event that such a yachtsman existed.

Darwin Sailing Club is situated right on the beach in an area called Fannie Bay, about fifteen minutes by bus from the city center, where it overlooks the waters of the Beagle Gulf. Beyond lies the Timor Sea, that pesky stretch of water that separated me from the next feasible chunks of land—East Timor or, slightly further to the east, the Indonesian Island of Bali. Either would be fine by me. At only four hundred miles across the water, East Timor was significantly less than I had sailed from Hobart to Sydney, so distance wasn't an issue; the problem was the weather. Cyclone season was in full swing in the tropical north, a time of year (October to March) when, generally speaking, no one dared negotiate the route. (Being in the temperate south of the country, the race from Sydney to Hobart is unaffected.) Would anyone be foolhardy enough to risk it now? And if so, would they need crew? I wasn't optimistic. With zero commercial ferries leaving Darwin, the only other possibility was to approach a container ship. But no matter how much of a long shot finding a yacht seemed, I was here now, so it was damn well worth a go; and I intended to try every available option.

Swaddled in sauna-like tropical humidity, by the time I reached the yacht club my shirt was drenched in sweat. So much for looking dapper. I stepped into the plush interior and headed for the bar, uncharacteristically blowing some money on a Coke—more than I'd spent on food the last day and a half, having again made do with damper bread. Several locals whiled away the afternoon here, so I struck up a conversation with the nearest one, a weathered old mariner, telling him of my desire to get a yacht to either East Timor or Indonesia.

"It's actually quite simple," he replied in an optimistic and upbeat manner, as though such a proposition was wholly achievable.

This was a surprise. I was all ears and suitably encouraged.

"All you need to find a yacht out of Darwin at this time of year—" he paused for effect, leaving me hanging in suspense, before changing his tone "—is a bloody miracle!"

Thanks.

Similar responses came my way from several others in attendance, and after a failed attempt to speak to the club's commodore, who wasn't on site, I decided to try elsewhere. Despite the generally pessimistic feedback, I received a glimmer of hope from one of the locals who told me a crazy Frenchman had set off a few weeks earlier from the city's other yacht club, The Dinah Beach Cruising Yacht Association, situated on the other side of the sprawling peninsula on which Darwin sat. It was too far to get to before dark so I decided to make inquires in the morning.

* * *

"G'day, Jamie!" enthused a heavily tattooed middle-aged couple whom I had briefly chatted to the day before while waiting for a bus to the first yacht club. They were Tracey and Steve, a cheery and talkative pair of vacationers from the south of the country, who had been making their way to a casino when we first met.

"How did you get on at the yacht club?" asked Tracey.

I told them.

"What about you guys? Did you come out on top?" I asked.

"Fifty dollars up," replied Steve with a satisfied grin.

We chatted for a while about our respective stays in Darwin when suddenly, out of the blue, Tracey had a eureka-like moment of realization.

"You should go to our hotel for a free feed! They've got a full buffet breakfast and no one knows who's staying."

"Are you sure?"

"Yeah, they're all young staff there who are more interested in checking out the young diners than doing any work."

"Jamie," stated Steve emphatically, "They couldn't give a rat's arse!"

I thanked them for their counsel, got the details of the establishment and headed straight over.

With the confident air of a long-term resident I strolled into the Cavendish Hotel—or *The Cav*, as it was billed on a large sign outside. It was an airy, open-fronted establishment, beginning with a decked area of seating and tables leading to an internal courtyard, where a large swimming pool was located. To the right of the decked area was, just as Tracey and Steve had described, the buffet room. No staff or residents were currently inside it, so I headed straight in. Awaiting me was a smorgasbord of culinary delights.

Retiring with a feast to the decked area, I settled down to an obscenely large breakfast of fresh fruit salad, yogurt, croissants, pastries, muffins and cereals, all washed down with several glasses of juice and a large cup of tea. I took my time, and over my banquet picked up the local paper, *NT News*, for a perusal of Darwin's goings on. Splashed across the front page no less, was a big circular red prohibited sign, within which a buxom young lady was showing off her ample assets in a tight fitting wet t-shirt.

"Is this the end for TOT?" screamed the headline.

I read on, intrigued.

Protest to spell the end of TOT? The days may be numbered for one of the Territory's raunchiest nights out. Discovery nightclub will front the Liquor Licensing Commission next week after a complaint was lodged about its weekly TOT night, the ABC reported. The nightclub claims TOT stands for Tequila On Tuesday, but to locals it is known as Tits Out Tuesday. The event features scantily-clad female patrons dancing on stage often baring their breasts. "We are not strippers so much, just people flashing our boobies," a patron said.

And that, I think, tells you just about everything you need to know about Darwin, as does the fact the story warranted the front page lead article, possibly after a frantic "stop the press!" cry at the printers when the story first broke.

With a satisfied stomach I headed to the city's Parliament House—an imposing rectangular modern structure, with a gleaming white façade and a flat roof, located within an orderly little park. Here, I knew, free internet was provided in its library.

It was a building I was well accustomed to.

It's got to be said, when previously marooned in Darwin I didn't really have the best of times. Thanks to getting scammed by the aforementioned fake checks, I'd arrived there so out of pocket that on Christmas day my only meal was a bowl of Weet-Bix cereal, served with, and I'm not making this up, water—I simply couldn't afford any milk. So when I entered Darwin's parliament just after Christmas for one of my regular email checks, and was greeted there by the sight of distinguished-looking guests milling around the building's grand hall while attentively being served glasses of wine and assorted canapés, I decided to try my luck.

I didn't exactly look the part, being dressed in a surf t-shirt and shorts, and would have been hard pushed to look any more different from the other smartly turned-out guests, who included several high ranking military officers in crisply pressed uniforms. But what the hell, it was worth a go. Doing my best to remain incognito, I ambled around the opulence of the grand hall's high-ceilinged, marble-floored interior, stuffing as much food and drink as I could get down my neck in readiness for when someone had the good sense to ask me to leave. Nobody did.

Much free food and booze later, feeling pleased with myself as well as tipsy, one of the guests, a high ranking American military officer with a shirt full of striped rectangular commendation ribbons, got up on a small makeshift stage to address the assembled dignitaries.

"Ladies and gentlemen," he said gazing out across the hall at the cream of Darwin's society, luckily not spotting me in the process, "I'd like to raise a toast to our dearly departed friend, George Brown."

Bloody hell. I'd crashed a funeral! This was a first, even for me.

I made a swift exit to the library, sending an email there to my brother in which I recalled my funeral wake antics. The following day a friend of his from Sydney, to whom my brother had forwarded my email, sent him a scan of an article from national newspaper, *The Australian*, entitled, "Darwin Toasts Dead Mayor," in which I warranted a mention:

> Darwin's lord Mayor George Brown's favourite tipple, red wine, was the first to run dry at his wake in the Northern Territory Parliament House yesterday. Political, military and judicial leaders, as well as the odd barefoot commoner, accepted an open invitation to have a drink on the territory Government in the parliament's main hall to farewell Darwin's longest-serving mayor.

Back in the library this time, I got straight on to the Internet to look up the town's major container shipping company, Perkins Shipping, with a mind to pitching someone in authority there with the idea of me traveling on one of their weekly freighters to East Timor. Perkins, I knew, was going to be a very tough nut to crack. I had briefly corresponded with an American woman, Marie, who back in 2001 had managed to get passage out of Darwin on one of Perkins' ships to the capital of East Timor, Dili. She had written about her trip on a travel blog, which was how I found her email. Her advice was clear:

> Darwin to Dili. Don't. That's where everyone gets stuck. And when they get stuck, they start googling. Eventually, they find me and e-mail me. That's how I know everyone still gets stuck, and that the guys I convinced to take me on that route say no to travelers nowadays.

Although it seemed unlikely to me that I could convince anyone at Perkins to take another traveler across the Timor Sea, I stood to lose nothing by trying. I scribbled down the name of Perkins' boss, made a note of the company address and headed on over there.

Perkins Shipping was based at an industrial wharf, lapped by green and murky waters, to get to which required a sweltering walk through tropical humidity—and a wasted walk at that, with a categorical "no" to passengers boarding any of their ships coming my way.

My next port of call was the city's second yacht club, Dinah Beach Cruising Yacht Association, located further along the coast. It was much more rustic than yesterday's club, consisting of little more than a marquee-like roof on pillars with open sides, beneath which multiple tables and chairs were arranged. Tagged onto the front of the structure was a small bar.

I stuck a flyer up on a notice board and went over to the bar to make inquiries. Feeling duty bound to buy a drink, I ordered an ice-cold bottle of Carlton beer and got chatting to the bar manager—a hardy-looking, personable and upbeat middle-aged man named John, the only person currently around. John gave me the low down on the yachting situation and shared plenty of interesting stories of his time working in England as a sheep shearer. His yachting info pretty much mirrored that of the day before: there had been a crazy French bloke who'd left a few weeks back, but no one since.

"It's pretty suicidal at this time of year," he said. "To be honest, I shouldn't think you'll find anyone."

"What if I offered someone ten thousand dollars to take me?"

He laughed. "Now that's a different story. Just when is it you want to leave, Sir?"

I explained my odd inquiry. When searching online for ways across the Timor Sea I had happened upon a travel blog of someone who'd worked on board a private yacht chartered out of season by the BBC for ten thousand dollars, so that their travel show presenter—a well known travel writer with a penchant for motorcycles—could get across in the other direction without flying.[20]

I bade John goodbye with a promise to check in daily for any updates, just in case another crazy Frenchman arrived on the scene.

Back in the town center I picked up a most welcome email. With a view to avoiding a protracted stay in a hostel, I had previously sent a number of prospective emails to the Darwin members of a website I had used when traveling in Venezuela, couchsurfing.org. This wonderful site puts travelers seeking free accommodation in contact with travel-minded locals willing to open up their home and provide somewhere to crash. I had an offer from a member of the Australian Navy. Using a public pay phone I called the couchsurfer, and come the evening met with him at a watering hole in town.

"Welcome to Darwin," exclaimed a big athletic and enthusiastic sailor in a tight black t-shirt, thrusting out a meaty hand to shake.

This was Carl, who was accompanied at the bar by a similarly proportioned naval colleague, Mike. We hit it off immediately, with both possessing a quick-witted, dry sense of humor, and a love for multiple ice cold beers.

After finishing up at the bar, we headed back to Carl and Mike's apartment. I couldn't have asked for a nicer place. It was clean, commodious and modern, with a spacious open-plan sitting room and kitchen, off which were the guy's bedrooms. Through the open door of one could be seen a big Marilyn Monroe poster above the bed.

"Dump your pack by the couch," said Carl. "It folds out as a bed, I'll set it up for you later."

Next to this was a coffee table with an interesting item on top of it: a samurai sword.

"D'you wanna take a shower or fancy a cuppa?" asked Mike.

I did indeed, and went for both in that order.

This is what I love about couchsurfing. I barely knew these guys, but simply by sending an email to Carl, I had scored a nice roof above my head from a couple of first rate hosts.

"Help yourself to a cupcake," offered Carl, as we drank our teas leaning against the kitchen's marble work surface. I selected a delightful little sprinkle-covered chocolate one from a tray nearby, next to which, by contrast, resided a jet-black pistol.

Carl picked up and cocked the weapon.

"Want a look?" he asked, offering it my way, before quickly adding, "don't worry, it's decommissioned."

Several photos of me packing a piece in one hand and a nice cup of tea in the other followed, after which we settled down to a pizza. Over the meal the guys told me a bit about their experiences in the Navy and of their plans to soon depart from it. Neither sounded particularly enamored by their time thus served.

"The Navy is the government's way of taking people who don't function in society and sticking them all together on a big tin can out at sea so they can't harm the rest of society," said Carl, clearly excluding himself and Mike from this summation.

The guys had the day off tomorrow, so they offered to take me onto their naval base in the morning for a look around.

This, I was well up for.

We approached the security barrier at the start of Darwin's sprawling Larrakeyah Barracks where Carl and Mike quickly flashed their I.D. in the direction of the sentry stationed there. He didn't so much as glance at these before waving us through.

"One of our mates took a photo of his own poo in a bowl to use as his photo I.D. and it worked for months," said Carl with a laugh.

We drove on round the base going past several barrack buildings and a section where, Carl explained, some unfortunate soul from times gone by had been imprisoned behind bars for seventy-three days, in a building with no roof to protect him from the elements.

"Can you imagine what that was like in Darwin's weather?" he asked.

With brutal tropical temperatures, cyclones, and monsoon-like floods, it must have made for one hell of a trying stretch.

We parked down a small hill by a dry-dock hangar, next to a man-made harbor with a large wave-break wall. Inside the harbor stretched a substantial concrete jetty where several huge, mean-looking gray patrol boats were docked.

"We have to clean their hulls in little dinghys," said Mike. "Got to watch out for crocs and box jellyfish in the water though."

To mention a squishy jellyfish in the same cautionary breath as a mighty sharp-toothed crocodile might, to some, sound a little too elevating of the jellyfish's harm causing capacity; but don't be deceived. The box jellyfish is the nastiest of Australia's long list of animal nasties, and is loaded with millions of venom packed stingers along every centimeter of its multiple tentacles. It is the most poisonous creature on the planet, packed with enough venom to wipe out a football team. Brush against one of this translucent little invertebrate's tentacles when out for a dip, and you can go into such convulsive shock as to end up drowning on the spot. Its toxins attack the heart, nervous system, and skin cells in a manner unlike any other creature, causing such unfathomable pain that victims have been known to continue screaming even when completely unconscious and heavily sedated.

For such a fearsome creature you might expect it to have evolved this way to contend with some pretty hefty and armored prey, but it actually feeds on tiny fish and shrimps, surely qualifying as the animal kingdom's ultimate example of overkill. Since box jellyfish are present year round in the seas off Australia's tropical north—with the peak season being October to May—it makes the coastal waters around Darwin all but unusable for bathers at the hottest times of year, despite their "oh so tempting" appearance. Yet another reason you don't want to get stuck in Darwin.

Carl led us into the dry-dock hangar where a huge patrol boat was being renovated after an electrical fire.

"Want to go on board?" he asked.

"Sure."

The guys cleared it with some nearby colleagues and then led me on board the boat.

It was an interesting vessel that had apparently taken quite a beating from the fire, although much of it was now patched up. It had, Carl explained, been used in the highly politicized interception of boats carrying asylum seekers trying to make it to Australia, something both he and Mike had been involved in.[21] There were lots of people on the lower decks fixing it up, so after a quick look around the cabins here, and at a massive gun towards the bow, we made our way to the cockpit where I plonked myself in the captain's revolving chair. We had this area to ourselves and stayed here chatting for a while, before Mike showed me something sinister nearby, which he referred to as a "sound weapon."

"Its frequency can make people you aim it at convulse, spew, and shit themselves," he said.

This delightful coercion aid was apparently used to get boats full of asylum seekers to comply with the Navy's orders.

After a further look around the base we headed back to their apartment, where Mike crashed out in his room while Carl and I sat having a cup of tea and another little cupcake. A few minutes later, when discussing some of the operations Carl had been involved in, he told me something truly shocking. Now I'm not vouching for the validity of what he claimed, but the details are thus.

One particular patrol boat that Carl had been on board, HMAS Larrakia, had, according to him, received a distress call from a boat full of asylum seekers that was sinking in an area near the Cocos Islands. At the time, HMAS Larrakia was, apparently, just two hours away from reaching the stricken vessel but the captain received orders from his superiors not to assist. The asylum seekers' boat then sank, killing all the men, women, and children on board. Despite being close enough to have attempted a rescue—a legal obligation under the circumstances—the official version reported in the press claimed that the nearest Australian naval vessel was two days away. According to Carl, the ship's logs could prove this as untrue. "It was all a political decision," he told me ruefully.

*   *   *

A week is a long time in Darwin, especially if you're living off damper breads cooked up in the oven of your hosts' apartment to preserve your travel funds. After seven painfully long days stuck there, I couldn't really claim to having much, if anything, to show for it. Perkins had, of course, turned me down, as had the town's sole remaining freight shipping company, Swire. My daily trips to the city's yacht clubs to check whether anyone had arrived who was planning on crossing the Timor Sea had come to nothing. I had also pitched a local pearling company after being told (incorrectly) that their boats traveled to Timor, made inquires with my Navy contacts in the unlikely event that one of their vessels was going to East Timor or Indonesia—and the unlikelier-still scenario that I could get permission to come on board—and even approached a local aviation club to see if I could hitch a ride on a light air-plane heading over the water. All avenues of inquiry came to nothing.

The key to crossing the Timor Sea from Darwin was clear. You either had to do it out of cyclone season when the trade winds were favorable and you could crew on a yacht—either pleasure cruising or taking part in one of two sailing rallies that crossed the Timor Sea from Australia in July, *The Darwin to Dili*, and *Sail Indonesia*—or have crazy amounts of money in order to convince some nutter to risk sailing the route at the wrong time of year. Other than that the only feasible option was to jump on a commercial plane.

I bit the bullet.

CHAPTER NINE
Gangsta's Paradise

Balancing myself on the rear of my old school friend Dan's scooter was no mean feat, even before we got on the move. To fit myself and my cumbersome backpack on the passenger seat required some up-close and personal rearranging of the space between passenger and driver, to the extent that I was practically spooning on the back with Dan.

Not a pleasant experience.

We made our way from Bali's western Uluwatu Peninsula through thin, twisting, and potholed streets, crowded with bikes, mopeds, trucks, cars, buses, taxis, pedestrians, and no small quantity of chickens, all of whom seemed to be following their own arbitrary "make it up as you go along" rules of the road. The chickens were the most orderly. Cars pulled out on the wrong side, mopeds overtook on blind corners, pedestrians walked in the middle of the road, and trucks just did as they pleased—with the right of way belonging to the biggest. Dan swerved from left to right, avoiding several near-collisions in the process, while yelling abuse at other road users where appropriate.

"They don't have a clue how to drive here!" shouted Dan so I could hear him above the sound of hot tropical air rushing past me on the back. "A truck wiped out a whole crowd of people just down the road from here. Its brakes failed at the start of the hill and instead of trying to pull over into a ditch, the driver just jumped out. Picked up more and more speed the further it went downhill until it careered off the road. Killed fifteen people, smashed ten shops, about thirty bikes, two pickups and another yellow truck. It looked like an airplane had crashed!"

It was clear hitchhiking in Indonesia was going to be a very different experience to the long straight empty roads of Australia.

After about twenty minutes we reached, and then made our way through, the central city streets of downtown Kuta—the raucous main tourist district of Bali—heaving with early morning commuter traffic, a mass of multicolored metal that erupted into a triumphant chorus of throaty exhaust-pipes and high-pitched horn blasts. The majority were on scooters, many with several passengers crammed onto a single bike. Thousands thronged the streets in bewildering chaos, screaming along like a giant collective entity past war-like statues of Hindu gods, standing proud and strong beside intersections and roundabouts; the sheer quantity of traffic creating huge congested backlogs at junctions. When the center of the city was finally cleared, we pulled over at a small convenience store in the area of Changu. From here I was on my own. Dan had to head back to Uluwatu where he worked, so after thanks from me and best wishes for my trip ahead from him, we bade each other farewell.

I had met up with Dan and another great friend from school, Mark, on my first morning on the small Indonesian island of Bali. They had been out here for years, living and working, but more importantly surfing, something that had drawn them to Bali in the first place. The waves were world class and waters warm, pretty much the diametric opposite of the U.K. We'd spent most of our time together on Bali split between the beach and a miniature "British pub" that Mark had constructed, in questionable taste, in the backyard of his Bali home. It had been great to catch up, but I yearned for fresh adventure and the clarity of spirit that came with it. The open road was beckoning me back and I had a tantalizing new objective driving me onwards: Mt. Bromo, a dark, cone-shaped volcano on neighboring island Java that according to reports was in a seriously tempestuous mood, spewing lava down its sides and a colossal ash cloud miles into the skies above. I had never visited a volcano before but I could feel its primal calling. A new experience awaited.

Today was going to be an interesting experiment. Mark had been convinced that I would need to offer some sort of financial inducement to get a ride in Indonesia, but I wasn't so sure. Nor was I prepared to do this. I was going to hitchhike, and that meant for free. If this entailed multiple drivers turning me down when it became apparent that I wasn't going to cross their palm with silver, then so be it. I'd play the numbers game and wait it out until someone gave me a lift for gratis. After all, if I was to start paying for transport then it would be cheaper, and far easier, to catch a bus or train. Even if I handed over only half a dollar per driver, this would still equate to far more than public transport—considering the multiple scooters, trucks and cars a similar journey would no doubt entail on Indonesia's heaving roads.

Carrying a red scooter helmet that Dan had given me, I set off on foot along the road, prominently displaying my thumb. Streams of vehicles poured past and although plenty looked my way with a marked degree of confusion, for the first ten minutes none stopped. My luck changed when I had dropped my hand for a second and was, to all intents and purposes, just walking in my desired direction.

A scooter ridden by a guy in his early twenties pulled up. The sight, it seemed, of a Westerner with a backpack hiking along a non-tourist road being sufficient to pique his curiosity.

"Selamat Pagi," I said, reading from a piece of paper that Dan had scribbled essential Indonesian phrases on—this one meaning "good morning." "Err, Tanah Lot Temple," I continued, pointing at myself, then gesturing down the road.

"Thirty thousand," he stated matter-of-factly in English.

"It's okay, I'll walk," I said, turning to do just that.

"Wait," he said, stopping me to discuss the situation.

It took a couple of minutes to convince him that I wasn't interested in paying for a ride, no matter how small the fee, and that I was, essentially, going from place to place relying on the generosity of passing road users.

"You are like Buddha!" he said with a smile, then gestured for me to get on.

As we made our way along the road, it immediately became clear that covering anywhere near the sort of distances I had managed daily in Australia, would be utterly impossible in Indonesia. With a population of over 240 million people, even if I got lucky and scored a ride with a truck or car, there was simply too much traffic, on roads too twisting, too minor, and in too poor a condition to get anywhere particularly fast.

New life and intrigue presented itself around every corner: Hindu temples, grotesque angry-faced statues, mountainous piles of old coconut husks, street stalls hawking pink-tinged gasoline in see-through incremented containers, stray dogs, sparks exploding from angry-looking disk-cutters on workshop floors, consolidated mounds of discarded plastic bottles, puncture-repair shops, mechanics' garages, otherworldly tropical trees, curious tube-shaped cages containing live pigs; and everywhere people, going to and fro, busying themselves with all manner of tasks ranging from the backbreaking to the casual. Some lugged towering bundles of unidentifiable vegetable matter or bits of steelwork, others stood chatting outside local roadside stores. At one stage a religious parade, complete with banners, gongs, and chanting, made its way along the street, holding up the traffic until it passed. My surroundings had changed beyond all recognition since Darwin, and I couldn't have been happier. This was what traveling was all about.

It wasn't long before the crowded streets gave way to lush green rice paddies, offering expansive views across the rural heart of the island, and we were nearing the ticket office for Tanah Lot Temple, where the green and pleasant abruptly ended, replaced now by a large car and coach-lot surrounded by tacky commercialized tourist infrastructure. Somewhere, hidden from view beyond, was the sacred temple, an iconic symbol of Bali thought to date from the sixteenth century, and a place Dan had recommended I stop off at on my way across the tiny island. Purchasing a ticket from a little office, I made my way past a barrage of gift shops and market stalls, piled high with mountains of tourist junk: beach sandals, random bits of coral, sarongs, wind chimes, baseball caps, jewelry, and other tasteless souvenirs, before finally arriving at a coastal clifftop where the temple came into view.

Perched on top of an exposed rocky sea stack, stranded a couple of hundred feet off the coast, was a collection of multi-tiered shrines that rose from the center of this craggy island. Being semi low tide at the moment, the foreshore of the island was accessible for those willing to get their feet wet, so I made my way down onto the shore, threw my shoes in my pack and waded into the warm but sloshing water for a closer look. There wasn't much to see. Staircases led up the perimeter of the rock to the temple above, but they were prohibited for all but true devotees, and over a third of the "rock" turned out to be fake; an artificially enhanced sham, sculptured like a prop from a movie set to look like the real thing. I can't say I was particularly impressed, a feeling hardly helped by the hordes of tourists and nearby infrastructure, which included an 18-hole golf course and spa resort, roughly 1500 feet away.

The large scale commercialization of such a sensitive part of Bali's historic, religious, and cultural heritage was initiated in the early nineties, to huge outrage among the Balinese. Developers with close ties to the country's then dictator, General Suharto,[22] skirted around planning rules, forcibly removing locals from their property surrounding the site to make way for the resort, and bulldozing land before owners had even agreed to sell.[23] Protests erupted in what became the first proper challenge by the Balinese to unrestrained tourist development on their island. With as much as 85 percent of tourist assets on Bali owned by foreigners,[24] all too often local communities shoulder the burdens of development, but reap very little of the benefits,[25] with the lion's share of profits going abroad.

Furious landowners presented a petition to the head of the regional government stating their grievances: that they had been told their land was to be appropriated "in the national interest" only to find it handed over to a private conglomerate, that lives had been threatened, land impounded by the courts, and irrigation water cut off.[26] Despite protests succeeding in stalling the development, the military finally stamped them out,[27] and the project went ahead. That there were protests in the first place is testament to the strength of feeling for this holy Hindu site, especially when you consider who was running the country at the time: General Suharto, a man the C.I.A. attributes as carrying out "the worst mass murders of the second half of the 20th century,"[28] and whose former atrocities on Bali alone account for at least 80,000 dead in a single year, many of whom, unbeknown to most tourists to the island, are buried in mass graves under the car-lots of major hotels.[29]

Leaving the temple, I strode off along the road leading from it, waving off taxis as I went. From now on I would head straight to neighboring island, Java, the most populated in the Indonesian archipelago, which is made up of a mind-boggling seventeen thousand islands. If all went well I hoped to reach Java by the afternoon.

Without any outward request for a lift from me, a second biker pulled over. This was a strange but welcome feature of hitchhiking in Indonesia, where simply looking out of place and making a journey on foot was enough to get a ride.

"Where are you going?" asked its middle-aged male rider.

"Kediri," I replied.

He asked for money, and this time really wanted it.

With a polite decline I carried on my way, determined to clear a good distance from the temple where it seemed likely everyone would want remuneration for a ride.

Endless fields of rice stretched into the distance, dotted with workers in wide-brimmed, circular hats with a central point, who bent down at the knees with flagpole-straight backs to gather in the harvest. A few minutes later another bike stopped. The rider was in his thirties and despite the scorching hot and sticky temperature was decked out in a chunky padded jacket and a pair of stone-wash jeans. Like most of the bikers I had seen, he wore no helmet. He spoke next to no English, so to secure the deal I resorted to mime. Rubbing my thumb and forefingers together, I indicated money, then waved a hand across my chest while shaking my head and politely saying "no," punctuating it with a hand on heart gesture at the end, to say "please."

It did the trick. I was on the move again.

For a scooter ride it felt long, coming in at around ten miles and continuing until the high-street of busy regional capital Tabanan. Such was the pattern for the next couple of hours, with scooter rides coming and going with varying ease, and for differing lengths, until I found myself walking along a section of road surrounded by verdant fields, bordered by a thin grass verge that dropped away steeply into a bank below. It began to rain. However, when hitchhiking, rain is your friend. The sight of a soaked-through hitchhiker on the side of the road elicits a big dose of sympathy. Within a minute of the first drops falling a battered truck with the words "Trust to God" emblazoned in English above its cab pulled over.

The passenger door swung open revealing three guys in their late twenties with deep cola-colored skin. None spoke English so the usual miming ensued to establish the lift was for gratis. It was. I moved to haul myself inside, but then slipped on the wet grass underfoot. My backpack's weight added momentum. Over I went, toppling down the muddy bank, falling about a hundred and thirty degrees backwards, landing with a thud. My humiliation wasn't over. In cartoon fashion I began sliding head first down the bank, legs splayed wide apart behind me. Leaping from the door, one of the guys lunged for my ankles, grabbing a hold of them and dragging me feet first up the bank through a carpet of mud and rain-soaked grass. It didn't make for the most dignified of introductions.

Despite the language barrier between us, I established my companions names—Antok, Opik (the ankle grabber) and Ahmad (the driver)—and that they were heading to Bali's ferry terminal for Java. As we bumped along a poorly maintained road, the gentle shower of rain turned suddenly into a giant block of descending water, lashing the truck and the world outside, sending locals scrambling under cover or those caught out in it on motorbikes to hastily don large plastic ponchos. Water began pouring from the foliage of trees, ripping into the gravely road and peppering its surface with a thousand miniature explosions. Then it was gone, expiring, as if by the flick of a switch, into waves of faintly visible humidity, driven from the land by a huge tropical sun.

Standing across two and a half miles of shimmering sea appeared Java, a world of fertile greenery, rising steadily in elevation to form the smooth conical peaks of the distant Ijen plateau. Soon we were skipping across the waters of the Strait of Bali, riding the ferry between the islands and landing on the other side where things took an interesting turn.

Opik made a call on his cell, then passed it over to me.

"Where do you want to go?" queried a man on the other end in reasonable English.

It was a good question, which in many respects depended on where the guys were going. Having initially just asked for "Java," now that we had reached it some specifics were called for. Java is a sort of mutated cigar shape stretching from east to west, and since we were at its far eastern point, and I was ultimately heading west to Mt. Bromo, just about anywhere they were going was in the right direction. But a nonchalant "anywhere" is hardly the sort of reply you expect from a hitchhiker when asking where they desire to go, so I decided to request logistical help instead.

"Somewhere I can buy a map."

"Map?—oh, atlas. Okay, give the phone to Opik," said the man.

I did, and kind of assumed I'd be dropped at a local store where I could buy one, but to my surprise we came to a halt outside a shady-looking pool hall where a row of motorbikes was lined. We were in the city of Banyuwangi, about fifteen minutes drive from the docks. The guys led me inside. Sitting around drinking, smoking, holding court and playing pool and billiards were several groups of tough-looking locals. On a stool at a central bar section sat what looked like the boss, a flinty-eyed tough guy with a neat, well-trimmed goatee beard, wearing a white "wife beater" vest, and black, belted dress pants. His arms bore several chunky scars as well as multiple U.S.-style gang tattoos, including one that depicted a medieval scroll-like document upon which was written "Game is Over." The guys who'd given me a ride approached him.

"I run this town," said the man, remaining seated on the stool. "You will be safe here, no one will harm you."

Up until now I hadn't felt unsafe.

"I have sent someone to buy your atlas," he said, revealing himself as the guy on the phone.

He introduced himself as Rio Rossano Hansa.

Rio summoned a lackey from behind the bar who promptly poured two shots of unknown liquor into dainty glasses.

"Welcome," he said, handing me a glass. He was friendly, yet somehow still menacing.

I have no recollection of what the booze tasted like other than being very alcoholic.

"You speak good English," I said, just making conversation. "Where did you learn?"

"The United States, I spent eight years in a Californian penitentiary."

I was surprised at nothing but his candor. Was it bad criminal etiquette to ask what he had been inside for? I didn't know but couldn't resist.

"Narcotics and shooting someone," he replied, unperturbed at my inquiry. "I used to be a gang-banger."

This was a most odd situation to have suddenly found myself. Moments earlier I had been happily plodding away on the road, and now, out of the blue, I had been thrust into the Indonesian equivalent of the Sopranos and was making the acquaintance of a bona fide gangster. Despite this, I can't say I felt uneasy at my change in circumstances. After all, Rio seemed welcoming to me, as had his three stooges who introduced me, and so instead of concern, I felt intrigued.

"Would you like something to eat?" offered Rio.

I accepted, and on Rio's say-so the barman began ladling out a serving of tofu and noodle-based stew laced with red-hot shaving of chili, taken from a large urn behind the bar. Rio pointed the barman towards a nearby table.

"Take your time," said Rio, gesturing me to the table—the unspoken implication being that we would only converse again once I had finished.

Moments after tucking in, my "atlases" arrived. I owed the delivery man roughly four dollars, but gave the equivalent of five. They were two big fold-out road maps: one of Java; the other of the next island to the west, Sumatra. Both islands are far larger than Bali and would require several days of hitching to cross.

When I finished my stew, Rio came over and asked about my plans in Indonesia.

"It is too dangerous to wait on road," he stated on hearing my intention to hitchhike. "You must get bus or train."

I did my best to explain that this was not within my remit, but it fell on deaf ears, with him just repeating himself several times, until it sounded more like an order than a suggestion. In the end I just pretended to agree.

"Okay," I said, "You're right. I'll catch a bus."

He seemed happy with that.

By now it was early evening so I made inquires with Rio as to local accommodation, with the intention of crashing out and hitting the road at first light—and not in a bus.

"I will arrange for you," he stated.

The same guy who had delivered the maps was sent out again, this time with the task of visiting local boarding houses and reporting back on their availability and price. While he was gone I queried Rio on his time as a guest of the U.S. government.

"You have to have these experiences," he said with an air of the philosophical, as if prison was just one of those things everybody had to go through once in a while.

"In England we say you have to take the—" I paused, having intended to say, "rough with the smooth," but then concluded this might not translate, so just said, "good with the bad."

It was hardly a deep and nuanced insight worthy of passing on, just bullshit conversation making, but Rio saw different.

"Yeesss!" he responded enthusiastically as if I had imparted something terribly apt and astute, and he had finally, after all these years, come across a fellow great thinker of depth and gravitas whom he could converse with on the same highbrow philosophical wavelength. He looked at me with a touch of admiration. We were buddies now, and while waiting for his associate to return, Rio chatted more openly with me; mainly about himself. He'd been married four times, had children who still lived in the U.S., and had just got out of prison in Indonesia. This time though he was adamant he'd been framed.

"My sister is running for mayor," he told me. "They did this to me to make her look bad."

Accommodation-wise, it turned out that my best option was a little motel across the road, where I could get a room for about seven dollars. For the next hour or so I hung out with Rio. When it finally got dark outside I thanked him for his assistance, then made my excuses and headed to the motel—after falsely agreeing to consult with him in the morning about a bus or train.

The room was miserable, a gloomy little hovel that could have been out of a horror film. Several recent blood splats decorated the woodchip wallpaper, and creeping over the walls and floor was an army of cockroaches whose numbers increased in concentration in a dingy shower cubicle where the plug hole was thick with human hair and a horrible sludge; a cocktail of what looked like dead skin, dirt, and soap scum.

I made the best of it and settled in for the night with a book, the only one I had with me, and one that I had already read: *Unpeople, Britain's Secret Human Rights Abuses* by Mark Curtis. Emily had been reading it on the plane to Australia, but somehow it had found its way into my backpack during my frantic high speed packing in Hobart. The subject matter seemed unlikely to lighten the atmosphere of the room, but I delved into it once more nonetheless, turning to its section on Indonesia, which began in somber fashion: "Few people have suffered as much from

Britain's backing for repressive regimes as those living in the islands of Indonesia . . . [Britain's] strategy has been remarkably consistent: forces are supported according to their ability to do Whitehall's bidding; the Indonesian people are an irrelevance."

CHAPTER TEN
A Little Shooting

If you want to understand modern Indonesia, then you have to understand the bloody legacy of the country's former dictator, General Suharto, and the role Western governments—particularly the United States, Britain and Australia—played in his rise to power. This, and their subsequent collusion in his atrocities, is something very often skimmed over, whitewashed or swept beneath the editorial carpet by his Western corporate media apologists; but not by me. After all, when the truth is replaced by silence, the silence is a lie. It is an episode they might well like to forget, for it speaks volumes about the true designs of Western power and how the world is run, where governments say one thing and do another, and justify murder on an industrial scale in resource rich countries for strategic and economic gain.

In 1955 a great conference full of hope and optimism was held in the Indonesian city of Bandung, where leaders from twenty-nine African and Asian countries, many of them newly independent states, met to discuss a peaceful coexistence, where non-aligned countries—states seeking a third way, unaligned to the major capitalist or communist power blocks—could join together, forge common interests and find a powerful harmonious voice on the world stage, distinct from the agenda of rapacious corporate or imperial power. Such a viable alternative model for development was seen as a direct threat by the Western powers.

Hosted by Indonesia's President Sukarno (not to be confused with the above mentioned General Suharto), who had led his county's struggle for independence from the Dutch who colonized Indonesia in the sixteenth century, the conference declared a path of mutual respect and neutralism for the underdeveloped world, the majority of humanity. To the C.I.A. it was little short of heresy. U.S. Secretary of State John Foster Dulles condemned neutralism in the face of communism as "immoral."[30] His younger brother, Allen Foster Dulles, held the same view; and he ran the C.I.A.

"I think it's time we held Sukarno's feet to the fire," said Frank Wisner, the C.I.A.'s Deputy Director of Plans (Covert operations), in 1956.[31]

And so began a sordid U.S. and British campaign to discredit, oust or kill the president of a resource rich country of "great potential wealth,"[32] which sat as the jewel in the crown of a region that declassified British Foreign Office files called for the "defence" of Western interests in, noting that "the region produces nearly 85 percent of the world's natural rubber, over 45 percent of the tin, 65 percent of the copra and 23 percent of the chromium ore."[33]

Sukarno was a nationalist, not a communist, a non-aligned populist who did his own bidding, by and large, using the Indonesian Communist Party (the PKI) and army as counterweights, granting concessions to both to create a workable balance of power. But with the PKI playing a role in a Sukarno-led coalition, his enemies could label him a protector of their party. Over a million strong, and having made significant electoral gains, if true democracy was to be served, then the PKI could not be excluded by Sukarno, who stated, "I can't ride a three-legged horse."[34] Such pragmatic accommodation to the subtleties of governance played badly with the black and white, with or against us, politics of Washington and London. They cared not that the PKI was a peaceful or law abiding constituent of the Indonesian political process, who had, in the words of Australian historian Harold Crouch, "won widespread support not as a revolutionary party but as an organisation defending the interests of the poor within the existing system,"[35] only that they were the PKI.

The size and breadth of the C.I.A.'s planned military operations against Sukarno required substantial resources from the Pentagon, something only obtainable if deemed necessary and appropriate by top officials of the National Security Council acting on behalf of the President. To garner such approval, the C.I.A. cooked the books, a classic case of intelligence and facts being fixed around policy, long before the *Downing Street Memo* revealed as much about Iraq, only this time it was the C.I.A. determining policy over the government. As then head of the C.I.A.'s Indonesia desk, Joseph Burkholder Smith, reveals in his memoir *Portrait of a Cold Warrior*, before suggesting any plan to officials from the National Security Council, where "premature mention . . . might get it shot down," first they laid the ground work (emphasis below is mine):

> [W]e began to feed the State and Defense departments intelligence ... [w]hen they had read enough alarming reports, we planned to spring the suggestion we should support the colonels' plans to reduce Sukarno's power . . . In many instances, we made the action programs up ourselves after we had collected enough intelligence to make them *appear* required by the circumstances. Our activity in Indonesia in 1957–1958 was one such instance.[36]

In November 1957, the top officials from the National Security Council gave the C.I.A. the go ahead,[37] who used their newfound assistance from the Pentagon to arm, equip, and train tens of thousands of separatist rebels[38] centered around Indonesia's outer provinces, led by dissident colonels in Indonesia's army. Britain provided the use of her military bases in nearby Singapore and Malaya for arms drops and covert operations.[39] As declassified documents from the British Foreign Office make clear, although the separatists' aims centered around a desire for more self-government and an end to what they saw as Sukarno's inefficient economic policies; this wasn't the line that Britain or the U.S. would be pushing. They opted instead for "anti-communism," which was expediently added to the rebels' official aims. "[I]n order to attract Western support, it [anti-communism] has been made to *appear* one of the main purposes of the rebellion,"[40] (my emphasis) wrote Britain's ambassador to Indonesia in a Foreign Office report. In Singapore,

Britain's Commissioner General, Sir Robert Scott, had told the Foreign Office, "I think the time has come to plan secretly with the Australians and Americans how best to give these elements the aid they need . . . The action that I am recommending will no doubt have little influence with President Sukarno. They are not designed to; I believe it should be one of our aims to bring about his downfall."[41]

They certainly gave it a good go. U.S. Navy submarines provided weapons, supplies and communications equipment to the rebels;[42] on Okinawa an army of Indonesians, Americans, Filipinos, and Taiwanese were amassed, along with other "soldiers of fortune;"[43] and the C.I.A. formed a rebel air force of around 350 pilots.[44] Made up of Americans, Filipinos and Chinese nationalists, it consisted of a sizable Air Transport force tasked with dropping thousands of weapons, ammunition and equipment deep into Indonesia, and of a bomber fleet comprised of fifteen B-26 bombers, which rained explosives down on cities, towns, villages and civilian shipping— the latter done to dissuade commercial tankers from entering Indonesia's waters in order to strangle the county's economy.[45] Declassified British files record an attack on a 12,000-ton Panamanian steamer, causing the death of twelve of its twenty-six crew, and of the sinking of a 5,000 ton Italian ship with twelve of its crew missing.[46] A British freighter was also sunk, promoting head of the C.I.A., Allen Dulles, to describe the air strikes to President Eisenhower as "almost too effective."[47] As well as providing arms and the use of their regional military bases, the British flew war planes on reconnaissance missions over Indonesia,[48] and were reported to have used one of their submarines to rescue U.S. paramilitary advisers when the rebel positions collapsed.[49] And collapse they did.

Despite the rebellion spreading to several different regions, and the devastating effect of the bombing and strafing raids, the C.I.A.'s operations were soon curtailed, following an assault on the Indonesian island of Ambon. It was here, on May 15, 1958, that a C.I.A. plane bombed a marketplace, killing a large number of civilians making their way to church;[50]—not that this was a concern for the C.I.A., but rather what happened during a subsequent raid three days later, when U.S. pilot Allen Lawrence Pope was shot down. Quickly captured, Pope was paraded, along with incriminating documentation found on him, in front of the press, thus exposing the lie that had been fed to the world a couple of weeks earlier by U.S. President

Eisenhower: "Our policy [on Indonesia] is one of careful neutrality and proper deportment all the way through so as not to be taking sides where it is none of our business."[51] Interesting to note that unlike Indonesia, supposed neutralism was a perfectly acceptable path for the United States to tread.

A month later the Indonesian army effectively crushed the U.S. and British sponsored rebellion. As for Pope, he spent four years in an Indonesian prison, before being released after an intercession by Robert Kennedy. Following release he stated of his time in Indonesia: "I enjoyed killing Communists . . . we knocked the shit out of them. We killed thousands of Communists, even though half of them probably didn't even know what Communism meant."[52] In other words he enjoyed obliterating peasants; poor families aspiring for a better, happier, and more equitable life.

Sukarno had escaped the U.S. and British wrath for now, but his card was marked; they would soon try again, as shown by a C.I.A. memorandum of June 1962. According to the memo, President Kennedy and British Prime Minister Macmillan had agreed to "liquidate President Sukarno, depending upon the situation and available opportunities." The memo's C.I.A. author added, "It is not clear to me whether murder or overthrow is intended by the word liquidate."[53]

Two and a half years later, Pakistan's ambassador to France would send a secret report to his country's Foreign Minister detailing a conversation with a Dutch intelligence officer attached to NATO, who had informed him that Indonesia was "ready to fall into the Western lap like a rotten apple." But the real bombshell revelation regarded Western intelligence agencies, who, it was said, would organize a "premature communist coup . . . [which would be] foredoomed to fail, providing a legitimate and welcome opportunity to the army to crush the communists and make Sukarno a prisoner of the army's goodwill." The date on the report: December 1964.[54] Less than a year later, an exact carbon copy of this prediction would come to pass, when, on September 30, 1965, six army generals were murdered by junior officers, who seized several strategic locations in the Indonesian capital, Jakarta. The army quickly retook the captured points, and under the direction of General Suharto—a man who had served both the Dutch colonialists and Japanese invaders[55]—the junior officers were crushed and accused of staging a "coup attempt" on behalf of the Indonesian Communist Party. As investigative journalist John Pilger has remarked: "Certainly, if it was a 'communist coup,' it had the unique feature: none of the officers accused of plotting it was a communist." But no matter, General Suharto's version of events would be the one disseminated in the West. Suharto seized power from Sukarno, who was deposed and held "prisoner of the army's goodwill" under virtual house arrest, until his death five years later.

With General Suharto in control of the country, an unimaginable wave of killing was unleashed against anyone suspected of being a communist. So barbaric was the slaughter that followed, that it is no exaggeration to draw comparisons to the Holocaust. American historian Gabriel Kolko writes:

> The "final solution" to the Communist problem in Indonesia was certainly one of the most barbaric acts of inhumanity in a century that has seen a great deal of it; it surely ranks as a war crime of the same type as those the Nazis perpetrated. No single American act in the period after 1945 was as bloodthirsty as its role in Indonesia, for it tried to initiate the massacre, and it did everything in its power to encourage Suharto, including equipping his killers, to see that the physical liquidation of the PKI was carried through to its culmination.[56]

To help kick start the massacre, which it is estimated extinguished the life out of between 500,000 and more than a million human beings,[57] U.S. officials supplied comprehensive lists to the Indonesian army of "communist" operatives to be hunted down and killed.[58] As the bodies piled up, U.S. officials checked their names off the list.[59] "It really was a big help to the army," stated Robert Martens, a former political officer of the U.S. Embassy in Indonesia, in an interview in 1990. "They probably killed a lot of people, and I probably have a lot of blood on my hands, but that's not all bad."[60] From Suharto's headquarters came confirmation of the killings. "We were getting a good account in Jakarta of who was being picked up," revealed the C.I.A.'s former deputy station chief, Joseph Lazarsky. "The army had a 'shooting list' of about 4,000 or 5,000 people. They didn't have enough goon squads to zap them all, and some individuals were valuable for interrogation. The infrastructure [of the PKI] was zapped almost immediately. We knew what they were doing . . . Suharto and his advisers said, if you keep them alive, you have to feed them."[61]

In *The New Rulers of the World*, John Pilger details examples of some of the wholesale savagery visited upon Indonesia—of rivers jammed with bodies like logs; of village after village where young men were slaughtered for no reason, their murders marked by rows of severed penises; of people snatched in the night and beheaded; of men taken from holding cells in batches to be shot; of so many bodies that they were being washed up on the lawns of the British consulate; of British warships escorting ships full of Indonesian troops down the Malacca Straits so they could take part in the slaughter; of torture, mass graves and the systematic execution of teachers, students, civil servants and peasant farmers. Chronicling a typical case, Pilger reports on a primary school headmaster suspected of being a communist, who, in full view of the school's children, was dragged into the playground and beaten to death: "He was a wonderful man: gentle and kind," a former pupil told Pilger. "He would sing to the class, and read to me. He was the person that I, as a boy, looked up to . . . I can hear his screams now, but for a long time, years in fact, all I could remember was running from the classroom, and running and running through the streets, not stopping. When they found me that evening, I was dumbstruck. For a whole year I couldn't speak."

Such horror was commonplace; not that the United States, Britain or Australia cared; they approved. "With 500,000 to a million communist sympathisers knocked off," remarked Australian Prime Minister Harold Holt, "I think it's safe to assume a reorientation has taken place."[61] As the frenzy of killing reached its peak, General Suharto was told by America's ambassador to Indonesia, Marshall Green, that "The U.S. is generally sympathetic with and admiring of what the army is doing."[62] Britain's ambassador to Indonesia, Sir Andrew Gilchrist remarked in a cable to the Foreign Office: "I have never concealed from you my belief that a little shooting in Indonesia would be an essential preliminary to effective change."[63]

Some change. In less than a year of the genocide, a corporate takeover of Indonesia would occur that saw the country's vast hoard of natural resources—its minerals, nickel, tropical forests, bauxite, oil, etc.—essentially gifted to Western mega corporations, and the Indonesian economy rewritten in their favor. Described by President Nixon as "the greatest prize in south-east Asia," Indonesia's staggering natural wealth was divvied up at a remarkable three-day conference attended by major Western companies and banks. Professor Jeffrey Winters of Northwestern University, Chicago, has said of the conference: "They divided up into five different sections: mining in one room, services in another, light industry in another, banking and finance in another; and what Chase Manhattan did was sit with a delegation and hammer out policies that were going to be acceptable to them and other investors. You had these big corporation people going around the table, saying this is what we need: this, this, and this, and they basically designed the legal infrastructure for future investment in Indonesia. I've never heard of a situation like this where global capital sits down with the representatives of a supposedly sovereign state and hammers out the conditions of their own entry into that country."[64]

A bonanza of rapacious capitalist feeding began, a methodical vacuuming up of huge sections of the Indonesian economy out of the hands of the toiling local masses, into the claws of the moneyed foreign few—with generous kickbacks of course for Indonesian politicos brokering the deals. It was a blueprint for what would later gain the fluffy sobriquet, "globalization." One of globalization's early architects, Margaret Thatcher, would tell Suharto, "You are one of our very best and most valuable friends."

For the next thirty years General Suharto would rule Indonesia with an iron fist, a period of governance he referred to as the "New Order," hallmarked by brutality and rampant corruption. His ousted predecessor, Sukarno, had attempted to deliver economic independence for Indonesia, by holding the Western corporations at bay, incurring little in the way of debt, and showing the door to the World Bank and the International Monetary Fund. Under General Suharto these twin agents of the world's wealthiest nations were welcomed back, bringing with them an influx of loans, a result described by an official of the bank as "the best thing that's happened to Uncle Sam since World War Two."[65]

And so Indonesia, a country that at one stage owed nothing, was swamped in a burden of debt of enormous proportion, and Suharto and his cronies became fabulously wealthy. A World Bank internal report on Indonesia reveals that somewhere in the region of 30 percent of all loans made by the bank to the country were siphoned off by the Suharto regime. "At least 20–30% of government of Indonesia development budget funds are diverted through informal payments to government staff & politicians," states the incendiary document.[66] It is estimated that Suharto stole more from his country than any other leader in history.[67]

Suharto attempted to legitimize himself on the basis of supposed economic progress, but in 1997 his economic house of cards based on debt, plunder, and a vast pool of dirt-cheap sweat-shop labor, came tumbling down. Short term capital fled the country, the stock market crashed, currency imploded—losing 84 percent of its value over a short period[68]— and those living in absolute poverty hit 70 million.[69] Ordinary Indonesians lucky enough to keep their jobs saw their real wages plummet: by 40 percent for agricultural workers, and by 34 percent for those in urban areas. Unemployment went up tenfold.[70] Suharto was forced to resign, doing a runner with an estimated 15 billion USD, roughly 13 percent of his country's foreign debt, a large portion owed to the World Bank. Regardless of where it went, the Indonesian people still have to pay it back, with crippling interest, of course. Today Indonesia spends around eight times as much on debt repayments as on either health or education spending;[71] 39 million Indonesians exist in appalling poverty, struggling to live on less than one dollar a day, while another 140 million scrape by on less than two dollars a day.[72]

But that's not all bad, at least if you're the foreign C.E.O. of a company exploiting the labor "market," or if you're a Western consumer buying products made there. Poverty equals cheap labor, which means bigger profits and artificially low prices on the high street. Everyone's a winner; except of course if you're one of the millions of invisible "unpeople" toiling away in sweat-shop misery. But, hey, out of sight out of mind.

CHAPTER ELEVEN
Nature Bares Her Teeth

Unlike Bali where the majority of inhabitants are Hindu, on Java they are Muslim, a change in religion made obvious by several roadside mosques, and by the set of Islamic prayer beads that dangled from the windshield mirror of the aged farming truck that picked me up after a hectic morning of hopping on and off multiple bikes. The driver was a kindly old fella called Muhammed, with a weathered face and a warm smile, who chain-smoked the entire way, holding his cigarettes in a curious manner—between his ring and little finger. He spoke no English, so I took in the view and by early afternoon we were winding our way together through a forested, twisting mountain gorge.

Stationed at intervals along the side of the road, about a minute's slow drive apart, were utterly demoralized-looking people waving the traffic along, despite there being no discernible reason for doing so. Some didn't even put on the pretense of assisting traffic, and instead just stood with an outstretched palm and a forlorn expression. There were men and women, young and old, able-bodied and disabled, even a mother cradling a child. Some sat beneath basic self-made shelters, little lean-tos no more than a couple of feet off the ground that had been thrown together with old bits of bamboo and jungle leaves to provide shelter when the ferocious tropical rains arrived.

My heart went out to them. I might know something of what it is like to stand on the side of the road, but not like this. Whenever I waited it was with a sense of optimism at the adventure ahead and of the progress I would make. How demoralizing it must have been to wait, rooted to the same spot, staring day after day at approaching traffic, hoping for a hand out. My life had incomparably more opportunities than theirs, simply through the nationality on my passport; an accident of birth that I felt both thankful and guilty for.

Muhammed dropped me by a gas station in an unknown minor town, from where it took me multiple rides, and plenty of walking in between, over several hours, to reach the small remote village of Sukapura, about eleven miles from the volcano Mt. Bromo. Bromo still remained unseen, hidden behind distant, gradually climbing, green terrain. With roughly an hour of sunlight left I began to wonder if I would catch a glimpse of it before nightfall.

By now traffic had all but ceased to exist. If need be, then from here on in I was willing to walk to Mt. Bromo. It seemed likely to be a difficult hike, especially given the incline and how ridiculously heavy my backpack was, which still held all the superfluous items hastily packed in Hobart that I had yet to jettison. After plodding my way towards the end of the village, I came upon three middle-aged guys loading up an old black four-wheel-drive Mercedes SUV, who looked like they were just about to depart, and in the direction I needed.

"Hi, there," I said waving in their direction. "Do you speak English?"

None did, but the ball was rolling. A bit of gesturing, with the occasional inquisitive "Mt. Bromo?" dropped in, and it soon became apparent we were all heading to the same place and they were willing to take me for free. I was back on the road and my timing couldn't have been better. Soon after squeezing on board between assorted mechanical knick-knacks and two humongous canisters of gasoline it began to rain. Contained within it was a dark sludge that built up on the windows and the windshield beyond the area reachable by the wipers. It was laden with volcanic ash. The sky began to darken prematurely, throwing the interior of the vehicle with its exposed jet-black metal panels and identically colored seating into near total darkness. I clambered over to the window and squinted out into the slashing deluge. The landscape had turned black too, blanketed by a thick slushy coating as if covered in a layer of satanic snow. I'd never seen anything like it, and as we climbed in elevation, bumping our way along a twisting mountain path with fear-inducing drops, my heart began thumping hard in anticipation. What on earth awaited me at our final destination?

Then I caught sight of it. An enormous dark-gray volcanic dust-cloud rising ominously into the sky, riding eastward on the prevailing wind, mutating as it went. There was still no sign of the volcano it came from, but the cloud itself was epic. It looked like something out of an apocalypse movie, bestowing a truly foreboding beauty on an already eerie landscape. A bolt of lightning flashed within it.

"Wow!" I cried, unable contain my excitement.

The guys were pleased I liked it, and began pointing its way with enthusiastic musings. I watched, transfixed as the cloud grew larger and more daunting the further we drove. This was real adventure hitchhiking. This was living.

When we pulled up in the village of Cemoro Lawang and as I stepped from the SUV, I was on a high, nearly shaking with excitement. The rain had stopped now, and in the open-air the eruption cloud looked even more impressive. Its turbulent beginnings rose just over the brow of a distant hill, past homes caked in ash, providing a ghostly backdrop to the village. Mt. Bromo itself was still out of sight, making it look like a giant warhead had detonated nearby.

Gesturing to a little café, the guys invited me to join them for some food. Waiting outside, propped up against the wall, was their friend Gondo, an excellent English speaker.

"You are extremely lucky to be here at the moment," he told me. "Bromo is very active, the best for many years. The nighttime lava viewing area has been amazing."

The viewing area, Gondo explained, was a location with clear views of the volcano, where, come nighttime, the bright red lava would be clear; something you could see being thrown hundreds of feet into the air.

This I had to witness.

Gondo led me inside the café, whose interior was near pitch-black.

"Power cut," he stated.

A couple of candles soon solved the problem, their gently pulsating light revealing little more than a cramped low-ceilinged room with a bare concrete floor, tiny windows, a solid counter around its walls, and several plastic stools. We all settled down to some food, with me going for a chicken broth that also contained a boiled egg, chunky noodles and tofu. It was delicious, as was the cup of vanilla tea I washed it down with.

The bill came to just seventy cents.

Stepping outside again I shook my head in disbelief at the sight that had gone unseen indoors—the volcanic cloud, writhing only a few hundred feet above the village. Through Gondo, the guys offered to drive me further up the hill to a budget hotel on the outer edge of the village. I accepted, and minutes later was bidding them farewell and checking in. There was no time to hang around inside. Dumping my pack in a tiny room barely big enough to accommodate its single bed, I immediately headed out to find a spot where I could finally gaze upon Mt. Bromo, to see where the fury was coming from before the last of the daylight slipped beyond the horizon.

An almighty, earth-reverberating boom threw me into a frenzy of excitement as I made my way along a thin track compacted with thick wet ash. A few steps further and another rumble erupted, its sound wave passing through me. Suddenly the earth dropped away, exposing an expansive ash-covered valley below that stretched off into the distance. Standing proudly in the middle of it, a couple of miles away, was a partial cone, some 7,641 feet high, the top blown clean off revealing a cavernous crater within. Billowing violently from here was the eruption cloud; it was mighty Mt. Bromo in all her glory. To her right flank stood Mt. Batok, the quintessential perfect mountain, a symmetrical cone of 8,103 feet with deep ribs running down her sides; and behind them both, providing the perfect background to a wondrous scene, was a taller distant mountain, another perfect cone and active volcano, Mt. Semeru, the highest peak on Java at 12,060 feet.

An explosion erupted from within Bromo, throwing debris skyward. Just how safe was it here at the moment? Days earlier I had seen footage on television of residents being evacuated from the vicinity around another one of Indonesia's mighty volcanoes. At what stage would Mt. Bromo warrant the same precautions? I watched engrossed until nighttime fell, then decided on a closer look.

Walking along a darkened trail of slushy ash that led southward from the village, I arrived at the lava viewing area, situated on the rim of the giant valley in which Bromo sat—actually a ten mile wide caldera, that is, a vast, cauldron-shaped depression in the earth formed by the collapse of land following a volcanic eruption. I had the spot to myself. For the first few minutes there was nothing visible in the dark beyond a faint brown-tinged glow coming from the distant base of Bromo, where the volcanic cloud spewed into the cold night air. Then it began. Exploding from the earth's depths, showers of deep-red molten matter shot upward in arcing trails that careered down Bromo's sides. Seconds later, the eruption's sound-wave hit me. I stood for a couple of hours, mesmerized as jets of lava greeted the night. Every so often the occasional streak of lightning joined the fray, scurrying from ash-cloud to ground, bringing forth vivid colors of incandescent white, blue and purple, as it released its pent up charge. It was one of the most captivating sights I've ever seen.

Lifting my jaw up off the ground, I headed back to the village. Strolling down the street was another Westerner about my age.

"How's it going?" I asked, in the hope of striking up a conversation with a potential English speaker.

"Good thanks," came the reply in a thick Dutch accent.

He introduced himself as Wim—pronounced "Vim"—who, it turned out, was doing a very similar trip to mine. Starting off in Sydney, Wim had traveled overland to Darwin where he flew to Indonesia, and was now making his way home to the Netherlands, a trip he had allocated a year to complete. It was time he might well need—he was cycling it!

Wim was hitting the sack soon; an alarm call beckoned for him at 4 a.m., set so he could complete a two hour hike to a scenic lookout on nearby Mt. Penanjakan, a popular spot to watch the sunrise from and take in its panoramic views of Mt. Bromo and the sounding area.

"You should come along," he suggested.

I agreed, and after arranging to meet outside my hotel at 4:15 a.m., I headed in to get my head down.

* * *

A soft dawn light diffused by a cool morning mist crept across the horizon, slowly revealing a ghostly panorama that could have been on another planet. Far off below lay the giant valley floor of the Tengger caldera, its towering cliffs reaching down to a sea-like swathe of black volcanic sand. Standing in the middle was Mt. Bromo, as active as ever. Blown by a brisk morning wind, her ever-changing eruption cloud drifted for a mile or so just above the caldera's floor, before climbing thousands of feet into the air. In front and to her right was the noble-looking cone of Mt. Batok, and in the distance, many miles away, Mt. Semeru.

Wim and I stared out at the classic picture-postcard shot of Java, often reproduced from Mt. Penanjakan's lookout; but with one notable exception. Normally captured is a quaint Mt. Bromo, emitting a gentle whisper of white gas into the still morning air; but that wasn't the case today. Bromo was enraged, hurling rocks the size of houses hundreds of feet up and spewing thick noxious fumes into the atmosphere, painting the air a dense dark gray for miles around. We were tremendously lucky to catch Bromo at her best, and she made for some fantastic photos.

Sharing the scenic lookout with us were a handful of other tourists who were doing the rounds swapping cameras to get a once in a lifetime photo of themselves against such an incredible backdrop. Staying behind long after everyone else had departed, Wim and I remained spellbound, watching Bromo's fluctuating mood unfold before us.

"Can you see that motorbike?" asked Wim, pointing down at the tiny figure of a lone rider transporting a bundled-up cargo of plant matter on the back of his bike, who was skirting along next to one of the towering valley walls at the bottom of the huge caldera in which Mt. Bromo sat.

"Apparently there's another track that leads from the village to Jemplang," said Wim.

This was currently invisible from our location high up Mt. Penanjakan, but Wim pointed out the rough route of the track. It went from near the lava viewing area, down the huge cliff wall of the caldera to its floor below, where it led towards an area directly under the volcanic cloud, which was currently depositing a hazy rain of ash.

"I'm thinking of cycling it," he added.

Wow. This was ballsy, if not foolhardy.

An exclusion zone was currently enforced around Bromo, which meant the entire caldera valley in which Mt. Bromo and Mt. Batok sat was strictly off limits. The local on the bike had broken this, but had done so along a different trail, far from Bromo herself, somewhere the track Wim was suggesting would end up pretty damn close to.

"Fancy coming along?" he asked.

My initial reaction, at least to myself, was a resounding, "No chance!" But when Wim explained that the village of Jemplang was located only seven and a half miles beyond Bromo, and that from there the track continued due west to the city of Malang, I began to consider it. This would cut out a hell of a lot of back-tracking, which, if I didn't come along, would be necessary in order to reach a distant road that skirted around the mountains in a big time-consuming loop.

Looking down at Bromo, I wondered if it was doable. I would need another local on a motorbike to do it, but whether any were using this particular track, and how frequently, I didn't know. To go so close to an active volcano while it was erupting was likely an opportunity I would never get again, but would it kill me? I had seen plenty of explosions throw material upwards but none had cast this particularly far outwards, in the sense of it reaching a long way beyond Bromo's flanks; and so, unless she came out with a big one while I was nearby, I figured I should survive.

"Okay then," I said to Wim, hardly believing the words coming out of my mouth, "I'm up for it."

Back in the village we stopped off at a small official national park office to confirm that the caldera and track was closed. I'm not sure what prompted us to do this. Maybe it was in the vain hope that the official there would tell us that although the exclusion zone was indeed in force, it was actually an over cautious bureaucratic response to the eruption, and, in fact, the route we wanted to travel was quite safe.

He told us the opposite.

We told him nothing of our intentions of venturing along it anyway.

A quick pit stop at my hotel to collect my backpack, and at Wim's so he could get his bike, and we set off, making our way along the beginnings of a bumpy road that led from the village to the edge of the caldera's cliff. Straddling the road at the top of the cliff was a chunky metal barrier, blocking access—at least for Jeeps and the like—to the exclusion zone of the caldera's floor below, which the road led steeply down to. We slipped around the barrier, Wim coasting down the annoyingly angled road, leaving me to walk it solo towards the sea of black sand-like ash at its base. With every heavy footstep my heart pounded harder and my adrenaline elevated, racing around my veins as the raw and unrestrained power of Bromo grew closer, until I was no longer looking down on her but up.

If ever somewhere could be described as a moonscape, then the caldera's belly was it. A desolate world of dark ash blanketed the expanse that stretched before me, from which Bromo's shattered cone rose, a little too close. Huge quantities of dark matter spewed into the air, as great sheet-like offerings fell across the area we planned to travel. There was zero sign of any track. It was without doubt the craziest place I have ever stood waiting for a ride.

Sometimes when hitching you can be in what is theoretically a great spot to wait, but for whatever reason no one stops. Other times you can be in what on paper is a ridiculous place to hail a ride but you strike it lucky and one materializes. There was no doubt which of the two I was in today, but was I feeling lucky?

I walked over to Wim, who stood nearby taking photos. We took a couple of each other, and then, with little further ado, he wished me well and set off.

Sitting on my backpack, I watched as he struggled to ride in the conditions. In less than a minute he had given up, and was pushing his bike through the sludge, getting closer to the volcanic cloud, which descended, every so often, to just above ground level, threatening to envelop him. Sitting here, I really didn't think I would get a ride. I foresaw a demoralizing trek back up the caldera's cliff face and a protracted detour along roads I'd hitchhiked the day before.

Soon Wim had disappeared from sight into the abyss.

Bromo let out a groaning rumble that cast huge rocks into the air.

"Bloody hell!" I said out loud, feeling more than a little too close for comfort.

The sand-covered caldera floor felt like Bromo's domain and I was trespassing.

Ten minutes later it happened: an amazing stroke of luck; a local on a motorbike slowly made his way down the steep cliff-face road to the caldera floor, and on reaching it set off in my general direction. I frantically waved him over. The rider was a middle-aged man with a big cheesy smile and a set of teeth so gap ridden he could have flossed with a skipping rope. He spoke no English, and so to establish where he was going I employed the medium of sign—after considering contemporary dance but then discounting it. A few additional utterances of the village name I was heading to (Jemplang) and I achieved the task. Not only was he going there, but, more importantly, was willing to take me. I could have jumped for joy. Clambering on the back of the bike, I sucked a deep breath into my lungs and held on tight.

It was tough going across the ash, and the bike struggled from the outset with the back tire sinking from the additional weight in the deep sand-like conditions. Perching on the back was a surreal experience. I was hitchhiking across a sea of ash with an erupting volcano to my immediate right, the morphing cloud from which approached like some mythical beast getting ready to swallow us whole. Our world began to darken as the cloud came in around us, skimming our heads to the point where I could feel its warmth. Debris started falling from the sky, a torrent of sand-like particles, only far chunkier, leaving a sting on my exposed legs and arms, like being lashed by a sandstorm in a desert. I pulled the thin rolled-up sleeves of my sweater down to minimise the effect. My local comrade had wisely come prepared, wearing a chunky jacket and a helmet with a visor.

The downfall's ferocity intensified, severely diminishing visibility and forcing me to screw up my eyes and angle my face towards the ground so that the back of my helmet took the brunt—amplifying the falling debris' sound around my head until it resembled TV static with the volume up. We plowed deeper into the storm until a pocket of loose silt thwarted our advances. Clambering off, we began trudging through a hail of falling grit, grappling with the bike as if forcing a reluctant animal forwards against its will.

Bromo groaned.

Through squinting eyes, I looked out across the bizarre downpour of dry and solid rain, at a near biblical vision of Armageddon, a literal world of fire and brimstone. I smiled. Both with incredulity and contentment. Incredulous at the insanity of my reality at this precise moment, and content that I was here, living on the edge, as far as I could get from the repetitive doldrums of normal life that had so frequently imprisoned me at home. Such desperate mediocrity seemed a universe away now; I could feel the overwhelming power of nature reverberating beneath my feet and all around me, affirming my existence and energizing my being with a feeling of complete exhilaration, to the point where I felt likely to burst at the seams. I let out a war cry, muffled almost immediately by the sound of slashing silt, but which thundered in my heart.

When the terrain allowed, we resumed our passage through shrouded oblivion, until, suddenly, we burst through to the other side. We had entered the promised land. Ahead lay an expanse of sunshine amid a green and pleasant world. Rising up the immense sheer cliff-face of the caldera's southern side, which protruded skyward by nearly a thousand feet, was lush vegetation. The cliff curved in an arc to the right, where it formed part of a narrower gorge—made up by the cliff itself and a giant internal ridge jutting up inside the caldera. A muddy track became visible ahead, and soon after a familiar figure cycling along it. As we got within earshot I called out to Wim. Turning around, he looked at me in shock.

"I didn't think I'd see you again!" exclaimed Wim as my lift pulled over beside him so we could chat.

"Me neither," I replied. "I didn't think I had a hope in hell of getting a ride."

For the next few minutes we swapped notes on our experiences beneath the volcanic cloud, before my motorcycle captain finally indicated it was time to wrap things up. I wished Wim well, and before I knew it he had disappeared from sight behind me.

As we made our way into the gorge along a twisting, partially waterlogged, track, I looked back towards a dichotomy of sky. To the west stretched a perfect unblemished blue, to the east a frenzy of dirty gray and brown that looked like the fallout from a nuclear explosion. It wasn't long before the last signs of Bromo had disappeared from sight behind the gorge's towering walls. The further we traveled the more serene it became. Lining the gorge's lower reaches were purple-petaled wild flowers, gently swaying long grasses, dense clumps of bracken and princely-looking plants with ripe clusters of umbellifers.

When the track reached the caldera's southwestern wall it began to climb, meandering though sparsely wooded terrain until the summit, where it formed something resembling a road; forking now in two directions. A couple of little huts with odd two-tiered roofs stood here, as did what appeared to be a forest fire lookout tower. This, my lift indicated, was where we departed. He was continuing left whereas I needed right. I thanked him for an unforgettable ride and set off on foot. Ten minutes into my walk, two scooters approached from behind—one carrying two girls in headscarves, the other ridden by a lone male. Without any request from me to do so, they all pulled over.

"Can I have my photo taken with you?" asked the girl riding on the back of the bike.

"Sure."

I posed for a couple of shots with her.

"Can we become friends on Facebook?" she asked.

I agreed, and gave her my name so she could look me up; hers was Farah.

By way of thanks, Farah got her male friend to give me a lift to the beginnings of the next little village, a place called Ngadas, about a mile and a half down the road. Situated on top of a ridge with steep inclines on either side, Ngadas was perched between two separate valleys, the combined sides forming a W-like shape, with the village on the middle peak. Running down all four slopes and stretching into the distance were fields of vegetables, laid out in neat patches on the super steep terrain, leaving the landscape resembling a quilt.

We stopped on the edge of Ngadas by another fork in the road. To the right it led upwards into the village; to the left the road went downhill, skirting around the settlement in the direction of Malang, about thirty miles away. Situated nearby was a little food stall with a multicolored umbrella sticking out the top of it to shelter the food when it rained.

"Would you like some meatballs?" offered Farah.

I accepted.

From a big metal pot came three white bun-shaped forms that to me resembled anything but meatballs. To my eye they looked more like dim sum dumplings. These were placed into a little china bowl filled with a noodle soup that was ladled in from another metal pot. Reaching into my pocket I attempted to pay but Farah was having none of it and promptly thrust some money towards the guy running the stall.

"I am sorry but I have to go now," she said, passing me my food. "It was nice to meet you."

And with that she got onto the back of her friend's scooter, waved me goodbye, and rode off into the village.

Standing next to the street stall was a grubby concrete rain shelter with an internal seating ledge where several other diners ate. I went inside and joined them. The food was curious, in a gritty kind of way that induced super cautious chewing, done out of fear of breaking a tooth on the durable foreign matter conjoined within the dumpling's meaty core, which had to be inquisitively probed with the tongue, to winnow particles better suited to resurfacing a road from those theoretically digestible. I finished full, but not satisfied.

Stepping from the shelter's shady interior, I emerged back into wondrous sunshine where a familiar voice greeted me.

"Jamie!"

Free-wheeling downhill towards me was Wim.

"That was quick!" I exclaimed as he pulled up next to me.

I couldn't believe he'd managed to cover such a long distance over such difficult terrain and in only slightly longer than it had taken a motorbike. We chatted for a while before Wim set off again, disappearing from sight down a bumpy road into a landscape dominated, in the immediate valley, by orderly vegetable patches, behind which lay more mountainous uncultivated terrain. As I set off on foot, it just felt wrong. Here I was taking lifts from transport propelled in motion by the internal combustion engine, whereas Wim, through pedal power alone, had overtaken me. I continued on my way for about twenty minutes, soaking up the scenery, when, all of a sudden, the sound of a vehicle approaching from behind snapped me back into hitching mode. Lurching from side to side and bouncing up and down was an old red Jeep. I stuck out my hand and smiled. Being in such a remote location I had high hopes of getting a ride, and so it came as little surprise when the driver stopped to offer me one. By the looks of it, three generations of the same family sat inside, making for a tight fit. I squeezed in next to ganddad and two grandkids, a boy and a girl aged about three and five, respectively, while Dad drove and Mum sat up front.

None spoke any English but it was easy enough to establish where they were going: Malang. The further we went the worse the "road" became, until it could barely be described as such, more a partially cobbled downhill track that definitely required an off road vehicle to dive along—in Wim's case his touring bicycle. He appeared in the distance through the Jeep's windshield, standing high on his pedals to negotiate the crevices of the road. As we slowly overtook him he spotted me in the back. We shared a wave and a smile, and not long after he disappeared from sight behind us. It was the last time I saw him.

After much slow and painful driving we eventually made it down to much lower, flatter ground, where the road quality improved. Multiple rural villages and towns separated by characteristic Indonesian greenery passed by on our way to Malang, where I was dropped at a chaotic junction in the north of the city. The whole family took their time waving me goodbye, holding up plenty of agitated traffic in the process. When they finally pulled off, a flood of heaving cars, trucks, bikes and buses surged around their Jeep in a pincer-like move that seemed to swallow them up.

I didn't have a particular destination in mind that I wanted to reach today; so long as I kept pushing in a northeasterly direction until nightfall, then that was good enough for me. In the end, daylight finally departed on my arrival in the eminently forgettable city of Jombang. Despite the effort, as the crow flies I had only covered sixty miles from Bromo—on paper a truly pathetic distance for a day's hitching. I wondered if Wim had got further on his push bike? But no matter, it would take more than this to demoralize me today. Mt. Bromo had given me one of my most remarkable hitchhiking experiences ever.

Rain poured down as I walked through Jombang's dark backstreets in search of a cheap hotel, and by the time I found one I was soaked—my hair slick, shorts waterlogged and feet squelching in my shoes. The weather may have left me cold but it couldn't touch the warm internal glow of satisfaction I felt at having visited Mt. Bromo; and neither could the room I booked into. Lying back on a concave bed, in a mosquito-rich interior, I felt strangely satisfied. Sure, the accommodation could have been nicer; I could have covered greater hitchhiking distance too, and experienced more clement weather, but a better more fulfilling day, I really couldn't have asked for. And for that, I fell gratefully asleep.

CHAPTER TWELVE
Forgotten Temple

T he thing about hitchhiking in Indonesia, is you often require such a ridiculous number of lifts to get between two moderately spaced apart points, that from a writing point of view, huge swathes of travel time can never see the light of day on the written page, or if it does, can only receive but nodding recognition, betraying the often arduous effort that went into completing a given journey. So it was today, with no less than thirty-two separate rides stretching from pre-dawn to post-dusk, through the green rural heart of central Java, that I arrived, tired, bewildered, and weary, in the village of Borobudur, having covered barely 138 miles—an average of just 4.3 miles a lift.

A UNESCO World Heritage site and the world's largest Buddhist monument, the huge pyramidal Borobudur Temple rises majestically from an expansive fertile plain enclosed by three towering cone-shaped volcanoes and a distant jagged ridge of limestone. Considered one of Southeast Asia's greatest Buddhist relics and the single most important piece of classical architecture in Indonesia, this ninth century temple was for a long time completely buried and forgotten under hundreds of years of tangled jungle growth, until it was rediscovered and unearthed in 1815 by Englishman, Sir Stamford Raffles. I had heard much about Borobudur, and couldn't wait to see it for myself.

My final lift of the day was on the back of a scooter, ridden by a charming local girl wearing a headscarf and a long overcoat, who spoke good English and worked at a local bank—where I met her while using its ATM. She dropped me at a little hotel opposite an extensive parkland that contained Borobudur. Despite the park's close proximity, Borobudur remained hidden, shrouded by foliage.

The hotel was another grubby place to crash, with no shortage of cockroaches or stains on the bedsheets; but on the upside, it was cheap, included a breakfast of fried eggs and coffee, and all guests received a three dollar discount voucher redeemable off the entrance fee to Borobudur, which cost the equivalent of fifteen U.S. dollars for non-Indonesians.

I set off for the temple at dawn, and was surprised to be offered a complimentary cup of tea by the security staff at the entrance gate, taking the edge off the entrance fee—oh, how the little things make me happy. The park was quaint, manicured civility, with long stone paths, beautiful lawns, towering specimen trees and lovingly tended flowers and shrubbery, all shrouded in a gentle morning mist. According to my map, a major path circumnavigated Borobudur itself, from which four additional straight paths led inwards towards the temple, approaching it from the four points of the compass.

It took a while ambling about before I located the major eastern approach route. Split down the middle by a raised bed of shrubs, and lined on either side by palms and other tropical trees, it channeled my gaze towards a distant staggered staircase leading up a lush green hill, where, poking through the slowly evaporating mist, was Borobudur. Obscured by much of the park's surrounding trees, little more than Borobudur's central bell-shaped stone stupa tower was visible from afar. Known as the sacred path, the eastern approach route was traditionally used by Buddhist pilgrims, who on arrival at Borobudur would proceed in a clockwise direction around its enormous base—repeating the process on every one of the enigmatic pyramid's nine graduated tiers, to finally reach the top. Ascending it in this ritualistic fashion is symbolic of the path from the earthly world to enlightenment, and apparently encompasses a walk of over three miles; but no matter how big on paper, as I gradually approached the base of the hill on which Borobudur sat, I began to wonder whether the place was somewhat over-hyped. It's just, when looking from below, it was difficult to gauge a true sense of its scale, as little of it was visible. And so, as I climbed the hill, my expectations were somewhat subdued as to what would greet me at the top. Ascending the final stairs and stepping out onto a broad terrace, Borobudur's majesty finally revealed itself, and my pessimism evaporated in an instant.

Sprawling in front of me was a magnificently detailed temple, meticulously constructed out of dark volcanic stone on a truly colossal scale, whose staggering width seemed completely out of proportion to its moderate height, creating an intriguing squashed pyramid. Built around and completely enveloping an existing hill, it was constructed on a giant, generally square base, the simple geometry of which was broken up by additional square forms jutting sideways from the overall structure, leaving it resembling a Buddhist mandala. (A spiritually significant Buddhist and Hindu symbol made up of concentric squares with a circular central point). Stairways led up from the center of all four sides, and also gave access to nine terraces, comprising the pyramid's individual levels. Stretching their entire length were finely carved bas-reliefs, and above them, squatting in little alcoves, hundreds upon hundreds of Buddha statues, all wearing the same timeless expression of the stoically unmoved. It was remarkable, and I was very lucky to be sharing it with but a handful of other early risers whose diminutive figures could be seen on Borobudur's various levels, providing the perfect scale of reference to the structure as a whole.

The traditional three mile concentric climbing to the top seemed too much like hard work, so I skirted around part of the temple's lower base to get a sense of its presence, then headed on up. Scaling the stairs, I fixed my gaze on the temple itself, with a mind to only turning around and looking at the vista behind me once I'd made it to the summit. Ornate stone archways separating the different tiers passed overhead, then came multiple bell-shaped stone stupas of the upper levels, inside which life-size statues of the Buddha could be seen, visible through lattice brickwork. Finally I arrived at the upper terrace and slowly turned around.

Expanding in front of me and reaching out to the distant horizon, was the fertile agricultural basin of the Kedu plain, a green vista consisting of a medley of rice paddies, fields of sugar-cane and coconut palms. Shrouding the scene was a delicate blanket of slowly evaporating mist, which climbed skyward from the earth like some great ethereal spirit. Trees glistened; their dew-heavy foliage sparkling like precious stones in the low morning sun. Through the hazy vapor the distant mountains could be glimpsed: three perfect cones, two dead-ahead and one to my left, which along with the jagged range behind and to my right, gave the plain a paradoxical feeling of both extreme spaciousness and enclosed security.

Stories from the Buddha's life and other Buddhist tales are immortalized in the stones of Borobudur, as is an unintentional, although highly valuable, historical record of Javanese life from a millennium ago. Ships with billowing sails, flamboyant dancers, towering elephants, voluptuous maidens, regal kings and fearless warriors line the embellished walls. At the base of the pyramid, in an area known as the hidden foot, are carvings of man's most elemental desires. These particular reliefs were only discovered during a UNESCO restoration project and were originally intended to remain unseen by the temple goers, buried in the earth as part of the structure's foundations, despite them being every bit as intricate as carvings elsewhere. The UNESCO team decided to leave four panels exposed for posterity.

While studying these, I was practically mobbed by a mixed group of teenage students on a school trip; not to study the temple as you might imagine, but so they could practice English with the foreigners found around the place. Everyone wanted to chat and have their photo taken with me, so I obliged them for a while until the group dispersed in favor of some foreign new arrivals. Over in a corner, sitting by themselves on a bench, was a young European-looking couple of the hippie variety. I ambled over to say hello, meeting Lucy from France and Edgar from Lithuania, the latter of whom sported a head of flaming red dreadlocks. They were traveling overland together through Southeast Asia and had arrived in Indonesia by way of a ferry from Malaysia. This was my plan but in reverse, so I inquired as to the ferries' costs, regularity, and departure locations.

"If you go from Sumatra then you have to leave from Dumai. There used to be ferries further north but low cost airlines have put them out of business," explained Lucy.

"They'll probably cease from Dumai soon too," added Edgar.

This was an interesting development. The next big Indonesian island that I would come to, and my last en route to Malaysia, was Sumatra, but on it I had hoped to travel much further north than Dumai in order to visit Gunung Leuser National Park, an area where it is possible to see orangutans in the wild. But with no ferries leaving north of Dumai, this was now unrealistic. Sumatra's roads were, apparently, even worse than Java's, and the ones I needed wound much of the way to Dumai through dense jungle—a route with reportedly nothing worth stopping off at along the way. Distance-wise, Dumai was about a week of hitchhiking away, and the orangutans about a week after that. I just couldn't justify it. I would have to leave for Malaysia from Dumai. The orangutans could wait for another visit.

I got moving soon after, heading up a road with a slight gradient away from Borobudur village, into a steamy morning. On spotting me, several well-meaning locals frantically pointed back towards the village where the bus terminal was. Five minutes later and a small black car pulled over whose driver gave me a ride to the next cross roads. A lift on the back of a motorbike soon followed to the town of Salaman, and from there I scored an excellent ride in another car, this time driven by a super friendly young couple: Lisa and Andi. Despite their Western sounding names, both were Indonesian. Of the two, Lisa spoke the best English. They were heading west to the town of Kebumen, about fifty miles away.

"Have you tried our famous Durian fruit?" asked Lisa, after plying me with several mangosteen—a delicious purple-skinned tropical fruit about the size of a small orange, with several white segments and a wholly unique tasting pulp.

"No. But I've heard they're disgusting. Is it true?"

"For Westerner I think so! They say it smells like, how you say, bad feet."

"Would you like to try one?" asked Andi.

"You're not exactly selling it to me you know; but yeah, why not."

We pulled over by a lone roadside shack where several spiky fruits the size and shape of heads were dangling on strings from the shop's overhead wooden shutter. Lisa and Andi walked carefully from fruit to fruit inspecting them with a discerning eye. This seemed like serious business. The day before, a truck driver had picked me up and stopped at a total of four different stalls to inspect their Durian, but, unimpressed, decided not to purchase one. I knew that Durian fruits were considered a delicacy in Indonesia, and as such expensive, so when Lisa and Andi settled on one I tried to pay.

"No," insisted Lisa. "It is our gift."

The woman working the store placed the fruit on a bamboo table and with a machete prised it open—splitting it into four sections, each consisting of a white fleshy casing containing a slimy-looking yellow pod.

"Take one," insisted Lisa with excitement.

I did.

"Try not to smell it before you eat it!" she instructed with a laugh, which of course meant I became acutely conscious of its aroma.

It was odd smelling, that's for sure. To me it didn't so much bring smelly feet to mind, more a suggestion of vomit. I took a tentative nibble, and in so doing recalled a television travel show I had seen on Indonesia where the presenter had enthused that the Durian's taste was "quite heavenly." Well, if that's what heaven's like, then you're welcome to it. It was like a fermenting, slightly alcoholic, onion-flavored custard. Like the sound of that? No, didn't think so. But Indonesians go mad for Durians—although unfortunately, not today. Since Lisa and Andi purchased the Durian for me, they took the merest of bites, purposefully leaving me the lion's share. I had no desire to continue, but put on a brave face and polished it off—along with the contents of my water bottle to wash away the taste.

Our next stop was a police station in a town called Purworejo where Andi had, as he put it, "some business." He seemed a bit cagey when venturing this information so I didn't pry as to which side of the law his business was on, and waited in the car while he and Lisa disappeared inside. Ten minutes later and they returned. We drove for another hour or so through more green fields and villages, before pulling over at a little roadside shack constructed from split bamboo. Here Lisa and Andi insisted on buying me lunch, and very nice it was too. A delicious meal of duck and soya fritters, served with cucumber and a spicy spinach-like vegetable came our way, as did a shared pot of tea, served in little patterned glasses. It was the most I'd eaten in days.

"What is your job?" asked Lisa.

"Writer," I answered, which elicited the standard impressed response, with mutual nods of the head shared between both of them. I didn't want to spoil their illusion by explaining the reality of scraping by in all manner of less glamorous sounding professions, and so for the next few minutes indulged them, and myself, in a thorough massaging of my ego.

"And what is your job?" I asked Andi afterwards.

"I am secret service."

"Ah, like James Bond," I responded.

"No," laughed Lisa. "James Bond is handsome!"

I gestured to Andi's face. "What's your problem?"

They both laughed.

Further up the road and we stopped at another police station, this time in Kebumen. Andi went inside again and came out moments later with several cops in tow who it turned out wanted to meet me, shake hands and say hello.

Kebumen was as far as Lisa and Andi had planned to travel, but instead of dropping me on the main road out of town, these wonderful people insisted on driving me a further thirty miles to the town of Buntu.

"Are you sure?" I asked Andi as we set off.

"Don't worry. Your luck will be my luck."

I hoped so, and was touched by his generosity.

We arrived in Buntu by late afternoon, having spent most of the day on the road in order to cover a total of barely eighty miles.

I could have just stood still at Buntu, gesturing for a ride north to the city of Purwokerto, but I seemed to have far more luck in Indonesia when I took the initiative and hiked along the road. Within minutes a car pulled over. Inside sat three young guys in their late teens: two up front and one in the back, currently using a laptop. By the time we arrived in Purwokerto it was raining with such ferocity that is seemed likely to tear through the roof of the car. Outside was a world of water. Streets were flooded, pedestrians were crammed in together sheltering under awnings, and cars and trucks crawled though river-like conditions. Few bikers currently braved the downpour, even those with ponchos. I hardly wanted to get out, but this was the end of the line.

Stepping from the car, my foot sank into about ten inches of water, as the rest of me got battered by the cold power-shower coming from the sky. I hastily dragged my backpack from the vehicle and sprinted for a nearby car mechanics with an overhanging tin roof. From its corrugated channels gushed murky individual jets, their collective appearance resembling a waterfall. I slipped around its side just as a bolt of lightning exploded nearby, its almost instantaneous thunder echoing through the streets.

I was keen to get back inside the warm, dry interior of a car or truck, so stood here attempting to wave one down. After ten minutes, a car that had passed moments earlier began reversing in my direction through a near-lake of water, creating a stern wave in the process. The passenger window wound down the merest of cracks so that conversation could ensue without soaking the car.

"We're only going to our house around the corner," said the middle-aged male driver, leaning across his wife in the passenger seat. "Would you like to wait there until the rain stops?"

My heart swelled at their kindness. I jumped in.

They introduced themselves as Herwin and Jrawati. Moments later we were reversing into the garage of their humble bungalow, or at least trying to, the downpour making visibility so atrocious that poor Herwin botched the operation, hitting the garage wall twice before finally slotting the car inside. While Herwin inspected the damage, both to wall and car, Jrawati led me inside the house. Here she introduced me to their three children, the oldest of whom had been babysitting. They were Krisna and Haryo, both teenagers, and their adorable little sister, Andari, who was about seven.

"Would you like a tea?" asked Herwin when he returned from outside.

We sat on a rug sipping our drinks, while rain reverberated on the roof and thunder discharged outside. It was great to be indoors, but more so to be amid such welcoming people.

I'd been in plenty of situations like this, where strangers had shown me touching generosity, often culminating in an offer of accommodation. And sure enough, before I'd finished my first cup of tea, Herwin asked if I needed a place to stay for the night. It couldn't have come at a better time. By now it was growing dark outside and the rain was unabated. I accepted and thanked him.

"I do not discriminate between Indonesian, European, Japanese, or Australian. I have a responsibility to help others. You will find this often in central Java, much more than the west of the island. You could say that helping people is very much the tradition here."

Next up he offered me a meal.

His hospitality was indicative of other Muslim countries I had traveled through before, and I immediately felt at home and a strong kinship towards Herwin and his family. Meeting people like them was the essence of traveling.

While Jrawati organized a meal, Herwin and I sat down and conversed over several additional teas. I told him of my journey so far and plans to reach the western town of Merak tomorrow, where I would catch a ferry to Sumatra; he told me of his life on Java and work as a government attorney.

Jrawati served up a traditional Javan meal called Rawon, or beef black soup, made up of diced beef mixed with black nuts of the keluak mangrove tree, which, although poisonous, are made edible through fermentation. Added to this base is a medley of exotic herbs and spices including red chilli, turmeric, ginger, garlic, lemon grass, lime leaves, and sugar. We ate together on the floor, and very nice it was too, with a rich nutty flavor and sweet aroma. When finished, the family sat back and watched the nightly news on television. Reports of two fatal transport disasters dominated the program, both of which had struck Java earlier in the day. Two passenger trains had collided head-on near the town of Bajar, roughly forty five miles away, and then thirty minutes afterwards a ferry sailing between Java and Sumatra had caught fire. Hundreds were injured in the twin disasters and at least 16 people killed. The ferry had been traveling the route I intended to take tomorrow. I was pleased I hadn't made it there today. After discussing my onward journey with Herwin, he recommended I change my destination from Merak to the country's capital, Jakarta, and to catch a ferry from there to Sumatra instead.

If I wanted to hit Jakarta in time then I would need to be up at the crack of dawn, so I asked Herwin and Jrawati if they'd mind if I let myself out in the morning without saying goodbye so that I didn't wake them up. Amazingly, Herwin said he normally got up between 3 and 4 a.m. I wondered if this was to pray. Nearly every morning on Java, I had been awoken around this time by the infuriating sound of loudspeakers on mosques pumping out a calling to prayer. When it was time to hit the sack, Herwin said that I should share his son's bed, which was arranged with a long separator pillow down the middle. This was fine by me, but in the end his son, who went to bed after me, slept on a mat in the sitting room.

I awoke to the sight of light streaming through the slats of the bedroom window blind.

Shit. I had overslept.

I checked my watch but it was only 3 a.m. This was far earlier than I had intended to get on the road but if there was light then there would be vehicles, and the less crowded the roads were then the faster I could move along them. I quietly got dressed, picked up my pack and slipped into the living room. Sitting there was Herwin, wide awake. I couldn't quite believe that he was up at this hour, or work out whether it was the sound of me getting up that had roused him.

"It is too early for you," he said on seeing me.

"No, I think if there are cars then I should go," I politely countered, keen to get moving and hit Jakarta by nightfall.

"But the road will be empty at this time."

"Even if there are one or two vehicles, I think it's best I set off now."

The conversation went back and forth like this for a bit until Herwin finally conceded, but only after insisting that we share a final departing tea before I leave. I agreed. Having expected him to throw the kettle on the hob, it came as something of a surprise when he woke Jrawati up to do the honors. On finishing my tea I quietly thanked them for their touching hospitality and bade them both a warm farewell.

Getting into hitching mode I took a deep breath and opened the front door—stepping out into pitch darkness. This didn't make sense. The source of "sunlight" that had woken me in such a panic to get on the move was now all too clear to see—a lightbulb on the front porch positioned directly in front of the bedroom window. I made an apologetic about-turn and stepped back inside. I felt like a right numpty, and a complete shit too, especially after Jrawati had been woken to make me tea.

"What time is it light?" I asked in a cringe-worthy reversal of my position of moments ago.

"Five o'clock," said Herwin. "Shall I wake you then?"

"Yes, please," I replied in as contrite a manner as I could muster, then crawled back into bed.

* * *

By the early evening I made it to Jakarta, a city of 10 million people, that thankfully I skirted around in a family car containing a middle-aged couple and their two young daughters, who went out of their way to drop me in the city's port located in sub-district Tanjung Priok. The place was colossal. Mountains of containers from huge cargo ships lined the surrounding docks. Where the hell did I need to go?

Eventually I worked it out and strode towards the passenger ferry office, where several private ticket sellers approached me to do business. I continued without breaking step. Inside sat two headscarf-wearing girls working the desk. After confirming that they spoke English, I inquired after ferries to Sumatra.

"The next one leaves on Friday," the nearest one stated bluntly.

That was six days away!

I asked after ferries to the port of Merak further down the coast, with a view to catching a trans-island ferry from there to Sumatra instead.

There were none.

I wondered if yesterday's disaster had played a part in their apparent scarcity.

"Are there no ferries leaving tonight for anywhere at all?" I asked.

At first the girls seemed to say there weren't, but then changed their minds and answered, "Yesterday"—hardly an improvement. Eventually though, after further prying it transpired that there was in fact a ferry leaving, and tonight at 10 p.m. for the tiny Indonesian island of Bintan.

"Where is that?" I asked.

With the assistance of a big map on the wall they pointed out its location. It sat just off the coast of neighboring countries Singapore and Malaysia, both of which you could apparently catch a "speedboat" to from Bintan.

My options seemed three-fold, and all presented their own problems. One: stay in Jakarta for six days until the next ferry departed, by which time I'd have burnt significant travel funds on the capital's Western-priced accommodation. Two: crash here tonight and then hitchhike to Merak in the morning in the hope that I could get a ferry to Sumatra once there. Three: buy a ticket for Bintan and set off tonight but bypass Sumatra altogether. In the end the third option clinched it. Hanging around just didn't appeal at all, nor did the uncertainty of another Javan port, and what with Sumatra's orangutans being located far north of its ferry terminal for Malaysia, the island no longer held such interest for me. I purchased a ticket and hoped for a smooth voyage, which the girls informed me could take anything between one and two days, depending on weather conditions. Their other advice: be wary of thieves on board.

I had several hours to kill before departure, and spent the first thirty minutes in the office with the girls, who challenged me to a go on a "shoot-em up" computer game, in which these petite headscarfed Muslim girls, gleefully played the role of a U.S. solider, wantonly taking out stereotypical Middle Eastern "terrorists."

A couple of doors down was a tiny travel agency, where I got talking to the competent English-speaking staff member, Mohammad.

"Would you like a coffee?" he offered.

I did, and so we settled down to a cup. Minutes later we were joined by two tough-looking individuals with whom Mohammad was familiar. They spoke little English but when they heard that I was British said, "SAS, good. SBS, good," accompanied with a muscle-flexing thumbs-up. Their reference to Britain's special forces—the Special Air Service and the Special Boat Squadron—was an odd one, but became clear when Mohammad explained that both were members of Kopassus, and had trained with the British. I knew the name. Kopassus is an infamous brigade of killers, the Indonesian equivalent of the Nazi Gestapo or Waffen SS, notorious for carrying out horrendous war crimes during the country's genocidal conquest of tiny neighboring country East Timor in 1975, and its subsequent quarter of a century's occupation, which killed over 200,000 people, a third of the population;[73] a number proportionately higher than those killed in Cambodia by Pol Pot.[74] Kopassus led the heinous invasion and were almost certainly responsible for the brutal murder of an Australian, British and New Zealand film crew attempting to chronicle the beginnings of the genocide, most of whom, witnesses say, were captured alive, strung up by their feet, had their genitalia cut off and stuffed into their mouths, before being stabbed; dying from either choking on their own sexual organs or bleeding to death.[75] (One senior Kopassus officer to receive training in Britain was the man an Australian inquiry identified as having ordered the films crews' murder.)[76] Other atrocities carried out during the invasion of East Timor include the systematic killing of children, with soldiers swinging infants by their legs and smashing their heads against rocks.[77] "When you clean the field, don't you kill all the snakes, the small and large alike?" explained an Indonesian officer.[78]

Once again it was an American, British, and Australian sanctioned slaughter. East Timor posed no threat to mighty Indonesia, which at the time was the fifth most populous nation on earth (now the fourth), nor did Indonesia hold any historic or legal claim to East Timor that could be used as a pretext to justify its annexation. But with East Timor residing next to a strategically important shipping lane and possessing resources described by Australia's foreign minister, Gareth Evans, as a prize worth "zillions" of dollars,[79] Indonesia decided to take it for her own. With foreknowledge of an imminent invasion of East Timor, British Ambassador to Indonesia Sir John Archibald Ford cabled the Foreign Office: "It is in Britain's interests that Indonesia absorb the territory as soon and unobtrusively as possible and when it comes to the crunch we should keep our heads down."[80] During a visit by U.S. President Gerald Ford and his Secretary of State Henry Kissinger to Indonesia that was described as "the big wink"[81] by a State Department official, the President and Kissinger gave the country's military dictator General Suharto the go-ahead to launch the invasion and conquest of East Timor. "You can be one hundred percent certain that Suharto was explicitly given the green light to do what he did," revealed C. Philip Liechty, a Senior C.I.A. Officer to Indonesia at the time.[82] In 2001 the transcript of the meeting between Ford, Kissinger and Suharto was finally released in uncensored form, disclosing exactly that:

> Suharto: I would like to speak to you, Mr. President, about another problem, Timor . . . We want your understanding if we deem it necessary to take rapid or drastic action.
> President Ford: We will understand and will not press you on this issue. We understand . . . the intentions you have.
> Kissinger: You appreciate that the use of US-made arms could create problems . . . It depends on how we construe it, whether it is in self defense or is a foreign operation. It is important that whatever you do succeeds quickly, we would be able to influence the reaction in America if whatever happens happens after we return.[83]

As the U.S. Presidential plane lifted off the Indonesian runway, the invasion of East Timor was launched, and the genocide commenced. On arrival back in Washington, Kissinger plotted how best to justify the aggression, opting for the 1970s catch-all equivalent that "fighting terrorism" is today. "Can't we construe a Communist government in the middle of Indonesia as self defense?" he asked an emergency meeting at the State Department.[84] (For more on this repugnant Western-armed and sanctioned crime against humanity, see acclaimed documentary film "The Timor Conspiracy," viewable online: www.johnpilger.com/videos/the-timor-conspiracy-update-).

As nightfall arrived and the departure time of the ferry approached, hundreds of people began congregating on the poorly lit terrace outside the ticket office. I was the only Westerner about, and with my oversized pack stuck out in the crowds. Despite the numbers, for some reason the proper waiting room for the terminal was all locked up. Ten o'clock came and went, and the ferry was nowhere to be seen. By midnight half the crowd was lying down asleep.

Suddenly an announcement came over a loud speaker and the terminal waiting-room door was unlocked. Chaos erupted and a stampede of people funneled inside. I took my cue. Getting swept along in the flow, I passed right through the building to the dock itself on the other side where, through tired eyes, I stared out across a foggy quay accentuated by murky yellow lighting of several lamps, at a huge rusting heap of a ferry.

No apparent logic led to the boarding or departure, with everyone just pushing and shoving, dragging themselves and their luggage on and off the ferry. I headed up a giant gangplank enclosed on either side by a safety net constructed out of oily knotted rope, and entered the ferry proper. It was in a terrible state. Rust, dirt and trash were everywhere. The vessel was probably older than I was. Accommodation consisted of several floors of sweat-reeking windowless open barracks, lined with long communal wooden platforms, where super-thin plastic-coated mattresses were placed—the sort of thing you might use for judo or wrestling. Throwing my pack down, I claimed a space by the wall so that I slept next to one person, not sandwiched between two. In minutes the place was full to the brim with hundreds of people, all crammed in here together side by side, trying to organize their tiny bit of platform space. Cockroaches outnumbered the human passengers. Many people lit up cigarettes, then casually discarded them on the floor, all but inviting a repeat of yesterday's ferry inferno. I familiarized myself with the exits in case I needed to make a run for it. Departure arrived at 1 a.m., and with it I decided to get my head down. Before doing so I tactically tied up my backpack to prevent any pilfering when asleep, then slipped into my thin bivvy to use as a sleeping bag—it was far too hot to use the bag itself.

* * *

Time dragged by on board, broken only by periodic games of cards with those surrounding, none of whom spoke any English, and at the thrice-daily food handouts. These consisted of three meals: rice and a limp pancake; rice and a sliver of shoe-leather meat; and rice and a mouthful of rehydrated fish. Others, wisely, had brought their own sustenance.

In the end the voyage encompassed two full miserable nights on board, arriving on the tiny green island of Bintan at about eight in the morning.

Passing though customs was a painless experience. It was satisfying to be on the brink of another country. Right on time a nifty catamaran ferry arrived that looked capable of holding about a hundred people. It was a quick but bumpy ride across the windswept waters of the Singapore Strait that separated Bintan from the coast of Malaysia. In the distance, swaddled by an uninspiring cloudy sky of gray, appeared Malaysia. From here on in it would be overland for a seriously long way. The next oceanic body of water I would meet would be the English Channel.

CHAPTER THIRTEEN
Meat Cleaver Madness

I waited on the outskirts of clean Malaysian city, Johor Bahru, about a hundred yards up the road from a gas station forecourt on a wide gravelly area that was tailor made for passing motorists to stop, having arrived here minutes earlier on the back of a motorbike. As it was a small country with a good road system and modern infrastructure, my stay in Malaysia seemed likely to be a short one.

The city's morning rush hour was in full swing and it wasn't long before a car began to pull over for me. It narrowly missed my pack but hit the helmet Dan had given me back on Bali, jamming it between the bumper and the gravelly roadside. It took a considerable effort to yank it free, and although in one piece, it now sported several deep grooves from the stony surface along which it scraped.

Needless to say, it was with a distinct air of caution that I approached the passenger side of the vehicle. Did I really want to get in? But then again, a lift is a lift. The driver was a short and skinny old bloke, with a deeply furrowed face, and wild angry eyes, who wore an Arab-style one-piece body-dress, and a red and white checkered headscarf.

"Where you go?" he not so much asked as demanded.

"Melaka," I replied, but sensed that he was after money, so told him I couldn't pay.

It was as if I'd flicked a switch in him. He went crazy and started shouting and cursing at me with uncontrolled venom.

"You fucking!—You donkey!—FUCK!" he screamed as if trying to remember how to insult someone in English.

He began to pull off, but then hit the brakes so he could give me some more.

"Why you come Malaysia if no money!" he yelled, pulling off now, shouting more abuse and swerving wildly into the road.

"Freak," I muttered to myself, turning back to face the oncoming traffic.

I thought nothing more of the incident, until, a minute later, I spotted the weirdo sitting in his car on the gas station forecourt, staring my way with a fixated glare. His car faced towards me and the oncoming traffic. He had initially passed the gas station so must have hung a U-turn to return, and it didn't look like it was to purchase fuel; he couldn't pull out onto the road this way so I began to wonder if he had come back with the intention of running me or my pack down. No sooner had the macabre thought popped into my head, he floored it in my direction. Grabbing my pack I hastily stepped forwards and to the side, finishing up past a curb leading into the station, over which he couldn't drive. He came skidding to a halt nearby, looking none too happy I'd thwarted him.

"Why you have no money!" he yelled at me through his open window.

"Oh, just piss off, you old bastard," I replied.

It didn't have the desired affect.

"This is Muslim country!" he screamed back at me repeatedly like a stuck record, as if that meaningless utterance was somehow relevant or justified his attempt at running me down.

"Why you come Malaysia if you have no money!" he yelled once more, fumbling now in his wallet for a handful of banknotes, which he waved sarcastically in my direction.

Despite attempting to run me over, for the briefest of moments I stood watching, almost entertained. I wasn't the only one. Motorists passing in the now slow-moving, congested traffic began staring towards the both of us.

More inane invective flowed from him towards me, and it wasn't long before I found it tedious. With no sign of him moving on, I looked further up the road to see if there was anywhere else feasible for me to wait. Nothing was within sight.

I tried to wave him off but it was no good.

"Fuck! Fuck! Fuck!" he yelled among other nonsense; baiting me, desperate, it seemed, for a row.

I took the bait.

Pointing his way I mimed, "You're crazy!" It hardly calmed him down.

From his glove compartment came something wrapped up in a clump of fabric, which he hastily unraveled, revealing—a meat cleaver!

Bloody hell. This guy was a complete fruitcake!

Brandishing it in my direction he began screwing up his face, no doubt trying to look intimidating. He looked like a twat. Thrusting the cleaver down the side of his seat he opened the car door and got out. Walking aggressively towards me, he stopped just outside my personal space and then really embarrassed himself. Striking an over-the-top theatrical martial arts-style pose—the sort of thing you might expect from a nineteen-seventies kung-fu flick titled, Praying Mantis and the Rum Soaked Fist—he beckoned me on, challenging for a fight.

I laughed in his face and told him to "fuck off."

If he had been thirty years younger, a foot taller and a hundred-and-fifty pounds heavier then I might have afforded him a little more caution, but without his battering ram of a car he was as much threat as an angry sparrow. The old bugger abandoned his Jackie Chan antics when a packed public bus came to a standstill in the traffic next to us, and its passengers began pointing and staring his way. He reverted back to yelling, now almost exclusively in Malaysian. As the bus began to pull off I pondered giving the crowd a laugh by yanking down his headscarf, but then spotted a couple of motorcycle cops and decided to flag them down. Maybe they could move him on.

They dutifully came to a stop, and after a brief consultation with me, quickly pulled the old guy to one side. He started remonstrating with them, pointing my way and no doubt describing me in the darkest possible manner.

With the cops' backs turned, a mischievous idea flashed across my mind.

I flicked the old bastard the bird.

He went ballistic. Yelling and pointing, he tried to replicate for the police what I had done, but in his fury used his index finger instead of middle one. The cops turned around to look at me.

Butter wouldn't have melted in my mouth. I was the picture of innocence, and looked their way with a confused expression, as if to say, "Is there a problem officers?"

They turned back to him. No sooner had they done so and I did it again.

The same result followed but this time he got the correct finger when demonstrating. Once more the cops looked my way, and once more they found me standing there, hands by my side, innocent as a lamb.

I really should have quit while I was ahead, but couldn't resist a third go, and this time got complacent. Flicking him the middle finger, I let it linger in the air a satisfying moment too long, and before I knew it, one of the officers had whipped his neck around and caught me in the act.

He was not best pleased.

"If you do that again I will take you to the police station."

I apologized, and probably shouldn't have been so gung-ho with the law in the first place, but I can't say I was particularly concerned.

"You must leave now or get a bus," he instructed.

I did as I was told—leaving that is—hiking up the road, doing so with periodic cautionary glances behind me, just in case the geriatric nut-case had a mind to follow and run me over.

It took a while before I located another suitable place to wait, and after about five minutes a medium-sized truck pulled over. Two guys sat inside. Both were cheery souls but only the driver spoke English. From his traditional songkok cap and the prayer beads hanging in the cab, it was clear that he was Muslim. Unlike his brethren down the road, he couldn't have been nicer. In good English he told me how he always picked up hitchhikers and tried to help others whenever the opportunity arose.

"If you do good, then good will be done to you," he said.

And, as if to emphasise the point, he drove me a significant distance out of his way, dropping me on a highway turning for the historic colonial port city of Melaka; once part of the Portuguese Empire, then the Dutch, then British, as well as having a brief stint under Japanese rule during the Second World War. It was my intended destination today. Apparently a toll section began about a mile along the highway, but having no idea whether or not it was illegal to hike along a highway in Malaysia, I did so at a considerably fast pace, so as to reach it before any further shenanigans with the law.

On arrival I slipped through to the other side, using a coach to block my view from the official working the booth, just in case this turned out to be prohibited. Vehicles streamed past for about ten minutes before an almighty modern truck came to a stop next to me, letting out a loud pneumatic hiss. To reach the cab required climbing several metal steps. Inside were a couple of ultra enthusiastic guys in their late thirties, Isa and Botak. Both were delighted with some foreign company and although neither spoke much English, we hit it off from the start, with us all singing karaoke-style to their *Eagles* CD less than a minute into the drive.

After the roads of Indonesia, traveling in Malaysia was a dream. The highways were modern, and the vehicles likewise. Whizzing through a generally flat and green landscape, we passed an area where a river had burst its banks, flooding the surrounding fields and reaching just shy of the road.

"I see twenty dead cow on other road," said Isa, pointing to the floods.

Further on and we stopped at a rest area where Isa kindly presented me with a can of "100" energy drink, as well as some fresh pineapple and watermelon, served with an odd covering of seasoning called "lam powder."

"What is it made from?" I asked.

He struggled a bit with the words, but left me with the impression that it was dried mango.

"Eat too much, not good stomach," he said.

Our journey together came to an end at another toll, roughly twenty miles from Melaka.

"Jamie, you no forget me," requested Isa as we parted.

I promised him I wouldn't.

I had no problem picking up another ride, this time in a car driven by a former Olympian hockey player, now a coach, named Shaiful, who took me to another toll. From here a charming couple in their sixties, Ester and Albert, drove me in a car with a crucifix hanging from its mirror into Melaka, where they downright insisted on buying me lunch at a quaint little "satay house" near the banks of the Melaka River.

"Eat as much as you like," instructed Ester in the packed restaurant as a waiter delivered the first of multiple servings of Malaysian delicacy, satay— tender marinated pork on sticks, served with peanut sauce, cucumber and onions.

"The price of onions is very expensive due to a bad harvest," said Albert, a stockbroker by trade, when a measly second portion was brought out.

After lunch they took me into the historic heart of the city, and before dropping me at a centrally located hostel, handed a little patterned red envelope my way.

"For Chinese new year," said Ester with a motherly smile.

When they'd disappeared I opened it. Inside was twenty ringgit (about seven dollars).

After dropping off my pack in a stuffy windowless room, I strode off to get a better look at Melaka. It was a clean, modestly-sized port city with a medley of historic architecture; a pleasant enough location to spend the day, but somewhat tame, lacking in the buzz of Indonesia, and crawling with foreign tourists—the first I'd seen since Borobudur. For the next few hours I strolled around this one-time maritime trading hub of three successive European powers, perusing salmon-colored Dutch architecture from the seventeenth century, the ruins of an old sixteenth century Portuguese fortress, the roofless shell of a hilltop Catholic church, and a landlocked full-size replica of a 500-year-old, 400 ton sailing ship. It was relaxing and interesting, but hardly high adventure; come the morning I decided to push north towards Thailand.

* * *

Now here's a tip. If you're hitchhiking through a foreign land and can't speak the language, then do yourself a favor and have a map. Having previously navigated from Johor Bahru to Melaka after glancing at Google Maps in the lobby of my hotel, I felt confident of doing the same again in Melaka in order to travel the far longer journey to the country's border with Thailand. On screen was a long straight highway heading there by way of the capital, Kuala Lumpur, so it seemed simple enough. But with no map in my possession to point at for drivers, things got a little confusing, especially with non English speakers. It was a stupid mistake that cost me a good couple of hours after the inevitable happened, and I was taken off course.

As a result, by mid-afternoon I found myself riding along a minor road, past foliage-covered sugar-loaf mountains, one in the process of being torn down as part of a mining operation. Behind the wheel of the car sat an interesting character; a traditional Malay restaurant owner from the north with an odd sense of distance.

"Thailand is long way," he told me. "You should get bus."

I reassured him that it really wasn't very far—roughly a hundred miles—especially given that I had already hitchhiked here from Tasmania.

"Noooo!" he stated in a manner that all but invited the conclusion he thought I was lying. "That is *very* long way."

"Yeah, it's a bit of a distance," I concurred with a good dose of British understatement.

"You like Thailand," he told me with wide-eyed enthusiasm further up the road. "They got lady boy. You know lady boy?"

I told him that I was familiar, in a strictly academic sense, with the concept.

"Thai girl, twenty for night. You think okay to come three time?"

"Depends on the small print, I guess."

"They like European, they have big cock! I watch movie and they have very big COCK."

He emphasized the last word with a perverse smile as if deriving a thrill out of uttering it, and mimed grasping a hold of something the size of a football.

"Do you have big cock?" he asked. "You got BIG COCK?

"Erm, sufficient," I answered.[85]

Deeming this conversation to have gone far enough, I not so much faked tiredness as finally gave in to the nagging blanket of fatigue that had, for the last few hours, been threatening to envelop me. I closed my heavy eyes and almost instantly fell asleep.

Sometime later I was rudely shaken to a jolted state of consciousness.

"Look! Look!" he cried.

By the side of the road was a twisted five car pile-up, one belching dancing flames and thick black smoke into the filthy air. Victims stood around in various states of distress. A mother cradled a baby by the roadside.

Then they were gone.

We parted company at a toll. As I stood here by the roadside my gaze fell towards the setting sun, now big and bright orange, and soon to drop beneath the horizon. The oppressive heat of the day had now departed. Fatigue took a hold of me again, gnawing away at my resolve to push forward to the border. It had been a long day, and with a reluctant sigh I began to glance around for somewhere to throw my tent. A gas station stood nearby, where about twenty young guys sat on their motorbikes, revving them in unison, creating a deafening roar. Further on were a few random buildings—cafés, bathrooms and the like—where several cars were parked. Beyond lay a generally undulating terrain with occasional random strips of greenery. Nowhere looked particularly feasible. I decided to try my luck a little longer.

Somewhere in the region of twenty minutes passed by, when one of the cars that had been parked in front of the bathroom-block began reversing in my direction. Behind the wheel sat a pretty girl in her mid twenties, next to whom was a guy in his late teens.

"Where are you trying to get to?" asked the girl in excellent English.

"The border with Thailand."

"Oh. That's a long way."

It really wasn't, but Malaysians, it was confirmed once more, had their own thoroughly distorted sense of scale.

"Where are you going?" I asked.

"Alor Setar."

This was perfect. Having previously got my cock-obsessed lift to write down the major towns on the way to the border, I knew Alor Setar was one of them, and only thirty miles from Thailand. It really is an odd thing about hitchhiking that often people conclude that unless they're going right to your final destination, then any lift along the way, even if it's for a good distance, is somehow not worth offering. From now on I would only request a ride to the next town; if the driver was traveling beyond this then I'd negotiate something further once on the move.

I explained that Alor Setar was a fine destination and that a lift there would be much appreciated.

"Get in," said the girl, reaching into the back with a smooth and delicate hand to shake as I clambered on board. "I'm Ann. Oh, and this is my brother, Jalal."

He nodded my way.

Jalal spoke little English, so Ann and I chatted between ourselves as she drove.

"Many years ago my family picked up an Australian like you. We call him Uncle David, he stayed with us for a month and still stays in touch. He is part of our family now."

Ann explained that she had to rendezvous with her family at a distant truck stop, from where they would all drive on in convoy to Alor Setar. They would book into a hotel in readiness for the wedding of another brother in the morning. It grew dark shortly before we reached the truck stop, which was a scene of unremitting chaos, packed to the rafters with travel-weary motorists and passengers, which Ann attributed to the Chinese New Year.

By the looks of it most of her extended family was here: nieces and nephews, aunties and uncles, cousins and grandparents, all in attendance waiting for Ann and her brother in the truck-stop car-lot. With the exception of Ann, all the women wore traditional headscarfs.

"Ah, like Uncle David!" rejoiced Ann's mother as I was introduced.

She was a small elegant-looking woman with an infectious personality.

"Jamie," she said, leaning in towards me with a knowing smile after hearing my next destination. "When you go to Thailand, if you want to live a long time—" she paused for effect, tilting her head downwards and ever-so-slightly to one side while peered my way as if over a pair of imaginary spectacles "—then no sex with prostitutes!" She shook her head from side to side to emphasise the point, then repeated the last line, this time tapping out the syllables with a finger, "NO—SEX—WITH—PROS—TI—TUTES!" A beaming, smile crept across her face.

Recalling for me now the time she had spent in London, we chatted for a minute about the U.K. before she queried, "Would you like to come to a wedding tomorrow?"

I did.

Brief introductions with the rest of the family were made, and then we were on our way. Before I knew it we had arrived in Alor Setar. I can't say I paid much attention to my surroundings; by now I was ready for a sleep, and looked out on the darkened town through eyes almost comatose with fatigue.

"You can share a room with the boys at hotel. No cost," said Ann's mother.

I passed on my appreciative consent and hoped to soon become better acquainted with a downy pillow, but after checking in and dropping my gear on the bedroom floor, I was quickly bundled back into Ann's car and driven towards a restaurant. On the way Ann revealed a superstitious side.

"I had to move out of my house recently because there was a ghost."

"Did you see it?" I asked.

"No, but I spoke to my friend who can see these things and she told me to move out. So I did. She saw a ghost behind my car too."

"This one?" I asked.

"It has gone now," she reassured me. "This is our traditional belief. It may seem strange to you, but in England do you not have Dracula?"

"Erm, well, sort of," I replied, "In so much as there's a fictional book by that name, although it's by an Irish author."

"Exactly!" she replied.

Two titchy European cars sat on a terrace out the front of the restaurant as an odd sort of gateway to the venue, which we arrived at last after multiple wrong turns. Assembled around a long thin table on the terrace was the rest of the family. The food came out with our arrival. Fried prawns, chicken, assorted vegetables and rice made its way around the table. I was too tired to really do it justice but did my best, both to honor the generosity of Ann's family and out of obligation to myself. I'd consumed next to nothing today, and had been averaging one meal a day for weeks, so I figured that if food sat in front of me, then I should eat, if not for enjoyment's sake then for sustenance. As we finished up it came as no surprise that despite trying to chip in for the bill I was turned down flat. Before leaving, Ann poured water on her plate for "good luck." In a gesture of solidarity, I did the same.

* * *

The wedding was held at the home of the father of the bride. As a prison officer, he lived in one of many identical houses designated for prison staff, located right next door to Alor Setar Prison.

"My uncle has been taken to the doctor," said Ann to me before the ceremony. "Someone sent a ghost to him. Many people are jealous of his money. I have spoken to my friend who is going to help if I SMS her his photo."

Moments earlier another family member had told me it was due to high blood pressure.

I did my best to scrub up for the occasion by shaving, slipping on a polo shirt and giving my shoes a vigorous seeing-to with a wet rag. The other guests, of whom there were maybe thirty, wore colorful traditional dress, with the women cutting striking figures in long vibrantly colored gowns, many with abstract or floral motifs, accompanied, for those who chose to wear them, by similarly flamboyant headscarfs. The men wore fancy patterned shirts or baggy, but elegant, single-color shirt and dress pant combinations, along with flat-topped songkok hats.

Not knowing about local etiquette, before I entered the house I asked Ann's mother for a quick heads up. Apparently there wasn't much to worry about, just go inside and take a seat on the floor with everyone else. I did, realizing after a moment that I'd sat next to the groom. Was this a problem? It was too late to worry now. Proceedings were about to begin.

Three imams took up position. Two with lower status hats sat against the wall beneath a large embroidered picture of Mecca, while a third, wearing a white turban-style headpiece with a long drape at the back, sat in a central position within the room, presiding over the ceremony. The bride was nowhere to be seen. I hoped to God I hadn't taken her seat. All of a sudden the groom was called to sit in front of the main imam on a large cushion. After talking to him for several minutes—and what I can only assume were the pronouncement of vows—it all came to an end. The groom got up, walked over to the corner of the room, where, unbeknown to me, had sat his bride in a silvery dress, obscured by a mountain of presents. The groom knelt down in front of her, slipped a ring onto her finger, and they were married. Photos followed of the happy couple together, after which they posed with guests, including me.

Set up outside in the courtyard between houses was a feast of black beef and chicken, served with vegetables and sticky rice. Joining us for the meal were several prison officers in full uniform. They made an interesting accompaniment to a wedding party, as did the backdrop of a high security wall with razor wire.

Like the other guests, I ate in the traditional manner without cutlery, scooping up dollops of food with my fingers.

"Would you like knife and fork?" asked Ann's mother.

I politely refused, explaining that I wanted to try it the local way.

"This is good," she said proudly. "It is right that you should try new culture. You are one of the family now."

I was touched.

By early afternoon the wedding celebrations were winding down and my thoughts turned to the border. With a good sleep behind me and a full stomach I was willing to push it a bit today. A good friend of mine, Owen, was in Thailand, and if possible I wanted to reach him tonight. Owen was roughly 300 miles away, based on the popular Thai island of Koh Samui. Unlike your average island visitor, Owen was there not to sunbathe, but to fight; to hone his considerable *Muay Thai*—Thai boxing—skills at the prestigious Lamai boxing camp. The question was, could I reach him before the last ferry departed from the mainland? With Thailand's roads being an unknown quantity, I wasn't sure. Although one thing was certain, I would give it a damn good go.

To help me on my way Ann, had kindly offered to take me to the border. And so, after fond farewells between me and the other wedding guests, I climbed into her car, riding shotgun now. As we began to pull away from the gathering, her mother stopped the car to give me a final bit of parting advice.

"Jamie, don't forget what I told you—no sex with prostitutes!"

Was it something about the way I looked?

CHAPTER FOURTEEN
Boxing Clever

Thailand had a buzz about it even at the border. Multiple lines several hundred people strong stretched from little booths where officials stamped passports and processed visas. Tantalizingly close, began the dusty border town of Danok. Nearby, positioned on a wall across the road, was a large picture of the Thai king framed in pink and orange flowers, and further on, greeting new arrivals past the border, were depictions of Muay Thai fighters practising their art. The popularity in Thailand of the thousand-year-old fighting system is comparable to that of basketball in the U.S. or soccer in England.

It had been a long wait of over an hour, where I stood behind a large Swedish biker decked out in a studded leather jacket bearing the skull emblem of his club or gang. Next to him was his petite Malay wife wearing a smaller version of the same. I got chatting to them, half to pass the time, and half in the hope that when they finally got their passports stamped they'd offer me a ride. We shuffled along together and after what seemed an eternity, were only a few people short of the booth. As is all too typical of me, it was only now that I realized that everybody else who was waiting in line was carrying with them little immigration forms.

Shit.

"Where did you get your forms?" I quickly asked the biker, panic-stricken that I'd have to go back and fetch one. If I did, then by the time I returned they'd both be long gone and I'd lose my place. I could well imagine the new head of the line being obstinate to the point of revolt that I wasn't going to join it here.

"Have you not got one?" he replied, dumbfounded I could be so stupid.

"No."

"We were handed ours when we rode in."

What with Ann turning around before the actual border, I had done the last bit on foot and so had somehow bypassed the section doling them out to motorists or passengers from the multiple coaches parked up nearby.

The queue moved forward a person, bringing the biker to its front.

"Would you ask if they've got a spare?" I begged as he presented his passport and completed form to the official at the booth. After what seemed an eternity he reached back towards me. In his outstretched hand was a crisp new form. In the quickest I have ever filled out one of these documents, I scribbled down the requested details. Suddenly I was first in line.

My sole experience with the pliability of Thai border guards had come on a previous adventure when visiting Koh Lipe, a Thai island just across the border from Malaysia, which I had arrived at on a private day-tripping yacht. Serious irregularities had existed with the skipper's paperwork, but this was nothing that couldn't be glossed over with a little pourboire in the official's direction, who gleefully processed the "administration fee" to smooth things out.

With this in mind, as I stepped up to the border booth to present my documents, I subtly requested that the official switch the dates on his little passport stamp, to give me a slightly more generous time frame to conduct my visit than was officially sanctioned.

He shook his head.

I opened my wallet flashing some U.S. dollars his way with a suggestive look.

Thud. Down came his fifteen day stamp in unison with the word "NO!" It was worth a try.

Moving from the shade into blinding sunshine, I stepped onto the Thai mainland for the first time. Waving off several taxis with a smile, I made my way through Danok, heading uphill in the direction of an unseen truck-stop, which, according to my Swedish friend, was roughly three kilometers up the road. Looking back behind me, I kept a watchful eye out for them both, just in case I could get a ride out of them when they finally happened by. Soon after they did—sharing the same bike. The pair gave me a wave. After yesterday's navigational debacle, I made sure to visit an internet café before arrival at the border where I printed off a basic one page Google Maps representation of Thailand. This may sound inadequate to hitch across a country, but it's not. All you want is a layout of the main roads as well as major place names, preferably in English and the local language. Anything more detailed becomes an unnecessary complication, both for hitchhiker and driver alike. The problem with my current set-up was the printer cartridge used to produce the map. It had been so bereft of ink it made the map almost indecipherable. In desperation I was forced to sketch onto paper the image displayed on the computer screen.

It looked okay at the time. I just hoped it was up to the task now.

Twenty minutes of hot but rather buoyant walking commenced before a scooter rider responded to my gesture for a ride. After going through my standard "no money" routine, he flashed me a sunny smile and announced, "For free!"

Every now and again I had taken a motorbike ride without bothering to put my helmet on, but luckily today prudence got the better of me. From the outset the guy swerved all over the place, driving one-handed without a care in the world. Then, he spotted a friend by the roadside. Whipping the bike around, he powered off towards him on a thin sandy verge next to the road. He started to lose his balance. The bike began snaking wildly in the loose ground and I immediately knew what was coming. Almost in slow motion we began descending sideways towards terra firma, the earth rising to greet us. I twisted off the bike as best I could, landing with a thud, my helmet-protected head taking a glancing blow off the ground. We were unhurt but I'd had enough. This ride was over.

Dusting myself off, I continued on foot, and it wasn't long before I struck hitchhiking gold, picking up a ride with a couple of easygoing Thai truckers. Buddhist temples and large roadside statues of the Buddha passed by, which my two companions reverently bowed to while momentarily raising their hands in prayer. The landscape was still tropical like that of Malaysia but with a subtle yet indefinable difference that, for the life of me, I couldn't quite put my finger on. Having employed my new strategy of only mentioning the next major town down the road as my desired destination, for a long while I had no idea how far my new friends were ultimately traveling, but then, when nearing the town I'd mentioned as my destination, I got out my map and began gesturing to it. With a calloused finger the passenger pointed at Bangkok. I was delighted! To get to Bangkok would mean going within fifty miles of the ferry port for Koh Samui. I quickly conveyed that they should discard my initial requested destination. I would be riding with them for significantly longer. I sent a text to Owen:

> In truck heading to Bangkok. Where is best place to ditch lift to get boat to Koh Samui? Which bit you on? Should be there either tonight if there's a boat or in morn. Any idea if there is a direct road from Surat Thani to Dom Sak. Cheers!

The road query was due to a blank spot on my hand-drawn map where, I hoped, I'd inadvertently missed a road out. A moment later my cell buzzed.

> I'm away 4 the weekend 2moro. Will leave u my key u can use my room. Check Facebook for full details. Don Sak is where the ferry port is. Town of Lamai Beach on island. Last ferry is 6pm I think. First is 5am. I leave 0930 2moro. Back Mon morn. Get a map!

It was already late afternoon so there was not a hope in hell of me reaching the port in time to get to Koh Samui tonight; catching up with Owen would have to wait for a couple of days. Since I couldn't access the internet on my phone, I would have to find somewhere to do so in the morning. Despite these new developments I felt inordinately happy, both to have my own room at the Muay Thai camp awaiting me on arrival, and to have scored such a decent length ride. I watched the sun slip away with a grin.

The night seemed to drag forever. I felt too wired to sleep. We drove on through the darkness, finally reaching Surat Thang around midnight, where I discovered there was a direct road from here to Don Sak. This was as far as I went today. I was exhausted and needed a place to sleep.

Getting off at a gas station by the main highway, I went scouting for a suitable spot. At the edge of the forecourt was an old, derelict building. I made my way towards its rear to see if there was a way in, but stumbled upon a tiny late-night café tacked onto its end. Little more than a kiosk really, the smoke-obscured windows brought to mind the sort of establishment that in the U.K. might see late night taxi drivers hanging out at between jobs. To its right was an old carwash. Whether it was still functioning I couldn't tell, but several large tires were discarded at its entrance, in effect preventing anyone from using it. After wandering inside its eerie, near pitch-black interior, I discounted it as a home for the night, and so went off to look elsewhere. Next to the gas station's shop, on the side furthest from the road, was a little stony area partially shaded from the beaming lights of the forecourt by a couple of trees, next to which were piled some bins and old boxes; and sprawling behind the whole complex was a large building that appeared to once have been a department store or perhaps a mall, but which now looked thoroughly decaying, with trash and old bits of mangled concrete running alongside it.

I settled for the stony ground.

Once erected there was a strong chance my tent's dark green color would blend in and go unseen among the bins and boxes. This was crucial. The one thing that I didn't want was anyone knowing I was sleeping there, especially after being told more than once in Malaysia to be weary of getting robbed by "bad people" in Thailand. I had no idea whether these warnings were warranted, but it seemed prudent to be cautious. Crouching down in the limited shade provided by nearby trees from the glare of overhead lighting, I snapped together the four poles that provided structure to the dome and threw on its outer raincover. Suddenly horizontal lights were upon me; a car was approaching, illuminating the area with its turbid beams. I moved quickly towards the trunk of the nearest tree and froze behind it, blocking myself from view.

I turned to stone, listening as the car drove up and took the parking space directly opposite, roughly fifteen feet away. Its door clunked open and closed, followed by footsteps. The distinctive "psstt" and ensuant pneumatic humming made clear the person was inflating a tire. I stood rooted like the tree I hid behind, imploring him to disappear. Four times over he tended to the air pressure, until, finally, he drove off into the night.

I quickly clambered inside.

The tent and I were old bedfellows, my familiarity with its interior affording me a false sense of security. I could probably crawl inside it in the middle of a battlefield and be deceived into feeling safe, as if the world at large no longer existed beyond its walls. I threw my bedroll down on the stony surface, confident that fatigue would soon smooth out any ruffled protrusions underneath. Moments later I was asleep.

* * *

Already the sun was hot and every moment grew further still, its unimpeded strength producing a blinding glare off the ferry's brilliant-white upper deck. It was a short but enjoyable voyage towards Koh Samui. Several Western tourists were on board the ferry, but I sat surrounded by a big group of Thai women eating a picnic, who used interesting receptacles to bring their food on board: not Tupperware but plastic carrier bags—bowing in the middle like huge tear-drops, from which came mountains of cooked rice. Other foods placed directly into separate plastic bags included cooked fish, meat, and vegetables. One even held a sticky liquid dipping sauce. I hadn't eaten since yesterday's wedding, so when the woman opposite pointed towards some fish with an inquisitive look that could only mean "would you like some?" I nodded. She shrugged as if to say "suit yourself" and turned away; somehow my "yes please" conveying a "no thanks" instead.

I arrived hungry on Koh Samui where, after a brief stop at a dockside tourist information office to get a map, I strolled onto the island proper. I stood roughly at ten o'clock on a vaguely round-shaped island. Given the lay out of its roads, the quickest way to reach Owen's Thai Boxing camp at Lamai Beach was to travel counterclockwise to three o'clock. Strolling past a nearby row of cafés, bars, convenience stores, excursion agents, and ubiquitous Jeep and scooter hire shops, I came to a T-junction where I needed to turn right. There was no shortage of traffic, including a double-cabbed pickup truck with two middle-aged Westerners in it, currently waiting to turn in the direction I needed.

"Excuse me, is this the way to Lamai Beach?" I asked through the open window, pointing to the right, despite knowing full well that it was. "I'm hitchhiking there."

"Fucking get in, tourist!" called the white-haired and bearded driver in a broad U.S. accent. As we set off he introduced himself as Tom and the passenger as Rob. Both were Californian.

"Only other time we saw another hitcher out here was a Swedish girl. Blonde. Although the carpet didn't match the curtains!" said Tom.

"Oh, you got to find out, did you?"

"Not me. Rob did."

Rob, a man of few words, remained silent with a Snoop Dogg satisfied grin across his mug. Soon I was traveling across Koh Samui's lush interior, punctuated now by little roadside stalls and the occasional settlement, past billboards for buffalo fighting, and evidence of recent heavy rains. Further up the road and we passed another pickup, this time with a monkey in the back, wearing a chain around its neck.

"Farmers use them to collect coconuts," explained Tom. "One guy got his monkey drunk, it grabbed his machete and slashed him in the throat. Killed him stone dead."

Soon we were approaching significant tourist infrastructure and pulling into Lamai Beach, where I got out and began strolling up its high-street. Lamai was tourist central. Everything from McDonald's restaurants, travel agencies and Seven Elevens to dingy bars and "British Pubs" lined the crowded street. The British theme was a frequent one, with numerous establishments catering specifically to my fellow countrymen, of whom there are many in Thailand, with pubs showing English soccer games and soap-operas on TV, while offering "Full English Breakfasts" and other British fare on the menu for those who think the best way to spend a holiday is eating exactly the same food, watching exactly the same TV, and having exactly the same conversations as at home. The sort of person who sings a

Jamie Maslin 151

location's praises as being, "Just like England but you've got the weather," and whose idea of broadening their horizons, if feeling really adventurous, extends only so far as sampling the local beer. In short, the type of person I have contempt for. I did my best to ignore these establishments, but there was an additional element to the street I found harder to tune out.

Massage parlors were everywhere, both of the legitimate variety and ones offering an altogether more intimate service with, to use the local parlance, "happy ending," as indicated by the super-short skirts, fishnet tights, low cut tops, and suggestive looks and kisses blown my way by the girls hawking for business outside of them. When several buxom beauties tried to near-bundle me inside one establishment I hastily crossed the road, taking refuge in an internet café opposite. Here I tried to concentrate on checking my emails and the Facebook message Owen had sent, while the girls kept gesturing for me to join them in the parlor. Owen's message said to ask at the camp for Ricardo, a big, black Canadian fighter with a samurai sword tattoo running the length of his spine, whom Owen had left the key to his room with.

As I sat here, all of a sudden an uncharacteristic thing happened to me. Now I've thought long and hard about whether to include this bit in writing, and in truth it would be easy enough for me to brush over it, to sweep it beneath the carpet, and pretend it never happened. But I don't want to be that sort of writer, or indeed person. When I make a mistake, especially abroad, I want to hold my hand up to it and be held accountable. So it was today, for as I gazed out the window, what I can only describe as a sort of dark excited tunnel-vision of temptation took a hold of me. It started as a slightly alluring image squatting uninvited in my mind, but culminated in a pitiful act, which for a brief moment of gratification brought almost instant regret. At first I tried to be strong, really I did, but the more I struggled to cast off the lurid demon of temptation the more it ate away at my will, growing in power, feeding off my resistance, until it was an unshakable image clouding my reason. An internal conflict erupted inside me. I thought of what friends and family would say at home, then just as quickly lurched to the other end of the argument, attempting to justify it to myself.

"I've been on the road a long time, and hey, everybody has needs. And what's more with Owen out of town no one will know."

All of a sudden I reached tipping point. The attraction became too much and my defenses crumbled. Temptation smothered me, filling me now with excited resignation as I graphically pondered what I knew was about to transpire, and it may sound disgusting, but the thought made me salivate. Standing up from my PC I left the internet café and headed across the road, where, and it brings me no pride to write this, I indulged in a Full English Breakfast.[86]

* * *

The opening salvo to *Rocky* blared out from loudspeakers on the rear of a pickup truck decorated with billboards along its side, advertising a forthcoming Muay Thai event.

"Real international Muay Thai comes to Koh Samui," announced a pre-recorded message over the top of the music, "fighters from Australia, England, Sweden, Germany, Canada, the United States, and Thailand will battle for the ultimate championship belts. This event will be televised around the world. Kick off 9 p.m. tonight, Chaweng Muay Thai stadium. Be there!"

I heard the Muay Thai camp before I saw it. Making my way up a steep hill beyond the far end of the high-street, I began to detect the distinctive sound of shin and fist thwacking against leather, each blow accompanied by an explosive vocalisation characteristic of Thai fighters when striking. As the camp came into view—a big open-plan training area beneath a metal roof, decked out with kick and punch bags and a couple of rings—I saw that just one guy was training, taking, by the looks of it, a private lesson from one of the camp's trainers who was holding the pads for him. Both were glistening in sweat from the extreme exertion in the midday heat, which was considerable even in the shade. Owen had mentioned in his message that training was split into morning and afternoon sessions, and that in between these most of the fighters hung out at a resort opposite, lounging by the pool: the location I would most likely find Ricardo.

I made my way there along a little path going past expensive looking holiday chalets. It was a large pool complex, furnished with sun loungers and overlooking the sea, set amid landscaped surroundings with vivacious flowers, artistic boulders, palm trees and the occasional Buddha statue wearing a necklace of orange flowers. A most appealing place to recuperate between training it certainly was, but currently it was empty. I started back towards the camp and on the way saw two black guys, one big, one small, approaching in the opposite direction.

"Jamie?" asked the bigger of the two as I approached.

"Ricardo?" I replied.

After a brief chat he introduced me to his training partner and fellow Canadian, Manny, then handed me a key to Owen's room.

"Are you guys fighting soon?" I asked.

"In a couple of nights," said Manny. "Fancy coming?"

I did indeed, especially after Manny told me about Ricardo's last jaunt in the ring.

"Knocked the guy out in thirty seconds."

"Great stuff," I said. "Might have to put a wager on you."

They walked me back to the camp and showed me its accommodation. Rooms were situated just behind the main training area. Each came complete with a large bed, TV, fridge, wifi internet access, and a joint toilet/shower room. Owen's room was the nearest to the training area, with Ricardo and Manny a couple of doors down. I thanked the guys and arranged to meet up with them later, but for now, I needed a shower. Being such a roaster of a day I took it cold, its chilling effect not unlike drinking a triple-espresso—it was just what I needed.

On Owen's bed was a camcorder and a scribbled note:

> Thought you might like to watch one of my fights.
> Look for "KO Number 2." I think you'll like it.

I flipped out the contraption's little screen, located the recommended file and hit play. Shot from just beyond ringside, the shaky footage began with Owen wearing a shiny-red dressing gown, traditional flower necklace and decorative Mongkon headgear, being led into the ring by a flagpole-carrying official, hoisting the English colors. Flanking Owen on either side were his two corner-men wearing shiny-red waistcoats, who, after a quick pep-talk, left him to get on with business. It was a tentative first round from both fighters, but in the second Owen really got into the literal swing of things, offloading a brutal volley of kicks, punches, knees and elbows. One ferocious barrage after another culminated in a big left-hand that sent his poor adversary spiraling towards the canvas completely spark out. The ropes broke his fall; unfortunately he hit them windpipe first, leaving him suspended by his neck, bowing in the middle, until the ref could prise him off. The crowd went wild. Owen raised a hand in celebration.

"Bloody hell!" I said out loud, cringing.

I rewound and watched the finale several times.

I hoped for fireworks like that tomorrow night.

* * *

I had first set eyes on Owen the previous summer, standing near a multitude of giant speakers and lights at a packed-to-the-rafters Wembley Stadium. Firing on all cylinders, the speakers thumped out earth-shaking beats while the lights spun on their rotary axes, shooting colored beams onto the stage that I had assisted to assemble. Here, wiggling about in an interesting get-up of fishnet tights, a black leotard and something akin to an ill-fitting, armless white straitjacket with big eighties-style shoulder pads—which oddly looked like a sort of oversized baby's bib—was Barbadian R&B beauty, Rihanna. Mincing about with her were a platoon of greased up bare-chested male dancers in army-style combat trousers and boots, carrying what I took to be anything other than standard issue military kit—bright-pink plastic pump-action shotguns.

Three others, with whom I was familiar, stood near the speakers with a newcomer: a tall, blonde-haired, athletic, beast of a man, who brought to mind a Scandinavian Olympian. Even from afar the group was easy enough to spot, thanks to their regulation hard hats and bibs—this time of an orange Day-Glo variety. I was dressed in kind and approached my work colleagues for the start of our shift that would see us working though the night dismantling everything we had formerly put up. There was Steve, a cockney jack-the-lad actor, grafting here while waiting for his next theater job; "Metho Man," a muscular South African, so named for his penchant for smoking crystal meth in the stadium toilets; and Christopher, or simply "twat," to those who'd spent more than a couple of minutes in his presence.

As I reached them, the unknown newcomer stared at the show with uninhibited contempt. Shaking his head at the antics on stage he let out a deep frustrated sigh.

"The sooner I get out of this job the better," he said to all gathered.

"You and me both, mate," I responded, thinking of the long night ahead.

"You two could always go permanent you know," ventured Christopher. "There are several perks if you do."

I shuddered at the thought. The blonde one stared a hole through him.

"I would sooner be circumcised with a rusty butter knife," he stated with utter conviction.

It was, I think, in that moment that I knew I had found a kindred spirit.

Owen was, it turned out, a professional deep-sea diver who normally worked on oil rigs, a lucrative, and equally dangerous job that paid fantastic wages when the work was there; the problem was he never knew when it would be. Having gone through a dry spot of late on the diving front, he had seen his savings run out thanks to some seriously fast-living—to the extent that he had put his beloved racing motorbike up for sale, and had been forced, like me, to take a job erecting and dismantling stages.

"Make no mistake," he told me. "I will walk out of here the second the phone call comes!"

And he did, eventually. With a call that saw him earn a cool $180,000 dollars for just six months work. Not too shabby. With money in the bank again he relocated to Thailand, to spend his time training and fighting, while waiting for the next call. I was looking forward to seeing him.

I spent the rest of the day soaking up the peaceful ambience of the nearby beach. After so much draining travel, taking it easy was a beguiling experience to savor. I went for a leisurely swim, visited some nearby rock pools and a prominent phallic rock formation known as "Love Rock," then climbed to the top of a scenic lookout, where I gazed out across a sparkling emerald bay below. By the time I got back to the Muay Thai camp it was in full swing, packed with foreigners and locals alike, smashing the bags, pads, and each other while emitting a chorus of guttural grunts. Two girls, both Western, joined the ranks of those training. As I strolled through to Owen's room I passed the gym's main ring, where a sweat-drenched Ricardo was dancing around kicking the hell out of the pads.

Come nightfall I sat with Ricardo, Manny, and a host of other fighters from the club at a heaving outdoor food market off the high-street that served up myriad Thai culinary delights at cheap prices. A steaming hot meal of "pad Thai"—a Thai-style rice-noodle stir fry served with delights such as tamarind, chilli, crushed peanuts, lime juice, and sugar—came to just fifty cents. I selected a big seafood version filled with king prawns and squid, then got stuck into a fresh pineapple milkshake, before finishing with a Thai-style crepe served with banana and Nutella.

The stall selling these had attracted quite a crowd, both purchasing and spectating. The spectacle was all in the making. Unlike the liquid batter genesis of normal crepes, Thai crepes begin life as a sort of gloopy dough that has to be stretched out to the appropriate shape before cooking on a hot plate. The guy at the stall took the process beyond pure functionality, into the realms of art-form-cum-street-performance. Flinging the dough into the air, he whirled it around his head with adroit vigour, then, all of a sudden, slammed it down on his shiny work surface with enough force to make a few of the older tourists jump. A flurry of lighting-fast finger-tip movements followed to stretch the dough out, and then the whole process was repeated.

Over my food I got talking to "Scouse Bob," a heavily tattooed Liverpudlian with a lumpy-looking forehead that spoke of several recent elbows strikes.

"Fancy a game of connect whore?" he asked.

"How do you play?"

"Oh, you just have a normal game of Connect Four with one of the prozzies."

The "prozzies" were stationed at bars in and around the food court, dancing at poles trying to sell their wares, but were, bizarrely, also available for games of Jenga and Connect Four—so long as you sat drinking at the bar that they worked out of.

"Whatever you do don't challenge one of the older prozzies to a game. If they look a bit ropey, then they'll have been stuck at the bar practising all day every day."

We gave it a go. I won a couple, lost a couple.

It was an odd experience really, as despite the happy salacious masks worn by the girls—as well as those pretending to be girls—I was aware of what a grim business prostitution in Thailand really is.

Back at the table we found several of the fighters discussing one of the trainers at the camp with a sense of awe and intrigue, as rumors flew around as to the guy's colorful past.

"I heard he killed a taxi driver once, kicked him in the neck, went to prison and everything for it, but managed to buy his way out," said one.

"It's all true," confirmed Scouse Bob. "Apparently he was fighting at five, training properly at seven, had over two hundred fights by the time he was nineteen, then retired and became a gangster for a few years before becoming a monk."

A case of never letting the truth get in the way of a good story? Maybe. But I was sure looking forward to meeting the bloke.

* * *

"Mazza, you old bastard!" exclaimed Owen with a wide smile as he strolled into camp during the morning training session, reaching out a huge hand for me to shake—no hugs please; we're British.

The whole long lost buddies routine began with banter, followed by an exchange of wild stories that flew back and forth, each vying to outdo the other in our adventures. After dropping off some knickknacks Owen had purchased on his trip away to relax on a nearby island before his big fight tonight, we headed off to a café together to grab some food. While walking there Owen spotted something stuck up on a wall near the food court.

"They've only gone and done it again!" he said shaking his head in dismay.

I took a closer look. On the wall was a promotional poster for tonight's fights on the island. Splashed prominently across it were pictures of different fighters heading the bill, including Owen; only it wasn't labeled as such. Across his image was emblazoned, "Sebastian," juxtaposed next to a picture of the Swedish flag.

"What the—?"

"Happens all the time," explained Owen. "Promoters put up flags representative of the holiday makers currently on the Island to try and get them to come along and support their fellow countryman. Sometimes even follow through with it in the stadium. I've seen Canadians led out by guys carrying the stars and stripes, and being pretty pissed off and distracted by it too."

"And the Sebastian bit?"

"Different fighter from the camp. Must have mixed our names up. One guy at the camp only found out he was fighting when he went for a run and saw a poster of himself promoting that night's event."

With Owen's bout tonight, the camp trainers had prescribed him only light exercise today, so after a hearty breakfast we worked hard at taking it easy, hanging out for the rest of the morning by the pool and beach. In the early afternoon we went for a *legitimate* Thai massage at the only place recommended by the camp, a little nondescript establishment well off the main drag. This, apparently, was not your bog-standard tourist massage, but the real deal to prepare fighters before their bout. And good lord it felt like a bout. Joints popped, bones cracked, tendons stretched and muscles took one hell of a pummeling, as Owen and I were thrown into an array of contortionist-like positions by a couple of motherly-looking middle-aged women. Particular attention was given to the shin area—which Thai boxers kick and block with instead of using their foot. Here the masseuses jammed their elbows into the muscle alongside the shin, bearing-down and levering wildly, as if trying to prise meat from the bone. I can't say it was particularly enjoyable at the time, but it sure made me feel limber afterwards.

Come the evening we both did some gentle pad work at the camp in preparation for the big event. I'd done plenty of Western boxing before and even trained for a Muay Thai fight when in New Zealand—my opponent never showed up, so I was cajoled by one of the event promoters into participating with him in an "exhibition bout," which is not really a bout at all; more a friendly light spar with plenty of gentlemanly touching gloves and mutual nods of the head. Despite this previous training, I was surprised at how out of breath the workout with Owen left me, although it was hardly the real thing. Maybe it was the heat or maybe I'd just let my cardio slip, but I promised myself that when I got home I'd get back into it.

"I think I'm gonna have you as one of my corner-men tonight, Mazza," said Owen after a moment's reflection on the culmination of our training session.

I was honored, and excited.

Before I knew it we were clambering into the back of a pickup truck with several other fighters, making our way in the sticky evening air, along twisting and undulating roads, past resorts and towns teeming with people, shimmering coastlines and tropical bush, towards the island's main stadium. An almost palpable sense of anticipation pervaded the truck. Probably few would have admitted to it, least of all at the time, but I could tell everyone was already fighting their first battle of the night, an internal one against their own nerves. In Mike Tyson's early boxing career he used to get so nervous that he'd throw up before a fight. But no matter, he'd then go from dressing room to ring and destroy whoever was in front of him. It wasn't that he didn't feel fear, rather that he channeled that energy to his advantage. Tyson's legendary trainer, Cus De Ammo, used to say "fear is the friend of exceptional people" and that: "Fear is like fire. You can make it work for you: it can warm you in winter, cook your food when you're hungry, give you light when you are in the dark, and produce energy. Let it go out of control and it can hurt you, even kill you." Wise words. And in truth, there was legitimate reason for those on board to feel a touch of the nerves, if not outright fear itself, for before the night was out, some sitting among us would be brutally beaten in front of their comrades and a baying crowd; repeatedly struck about their legs, torso, arms, and head to the point where their very consciousness would depart them, and their unresponsive bodies fall to a bloody canvas at the feet of the person who inflicted such a fate, who would then be applauded for doing so.

Muay Thai is a tough gig, that's for sure.

Some sat in the back of the pickup chatting, others listened to music on their MP3 players, while a couple just stared warrior-like into the darkness, contemplating what lay ahead. Owen remained silent so I left him to it. What an odd reality, I thought. If your sport is, say, tennis, soccer, cricket or baseball, then if you lose a game, well, you lose a game. It might be a disappointment, possibly even a crushing one, but there it is. Lose in Muay Thai, however, and you face serious injury—arms and shins are no stranger to getting snapped—or even death, with fatalities occurring yearly in the sport.

We pulled up outside the Muay Thai stadium in Chaweng, where a war-like statue of a Muay Thai fighter was delighting visitors in a car-lot out the front, next to which multiple tourists stood posing for photos. Stepping into the stadium it was clear something big was scheduled to go down. The place crackled with excitement. An agitated atmosphere laced with manic nervous tension, not a calm before the storm, more like a group of storm chasers teetering on the periphery of a violent tempest, all hoping it would live up to the predicted forecast, but also with a modicum of concern. Tourists made up a large proportion of the crowd in this modern-day gladiatorial pit, seated on tiered benches that rose from near the center of the stadium, where, raised up about five feet off the ground, there was a large Muay Thai ring. For the high rollers, a section of comfy leather armchairs was situated near a bar, and towards the back lay an elevated area reserved for a traditional Thai orchestra. Made up of drums, cymbals, and Jawa flutes, the orchestra rhythmically reflects the fight itself, increasing in tempo as the action dictates, encouraging fighters into a maelstrom of violence.

Owen's trainer, Nokweed, a hard-as-nails, craggy-faced former world champion of the sport, led us through to a back room where several fighters were already in attendance, getting oiled-up ready for battle in tonight's opening bouts. With Owen's fight scheduled to be one of the last, we had plenty of time to settle down in an area near ringside reserved for fighters, and to watch the early fights.

After a long lonely walk to the ring, all fighters perform a pre-fight ritualistic dance known as the Wai kru, which roughly translates as "getting rid of fear from the heart." Done wearing a cord-like headdress known as a Mongkon, the Wai kru begins with a fighter paying respect to the crowd with a gracious bow. Homage is then paid to the fighter's trainers and camp before the stylized dance begins. Each particular camp has their own distinctive and recognisable Wai kru, with moves including the mimed firing of arrows from a bow, and the mimed catching and snapping of an opponent's. On completion of the Wai kru, fighters go back to their corner for a few final instructions. Their Mongkon comes off. A gong strikes. And battle begins.

Tonight's proceedings kicked off with some youngsters' bouts. They looked around their mid teens. By this age many Thais will already be veterans of scores of fights. No matter their age or stature, the level of skill, athleticism, speed and technical ability displayed was immense; so was the ferocity. Shin kicks chopped down into thighs in the manner of lumberjacks wielding axes against trees, while knees pummeled battering-ram-like into rib cages, and fists and elbows collided with thuds into wincing faces. I got to watch plenty of fights before Owen's bout—including a "lady boxing special" between two girls. Manny's bout produced a spectacular knockout for him in the form of a blistering uppercut. While Ricardo, the thirty second knockout man, lost tonight's one on a decision.

It was intriguing for me to see the difference between Muay Thai as practiced in its homeland, compared to bouts I had seen my more martial-minded friends compete in at home. The intensity was the same but here the ref seemed to push the boundaries a little further, letting the fight ride beyond the point where a referee in the U.K. might already have jumped in. Several full knockouts occurred, the worst suffered by a Canadian fighter from Owen's camp called CJ, who prior to the fight had enthusiastically asked me to immortalize his bout for him on his video camera. After a moderately paced first round, CJ came unstuck in the second, finding himself on the receiving end of a right-hand that could have been fathered by a gorilla—in actual fact a skin-headed British guy from a neighboring camp called "Stuey." CJ took it flush on the chin and was out cold before he hit the ground. Unfortunately, hitting the ground would be a while in the making. He had the misfortune of collapsing onto the top rope where, completely unconscious, he was momentarily suspended and at Stuey's mercy. No compassion was shown. Several completely undefended blows rained in on CJ's now limp head, which flopped from side to side with every punch like something out of a cartoon, erasing a year or more of high school education in the process. Eventually gravity got him out of there, sending CJ face-first towards the canvas, at which point Stuey, ever the gentlemen, threw a full power shin kick to CJ's head. The ref dived in but only made matters worse. In an almost carbon copy of the fight I had watched on Owen's camcorder, CJ landed neck first, face down on the lowest rope. Only this time he not only had his own weight to support from this most inappropriate and sensitive area of the body, but the ref's too—with him landing on top of CJ, arms waving about madly at Stuey to cease fire.

"YEAH! WOOHOO, STUEY!" screamed a lady friend of his, jumping to her feet with unbridled joy from the pew behind me.

To bring the stiff-as-a-board CJ around, several officials immediately hoisted him to his feet, and began massaging his temples—the exact opposite to what doctors do in the West, where fighters are made to remain prostrate to recover. Minutes after CJ's fight I headed to the changing room where I saw him slumped over on a bench looking thoroughly dejected. He glanced up at me as I happened by and simply said "sorry." Why he said that to me

I don't know, nor could I conceive of an appropriate response, so just smiled sympathetically. Despite the brutality of the KO, in a sense CJ was lucky. In neighboring Burma, boxers can be knocked out, only to find themselves brought around and launched straight back into the fray again, with all too predictable results. There's no two ways about it, Muay Thai is one brutal and violent sport where, should you lose, you might very well lose badly. But here's the thing, I'd be lying if I said I didn't find it thoroughly compelling.

Before I knew it, Owen was getting ready to make his entrance, and I was putting on one of the camp's red waistcoats to flank him, along with fellow corner-man Pi-Dang, on his way to the ring. I felt nervous just making my way there, and no one was going to be clubbing me around the head tonight—at least I hoped not. All I had to do was periodically stuff a wet sponge into Owen's ugly mug, and dole out a bit of tactical advice. Thankfully things got off to a good start, with the flag-bearer hoisting the proper colors as he led us out, and the MC using Owen's correct name in his announcement—a rarity for the night so far. Reaching the ring I scaled the steps leading up to the ropes and forced the top two down so Owen could clamber in behind me and begin his Wai kru.

Soon after, the gong rang out and Owen was squaring up against an angry-looking Thai veteran. Owen got off to a flying start, dominating the bout from the offset, capitalizing on his reach advantage with some stiff jabs and low looping leg kicks which seemed to knock his opponent off kilter, slowing his footwork and checking his advances. As the round progressed it suddenly struck me just how much fun this all was, for a corner man at least. It was a bit like playing a computer game only with real life characters, albeit with a slightly unresponsive and unpredictable key pad.

"Elbows, Owen! Elbows!" I'd yell at him when he was locked in a close range exchange, to which he would respond accordingly—once he'd heard me above the crowd and processed the instruction amid the understandable distraction of being lumped in the face.

"Right body kick!" I yelled when the chance arose.

This time the keypad worked and the requested shot fired first time, hitting home with a "BANG!" into his opponent's ribs. It really was the best of both worlds. All the fun and thrill of the fight, but absolutely zero danger of actually getting hurt.

As if in a flash, the round was over and I was in the ring with Pi-Dang, propping Owen's legs up on a stall and telling him to keep his guard high.

Another "BONG" and it was round two. Only this one didn't last very long. Dancing around his opponent, Owen threw out a few feints here and there, setting himself up to offload an almighty shin kick to his opponent's liver. Often described as the groin shot to the chest, a "liver shot" knockout is a rare treat indeed, and Owen delivered a peach. It landed with a wooden-sounding "thwack" that could be heard throughout the stadium. His opponent let out a yelp and collapsed to the floor motionless. A regular body-shot and a liver shot are two very different creatures. The former will knock the air out of you, but a liver shot . . . well, imagine that your "plums" are located not between your legs but below your right pec, and someone has just given you a full-power "hoof" straight into them—it's totally incapacitating. The liver is designed to filter all the nasties from your body, and when it's kicked, and hard, all those horrible accumulated toxins are released at the same time back into your system. The result is not a knockout in the strictest sense, since you're conscious throughout, but the effect is much the same, as you are momentarily paralyzed while the fires of hell race around your insides. The world around you goes fuzzy, and any pretense of fight drains from you quicker than a cheetah driving a Ferrari. All you want is to be tucked up in bed with a nice hot milky drink, and given a kiss "goodnight" on the forehead.

The referee waved an end to the fight.

I jumped into the ring and hoisted Owen's hand into the air.

CHAPTER FIFTEEN

Canine Carnage

"You must be very careful," stated the driver of an odd-looking van with a tiny cab but big square metal box-like protrusion for a rear. "There are many bad people," he exclaimed with a palpable sense of caution as he looked about at our nighttime surroundings, made up of scrubby waste ground, above which highway flyovers branched in a bewildering array of directions.

It was nearly midnight and, in truth, I didn't have a clue where I was—the edge of an unknown town with a turning for Pathum Thani, but beyond that, not the foggiest. To hitchhike at night is never an easy task, and despite having decided to throw my tent down after the culmination of my previous lift minutes earlier, when a new pair of headlights appeared on the deserted road behind me, I couldn't quite resist and found myself, almost involuntarily, throwing out a thumb—old habits die hard.

"Pathum Thani?" I asked. If my guess work was correct, then Pathum Thani was the direction I needed in order to bypass the sprawling madness of Thai capital Bangkok.

"Okay," he said. "You are lucky I stop. Do not trust people."

I stifled a laugh, as it was said with the unspoken implication that obviously such advice excluded him. He got out and led me around to the rear-end of the van's separate metal box-like storage compartment. A chunky padlock secured a door here. Selecting a key from a multitude on a keyring, he opened the door, revealing two big freezers inside.

"Is it safe?" I asked, concerned that I might well freeze.

He looked confused.

"Err, cold?" I said, miming shivering, accompanied with the appropriate noise.

"No." He pointed to a strange cage-like metal grate that comprised maybe ten percent of the flooring leading up to the door. "Air underneath."

On top of the grate were several wooden slats making it possible to clamber in. I did so, sitting with my back to one of the freezers and my feet resting on the slats.

"I will have to lock door," he said apologetically.

Oh, the irony. Trust no one, but hey, don't worry about me incarcerating you in a windowless metal box in the middle of the night. Images of the cage the "child catcher" used in Chitty-Chitty-Bang-Bang to snare his victims flashed across my mind. On previous hitchhiking trips, I had turned down ostensibly above-board rides, simply on a gut-feeling about the person offering the lift, but here, despite the insanity of the situation, I felt fine.

I nodded my approval. The door closed. My world went dark. "Clunk" went the padlock, making my commitment final. Then we were off. Despite the dark, I could make out the asphalt whizzing past beneath the grate, which somehow I found strangely reassuring. It was a very odd experience, that's for sure. I didn't know where I was, less so where I was being taken; I couldn't see out, nor had I any way of getting out.

After about thirty minutes, the movement of the tarmac slowed, then stopped altogether. Footsteps made their way towards the door, and suddenly there was light. With blinking eyes I stepped outside to survey my surroundings. In front of me, running parallel to the deserted road we pulled up on, was a wide grass verge, splitting the immediate vicinity in two. On its far side was an almighty elevated highway, beneath which a second highway ran at ground level. Vehicles raced along both, at speeds too great to hail a ride. Beyond these mighty tributaries lay a darkened urban sprawl. Behind me, on the near side of the verge, lay much the same. But the real downer to the area was the verge itself, along which ran a train track, flanked on either side by platforms of a tiny station.

"I bring you here so you can get train," announced the driver proudly. "It is safer for you."

Oh, for crying out loud!

It may have been safer, but it was somewhere I had specifically requested *not* to be taken; that and a city—something I had been clarifying repeatedly for drivers since Indonesia. I now had both. I was in a far worse position than before, in an area that afforded little in the way of hitchhiking or sleeping potential. And it was now well past midnight. I could have kicked myself. If only I had scouted out a place to sleep back at the waste ground. In vain I tried to encourage a lift out of him to the outskirts of wherever we currently were. It was no good. The guy was adamant: from now on I should only catch trains.

"But I have no money for a train," I said, issuing forth a white lie in the hope he'd change his mind.

He reached into his pocket to offer me some.

"No, no," I said, holding up my hands to stop him. "It's okay. I'm okay."

I was beyond tired now and just wanted done with this.

"Thank you for the ride," I said, then waved goodbye and headed up the road, resigned to make do wherever I was.

There were no hotels or boarding houses visible, and what's more, it was so late now that it hardly seemed worth the money if I did find one. The night that stretched before me looked unpleasant. But I was where I was. On and on I walked into the night in a fatigued daze, following the same route as the train tracks, hiking along the deserted road that ran parallel to them. Eventually, after much exertion, it looked like I'd found the spot: a vast empty and overgrown abandoned lot. Separating the lot from the road was a stagnant-looking canal. Leading across this were three concrete walkways, one at either end of the lot's boundaries and one in the middle. Ahead lay rocky and thoroughly uneven terrain but I didn't care. I was too tired now to give a damn. Starting across the middle walkway I scanned the area for somewhere remotely feasible to settle in for the night, but when halfway across I caught a glimpse of something out of the corner of my eye.

Squinting in the dark, I focused in on what it was, then let out a gasp of horror when the blur of motion registered in my brain.

Streaming across the first walkway to my left was a nightmare in action: an enormous pack of wild dogs, the front runners now heading my way at full-pelt along the empty road. And they weren't happy.

"Christ!" I said out loud as I began running in a panic back towards the road. My adrenaline hit red alert, taking hold of me as if I'd stuck my hand in a mains socket, jolting me from near-comatose to wide awake in an instant. If the pack reached the middle walkway before I did the road, then I'd be cut off, left with nowhere to run but back into the lot itself, where, as sure as day follows night, they would pursue me. And then I'd be royally fucked. Glancing back towards them as I sprinted, a blurred mass of hideous faces appeared out of the darkness, locking onto me like heat-seeking missiles, diminishing my thin advantage with every bound. One dog powered out in front, closing the gap and growling hideously. I pushed forwards, images of baying teeth flashing rapidly before me while barking rang in my ears. My mouth was dry and heart thundering in my chest as if about to explode.

I cleared the walkway and stumbled onto the road. Ahead lay a small concrete barrier separating the road from the railway verge.

Could the dogs scale it?

I had no idea but there was nowhere else for me to go. I ran possessed towards it, every step feeling paradoxically light yet ridiculously heavy at the same time—like running from danger in a nightmare, where you're wildly flailing your limbs about, commanding your body to move but it only responds in slow motion.

The barking was right on top of me.

I whipped my neck around, catching sight of the lead dog, eyes wild, full of destructive intent and blood lust, now only twenty feet away. With a mighty lunge I launched myself over the wall and stumbled onto the other side, throwing my pack down among the gravel.

Would the dogs leap after me?

I sure as hell wanted to dissuade any attempts. Panting like a steam engine, I grabbed the nearest rock to hand and hurled it with every ounce of aggression I could muster towards the closest dog—a powerful-looking Alsatian ready to rip me apart. I aimed to hit but soundly missed. The rock smashed on the ground in front of him, scattering debris across its surface.

He didn't back off but there was hesitation in his posture now and his advance ceased. Suddenly the rest of the pack joined the fray, venturing no further than the first but howling with such ferocity that they practically jumped off the ground with every vicious bark.

"FUCK OFF!" I yelled back at them, launching a barrage of rocks.

A few briefly scattered, yelping in response. Others jostled about wildly, feeding off their collective aggression, dynamically poised ready for a counter-attack, barking all the time.

The wall, it seemed, was enough to hold them off for now. I decided to get the hell out of here. Grabbing my pack I ran along the verge behind the wall, hoping the empty lot was their territory and not beyond, that they wouldn't follow me and find a way through to the other side, and would slink off instead back into the darkness. It was a theory that thankfully turned out to be correct. They stayed where they were. The aftershock of the encounter reverberated inside me for several minutes, as their vile-sounding cackles echoed in the distance.

I'd had encounters with wild dogs before when hitching but this one seemed a particularly close call. Had I not spotted the pack when crossing the walkway, I would have plowed deep into their unlit territory, and only realized after it was too late. Once there in the darkness I would have had nowhere to run or hide. The consequences didn't bear thinking about.

By now it was 1:35 a.m. and I was utterly exhausted. More than ever I just wanted to sleep, but I was damned if I was going to bed down anywhere like that again. Scarcely anyone was about at this hour. Even the traffic on the nearby elevated highway had all but ceased, so when a solitary pickup truck with a hard cover over its cargo unit began to approach on the minor road next to the verge, I figured it was worth a try. I clambered over the barrier and didn't really think it would stop, but it did.

Behind the wheel was a young guy who spoke very little English but somehow managed to convey that he was driving to a hotel he worked at, further up the road. It didn't sound especially far but any lift in the right direction was a bonus, so I got in. The motion of the drive almost had me asleep. Behind the cab, completely filling the enclosed cargo area, were row upon row of plastic vacuum-packs, filled with hundreds of T-shirts, compressed neatly into orderly bundles of what looked about twenty a pack. Their collective form resembled a mattress, at least in my current state. I asked if I could sleep there. It was a cheeky request for sure, but I was up for trying anything at this stage.

"No," he said, shaking his head with a smile as if surely I was joking.

I tried again, this time with slightly more conviction and a dash of mendicancy.

"No. Err, finish four."

"Until four?" I asked.

"Yes."

Result.

After driving for a while we reached his hotel, a huge super-expensive-looking venue of the corporate variety, the sort of place that might specialize in holding conferences. We pulled in past two big manned security gates, and arrived in a car-lot on the side of the building. I got out and walked to the rear of the truck with the driver, who opened up the tailgate door. I climbed in.

"Four," he said with a wave of the hands and a look that stated, "That's your lot."

I thanked him. He closed up and disappeared. My head near collapsed onto the comfy padding. As my eyes shut I was almost immediately asleep.

In what seemed a cruelly brief period of time I was shaken awake.

I couldn't believe that over two hours had passed—and with good reason; they hadn't. It was only 2:15 a.m. More than a little confused, I pointed the time out to the vehicle's owner who was now wearing a bellboy-like hotel uniform. I couldn't work out why, but there had been some change of plan. I would have to go elsewhere; namely, a little traffic-island security office positioned between the driveway in and the driveway out. Reluctantly, I followed the guy's lead and trudged off towards it. Inside a glaringly bright lightbulb blazed away. It would have to remain on. Stationed here were two night-guardsmen who were clearly up to speed on the arrangement. With little further ado one of them pointed out where I could crash—the floor. Having been so sublimely comfy only moments ago, this came as a bitter disappointment, but I made the best of it and quickly got my bedroll out. Suddenly it dawned on me that this cloud might very well have a silver lining. Maybe now I could sleep, not, as previously arranged, until 4 a.m., but right through until dawn. I tried to convey as much, doing so with sleeping gestures, some clock pointing and a splattering of monosyllabic dialogue. It seemed to do the trick. I settled in for the night, closing my eyes to a squadron of mosquitoes that did their best to torment me with their high-pitched wails.

Before I knew it I was being shaken again, this time by one of the guards. He handed me a little note:

> 4 o'clock, and good morning. Have a good trip in adventure if you problem in trip to call 085-1557*** My name is Ism. Good Luck.

It was still completely dark outside. I tried my best to reason with the guards but it was a no-go from the start. They just kept pointing at the piece of paper. I had to leave. As I got up to go I discovered my lower lip had a great big swollen lump on it. A mosquito bite. Or maybe several. It felt like I'd taken a punch from Owen. Heading out the front of the hotel, I plonked myself down on a bench to formulate a plan. Sitting here I couldn't help but gaze back longingly into the hotel's wide extravagant lobby area with its multitude of comfy-looking sofas. It was quite the temptation. Could I somehow slip in unnoticed? It looked big enough, and many of the sofas were located far from the reception staff's gaze. It was worth a crack. Entering the expansive lobby, I headed for some sofas off to one side when, all of a sudden, I felt someone grab a hold of my arm from behind. I turned around and it was Ism; standing there with a look of abject horror on his face. Next to him was a young colleague.

"What is it that you want?" asked his colleague in good English.

Was this possibly the author of my note?

"Err, I just came to say goodbye," I said.

A moment of awkward silence hung in the air.

"Goodbye then," I said breaking the deadlock, punctuating it with a wave. I turned around and left.

For a while I became better acquainted with the bench outside. Here I stretched out but I couldn't really sleep, so just mulled things over for a while. Hadn't Ism said that he finished at 4 a.m.? It had been a good bit after that when I'd seen him in the lobby, so why the urgency to vacate at that time? I didn't know, and probably spent far too long pondering it. I was outside again, and that was all that mattered. Despite being tired, I was also restless now. I got back on my feet and started walking.

Not far up the road and I arrived opposite somewhere that would have been the perfect place to sleep, had I known about it earlier—a giant airport terminal, situated just beyond the elevated highway. (Although I had no idea where I was at the time, I learned later that this was Don Muang Airport, one of two international airports serving Bangkok). At nearly 5 a.m., it hardly seemed worth it now. The sky was beginning to show the first signs of getting light so I trundled on. Eventually I found what I was looking for—a feasible place to hitch onto the highway. I decided to crash here until dawn, doing so on a stretch of gravel by the roadside.

* * *

It was only noon but already the day felt long advanced. I was drenched in sweat from the terrific heat that grew greater by the minute and seemed to suck the strength right out of me. I hiked up a long straight road that dissected the heart of a crowded unknown town. I couldn't say with any certainty exactly where I was, but my general direction and rough whereabouts were clear enough. I was relatively close to an attraction I really wanted to visit, the ancient Khmer temple, Phimai. Afterwards I planned to continue north to the border with Laos where tomorrow I intended to go to the Chinese consulate to apply for a visa—the first "proper" one required thus far. (For Australia I'd got an electronic one before leaving England; in Indonesia I'd got one on arrival; as a Brit I didn't require one for Malaysia; at Thailand I'd got one at the border; and I planned to do the same for Laos). Instead of going to Laos, I'd flirted with the notion of heading east into Cambodia then traveling north through Vietnam but it just seemed too much of a detour off route. Back on Koh Samui I had consulted Owen, who'd traveled practically everywhere in Southeast Asia, as to the main attractions in neighboring Cambodia.

"Angkor Wat, obviously. Or you can hire an AK-47 and blow away a cow."

"Do people really do that?" I asked, appalled, incredulous, but nevertheless intrigued.

"Apparently very popular with the Yanks. Rumor has it you can also do it with an RPG." (Rocket Propelled Grenade).

That sure as hell didn't appeal, but the famous Khmer temple, Angkor Wat, certainly did. In a sense, today's planned destination, Phimai, was to make up for missing out on this. Phimai was Thailand's largest Khmer temple and although not as big as Cambodia's Angkor Wat, it was older and in the same style. For the temple of Angkor Wat, think the film *Tomb Raider*, where much of it was shot.

As I walked through the town, I cast my trusty upward thumb into the waters of the thronging approaching traffic, but despite a few nibble-like inquisitive glances, none pulled over for the full bite, except several local buses known as "bemos"—little vans with pew-like internal benches stretching along their rear length—that I waved off. I continued up the road, convinced that I could get a free ride. I hadn't succumbed to catching a bus through a town or city yet (with the exception of Darwin where I caught one to the yacht club) so was determined to only do so if absolutely necessary. It was a fair size place, heaving with vehicles and people, plenty of whom stared my way, but from what I could see of it, it didn't appear so big as to preclude crossing it on foot. Eventually, after about forty minutes' slog, I got another ride. This time from a young guy who dropped me on the town's outskirts.

Once there, getting on the move again proved a formality, with two middle-aged women picking me up. Both were caked in make-up and wore glitzy stick-on nails. After little in the way of introductions, the driver asked me—rather strangely to my mind—to guess her age.

"Err, thirty-five?" I said, lying through my teeth.

"I am fifty-two," she boasted.

"Goodness. You don't look it," I said. Again lying.

Her clone in the passenger seat sat with two rolled up laminated posters on her lap, which she proudly unraveled for me. Both were of the Thai king.

"In Thailand we love our king," she said dreamily.

From the glove compartment she produced a CD of songs recorded by none other than His Royal Highness, the King of Thailand.

"Would you like to hear?"

It was super-bland and eminently forgettable.

It proved an odd ride, but it took me to the turning for Phimai, a small but bustling town that had grown up around the temple, which I arrived at after a long walk, and a short lift on the back of a pickup truck.

Although mainly obscured by trees and foliage of a surrounding parkland, Phimai Temple revealed tantalizing glimpses of her ragged splendor from the sidewalk skirting this green exterior. Milling around outside the main entrance was a large exuberant group of school kids whose teacher was having a frightful time trying to marshal the little urchins into an orderly line. By the entranceway congregated a bunch of tourists, Thais and Westerners alike, the latter comprising a small tour group of senior-aged vacationers, several of whom wore matching ill-fitting baseball caps. Also present, cloaked in yellow robes, were about a dozen Buddhist monks. Buying a ticket for 100 Baht (about three dollars) I entered the park, and in so doing stepped back in time.

Ancient paving led through ordered greenery towards a distant row of rusty-colored stone buildings, decorated along their façade with gaping stone windows and elegant columns. Behind this prelude lay the main event; three towers, two shaped like arrowheads, the third crumbled into a decrepit remnant of its former glory. Between here and there were smoky-gray pillars and multiple sunken stone beds—mysterious indents in the ground resembling lavish drained swimming pools. I stepped into a cavernous entranceway and proceeded though a shady alley to a wide open sanctuary behind. Here the magnificence of the site became apparent. The best preserved of the three towers stood centrally, dominating the surroundings. It was a triumph of layered complexity, bedaubed and emboldened with countless pointed protrusions, rising from its extremities like little flames licking at the sky. Multiple stairways led up into the towers and their adjourning buildings, but for now I chose to remain outside.

Phimai temple was constructed by the mighty Khmer Empire around the tenth and eleventh centuries, making it a century older than its more famous cousin Angkor Wat, the two once marking different ends of the ancient Khmer Highway, an important trade and pilgrimage route that stretched 140 miles between the two sites. Although the Khmer were Hindu, Phimai was built as a Mahayana Buddhist temple, making it unique among other Khmer temples of the same period, which, although closely related architecturally, were built as Hindu sanctuaries.

Eventually I moved on to the largest tower, climbing a set of well-worn stone stairs and stepping into the structure's shady heart. It was far less spacious than I imagined, and less embellished too, just a simple main chamber of basic stone-block walls and flooring, contrasting with the intricacies of outside. Providing interest in this plain interior was a large solitary statue of the Buddha, regarding the world from the lotus position, hands cupped upwards holding a bouquet of orange Chrysanthemums. Several visitors congregated in the cool interior, but all moved about with quiet respect. After a good look around, I explored a sort of cloistered walkway adorned along much of its length with beaded columns, then headed onto the smaller of the two intact towers. Inside was another Buddha in similar surroundings to the first, except here the light streaming though the tower's open doorway cast the inner chamber a warm honey color, imbuing it with a faint glow.

I spent a good long while exploring the rest of the site, delving into every nook and cranny, and soaking in its grandeur. When the sun had descended in the sky, and long shadows stretched across the ruins, I decided to get on the move again.

One ride got me back onto the main road heading north, and another to a T-junction about fifteen minutes further on. It was a good spot to wait, and although already late afternoon, I was confident I could reach Laos, and hopefully its capital just beyond the border, by tonight. Thirty minutes of being stared at like an alien from outer space by passing motorists followed, but eventually a double-cab pickup that had just driven past began reversing towards me. Inside sat two girls in their twenties.

"Where are you going?" asked the driver, a petite and pretty girl wearing big "celebrity" sunglasses.

"Khon Kaen," I said, naming the next town on my map, so as to at least "lock in" a short ride. "What about you?"

"We are going to That Phanom."

I scanned my Google Maps print off but couldn't see it, so asked where it was near.

"It is just across the border from Laos."

I was chuffed, absolutely delighted, and promptly got in.

"I am Mao," said the driver. "And this is my friend, Mai."

"Jamie."

We all shook hands and promptly got moving. Mao spoke quite good English, whereas Mai—an arty-looking girl with a haircut that rose up in a central point—spoke none.

A few typical ice-breakers flowed between us including each other's occupations.

"It is difficult to explain," said Mao. "We are, how can you say, we do work for society."

"Social workers?"

"Yes, we are Buddhists and help those with problems of drugs and alcohol, and other problems."

Mao was keen to know about my trip and asked where I'd been, so after reeling off some place names, I handed my digital camera into the front so they could flick through my photos. Suddenly a particular picture caused quite a stir—Owen, in his little shorts backstage at the Thai stadium, all oiled up, pecs and abs on display, ready to raise hell. The girls certainly approved. And who can blame them; a fine figure of a man.

"Do you like Muay Thai?" I asked.

"Oh, not really," said Mao. "I always feel so pity for the loser."

We chatted for some time, but I was still tired from last night's wandering, so when darkness fell I asked if they'd mind if I closed my eyes. They didn't.

When I awoke I checked my watch. It was late. Surprisingly so, considering we had still not reached our destination. If we didn't arrive soon I would struggle to make it to the Laotian capital, Vientiane, tonight. If that happened, I would likely miss out on getting the visa application process rolling tomorrow, as the Chinese consulate was said to close at 11:30 a.m.

"How far is Vientiane from where we're going?" I asked, trying to work out if it was still feasible to get there tonight.

"Urm, about five hours," said Mao.

Say what? That couldn't be right. It had only been five hours away when we'd set off, and that was about five hours ago.

I explained this, and that surely Mao had made a mistake. The mistake was all mine, at least in not checking *which* border with Laos the girls were going near, not Thailand's northern one, a stone's throw from the capital of Laos, but it's distant eastern one, by the Thai town of That Phanom. Poor management on my behalf, for sure, although in my defense, the road we met on was the one that led straight up to the northern border, so on hearing the girls were going "near the border with Laos," it was perhaps not unreasonable to assume it was the nearest one.

"Oh dear," said Mao, concerned at the misunderstanding. "What are your plans for tonight now?"

It was a good question. I was significantly off course, heading along a minor rural road in the dark. If I terminated the ride here, then I would have, in all probability, little hope of getting another ride until the morning. Did it make more sense to trudge on and cross into Laos at the eastern border and then travel from there onto Vientiane, or head back to the northern border come daybreak?

Mao strongly recommended the second option on account of the roads in eastern Laos, which apparently were "terrible."

A brief conversation in Thai ensued between Mao and Mai, which concluded with a mutual nodding of heads.

"If you would like you can stay in Mai's family home tonight. You must know it is not very big."

"So long as it's got a roof and a floor it will be big enough for me."

This was good news. And in truth, I was borderline pleased to be heading east now; an opportunity to stay in a Thai home was not one to pass up.

We drove on into the night and eventually made our way along a thin road running along the banks of a giant river.

"You see those lights," said Mao pointing to some random twinkles among the overall darkness of the other side. "That is Laos."

The river was the Mekong.

We came to a stop at the start of a long thriving section of food stalls flanking the road—now little more than a path—constricting forward motion for all but scooters, that snaked their way through a chaotic crowd of people ambling merrily from stall to stall. In the distance dangled drapes of colored lightbulbs, highlighting clouds of steam and smoke that rose like great apparitions from multiple hissing woks and charcoal burners. Music blared and a vibrant party atmosphere was detectable in the air. Something big and out of the ordinary was going on.

"Once a year for a week is a big festival and market," said Mao, anticipating my question. "We will take you there. But first—" she gestured to her side with a smile, "—We are here!"

Opposite was a simple two-story house with a little café out the front.

As we got out, waves and greetings flowed the girls' way from nearby stall owners, one of whom was Mai's mother, running a pitch selling kebabs, noodles, fish, icy drinks, and other aromatic food. A quick introduction by way of Mao, and we headed inside.

"Oh, you have to take your shoes off," said Mao, bringing me up to speed with local etiquette before I blundered through her friend's family home.

We made our way across a sparsely-furnished ground floor to a flight of stairs that led to an empty upper area with wooden ceiling beams and decking. Window frames bereft of glass cut gaping holes in the upper structure, blurring the line between inside and out, while a light breeze drifted in off the Mekong. We dropped our stuff and headed out.

Constructed mainly out of bamboo with tarps strung up above them, the stalls outside sold a bewildering variety of culinary treats, many coming our way from Mai's kindly mother. These included chips made from dried fish skin used for dunking in a spicy noodle soup, and shavings of desiccated pork. Stuffed, we strolled on into the thick of a crowded rabbit-warren of alleyways, the surging crowd sweeping us along, washing us up and spitting us out in the center of town. Here, stretching as far as the eye could see, was the beating heart of the festival. It was enormous, positively heaving with thousands of people of all ages, who all looked so very happy. There were no Western tourists, at least that I saw. Everything from snake charmers, to fairground rides, from dancing girls to traditional musicians was crammed into the area.

An elephant with its owner passed us by.

"Wow!" I exclaimed. The girls laughed.

"We see a lot of elephants," said Mao.

Making our way past a Ferris wheel lit up with multicolored lights, we came upon an odd display: a super-customized sports car, whose rear end and side doors were wide open, displaying the most ridiculously oversized speaker system imaginable. Practically half the car was boombox. It nearly burst my ear drums from fifty feet, so how the two bikini-clad dolly-birds gyrating next to it coped I've no idea. Mao, Mai and I covered our ears and quickened our pace.

It was a circuitous route, but after taking in much fun of the fair we found ourselves at a large flood-lit, golden-gilded Buddhist temple, Wat Phra That Phanom, which overlooked the festival.

"They say the Buddha bones are kept here," said Mao as we took our shoes off on the temple's forecourt.

It was a curious structure and temple complex situated at the end of a long straight tree-lined avenue that led back towards the silty waters of the

Mekong River. Within its walled confines stood several decorative temple buildings, embellished from top to bottom in red, white and patterned gold, serving as but a garnish to the site's centerpiece: a tall, sharply pointed stupa tower that rose high above the site and was patterned with decorative gold in the shape of what looked like a stylized tree's branches. Dotting the courtyard around the complex were neatly trimmed shrubs, golden lanterns and multiple shiny Buddha statues, some standing regally with perfectly straight backs, others lying down prostrate or meditating cross-legged in the lotus position.

Mai collected some candles and yellow Chrysanthemums from a nearby section providing these to pilgrims, which we placed as an offering at the foot of the great stupa. The girls clasped their hands together and bowed. I followed suit.

"You are allowed a wish now," said Mao.

I wished for a smooth visa application process at the Chinese consulate.

We moved on to an area around the back where a huge golden bell hung within a small open-sided bell tower. Gathered around this was a group of people taking turns to swing a rope dangling from inside the bell to make it chime. I gave it a go, producing a rather lackluster result, but this, apparently, was sufficient to receive a second wish. Having unintentionally stumbled upon such a wonderful and atmospheric spot, I was already pretty darn happy and satisfied with my lot, so simply repeated my earlier wish.

We ended up spending a couple of hours taking in That Phanom's sights, sounds, aromas, and tastes. On our way back to turn in for the night, we stopped at a food stall where the girls insisted I try some strange green-colored sugary bread, a delightful caramel-colored fruit called a lamoot, and the chilled milk from a fresh coconut that was fished from a huge slushy ice box.

I tried to pay, but Mao was having none of it.

"Maybe if we come to England you will help us too."

I promised that I would.

CHAPTER SIXTEEN

Evil from the Air

I had been wondering when I might first spot it, a sign of latitudinal region change, from the year-round intensity of the tropics to the starker fluctuating cycle of the subtropics and the temperate zone. An unknown tree announced the beginnings of this gradual adjustment, its leaves mottled in crispy shades of light green, yellow and brown, their nutrients getting sucked away and reclaimed in readiness for a period of rest. That's not to say the landscape wasn't tropical, the abundant bamboo groves, rice paddies, and lush exotic flora made sure of that. Rather, that the subtle process had begun, and the further north I pushed the more these differing circles of latitude would become apparent.

It had been a long hard day on the road. After spending a delightful farewell breakfast with Mao and Mai at the family-run food stall in front of Mai's riverside home, I pushed westward and then north, backtracking slightly to reach Thailand's northern border with Laos, which I arrived at as the last of the day's remaining light slipped beneath the horizon.

It proved a quick and painless crossing, with efficient corresponding border posts on either side of the Mekong River, spanned between no-man's-land by a large "friendship bridge." Some semaphore-like hand signals and map pointing got me a ride in the back of a pickup truck—driven on the right hand side of the road for the first time since setting off from Australia—to the country's capital, Vientiane, roughly ten miles away. Multiple grandiose embassy and consulate buildings passed by en route, which contrasted with the overall humble, almost provincial, feel to other parts of this modest capital. Pretty Buddhist temples drifted by, as did the occasional remnant of Laos' French colonial past: opulent European-style mansions, many built in Laos by its former colonial masters, now used as governmental offices or abandoned and slowly disintegrating from the cumulative effects of weather and time.

I was dropped on the main tourist drag running parallel to the palm-fronted Mekong, outside an array of bars, restaurants and hostels. After sourcing a cheap but clean room in a basic hotel on the outer edge of downtown, I headed out to have a look at Vientiane. It might have been dark, but I was too wired to rest, and so made the most of the cooler nocturnal temperature by exploring the central district. I investigated the exterior of several locations that would demand greater exploration during daylight hours: a former French colonial mansion, now presidential palace; a one time royal temple with a tiered roof and pillared veranda, now a religious museum; and a colossal floodlit archway monument, a Laotian Arc de Triomphe that stood like a giant squat fortress in the middle of a park, sandwiched on either side by opposing main roads.

For a long while I sat in the park just watching the world go by, then strolled beneath the archway where a sign caught my attention, prompting me to remember Laos' tragic recent past.

"It is the Patuxay or Victory Gate of Vientiane," stated the sign. "Built in 1962 (BE 2505), but never complete [sic] due to the country's turbulent history."

Turbulent indeed.

It said no more on this but I knew it well, and it seemed an apt time for me to reflect upon it. And for those who have taken me to task in the past, in reviews and in person, for including political history in my books, as if this somehow has no relevance to a book of the "travel" genre, well, you can skip this bit or buy yourself another book, for as Czech writer Milan Kundera once stated, "the struggle of people against power is the struggle of memory against forgetting." And I don't intend to forget the hell visited upon Laos as a sideshow to the Vietnam War any time soon, and neither should anyone else.

During America's illegal bombing of Laos an astounding 260 million bombs[87] rained down on this utterly defenseless, impoverished peasant society; over two million tons of explosives,[88] substantially more than the United States dropped on both Germany and Japan combined during the Second World War,[89] making Laos the most intensely bombed country on earth, with nearly a ton of ordnance dropped for every man, woman, and child.[90]

In 1958 the Laotian left-leaning nationalist political movement known as the Pathet Lao ("Lao nation") won nine seats in the country's elections, forming part of a coalition government that saw them, along with other leftists, control a block of thirteen out of twenty-one contested seats;[91] and their leader, Prince Souphanouvong, elected chairman of the National Assembly.[92] The United States was not pleased; U.S. Ambassador Graham Parsons would later admit: "I struggled for sixteen months to prevent a coalition."[93] With Laos inundated with American aid in an attempt to establish U.S. control—to the degree that Laos was "the only country in the world where the United States supports the military budget 100 percent"[94]—it proved easy to topple the government. "By merely withholding the monthly payments to the troops," wrote Roger Hilsman, who worked for the C.I.A. and State Department, "the United States could create the conditions for toppling any Lao government whose policies it opposed."[95] A coup was triggered that saw the country's "pro-Western" Prime Minister resign to establish a new government excluding the Pathet Lao. (He would later claim he was forced to resign due to America's opposition to Laotian neutrality.)[96] Things didn't work out for him, with the C.I.A. opting to support another man, leading to a bewilderingly complex series of coups and counter coups over the next few years in which one discredited government after another rose and fell in quick succession,[97] and the C.I.A. stuffing ballot boxes in farcical elections,[98] rigged, in the words of Noam Chomsky, "so crudely that even most pro-U.S. observers were appalled."[99] Hundreds of millions of U.S. dollars were pumped into tiny Laos, a country whose economy was primarily based on barter, and was 99 percent agricultural, causing "unimaginable bribery, graft, currency manipulation and waste."[100]

The immediate U.S. goal was to bring to power a carefully selected right-wing strongman, Phoumi Nosavan, while crushing the Pathet Lao, an organization whose leader, Prince Souphanouvong, insisted was not a communist movement—describing himself and the party he headed as "ultra-nationalist."[101] As American historian William Blum has noted, "The Pathet Lao were the only sizable group in the country serious about social change, a characteristic which of course tends to induce Washington officials to apply the communist label."[102] Fred Branfman, who first visited Laos as an educational advisor in the sixties, wrote of the Pathet Lao: "For the first time . . . [Laotians] were taught pride in their country and people, instead of admiration for a foreign culture; schooling and massive adult literacy campaigns were conducted in Laotian instead of French; and mild but thorough social revolution—ranging from land reform to greater equality for women—was instituted.[103]

Following the rigged 1960 election, civil war broke out,[104] and in 1961 the United States began serious clandestine military operations[105] against the Pathet Lao, with a secret mercenary force of about 30,000, the Armée Clandestine, made up of Meo hill tribesman (the same ethnic group organized in Vietnam), and citizens from the region's U.S. client states: Thais, South Vietnamese, Filipinos, South Koreans, and Taiwanese. Added to this contingent were U.S. military trainers and C.I.A. personnel, especially pilots of the agency's notorious Air America—infamous for its role flying heroin and opium across Indochina (Vietnam, Cambodia and Laos). Refined in a laboratory at the C.I.A.'s headquarters in northern Laos,[106] the C.I.A.'s drug running operations were undertaken to line the pockets of, and sway favor with, local allies, leading to an outbreak of addiction among American G.I.'s.[107] To keep this army secret from Congress and the American people, multiple covers were created for the 2,000 Americans directly involved,[108] including U.S. personnel working, on paper at least, as embassy attaches, and the C.I.A.'s Air America pilots contracting for USAID,[109] fighting a war under the guise of development assistance. Americans killed in Laos were recorded as having died in neighboring Vietnam.[110]

As their campaign against the Pathet Lao increased, the C.I.A. peppered the country with landing strips, hangars, radar installations, barrack buildings,

And so it begins. Sea hitching out of Tasmania. Photo credit: Jessica Nilsson.

The perfect breakfast stop. Wineglass Bay, Tasmania. Photo credit: Wolfgang Glowacki

Posing with one of Billy's multiple firearms.

Robbo smoking a little crystal meth.

Uluru.

To infinity and beyond, Australian outback.

Aussie road train.

Looking down on the Tengger caldera.
Photo credit: Wim Vanderstok

Borobudur, the world's largest Buddhist temple.

One of many rides on two
wheels in Indonesia.

Indonesian vegetable
patches.

Ferry dormitory on boat to
Malaysia.

Traditional Malaysian wedding with Ann
and family.

Thaiboxing corner man for Owen.
Opponent's foot in left hand corner.

Time for some RR in Thailand.

Phimai Temple.

Breakfast with Mao and Mai.

Almsgiving, Laos.

Scenic splendor, Laos.

Eye of newt and toe of frog. Laos market.

Traditional Laotian home . . . with massive satellite.

Asia's largest animal market, Kashgar. Photo credit: Etienne Margain

Night market, Kashgar. Photo credit: Etienne Margain

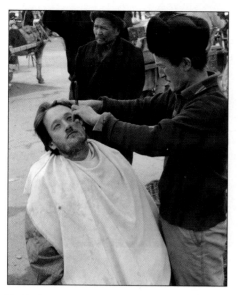

Indulging in a shave at Kashgar's
animal market.
Photo credit: Danilo Gartner

Tired. So very tired and cold.
Photo credit: Manon Margain

Journey to Shipton's lost arch.
Photo credit: Danilo Gartner

Sheer perfection. Shipton's Arch in all its glory.
Photo credit: Danilo Gartner

Kashgar bakery fires up the oven. Photo credit: Danilo Gartner

The Irkeshtam Pass.
Photo credit: Danilo Gartner

"I don't like the look of him."
Photo credit: Danilo Gartner

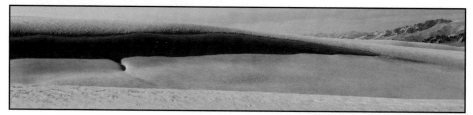

Wave Rock, Irkeshtam Pass. Photo credit: Danilo Gartner

The road to Kyrgystan. Photo credit: Danilo Gartner

Meal on the road, Kyrgystan.

Roadside accommodation, Kyrgystan.

Burnt out police station after riot in Bishkek.

Making friends on the road, Kazakhstan.

My friend Cokeh who shared his tiny squat with me.

Khoja Ahmat Yssawi Mausoleum, Kazakhstan.

On the road with Dmitriy.

Truck stop bathroom, Kazakhstan.

Kazakhstani highway.

Aktau. Kazakhstan's answer to Paris. Photo credit: Ethan Martin.

Male model shoot, Kazakhstan. Photo credit: Ethan Martin.

With Dmitriy and friends. Photo credit : Ethan Martin.

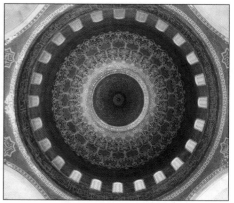

Mosque dome, Azerbaijan.
Photo Credit: Ethan Martin.

Caspian Sea cargo ship.
Photo credit: Ethan Martin.

Tank graveyard, Azerbaijan. Photo credit Ethan Martin.

Vardzia cave city, Georgia.

Cappodocia, Turkey.

Blue Mosque, Istanbul.

Hagia Sofia, Istanbul.

Roadside breakfast, Bulgaria.

The amazing Miodrag, Croatia.

The Julian Alps, Slovenia.

Securing my final ride with
Gerrit and Richard on the
ferry to England.

For more photos from the trip see: http://bit.ly/1pGaLk4

etc.,[111] to the extent that one secret base became the second largest city in Laos—an indication of just how underdeveloped, in an industrial sense, the country was; so much so that inhabitants of some villages were unaware they had a government. Loyalty in such remote regions was to the village or tribe, an allegiance cynically exploited by the C.I.A., who began recruiting local warriors "through money and/or the threat or use of force and/or promises of independent kingdoms which it had no intention of fulfilling, and then keeping them fighting long beyond the point when they wished to stop."[112] The most wanton exploitation of the populace began, where entire tribes were relocated; thousands of people, whole villages at a time, turfed out of their territories to cater for the C.I.A.'s strategic needs.[113]

Despite the offensive by the U.S. and its mercenary forces, the Pathet Lao got the upper hand and, according to a U.S. government assessment, by the spring of 1961 "appeared to be in a position to take over the entire country."[114] Its policy in disarray, The United States agreed to attend a multi-nation conference in Geneva in July 1962, aimed at securing an accord. Under newly elected President Kennedy, who described Laos as a country not "worthy of engaging the attention of great powers,"[115] a settlement was signed, but this quickly broke down after both sides violated the agreement, leading to resumed fighting. After Kennedy's assassination the following year, the Laotian coalition government was overthrown, and the C.I.A.'s old favorite, Phoumi Nosavan, rose to the forefront of a rightist executive excluding the Pathet Lao.[116] The ferocity of fighting increased, with the Pathet Lao making sizable gains. It was now that the U.S. bombing began; a campaign of unimaginable ferocity that between 1964 and 1973 saw the U.S. carry out a staggering 580,344 bombing missions[117] which equates to a plane load of bombs dropped on Laos every eight minutes, 24 hours a day, for nine years.[118]

Focused initially on areas in the north of the country under the control of the Pathet Lao, the bombing started several months before the regular bombing of North Vietnam.[119] It increased in intensity in 1966, and again in 1968 when it reached colossal proportions during the "bombing halt" in North Vietnam, which just saw planes diverted to the decimation of Laos instead.[120] "Village after village was leveled, countless people buried alive by high explosives, or burnt alive by napalm and white phosphorous, or riddled by anti-personnel bomb pellets," wrote American educational advisor in Laos, Fred Branfman.[121] "Any sign of life in enemy area is considered military targets," commented a U.S. pilot; another recalling "When it gets down to people in Laos, whatever moved was shot at; was bombed; was naped [napalmed]."[122]

And this is the real story of the bombing of Laos, the unreported bombing of the peasant civilian society in the north of the country, not the version propagated by the U.S. media at the time—and still a surprisingly common textbook orthodoxy—which focused on the more tolerable story of the bombing of the Ho Chi Minh trail in the south (the route by which communist north Vietnam supplied its southern comrades).

During 1968, Jacques Decornoy, the Southeast Asia correspondent of Le Monde, published extensive eyewitness testimony of the bombing of the north, reporting: " . . . a world without noise, for surrounding villages have disappeared, the inhabitants themselves living hidden in the mountains . . . it is dangerous to lean out at any time of the night or day because of the ceaseless bombardment that leads to the scientific destruction of areas held by the enemy."[123] The regional capital of Sam Neua district was described as being made up of "motionless ruins and deserted houses" much of which had been "razed to the ground," the houses and churches of this "population center" "demolished" by high explosives and phosphorous bombs, and the area strewn with fragmentation bombs designed to maximize civilian casualties.[124] Decornoy's reporting revealed the truth behind the United States' northerly bombing campaign: that it was a war waged against the civilian population. The following year the *New York Times* finally admitted that "the rebel economy and social fabric" are "the main United States targets now." Far from condemnatory, this war crime was almost portrayed as sound tactics: "both civilians and soldiers have retreated into the forests and hills and frequently spend most of their daylight hours in caves or tunnels. . . . The bombing, by creating refugees, deprives the Communists of their chief source of food or transport. ... The population... has been declining for several years and the Pathet Lao find it increasingly difficult to fight a "people's war" with fewer and fewer people."[125]

In 1970, the Hong Kong-based, Far Eastern Economic Review, reported:

For the past two years the US has carried out one of the most sustained bombing campaigns in history against essentially civilian targets in northeastern Laos . . . Operating from Thai bases and from aircraft carriers, American jets have destroyed the great majority of villages and towns in the northeast. Severe casualties have been inflicted upon the inhabitants . . . Refugees from the Plain of Jars report they were bombed almost daily by American jets last year. They say they spent most of the past two years living in caves or holes.[126]

Not that caves were safe refuge from attack. Advanced missiles were deployed to penetrate these natural shelters.[127] A direct strike on one killed 473 men, women, and children sheltering inside—the entire population of a village.[128]

In 1971, *The Guardian* of London reported that " . . . although US officials deny it vehemently, ample evidence exists to confirm charges that the Meo villages that do try to find their own way out of the war—even if it is simply by staying neutral and refusing to send their 13-year-olds to fight in the C.I.A. army—are immediately denied American rice and transport, and ultimately bombed by the US Air Force."[129]

The C.I.A.'s use of child soldiers in its war against the Pathet Lao was recalled by Professor of History Alfred McCoy in documentary film, *The Most Secret Place on Earth*, in which McCoy described a visit he made to a Laotian village as a young journalist: "The local headman . . . said 'we did a bargain with the C.I.A., we gave them our men, and all we ask is for them to feed us, now Vang Pao [the C.I.A.'s broker] and his men have asked us for the fourteen-year-olds. If we sent the fourteen-year-olds, who will be the men to marry the daughters of the village and produce the next generation of children? We'll die as a community. So we said no, and they [the C.I.A.] cut off the rice.'"[130]

That the U.S. Air Force bombing was targeted at civilians was even admitted to in a Senate report which stated that the purpose of the aerial assault was "to destroy the physical and social infrastructure of Pathet Lao held areas," noting that " . . . through such things as saturation bombing and the forced evacuation of population from enemy held or threatened areas we have helped to create untold agony for hundreds of thousands of villagers."[131]

"Untold agony" is about as accurate a description as I can think of for a campaign of terror that killed 350,000 human beings in Laos,[132] and somewhere in the region of 3 million across the rest of Indochina, employing a dark plethora of "anti personnel" weapons, whose nature could almost have been developed by Satan himself. Imagine, if you will, the horror you'd feel if your young son or daughter, niece or nephew, brother or sister, accidentally spilt boiling water on themselves; imagine then the uncontrollable rage that would consume you if a foreign government deliberately dropped a sticky substance onto them from the sky that generates over ten times that heat and is designed to continue burning under the skin.[133] "Napalm is the most terrible pain you can imagine," said Kim Phuc, the iconic "girl in the photograph," immortalized screaming naked in the middle of a road in neighboring Vietnam after a napalm attack covered her fragile nine year old body with sticky blobs of fire that vaporized her clothes on contact and tore into her skin and muscle, very nearly killing her. "Water boils at 100 degrees Celsius. Napalm generates temperatures of 800 to 1,200 degrees Celsius."[134] A U.S. pilot, talking about napalm, remarked:

> We sure are pleased with those backroom boys at Dow [Chemical]. The original product wasn't so hot—if the gooks were quick they could scrape it off. So the boys started adding polystyrene— now it sticks like shit to a blanket. But then if the gooks jumped under water it stopped burning, so they started adding Willie Peter [white phosphorus] so's to make it burn better. It'll even burn under water now. And just one drop is enough, it'll keep on burning right down to the bone so they die anyway from phosphorus poisoning.[135]

(For Dow's other famous contribution to the people of Indochina, this time specifically children, just type "Agent Orange" into Google and hit "Images"). The white phosphorous added to enhance Napalm was also used as a weapon in its own right; effects of which cause victims' skin to burst into flames when doctors attempt to scrape away dead tissue, and wounds to reignite days afterwards when bandages are removed.[136] Other weapons used on civilians by the U.S. in Indochina include a "pellet bomb," the forerunner of the cluster bomb, which worked by releasing hundreds of plastic dart-like fragments.[137]

If they didn't kill immediately, the darts would slowly squirm around inside the body of the man, woman, child, or baby victim, causing agonizing internal injuries; an excruciating, torturous death that could last several days. The intended design advantage of the darts being made of a plastic?—harder to detect under X-ray.[138] And then there was the standard cluster bomb, a weapon designed not for tanks or buildings but people. Each bomb bursts into as many as 400 individual bomlets that explode into jagged fragments of steel, creating a blizzard of shrapnel: a lethal airborne blender that tears limbs from bodies and pulps everything in its path. More cluster bombs have been spewed onto Laos than the rest of the world combined; some 260 million in total. Thirty percent of all cluster bombs used by the U.S. on Laos failed to detonate,[139] littering the country today with around 80 million lethal sub-munitions,[140] which have killed over 20,000 people since the end of the war,[141] and still claim an average of two new victims every week. Resembling small ball-like metal spheres, children are naturally attracted to them and make up the majority of casualties.[142] They are landmines from the sky. Recorded casualties are 98 percent civilian[143]—the equivalent of a policeman shooting forty-nine innocent bystanders for every supposed criminal hit. As Noam Chomsky has commented "[With] a failure-to-explode rate of 20%–30% according to the manufacturer . . . . The numbers suggest either remarkably poor quality control or a rational policy of murdering civilians by delayed action."[144]

The classic collective rationale for the protracted attack unleashed by the U.S. on Laos, Vietnam and Indochina's other victim of a "secret" bombing campaign, Cambodia, is, of course, "fighting communism." An interesting definition that implies much. Never is it expressed as fighting *for* capitalism— the unspoken assumption being that if you're fighting against something then whatever that something is must inherently be bad and therefore resisted. Perhaps a more accurate description would be fighting to *impose* capitalism, as neutralism, the historical record shows, was simply not good enough. And with the C.I.A. sponsoring coups, stuffing ballot boxes, using child soldiers and drug running in Laos, any pretense at "spreading freedom and democracy" is a farce. As historian Michael Parenti has noted, "when faced with a choice between democracy without capitalism or capitalism without democracy, Western elites unhesitatingly embrace the latter."

The specter of a much overworked doomsday scenario, the "Domino Theory," served then, and still does now, as a convenient simplified justification for the killing of more than three million humans across Indochina; its premise being, whereby when one country fell to communism, so too would another, and then another, engulfing Asia and far beyond. According to President Eisenhower, who first articulated the theory, even Australia and New Zealand might tumble in an unstoppable chain reaction.[145] But of course Vietnam, Cambodia, and Laos did fall to communism, and what happened? Did the rest of Asia and Australasia topple like dominoes into the fold of the red menace? In a word: no. In fact, if it wasn't for the C.I.A.'s meddling, then a neutral coalition government would have successfully been established in Laos in 1958.[146] However, if you want an example of a truly devastating, although rarely acknowledged, domino effect within the region, then look no further than neutral Cambodia. Declassified documents from the C.I.A.'s Directorate of Operations reveal that were it not for the death and destruction caused by the U.S. bombardment of Cambodia, which killed half a million people[147]—over ten times the number killed in the Luftwaffe's Blitz of Britain during World War II—then Pol Pot and the Khmer Rouge might never have come to power in the first place,[148] sparing Cambodia Year Zero, the Killing Fields, and all the unthinkable terror that followed, in which one in five Cambodians died at the hands of Asia's Hitler. (For more on this, see the superb but heart-wrenching documentary: *Year Zero, the Silent Death of Cambodia;* viewable online at: http://vimeo.com/17634265). And while on the subject of Cambodia, it's worth mentioning, for it's a rarely told hidden history, that when Vietnam liberated Cambodia from the nightmare of Pol Pot on Christmas Day 1978, the United States, Britain, and China began funding, arming, and training the Khmer Rouge in exile in Thailand,[149] their troops receiving training from Britain's special forces, the S.A.S., under Margaret Thatcher's government,[150] including "the use of improvised explosive devices, booby traps and the manufacture and use of time-delay devices."[151] The reason?—Pol Pot was the enemy of their enemy, the Vietnamese. (Despite China originally backing the North Vietnamese against the U.S., Cold War geopolitics saw the U.S. forging a strategic alliance with China as a counterweight to the Soviets after the fall of Saigon, using China as a surrogate to support Pol Pot against Vietnam—China's historic foe.)

In many respects the bombing of Laos served as a blueprint for how the West would wage war in the decades to come. The majority of the fighting was conducted by aerial bombardment against a defenseless enemy with no air force, who would rarely, if ever, get to see who was trying to kill them. They might catch fleeting glimpses of jets screaming past overhead but almost never get to look their attacker in the eye. It was a situation that suited the Americans just fine. "[The Laos operation] is something of which we can be proud as Americans. It has involved virtually no American casualties. What we are getting for our money there … is, I think, to use the old phrase, very cost effective," stated the U.S. Secretary of State, U. Alexis Johnson.[152]

For the Laotians it wasn't so cost effective. Hundreds of thousands of sentient, feeling human beings with lives of value died, many more were maimed forever, and Laos became a nation of nomads; refugees whose houses, villages and arable land was destroyed, forcing a wretched existence onto untold numbers who were reduced to begging or scavenging like animals for scraps of food. With Laos suffering such evil horrors, it is astonishing that this epic crime is not common knowledge, remembered globally with a vow to never forget. Had mainland America been attacked by a foreign power that riddled American toddlers with dart-like pellets, burnt American grandmothers alive with napalm and white phosphorous in front of their families, shredded pregnant American women with fragmentation devises, buried loving American fathers whole with 500-pound bombs, razed American communities to the ground, and callously bled the country and left it to die, then the screams of victims would echo through generations around the world. And rightly so. That the slaughter in Laos does not, speaks volumes of our inherent racism in the West. A world of worthy and unworthy victims exists, where we know much about the crimes of others but next to nothing of our own, and where the blood of an American is deemed infinitely more valuable than that of a Laotian. And what, I wonder, would be the reaction if the foreign power responsible for this hypothetical U.S. carnage, justified the worst of its atrocities with the flippant rationale that it gave them something to do? Think I'm exaggerating this final piece of moral equivalence? Not so. During Fred Branfman's work with refugees in Laos he was puzzled by one fact in particular:

> All the refugees said the worst bombing occurred from the end of 1968 until the summer of 1969. They were bombed daily, every

village was leveled, thousands were murdered and maimed. But I knew from U.S. Embassy friends that there were no more than a few thousand North Vietnamese troops in Laos at the time, and that there was no military reason for the sudden and brutal increase in U.S. bombing. Why, then, had this aerial holocaust occurred? And then, to my everlasting horror, I found out. At Senator Fulbright's hearing, he asked Deputy Chief of Mission Monteagle Stearns why the bombing of northern Laos had so intensified after Lyndon Johnson's bombing halt over North Vietnam. Stearns answered simply: "Well, we had all those planes sitting around and couldn't just let them stay there with nothing to do." [154]

Such callous emotional detachment to killing is, in an individual, a clinical indicator of a psychopath. What then does this say of us collectively in the West that so deafening a silence endures surrounding our own atrocities, and instead we are endlessly drilled in the false religion of American and Western virtue?

"We destroyed a civilization," stated Alfred McCoy, author of *The Politics of Heroin in Southeast Asia*, "We wiped it off the face of the planet . . . we incinerated, we atomized human remains in this air war, and what happened in the end? We lost."[153] Following the defeat and ousting of the U.S. from Vietnam, the Pathet Lao took control of Laos. As the U.S. Air Force shut down its radio station, it broadcast a farewell message: "Good-bye and see you next war."[155]

CHAPTER SEVENTEEN
Pleasure Island

Stray chickens, ducks, geese, even cows tottered along a poorly surfaced single-lane strip of road just outside of Vientiane. This was the highway heading north. A lift with two uniformed on-duty policeman got me here, and after a good deal of walking past the last remnants of housing, interspersed with green fields, I was picked up by a white SUV splattered with dried and flaky, bright orange mud.

Behind the wheel sat Stefan, a rugged German engineer who had lived in the country for the last few years with his Laotian wife, from whom he was recently separated. Stefan was a personable chap with excellent English, which proved something of a treat. We chatted with gusto from the get-go, with Stefan telling me much about his experiences and personal take on the country.

"Laotians have different priorities to us," he said. "Unless it's for food or alcohol, they're difficult to motivate. When building a house I became frustrated by the quality and speed of work so got rid of the workers and went to another village to hire my own team. I was instructing and intended to work too, but whenever they saw me try to lift something they would come running over. Laotians have no concept of a boss, particularly a foreigner, or farang as they call us, actually working themselves."

Suddenly a cow strode across the highway, forcing Stefan to hit the brakes. Taking its time, the creature nonchalantly drifted across to the other side.

"Does anybody own those?" I asked.

"Ah, now there's an interesting thing. It used to be the law that if you hit a cow, you had to compensate the farmer. Then the law was changed to the farmer having to compensate the motorist for damage, and suddenly no one owned the cow. You could ask about all day and nobody would admit to it being theirs!"

Further up the road (much was dirt track) the landscape became amazingly lush and verdant, broken only by the occasional isolated village made up of wooden homes on stilts with thatched walls and roofing. At one little hamlet, nearly every dwelling which backed onto the road had dried fish hanging up for sale, swaying gently in the breeze from strings attached to overhead awnings.

"They eat that stuff with saltwater to make a soup," said Stefan. "It's not bad. Quite tame compared to some of the food you'll find here. I once tried something that I thought tasted strange, so asked what it was. And once I heard, I didn't try it again."

"What was it?"

"Buffalo shit."

"Shit?"

"Yes."

I'd heard of indigenous people from the forests of the far northern hemisphere eating moss from the stomach cavity of a reindeer, so asked if this was what he meant.

"No. It is from the intestine. Proper shit. Apparently with enough sauces and spices it is okay for them. But it's not okay for me. It's eaten as a dipping sauce with minced beef."

"Yuck."

"Yeah. When it comes to food in Laos, logic gets turned upside down. A lot of the bits of meat we consider the best cuts, Laotians just aren't interested in. I have a German friend here, a butcher, who makes traditional

German sausages, and whenever the locals slaughter a cow they call him up so he can come down and take the fillets and sirloins—all the bits that they don't want. They want the tits and skin and tail—it's much more interesting to them. Dog is popular. If you hit one on the road the locals will be out to get it for the pot. Saw some of my neighbors killing cobras to eat the other day, skewered them with sharpened bamboo."

Stefan explained that his butcher friend was doing a roaring trade supplying steaks to restaurants for foreigners, and had pretty much got the market sewn up; but when the Laos tax office came to visit him they concluded quite the opposite.

"Because the profession 'butcher' doesn't really exist in Laos, when my friend's Laotian wife filled out the forms registering the business, the officials insisted she put down 'meatball factory' instead. So when the tax inspectors came to visit him this was what they were expecting, not a tiny premises with only him working there. They saw him covered in blood and said sympathetically, 'We will give you a discount.' In Laos, if people see a farang working manually they assume he's on very hard times."

We weren't long on the road together before the aesthetic splendor of Laos' mountain scenery began to reveal itself. The sort of peaks you might see depicted on a Taoist scroll jutted near-vertically out of a fertile countryside thick with foliage, above which bright cumulus clouds drifted; sky-borne beacons illuminated by a pure and radiant light.

My destination today was a place called Vang Vieng. I had heard it mentioned several times before in relation to an activity known as "tubing:" renting a tractor inner-tube and floating down the Nam Song River on it, while taking in the backdrop of limestone mountains and stopping off at riverside bars along the way. It sounded fun, but as we approached the town—little more than a few streets of colonial bungalows, wooden homes and low-rise concrete buildings—Stefan ventured that it might not be my kind of place; maybe, he suggested, I should continue on through, keep going with him further north. He wasn't forthcoming as to why this might be. So on having another look at the mountain scenery, I decided to stick with my original plan. After all, it looked like paradise. Unfortunately, as I was to soon discover, it was a paradise thoroughly defiled.

My initial mistake of deciding to stop here was compounded by a second— taking Stefan's recommendation of staying at a particular guest house on the outskirts of town, where he dropped me and we said our goodbyes. For had I wandered into the center of Vang Vieng before paying for a night's accommodation, I would indeed have decided to pass on through the place. What I found almost defied comprehension, at least to my mind. Row upon row of cafés and bars lined the town, where curious-looking creatures sat, young Western "backpackers"—and I use the term very loosely—staring like zombies at television screens playing reruns of three television shows, and three only: *Friends*, *Family Guy* and *Southpark*, but mostly *Friends*. I don't mean to say that a couple of establishments were showing these, but absolutely loads of them, one after the other, and playing them back to back. I couldn't quite get my head around why this might be, nor why the clientèle seemed so content to spend their time in such a culturally rich part of Asia mesmerized by such crap, but then I encountered up close the typical clientèle that came here and everything became apparent.

Making my way past places selling opium tea, magic mushroom pizzas, and marijuana-laced milkshakes, I headed down a side street and happened upon a large group of around fifty Western guys and girls in their early twenties, letting it all hang out in bikinis and shorts, drunk and high out of their minds, stumbling around by an inner-tube hire center, having seemingly completed their afternoon's "tubing." One girl displayed a deep cut on her knee that was streaming blood down her leg. Scribbled in body paint and marker pen over nearly all of the tubers' exposed flesh were imbecilic messages like "I love cock" and "kiss me: I'm wasted." Several were latched onto each other at the mouth swapping spit, near humping in the street. A girl with "bum bandit" scribbled above her backside started to vomit. Doubling over, she retched across the sidewalk in great heaves, showering her bare feet with sick, while others howled at the top of their voices with inane approval.

God, I hated this place.

I stared on as a detached outsider looking in, as if having arrived at some odd alien universe. But why had they gravitated here, in the middle of rural Laos amid such scenic wonder? And what did the locals, who traditionally cover up their arms and legs, and even refrain from holding hands in public, make of it? I felt embarrassed to be a Westerner. Making my way around the town past endless tacky cafés showing the same television shows as before, an odd uncharacteristic feeling enveloped me. It took a while before

I identified it, but then it hit me—I felt lonely for the first time since setting off from Hobart. A firm believer in the adage, "You are never less alone than when alone," I nearly never feel lonely when I travel, least of all when by myself, but in Vang Vieng, I felt it.

To escape the morons and formulate a plan, I made my way down to the banks of the beautiful Nam Song River, where, after a bit of searching, I found a spot to myself. Sitting on a large smooth, warm rock, I looked out across the quivering interplay of light and dark on the water's surface to the distant bank lined with towering stands of gently swaying yellow-tinged bamboo, banana trees with their thick sheet-like leaves, and innumerable other foliage that was wholly unidentifiable to me. Several trees had an ever-so-slight hint of autumnal color to them, indicating the imminent demise of perpetual summertime. Beyond loomed a splendid ridge of limestone mountains, a glorious ancient spine that stretched from left to right across a mysterious Garden of Eden landscape. A beer bottle drifted past.

It seemed to sum up the irony of the place and my dilemma here. The scenery held tremendous appeal but the thought of tubing, at least with the sort of crowd I had seen in town, held none. I made up my mind. Come the morning I would hire an inner tube and get on the river while the majority of the town was still in bed, presumably sleeping off the night before. I would drift down with the current, wholly to check out the scenery and then get the hell out of here.

Back in the town I stopped off at an internet café to send a couple of emails, and in the process searched YouTube for "Tubing Vang Vieng." The videos took forever to load but what I watched confirmed my decision as the right one. In video after video, juvenile numbskulls gleefully celebrated their ignorance and desecration of the river and local culture with alcohol and drug-fueled lecherous maraudings at little shack-like bars along the banks, whose specialty were plastic sand-castle buckets filled with hard liquor. A bit more searching and I discovered photos of other puerile marker-pen and body paint messages—actually car spray paint—scrawled onto the bodies of the tubers: "I've got aids . . . wanna fuck?" "I make Joseph Fritzl's basement look like a weekend in Butlins," "It's not rape if you yell surprise," and "I raped Steven Hawking," which was accompanied by a corresponding message on a girl's back that read, "I also raped Steven Hawking."

Opinions online regarding Vang Vieng ranged from those similar to my own, to others who couldn't get enough of it and defended what had become of the place by saying it brought money into the local economy. Which is basically an argument for destroying any area of outstanding natural beauty so long as it makes a select few people a quick buck.

Once a quiet and tranquil farming village, the seeds of Vang Vieng's destruction were sown innocently enough in 1998 when a local organic farmer purchased a few inner tubes so that volunteers on his thirty acre mulberry and vegetable gardens could have a cheap and ecological way of seeing the Nam Song River and surrounding area. Its popularity grew, and soon tubing was offered independently of the original farmer, and rickety bamboo bars sprang up along the river from which a liter of "Lao-Lao" (a clear-colored, locally brewed whisky, with a potent alcohol content of 45 percent) could be purchased in plastic buckets for as little as a dollar. Today backpackers outnumber locals in Vang Vieng by as much as fifteen to one, killing the town and in the process many who visit it, with no small number of "tubers" dying on the river. Twenty-seven tubing deaths were recorded at Vang Vieng's tiny village hospital the year I visited. Since many of the dead are taken straight to Vientiane—and therefore not registered locally—the true figure of fatalities is much higher. Many just get too drunk or high and then simply drown, while others bust their heads open on rocks after leaping from rope swings or pulleys into shallow water, despite signs claiming a safe depth underneath. In one incident an unfortunate girl scraped all the skin off her face on the rocks. There are no lifeguards and the nearest properly equipped English-speaking hospital is back in Thailand at Bangkok. For those who break their bones, a long and painful ride along a bumpy pot-holed road awaits to make it back to the capital.

Come the morning I did as planned, and was the first and only person at the inner-tube hire center when it opened. The grumpy guy running the place tried his best to encourage me to come back around midday when the backpacker crowd would be setting off, but he was onto a no-hoper from the start. Being the only person, he charged me extra for the songthaew taxi to get to the launch area upstream, which was opposite a mighty wall of blue-gray rock that rose almost vertically just beyond the river's far bank. Despite its angle, much of it was thick with trees and shrubs, clinging tenaciously in cracks and ridges that would have afforded random patches of sediment to gather. The water certainly looked enticing. Shimmering a reflective silvery glass, it created a near-perfect replica of the rock and bankside trees in its surface. A chorus of birdsong greeted me as I made my way down a little path and stepped into the cool, gently flowing river. I laid down my inner-tube, sat back in the middle and let the current do the work.

In no time little bankside bars with rope-swings and ramshackle diving platforms began appearing. "Fuck it get a bucket!" announced a sign dangling out over the water from an establishment called FU BAR—a helpful translation written below: fucked up beyond all recognition. On seeing me, some of the bars' proprietors turned on thumping dance music that blasted out from giant speakers, shattering the blissful morning solitude in an instant; others attempted to cajole me into patronizing their establishment by pointing to signs for free buckets of Lao-Lao—given away in the knowledge that you'll almost certainly purchase something more palatable afterwards. I wasn't interested and just floated on by, and must have looked rather ludicrous to them, drifting past, all by myself, with no intention of partying.

I eventually came across locals trawling with hand-nets in the shallows, probably for shrimp. Three guys ventured further from the bank in the hunt for larger quarry. Two swam with a big billowing net, while the third remained on a little wooden rowing boat, striking the water with an ore, so as to herd whatever it was they were after into the net by way of shockwave. The two in the water both wore face-masks, and ducked down and swam about to check on the location of their prey. I was keen to see if they were successful, but no sooner had my curiosity been piqued and I had floated past. With the exception of the music, it actually turned out to be a delightful jaunt, but the character of the river would change in a few hours' time. Just before I reached Vang Vieng I passed several water buffalo browsing by the bank and cooling off and drinking in the river; it was a stunning sight but one that reminded me of a photo I had seen online the day before—of a drunk clambering, for his own amusement, on top of a semi submerged water buffalo. I was thankful to have made my way downstream alone.

Dropping off my inner-tube, I grabbed my bag and said "never again" to Vang Vieng. My overriding image of the place: pleasure island from Pinocchio—although to be fair, most of the people I saw in Vang Vieng weren't turned into donkeys from visiting the place, but rather arrived in such a state.

* * *

The further north I pushed, the more inspiring Laos' scenery became. Amazing foliage-covered mountains dominated the view, many dotted around their lower slopes with tall elegant reed-like grasses, their fluffy heads glowing luminous white in the midday sun. The road became far more twisted, several sections displaying perilous drops. Villages of wooden homes on stilts came and went, of an increasingly impoverished nature. Beneath the stilts great mounds of firewood and bundled-up dry thatching-grasses lay, the latter used as roofing material for about half the dwellings, while others sheltered under rickety and often rusty metal sheeting. Intricately woven mats comprised many of the walls, interlocking in vertical and horizontal planes, creating a checkered pattern of rectangles. Several villages possessed but a solitary water tap, evident by the groups that gathered around them bathing and washing clothing. Other villages had simple wells where residents lowered little flexible plastic buckets on ropes. Occasionally a pig would scurry about on the dusty space between the wooden houses and the road, more so chickens, ducks, dogs, and geese. Barefoot children joined them playing, others as young as five or six lugged great quantities of firewood, doing so in baskets that sat on their backs like rucksacks but which were slung around their foreheads from straps attached to the basket's rim. It looked difficult and grueling work. One little girl of no more than four carried her baby sibling in a sling.

I rode in an SUV with a middle-aged Laotian couple. They didn't speak much English and had introduced themselves with an odd sense of formality: "Mr. and Mrs. Sourisak." Mr. Sourisak was a military man of some sort, manifest by the I.D. dangling from the rear view mirror. Both he and Mrs. Sourisak were on their way to a wedding party in Luang Prabang, a UNESCO World Heritage Site and my ultimate destination of the day.

Just as it was getting dark we pulled up at a little row of small, self-contained, apartments with huge satellite dishes out the front. Mr. and Mrs. Sourisak were staying here, and suggested I rent one for the night too. I did, paying 80,000 Laotian Kip, about ten USD. No sooner had I dropped my pack inside the room and my new neighbors were escorting me back into the car.

"Wedding party," stated Mr. Sourisak with a smile.

We arrived at a little house in a residential area of the town and walked through to its backyard, where several tables had been pushed together into a row and covered with wipe-down plastic cloths. Spread out across the tables were multiple lighted candles. Already sitting here, seemingly waiting for our arrival, were about twenty guests. Greetings flowed back and forth and I was introduced around. Since no one really spoke any English, I just smiled and nodded "hello." Food arrived soon after. Salad was first out and consisted of lettuce, spring onions, chopped mint, and succulent bamboo shoots. Next came steaming bowls of hot soup with noodles wrapped up into little balls, followed by strips of unknown chewy meat.

I ate heartily and followed my hosts' lead, taking a strip of meat and dipping it into a bowl of sauce on the table. But something was off about this sauce. No sooner had taste bud and sauce connected, and my body instinctively wanted to reject it. I smelled some. It was vile. Could this be the buffalo shit dip Stefan had told me about? Pointing to the sauce I tried to educe from the other guests what it was made from. Those nearby began to laugh. Then pointed to their stomachs. It wasn't proof positive, but it was a strong indication and more than enough to stop me dunking any more meat into it. Luckily the taste was soon wiped away with lots of beer and Lao-Lao whisky, used for multiple celebratory toasts.

With no one proficient enough in English to converse with me, the background chatter sent me into something of a trance, and after several "whiskeys" my thoughts turned to bed. But the night was far from over. Finishing up at the house, we all headed in a big convoy to a packed and vibrant restaurant nearby where a lively band played music of a style I either couldn't identify or immediately forgot, and more weird and wonderful foods were produced. Much unidentified meat of the ultra-chewy variety came forth, as did several servings of duck's feet, with a whole plate given to me. Let me repeat that: a whole plate. If you can form a rough impression of sticking the chewy, flappy little foot of a duck in your mouth, and gnawing on it, then, really, you're already there in understanding how rank an experience it was.

Come the morning, I was invited to the wedding. In all likelihood I had been asked the night before, but with the noise of the restaurant and Mr. and Mrs. Sourisak's limited English, if I had, then the invitation had gone unnoticed.

"Telephone, five," said Mr. Sourisak, pointing to his watch as he dropped me on the high street of Luang Prabang's historic center, so that I could do some sightseeing before the afternoon's wedding rendezvous.

My first impressions of Luang Prabang and its surrounding landscape were of the highest order. Sitting regally on a lofty inland peninsula carved by the mighty Mekong River and its sister tributaries, Luang Prabang looked out beyond these surging watercourses to a world of lushly forested limestone mountains, which enclose the town, to varying degrees, from all sides. The historic center was a gleaming jewel, a fusion of colors, exotic scents and architectural styles. Pastel-shaded colonial buildings of the French provincial style sat alongside Buddhist temples of shimmering golds, blinding whites, and fiery reds. Shaven-headed monks strode around with their young apprentices in tow, cloaked in orange robes, while tourists ambled about calmly. Everything was bathed in the cleanest radiant light, to the point where the town itself seemed to glow. Last night's accommodation had been nice, but it was too far out of town to be practical, especially when the time came to get on the move again, so I booked into a little lodging house out the back of a travel agency on the high street. For 50,000 Laotian Kip (about six dollars) I got a simple room with nothing in it but a bed. Located down the hallway was a shared shower-room and toilet.

I spent most of the day visiting temples and monasteries, drinking fresh fruit juice and coffee at little riverside cafés overlooking the Mekong, and generally recharging my batteries while soaking in the beauty of the place. It was quite intoxicating, with something new to feast my eyes upon around every corner. After climbing a centrally located forested peak with a spectacular view across the region, I strolled along a road high above the river where I happened upon a street stall with an utterly bewildering collection of glass jars. Inside, preserved for posterity in some sort of pickling liquid, was the most bizarre collection of snakes, lizards, centipedes, worms, and other creepy crawlies, all packed in together, probably in the order of fifty per jar. Was this the Laos equivalent of some nice pickled onions or peppers? I hadn't a clue, but it made for an interesting photo.

I continued along the Mekong, arriving at a section where a smaller river, the Nam Khan, met the main colossal body of water, flowing into it from a gaping cleft in the earth that formed one side of the peninsula's boundary walls. Upstream was a little run of rapids, where a couple of Westerners swam, purposefully drifting feet first through the flow, then getting out onto the sandy bank and walking back to do it again. It looked fun, and the perfect way to cool off in the roasting heat. I made my way down a little path to the beachy bank, where I took off my T-shirt, shoes, and socks ready for the plunge. Just as I was about to, the two river surfers strolled past, so I struck up a conversation.

They were Bill and Ben, brothers from the United States, traveling with their sister who was currently elsewhere in town. Bill in particular had done lots of traveling and ran a website—*mynameisbill.com*—detailing his adventures around the world, many chronicled via video blog, something that landed him a job presenting travel shows for *National Geographic Channel*, after an executive there stumbled upon his work. (I would just like to state for the record here, that should an executive at *National Geographic* similarly stumble upon my work, then the answer is a resounding "yes," I'd love to present a travel show).[156]

"So you're one of those rare internet success stories everybody reads about?" I said.

"In the flesh," replied Bill with a smile.

We chatted for a while about the "travel profession," and how people seemed to be doing more and more gimmicky trips to get noticed.

"I heard a group of Canadians set off with a film crew and a plan to visit every single country in the world in one year—" said Bill.

"What? In a year?" I interjected. "Surely getting visas for every country would take the best part of that."

"Yeah, that's what I said!" exclaimed Bill with hearty agreement. "And you wouldn't get to see anything either. Apparently they got to Central America, Guatemala, I think, and there was a mutiny among the crew and they all quit. Heard of another group who were traveling around the world in tuxedos."

"Why?"

Bill laughed. "No idea!"

We all hung out for a while and after much cooling off in the water and shooting the rapids several times, strolled back into town together, where the brothers were due to meet their sister for a meal. I wished them well and got onto contacting Mr. Sourisak. Stopping off at my lodgings, I inquired with the travel agency attached to the front of it if they knew the location of a public phone. The woman behind the desk simply picked up the one in front of her and handed it to me. After a quick "hello" to Mr. Sourisak, I marshaled the travel agent to converse with him. A brief chat and she hung up the phone.

"He will meet you here in fifteen minutes," she said.

I sat outside on a little swing chair, merrily watching the world go by, when, after about ten minutes, the woman came out to speak to me.

"Your friend call back. He has to pick up boss so can't come to see you now."

What? This made no sense, so after a quick request to use her phone I called him back.

"I meet minister from airport," he said, then promptly hung up.

And that was that. There'd be no wedding for me tonight. I was disappointed and confused, but decided to make the most of things. For the remainder of the afternoon I explored a beautiful golden-fronted temple, and when darkness arrived wandered about a vibrant night market that stretched along much of the high street, selling everything from textiles to bamboo lamps, from fresh fruit to silverware. It was so busy that it was difficult to walk through, but served as the perfect way to while away my time.

When I finally turned in for the night, it was with a sense of excitement for tomorrow.

China was calling my name.

CHAPTER EIGHTEEN
Touched for the Very First Time

As a much valued reader, would you feel short-changed if I summed up the next six days in a few paragraphs? I sincerely hope not, because that's what I'm about to do. You see, China is so damn big a country, and requires so many long highway rides to get from one point of interest to another, often in exactly the same type of vehicle, and almost always with people you cannot communicate with past a few basic gestures, that after a while, in fact after a very short while, you become completely and utterly dazed by the hitchhiking process; and I'm sure more so in the reading of such a venture.

I made it to China after a full day's hitching through majestic Laotian scenery and arrived at an ultra-modern Chinese customs building nestled in a little forested valley, just beyond the Laotian town of Boten. From here the nature of my journey changed dramatically. For the next six days my life became the road. I covered roughly 1,300 miles along modern highways and experienced much of what it is to be a hitchhiker in the People's Republic.

Soon the landscape shifted dramatically, no longer teetering on the brink of fall, but fully flushed in her brightest emblems. Forests of the deepest reds and yellows embraced the surrounding hills, setting the world ablaze with fiery color. I had reached a new climatic zone. Further north red-tinged mountains drifted in and out of frame, followed by pine forests and deep rain-soaked gorges, where hydrant-like waterfalls tumbled earthwards over huge slick rocks. Peasant farmers tilled away on giant swathes of agricultural land or worked beneath vast tunnels of plastic sheeting. Caramel-colored rivers lined with poplars meandered past, where little wooden rafts were pulled by hand from one bank to the other with ropes. Pagodas and temples rose up near the roadside, and eventually snow and ice appeared.

Having read that hitchhiking was not culturally understood in China, I had come prepared: armed with a note translated into Mandarin—acquired through my brother, a long time resident of China. The note introduced me, described the concept of my trip, and told the driver where I was heading (this section had a blank space for me to fill in with copied Chinese characters as appropriate). It also said that I didn't want to be taken to a train or bus station, and of course that I couldn't pay for the ride.

It worked beautifully, and, contrary to what I had read, I encountered no driver who on stopping for me failed to grasp that I wanted a ride. On several occasions I saw locals waiting patiently by the highway, holding signs stating desired destinations. Although probably expecting to pay for their rides, it showed that the concept of picking up strangers was not an alien one. How hard they found it, I don't know, but for a Westerner, hitchhiking in China is easy, very easy. The novelty value of a white face no doubt plays a part, as on three occasions I arrived at spots near sign-holding locals, but it was always me who got the first ride out of there. And the rides tend to be in nice cars; lots of comfy SUVs, driven by affluent thirty-somethings, with the better-off seeming more inclined to pick you up than the poor—again, if you're a Westerner. However, no matter who gives you a lift, just about everyone will want to drop you at a bus or train station, something you have to constantly resist and work your damnedest to avoid. Nearly every driver will nonchalantly throw trash out the window, and most will offer cigarettes your way. Over the course of a day you will almost certainly encounter one driver who insists on stopping to share a large multi-dish meal with you, which, try as you might, you will not be allowed to chip in for. Refusal is rude, and to pay is rude, so you may as well just accept it. Such generosity means that if you're okay with a single meal a day, then as a hitchhiker in China your only expense becomes accommodation. Sourcing cheap accommodation is an altogether different challenge, not for a lack of places to stay, but for lack of proprietors willing to let a Westerner book in—something I discovered on my second night in the country.

After a full day on the road I arrived, just after dark, in an odd little town, whose name I never discovered, set a couple of miles off the highway. I trudged my way through several long and darkened back-streets, where random piles of garbage burned and stray dogs roamed, creating eerie silhouettes against the fire's dancing orange flames. My arrival at a budget hotel caused quite a stir, with a little boy in the lobby literally jumping and letting out a high-pitched yelp at the strange sight of me. A guy in his early teens at reception was more composed and even spoke a tiny bit of English, unlike his older colleague who looked like his brother. Between them they booked me in—for now at least.

The room faithfully matched my expectations—or lack thereof. In a low resolution brochure photograph it might have actually looked rather nice, but on closer inspection it was falling apart. A plug socket hung off the wall exposing suspect wiring inside; its ceiling light shone with a remarkably dim and dirty-tinged yellow light, and the carpet was stained beyond the power of any known detergent. A lamp by the bedside should have been in a dumpster, and the bed itself was ready to join it, with nearly every spring in its bumpy mattress long since broken. The bathroom continued the cesspit theme and was swaddled in a damp and musty odour. Here were several striking features, including a sharp-to-the-touch crack running down a mildew-grimy mirror, and an interesting little complimentary by the sink—a plastic cup sporting a fresh red imprint of lipstick. But the real challenge was the door, which was self-jamming when closed, to the extent that it required a powerful shoulder barge or a tug of war just to get in and out. Not that I was particularly bothered by any of this, for the bedroom had a functioning kettle. I could have a cup of tea. And promptly did.

I headed out soon after in search of an internet café, entering a dark and noisy establishment lined with rows of computers in little booths. It was clearly the haunt of guys in their mid to late teens who packed it playing shoot-em-up video games. Officially I was not allowed to hire a computer without a government I.D. card, but after a bit of coercing I managed to persuade a local to briefly lend me his. With email open, I sent Emily, who was now back in London, a quick message, telling her that I was in China, and passing on the telephone number of my hotel on the off chance she could give me a call.

Back at the hotel, I tried to convey to the older non-English-speaking brother at reception, who was now by himself, that I might be receiving a telephone call from an English speaker, and therefore to put it through to my room. Twenty minutes later, when lying in bed writing up my diary, there was a knock at the door. Standing there was a rather worn-looking middle-aged woman in high heels, a low-cut top and short skirt; classic mutton dressed as lamb. She handed me a card announcing herself as a "masseuse," which listed the services she offered, including "Whale body massage." She didn't look like a big girl, so I assumed she got a friend in for that one. I kept the card but sent her packing. Moments later there was another knock at the door. She was back, this time with the reception guy who looked most confused. With his thumb and pinky finger outstretched he mimed calling someone on the telephone, then pointed inquisitively at the girl. I shook my head with a smile. He shooed her off down the corridor, throwing her a look of indignation as if for having the temerity to respond to his call in the first place. With a gracious nod, he disappeared.

At 11 p.m., when happily tucked up in bed, things took a turn for the worse. I received a knock on the door. Standing there was the English-speaking guy from reception, this time accompanied by a much older man.

"You must come police station," said the young guy.

I tried to protest but the older guy was steadfast.

After throwing on some clothes, we marched on down there. On the way the young guy conveyed two bits of information. "Father," he said, pointing at the older man; and "no problem," which he repeated several times in an indiscriminate generic kind of way, as if commenting on the situation at large.

Having been to China before, I can attest that it is a wonderful and varied destination to visit, but that's not to say every cultural oddity of my previous trips left me flushed with affection for the place. One particular Chinese habit that I am less than fond of was about to raise its ugly head on the way to the police station. With an almighty hacking cough, the father heaved some unpleasant green muck off his lungs and unceremoniously spat it onto the floor. It was a sound and sight I would get to see plenty more of in the coming days.

We reached a little police station off the main street filled to the brim with cops, none of whom spoke any English. Sitting behind a counter, lounging around looking decidedly bored, were about ten cops. My arrival perked them up, and a rapid-fire conversation commenced between them and the father and son. All of a sudden, at what seemed an arbitrary moment, the police demanded my passport.

"You can't stay in cheaper hotel. Foreigner must stay in other hotel," said the young guy.

"Which hotel?"

"You must stay at Red Apple hotel instead."

The Red Apple was across the road from their place and seriously expensive.

"Why?" I asked.

"For your safety."

This rule was a new one on me. During my previous trips to China I had stayed with my brother, so had no need to source cheap accommodation. On the couple of occasions I had stayed in hotels, it had either been with him or Emily. Since the former was a namby-pamby corporate type, he had always booked something upmarket, and since the latter was a delicate little flower, her sensibilities had deserved, and indeed demanded, better than the proviso for my current trip permitted. The night before I had inadvertently avoided this problem by staying at a nicer centrally located chain hotel in the city of Kunming.

I wanted to explain that I was happy where I was, that this was bureaucratic nonsense, and that the guy's father should have kept quiet once I'd booked in. Why he didn't just let me sleep out the night unnoticed in my room, I don't know. But in the interest of being understood, I kept it short.

"I can't afford to stay at the Red Apple."

He passed on the message. More debate followed before an interesting, and wholly unexpected, solution was posed.

"They will make for same price."

Mmm. I wasn't about to argue with a much nicer hotel for the price of a dirt cheap one. I confirmed that, yes, this arrangement would suffice. Off we marched up to the Red Apple with several cops in tow. Stepping inside its plush marble-floored interior, the main cop handed my passport to the girl behind reception and began to explain the situation to her. She listened respectfully and intently and then, when the cop was good and finished, let rip at him, shouting as if scolding a little schoolboy. All the while she yelled at him her frustration got worked out on my passport, which she bent back and forth against its spine with increasing angst. She looked about to tear the thing in two.

I nudged the young guy from the first hotel.

"Passport very important," I said, shaking my head in dismay while pointing at her antics.

He went over and reprimanded her, snatching the passport from her hands. I breathed a sigh of relief and expected him to hand it back but instead he proceeded to demonstrate exactly what she shouldn't do, now bending it back and forth himself. The situation was turning into a farce. By now it was midnight and all I wanted was bed, no matter where it was, but the woman, it seemed, wasn't about to get on board with the cops' program any time soon. More debate followed and then, suddenly, out of the blue, it seemed an agreement had been reached between all parties.

"You can return," said the young guy.

And so we did. Minutes later, when back in the same bed I had been kicked out of over an hour before, there was another knock on the door. I got up and yanked it open. Standing there was the young guy holding a note. He handed it to me sheepishly. It read:

> Sorry, only for your safety to the police station. The result foreigners can only stay at the Red Apple. Because this is a designated place to stay. Delay your time really sorry. I hope you can understand. Sweet dreams.

I thanked him for his help and finally crashed out.

* * *

Temperatures plummeted the further north I pushed, but also fluctuated wildly throughout the day with altitude until, by mid-afternoon of the sixth day, when on my way to the town of Tianshui, I encountered a small frozen waterfall on a minor back-road whose base created a thick glistening sheet of ice across the asphalt.

Further on, huge frozen desert hills riddled with caves and cloaked in dusty air gave way to rows of fruit and nut trees, then to vast tiered mountainsides. These were simply mind boggling. I'd seen tiered rice paddies elsewhere in Asia, but here the scale defied belief. They covered every hill and mountainside for mile after mile, leaving not a patch of ground unusable, transforming once unproductive highlands into vast terraced strips of workable fields. It was a truly monumental feat, so typical of the Chinese propensity for man-made scenic drama on a grand scale. And I was on my way to see their most renowned example: The Great Wall of China. I wanted to reach its terminal western section where a fortress was constructed during the Ming dynasty at a spot which signified the end of ancestral China.

Located just beyond the outer edge of the city of Jiayuguan, on the fringes of the desert, was the Great Wall frontier post, "The First Pass Under Heaven." It wasn't quite what I expected. In fact, first impressions left me decidedly underwhelmed. Having, on a previous trip, visited an eastern section of the Great Wall a few hours outside the Chinese capital, Beijing, I had conjured up similar dramatic images of a giant never-ending serpent of stone, rising and falling at insane angles over craggy mountains that stretched to the horizon as if encircling the entire globe. Not quite so at Jiayuguan. Here it was all a bit mediocre. The landscape of the immediate vicinity was flat, rusty-colored desert scrub, and the wall practically non-existent beyond the fortress. Little more than a few vague battered clumps dotted the landscape, broken remnants that boasted nothing of the wall's distant eastern glory or the epic two thousand mile journey it traverses to the shores of the Pacific. But if the wall was a disappointment then the fortress was an unexpected treat. Rising from the bare surroundings was an imposing barricade of pale vertical brick, incised along its length with battlements, radiating the sun to a degree that seemed wholly beyond the capacity of this morning's bleak exposure. Perched on top of it were several pagoda towers, faded in color, sterilized after seven hundred years of sand blasting from the desert.

The wall pre-dated the towers by almost a thousand years, and once signified the end of China. Beyond lay the wild hinterland, home to nomadic people: Mongols, Huns, Manchus. Here these supposed barbarians roamed free—hairy, milk-drinking undesirables that the wall was constructed to keep out. It was the ultimate "them and us" mentality, an ancient gated community of ludicrous proportion, drawing a physical and mental line between civilization and barbarism.

I made my way through a dark vaulted tunnel entranceway into an empty courtyard, silent but for the fluttering of red and yellow flags. On all sides loomed the clean lines of the fortress walls, thick barricades of brick that enclosed me within a neat womb of order, distinct from the wild beyond their reach. In an adjoining courtyard were a handful of Chinese tourists, all making their way down from the parapets above on a wide ramp that would once have seen rampaging cavalry clambering up it in a frantic effort to rain down fury on invaders below. At the summit sat one of the pagoda towers, its three layers of precise classical roofing rising up at the corners in embellished peaks, decorated here with the heads of miniature dragons. Fragile-looking lattice window paneling stretched along its two upper tiers, contrasting sharply with the thick and squat brick walling at its base.

Brick was the constant theme throughout the fortress, recalled in a nearby English placard:

> It is said that, during the construction of Jiayuguan, a highly skilled craftsman named Yi Kaizhen, proposed an accurate material-consumption scheme upon his careful investigations, calculations and designs. When the Pass was completely finished, all the building materials were just used up, with only one brick left. To commemorate this skilful craftsman, people kept the brick at the back eave of Huiji Tower, which stands in the West trap court.

To the west was the place China cast away its undesirables: the Gate of Sorrows, where countless numbers were exiled beyond the country, expelled into a life of uncertainty outside. Forlorn departing messages were scratched along the tunnel walls. As recently as the late Qing dynasty in the early twentieth century, common prisoners were banished here, thrown out with their entire families with no hope of ever coming back, their foreheads bearing the marks of the eternally ostracized, painfully tattooed with permanent black characters. I tried my best to soak in the place and appreciate its history, but in truth I was disappointed. I'd pushed hard over the last few days, and had done so often with the motivation of reaching The Great Wall. Even with the Jiayuguan fortress, it was nothing like the splendor to the east.

I got back on the road, this time with a new motivation. From here until the distant shores of the Mediterranean, I would be following a branch of the fabled network of ancient Silk Road trading routes that spanned the great cultural and geographic divide between the continents of Asia and Europe—the world's first superhighway along which technology, religion, armies, commerce, and ideas once flowed, threading their way across one of the greatest, most inhospitable land routes on earth, an environment so hostile that for millennia it served as a cultural firewall, allowing East and West to develop distinct characters totally independent of each other.

I was about to cast myself beyond the shadow of the Gate of Sorrows.

* * *

Three rides from Jiayuguan and by late afternoon I stood on a desolate expanse of road by a turning for the city of Yumen. Beyond stretched a barren landscape swathed in a low-lying opaque sky, tarnished by a coffee-colored diffusion of dust. It was bitterly cold, with a vicious chilling wind that tore straight through the thin fleece and sweater I had on. I would need to buy more clothing, not for comfort's sake, but survival's. I hadn't packed any winter gear when setting off as it would have been a cumbersome dead-weight through the Australian outback and the tropics, but those environments seemed a world away now. With practically no vehicles on the road out here, and only about an hour of light left, I was tempted to call it a day, to head into Yumen and find a room where I could warm up. But after a magnificently long ride the day before I was slightly more inclined to push my luck, if only for a little longer. Thirty minutes passed and on the distant horizon appeared a lone white SUV, its form, like my anticipation, growing steadily on approach. It began to slow, but sadly not for me, making its way instead onto the access road for Yumen, just before my position. I tried to remain upbeat, but as I cast my attention back towards the expanse of cold and empty asphalt, I couldn't help but let out a deep sigh. Suddenly, the sound of shouting stole me from my bout of self-absorption. At the bottom of the access road were two guys of about my age standing by the SUV, hollering my way, gesturing for me to join them.

My resolve faltered; Yumen it would have to be. It wasn't a long drive to reach Yumen, but in that short time I got the distinct impression that giving me a ride had been more for the guys' amusement than a desire to help. Neither spoke any English and both kept talking at me and laughing at my inability to respond, as if this, along with me simply being in their car, was the funniest thing imaginable. It was good to have a lift but since the laughter was *at*, rather than *with* me, I was keen for it to come to an end.

Soon I was riding into an ugly town, with little to distinguish it from the multiple other Chinese towns I had passed through on the way here. Clasping my hands together, I made a sleeping gesture to indicate a hotel. We stopped at a restaurant instead. I knew the routine. If they were eating, then they would want me to join them. I'd already had a meal today—my average daily consumption for a long time now—and considered declining, but in the end I decided to accept so I could warm up.

It was an interesting-looking establishment, containing multiple fish tanks to make sure that the "catch of the day" was seriously fresh, wriggling only moments before hitting the table. I hoped popularity was an indication of quality, as the place was heaving. Soon after sitting down, three of the guys' friends arrived, two men and a woman. They looked at me aghast, and the guys at them with an amused, self-satisfied expression of "look what we've found." Laughter followed, most of it aimed at me, which only came to a close when the food arrived.

First out was a communal fish stew in a large elegant porcelain bowl that contained the entire creature from head to tail. This was followed by a procession of plates containing everything from battered pork in a sweet and sticky bright-red sauce, to unknown meat served with succulent green vegetables. By now, I was fully used to sitting at a table with others talking a language I didn't know. I would nod and smile occasionally, but mainly just got stuck into the food, which, it's got to be said, was exceptional today. At one stage I was presented with a spoon—amid more laughter—but persevered with chopsticks and was pleasantly surprised at my increasing competence with these, which grew daily.

If my assumption that I was little more than an object of amusement had at all been in doubt, then it was confirmed when some beers arrived.

A rather obvious conspiracy was hatched among the group, who proceeded to take it in turns to toast me, doing so with increasing frequency between mouthfuls of food. For etiquette to be observed I had to drink with the one toasting me, but the others could sit it out until they were leading the toast. It wasn't like we were knocking back spirits so I plodded on, but after several bottles I decided to turn the tables. I sussed out the weakest link and proceeded to toast him again and again and again, eventually winning by way of submission.

On culmination of the meal and drinking contest, the driver of the SUV turned to me and began miming singing into a microphone, complete with contrived "la la la" sounds. More laughter followed and it soon became clear that he wanted me to tag along with them to a karaoke bar. If it hadn't been for several beers I would have probably bailed out, but instead thought, "Oh, what the hell." I agreed, but insisted on going there by way of a hotel to dump my backpack. A quick stop at a fair priced place nearby and on we went.

Just walking the short distance from the SUV to the bar was painfully cold. By now it was dark, and the light's departure had seen the temperature dive much further. Inside the entrance to the bar hung a thick drape of fabric, mitigating loss of heat whenever anyone opened the door. Pushing through, we entered into a dark hallway that led up a flight of stairs lined with colored lights. At the top was another drape, this time made of plastic cut into multiple strips, beyond which lay a small reception. Another red corridor gave the place a dodgy strip-joint or brothel atmosphere. We headed first to our left and into one of multiple private rooms decked out with the necessary apparatus: comfy seats, chunky microphone, big screen television, and a remote controller to select the songs.

Everyone wanted me to go first, but for now I managed to squirm my way out of it and sat back nursing a beer while the others took turns singing with gusto to Chinese pop. After a while we piled down the corridor in the opposite direction to a large communal room with a stage and a huge screen. We had the whole place to ourselves and this time refusal was not an option. My problem was there were only four songs in English: Celine Dion's *My Heart Will Go On*; Michael Jackson's *Thriller*; and two Madonna tracks, *Like a Virgin* and *Bad Girl*.

With a reluctant sigh, I got up on the stage and let them take their pick. First up was *Like a Virgin*. I can't really say my heart was in it, but I plowed on regardless, doing my best to vocally lament on being "touched for the very first time." They loved it, and immediately selected another, this time Celine. As I stood up there "singing"—although it could hardly have been described as such—and looked down on the audience below, my world took a surreal twist. I knew they couldn't understand a word I was saying, nor me them, so halfway through the song I decided, for my own amusement, to mix things up a bit. It was probably a symptom of spending too many long hard days on the road far from English speaking company, but I stopped singing and commenced a stand up comedy routine with the microphone instead, doing my best to remember jokes from an old Bernard Manning video I used to own, while effecting his guttural working-class northern English accent.

"This bloke goes into a Chinese restaurant and says, 'Hey, you!' and the guy working there replies, 'Err, how you know my name?'"

Blank expressions from the crowd. I launched into another.

"Burglar breaks into a house and he looks about him and thinks, 'I'll have that television, I'll have that nice antique clock over there,' and a voice behind him says, 'I can see you, and Jesus can see you.' He spins around and it's just a parrot on a perch. 'Fucking hell,' says the burglar, 'was that you?' And the parrot says, 'Yeah.' 'You scared me half to death you did,' says the burglar, 'what's your name?' 'Archibald,' replies the parrot. 'Archibald!' laughs the burglar, 'That's a funny fucking name for a parrot.' And the parrot says, 'Not as funny as that pitbull over there called Jesus.'"

I was rapidly running out of material so finished up with my favorite.

"Jesus is walking through Nazareth and he sees this great big crowd of people stoning this prostitute to death. He yells out, 'Oi, you lot, fucking pack that in! Let whoever is without sin cast the first stone.' And this great big rock comes flying over his head and hits the prostitute smack in the mouth. He turns around and says, 'Sometimes mother, you piss me off!'"

It was all in the delivery.

I signed off.

"You've been a wonderful audience. My name's Jamie Maslin. Goodnight. And God bless."

I promptly handed the microphone back, turned on my heels, and without so much as a glance backward, headed off to my hotel.

CHAPTER NINETEEN
Hypothermic Hiatus

In a sense, you could say I would be leaving China today, not officially, there was a long way yet before that, but culturally. If all went well I would make it to the country's Xinjiang province, a giant final-frontier wild-west, made up of sprawling deserts, vast arid plains and some of the world's highest mountains, bordered by eight countries: Mongolia, Russia, India, Pakistan, Afghanistan, Kyrgyzstan, Kazakhstan, and Tajikistan. Often described historically as "Chinese Turkestan," Xinjiang, or Xinjiang Uyghur Autonomous Region as it is officially known, has far more in common with the former Soviet Central Asian republics (Uzbekistan, Turkmenistan, Kyrgyzstan, Kazakhstan, and Tajikistan) than to China, sharing much of the "stans" culture, history and language, which belong to a larger closely related family.

Central Asia has seen a sweep of history as big, daunting, and complex as anywhere, covering thousands of years, punctuated by successive waves of conquest and migration, the rise and fall of mighty empires—including the Macedonian Empire of Alexander the Great, and the Mongol Empire of Genghis Khan—and dynamic cultural exchange brought about by the famous Silk Road trading routes that traverse its territory, linking the civilizations of East and West. It is a region of staggering diversity. The huge wider Turkestan region outside of Xinjiang was artificially splintered in the 1920s when the U.S.S.R. created the separate "stans." Before then the area's general populace had little concrete notion of borders or nation states, with people identifying themselves along religious, tribal, linguistic, occupational and social lines.

As for Xinjiang, it was declared an autonomous region of China in 1955. At the time its population was more than ninety percent non-ethnic Han Chinese, with the vast majority being Uyghurs, who speak a different language (similar to Uzbek), write in a different script (slightly modified Arabic) and practice a different religion (Islam). Today around fifty percent of Xinjiang's inhabitants are Han Chinese, forty-two percent Uyghurs, six percent Kazaks and one percent Kyrgyz, along with several minority ethnicities. Such a huge swing in the area's racial demographic is no mere accident, but the intentional result of "sinicisation," that is, the encouragement by Chinese authorities of mass immigration into the region by Han Chinese settlers, with the intention of diluting Uyghur nationalism. Despite the "autonomous" in its official name, Xinjiang is very much under the control of Beijing, with any political dissent or separatist desires being met, as in neighboring Tibet to the south, with an iron fist. In Chinese characters, the "jiang" in Xinjiang comprises the symbols for bow, field, land, and border, an appropriate amalgamation for this untamed frontier and historic mixing bowl of nomad and settler. Covering sixteen percent of the country's land surface, and an area slightly larger than Western Europe or Alaska, Xinjiang is by far the biggest of China's provinces, but is, nevertheless, largely empty, having only one major city, Urumqi, and a total population of just thirteen million. With Urumqi being the farthest city in the world from the ocean, and the province never nearer than two thousand miles from any coast, it is besieged by fearsome weather conditions, something it looked likely I would encounter today.

Come dawn I stepped out from the warmth of the hotel's lobby into a brutal all-encompassing freezer. I had on every item of clothing in my possession, whether clean or not, multiple layers of socks, underwear and T-shirts, all worn in a futile attempt to create enough dead-air space to keep the cold at bay. Despite my lack of winter attire, I decided to push on into the horrendous conditions, striding off along the road past a lone donkey cart. I could have stuck around in Yumen and tried to find somewhere local to buy winter clothing, but not being a particularly big place, it seemed unlikely to have the sort of modern lightweight gear that I was after; thick black gowns and fur-lined hats, perhaps, but I needed something portable that would fit in my pack and see me through the coming wilds of Kyrgyzstan and Kazakhstan. If I could just hold on until the next big city, Urumqi (the capital of Xinjiang), then I was sure I could find something appropriate.

It was an error of judgement that I would bitterly regret.

There is something about hitting the road at first light that pays dividends when hitching. People seem far more inclined to pick you up at this hour rather than later on, perhaps before the rigours of work have worn them down and clouded the optimistic and generous outlook that seems to spring naturally from the inception of a new day. So this morning, two easily sought rides arrived in quick succession, taking me past charmless gray architecture and rows of bare leafless poplar trees, ridged in the cold, to the main road north.

Ahead stretched cold and barren nothing. I decided to hike for thirty minutes down the road and then to turn around and head back again, just to get my blood circulating. After twenty minutes of trekking along a route that would once have seen caravans of camel trains a thousand-strong, a car stopped.

Four guys sat inside: two in their middle years, one elderly, and a driver in his twenties. I squeezed in the back. It was delightfully warm, and soon my core temperature was smiling again. The piece of paper that I gave the driver had the destination *Guazhou* on it, but it turned out to be a far better ride than that—all the way to Hami, about 330 miles away through the desolate no man's land of a frozen desert and on into Xinjiang itself. The low-lying cloud and steamed up windows prevented much in the way of a view for a lot of the journey, but every now and then a distant snowy mountain or sprawling wind farm on a barren plain revealed itself.

We said goodbye at the turning for Hami, where a convoy of eight identical mining dump trucks was parked by the side of the main road. They looked fresh off the production line, but it seemed that one of them had some sort of mechanical problem. Around the vehicle were gathered the trucks' collective drivers, one of whom lay on the floor poking a flaming piece of wood underneath the engine section. What this was for, I had no idea, but while they were stationary I took my opportunity. Ambling over, I presented a likely-looking driver, a guy about my age, with one of my notes. He read it and smiled, then went back to staring at the truck. I wasn't sure what this meant, but ten minutes later when the problem had seemingly been fixed, he waved me over. His truck had been the one receiving maintenance. I climbed into the cab, still covered in fresh showroom plastic, and we were on our way.

I managed to confirm that he and the other truckers were going all the way to Urumqi, making my decision to push on without acquiring winter clothing in Yumen seem a sound one. Or so I thought. Soon the weather took a turn for the worse. The little sun there was disappeared behind a layer of dark gray cloud with violent howling gusts lashing at the truck, churning the air into a fury of murky dust. We passed another bank of wind turbines, spinning in a frenzy amid a bleak and angry landscape of snowy rock and gravel. It was a comforting thought to be safely cocooned inside the heater-induced false micro-climate of the cab, looking out as a mere spectator on the unfolding drama of the landscape, not a ravaged participant within it. In total, the ride to Urumqi would encompass over 350 miles, making for a long drive and late arrival, and after several hours on the road nighttime fell. Darkness lay all around, broken only by a lone passenger train drifting into the black expanse on a distant track, its windows glowing a warm, cozy-looking yellow. I watched enviously as it overtook us, disappearing into the void ahead. The thought of simply buying a ticket in one city and hopping off at your desired destination seemed the height of luxury.

Around 1 a.m. our warmth and security became exposed for what it was—fragile, fleeting, and artificial. The truck released a spluttering retch from its inner workings and moments later let out a groan, slowly grinding to a halt on the side of the road. There was little passing traffic, and within minutes the cab went from comfortable to freezing. Our breath began billowing great clouds of steam and the windows started frosting over with a creeping incrustation of ice—the water vapour from our breath rapidly turning from steam to solid on the glass. Several attempts were made at starting the engine, every one concluding in failure. This was worrying. I had a rough idea where we were but retrieved my map and got my companion to pinpoint our location. It was pretty much as I had thought—we had broken down on the fringes of the Turpan Basin, the lowest and driest basin in all of China, about three hours outside of Urumqi. The region was renowned for its extreme temperature differentials, which in summer can see the thermometer soar to nearly 50°C (122°F), and in winter plunge below minus 40—and that's *both* Fahrenheit and Celsius, with the two converging at this point. I had no idea how low the temperature was tonight, but there was no doubt about it, it was the coldest I had ever experienced. My companion pulled his arms in from his fur-lined coat, approximating an upper-body sleeping bag. I retrieved my proper one, and, unzipping it, cast it over both of us like a blanket. We shared a stoic nod and huddled in together on the double seat of the passenger side. The cover helped, but not much. Without being enclosed inside the bag it trapped little air-space or warmth. Slowly the cold consumed me, its pervasive presence invading my person, leaching into the marrow of my bones. I'd never known anything like it, and wished to God I'd had the presence of mind to buy a proper jacket in Yumen, whether lightweight and portable or not. My flimsy fleece was practically useless.

After about an hour, one of the other trucks pulled up in front of us, its rear red lights emanating a diffuse aura that highlighted the almost horizontally sweeping snow. It must have doubled back to check on where we'd got to. Out jumped its driver. With his head hunched in against the cold, he battled his way toward us through the onslaught of wind and snow. He heaved open the passenger door. A gust of freezing air rushed into the cab, its icy chill attacking me as if imbued with a thousand tiny knives. Seeing us both huddled on this side, he shut the door and headed over to the drivers' side. Another momentary exposure to the bitter world outside, and he was enclosed within, plastered now with a layer of settled snow. For some time the two drivers discussed the situation, then, all of a sudden, the one from the other truck headed back to his vehicle. He drove off, disappearing into the frozen night. It was hard to tell what was going on, but from their shared mannerisms, it seemed that he had left to get an engine part to remedy the problem—presumably ascertained during their earlier collective examination of the truck back in Hami.

Ghastly hour after hour dragged by but I didn't sleep; neither of us did, it was too cold for that. We just sat there and shivered together in silence. Before embarking on my trip I had longed for new adventure and experience. I had got it now all right, although it wasn't quite what I'd had in mind. I thought back to a survival course I had taken years ago, where those instructing had told the class about two people trapped in separate vehicles on the same freezing night: one, a slight professional woman in a little hatchback, the other, a big macho backcountry guy in a pickup. The guy had died but the woman lived, doing so after having the wherewithal to rip the insulation out from her car's spare seats and stuff it into her clothing. If it wasn't for my sleeping bag we might have had to try it.

Time roughly equivalent to a full working day passed at an agonizingly elongated rate, doing so as if drawn from a clock near-frozen in motion by the cold, but finally our long and hideous wait was over, when, just after dawn, the truck returned, now accompanied by another. The two drivers came and joined us, and after a brief conversation, they and my icy comrade got out of the cab and began tinkering with the truck below. I knew very little about engines, but should I have gone out with them as a sign of solidarity? Maybe, but the hideous cold and my lack of a proper jacket stopped me from making any futile gestures. Eventually they returned and tested the ignition.

A long drawn-out stammer came from the engine, as if teetering on the edge of life, before finally it awakened. The driver wasn't about to lose her now, and began revving the engine into a wailing frenzy to the point where it almost begged for mercy. The other drivers ran back to their trucks and all of a sudden we were on our way, the heater blasting cold air before it finally began warming up. As we drove into a gradually lightening world of snow and ice, my thoughts turned to our arrival in Urumqi, and thawing out there under a steaming hot shower for an inordinate amount of time.

I'm sure it was my dazed perception of things, or possibly our route of approach, but Urumqi seemed to begin from out of nowhere, as if the tiny back country road suddenly metamorphosed into a sprawling metropolis of three million people, with nothing by way of middle ground in-between.

I was dropped near a bus stop crowded with people wearing thick puffy coats with fur-lined hoods, and chunky hats and gloves. Many of them were of Uyghur origin not Han Chinese. (Uyghurs are instantly recognisable from the Han, being larger, both in height and build, having darker skin and features that are more rounded and Central Asian in appearance. Many of the men also wear distinctive four-sided patterned skullcaps.) Ahead stretched frozen urban bedlam. Endless vehicles passed by, belching exhaust fumes into the frigid air like great industrial discharges. People hurried every-which-way on the slippy sidewalks, while municipal workers in padded blue and gray outfits scraped at the paving underfoot with shovels, creating an unmistakable tinny noise as steel clanged hard against concrete through a compacted coating of snow and ice. Endless gray buildings lay ahead, many brightened by colored Chinese characters running down their sides. Hawkers sold food from aged wooden carts: roasted chestnuts, patterned bread, sweet potatoes, colorful rice, and corn on the cob—skewered through the middle with rods that rested above metal boxes full of smokeless burning charcoal, throwing the surrounding air into a shimmering heatwave. I was hungry, but more for warmth than food.

This would be the third location where I had succumbed to catching a local bus since setting off. (The others beings Darwin and Kunming). I required two buses to reach my inner-city destination: a hostel. Although in most locations I loathe such places, not quite so somewhere like this. When you're this far off the gap-year backpacker track, the people you meet in hostels are of a different calibre: proper travelers, often with fascinating stories and invaluable tips for the path you intend to tread; and what's more, I fancied some English speaking company. I got off in a built-up area near several ice sculptures depicting curious abstract forms, located down the road from a towering skyscraper, whose glass top resembled a staggered frozen pyramid. After much bewildered searching, I finally located the hostel down an icy side-street. Climbing some snowy steps that led to its entrance door, I finally reached permanent shelter, and a great wave of relief washed over me.

My senses seemed out of sync, the blessed warmth of the interior registering before my eyes caught up and made sense of the surroundings. A large communal room containing a spacious central bar area stood before me. Sitting at a table with views down to the street below was a lone European-looking guy, studying a chunky travel guide with rapt attention. At a small reception was a Chinese woman stroking a ghastly-looking white cat with an unfortunate black square-marking beneath its nose, giving it the appearance of having a Hitler-style mustache.

Finally the moment I had been longing for had arrived. I beelined for the bathroom to check out the shower. The tank was cold. I tugged the cord and went over to my bed, swaddling myself in its covers. It was marvelous to be indoors, but it was going to take far more than that before

I fully defrosted. Eventually the shower was ready. It is no exaggeration to say that I found the shower emotionally warm. I stood beneath it for a very long time, trying to suck its glorious heat into my core as the room took on the rapid appearance of a sauna. I only stopped when the water's temperature began to turn. By the time I'd finished, my extremities of skin and superficial flesh were hot and flushed, but, nonetheless, I still felt cold. It was an unsatisfactory feeling, like eating a meal at a restaurant with stingy portions but sky high prices, where despite the expense you still leave hungry and wanting.

I dried off and got dressed, then headed to the communal room where I helped myself to a free cup of hot water from an urn at the bar. The European-looking guy was still seated at the window, now nursing a cup of tea. He had piercing blue eyes and a thin defined face that spoke of frequent exposure to the wind and sun. From his left ear dangled three large but slightly graduated silver loop earrings, and on his chin grew a bushy tuft of flaming red hair, contrasting with his short graying mop on top. I wandered over.

"Where you heading next?" I asked.

"Kashgar," he replied in a soft German accent.

"Nice spot," I said, inviting the inevitable.

"Have you been there?"

"A few years ago, yeah."

That was good enough for both of us; I sat down and settled in for a chat.

My newfound buddy was Danilo, a German fluent in English. Although quiet and unassuming, he was an accomplished traveler who after exploring Xinjiang planned to make his way around the rest of Central Asia before heading on to Iran and western Afghanistan. A male nurse by profession, he had the perfect arrangement with his employer: he would work in Germany for a few months at an old person's home, then, when the urge took him, set off and travel for an extended period, before returning and repeating the process all over. Like me, his main reason for coming to Urumqi was to visit the consulate of Kyrgyzstan and apply there for a visa—a process which he had a wealth of information on. Danilo had yet to apply, so we agreed to go to the consulate together when they were open next in two days time.

Through the window he spotted two cyclists down below, clad in chunky red and orange jackets, carrying their touring bikes up the hostel's snowy steps.

"French couple. They're going to Kyrgyzstan too."

A sprightly, cheerful-looking pair appeared at the top of the stairs, brushing off the remains of snow from their jackets and tea-cozy-like woolly hats.

"Ah, hello again!" said the woman enthusiastically on spotting Danilo.

They came over and joined us.

"How is it out?" asked Danilo.

"Freezing!" responded the Frenchman in a thick accent, accompanied with a beaming smile. "I check my thermometer. It is minus fifteen."

"So *that's* how cold it is," I exclaimed, intrigued to finally have a figure to attach to my unfortunate sleeping arrangements of the night before, which I briefly mentioned now.

"Oh no, it was far colder last night," said the Frenchman. "Went down to minus twenty, and that's in the city, it would have been much colder outside it."

No wonder I was still feeling it in my bones.

They introduced themselves as Etienne and Manon, a married couple traveling across China by bike, train, and bus, cycling some sections, catching public transport on others. Their next big section on two wheels would be from the distant western town of Kashgar (a famous Silk Road trading post), across the border to Kyrgyzstan. Like Danilo, neither had been to Kashgar before, so after asking what their plans were there, and listening to their itineraries, I ventured a suggestion of my own: to visit a place none of them had heard of, nor any of their guidebooks mentioned—Shipton's Arch, the world's highest natural archway at over 1,200 feet (taller than the Empire State Building), one of my all-time favorite places anywhere; a wonder of the world that barely anybody knows about.

I first became aware of the existence of this phenomenal span of rock after flicking through a *National Geographic Magazine* in a doctor's waiting room. "Journey to Shipton's Lost Arch" announced the headline of the article, which described how this incredible formation was found, then lost, then found again. The photographs of the arch and the amazing story of adventure undertaken to reach it, grabbed hold of me and set my imagination alight to such a degree that I knew, without doubt, I would visit it myself one day.

The arch was first brought to the outside world's attention by legendary British mountaineer and explorer, Eric Shipton, who wrote of its existence in his 1947 memoir, *Mountains of Tartary*. At the time Shipton, who was without the necessary modern equipment to measure the arch, estimated its height at around 1,000 feet. *Guinness World Records* featured the arch before subsequently dropping the listing after sending a team to verify it, who, failing to find the arch, wrote it off as a hoax. Largely forgotten thereafter, it wasn't until 2000, when *National Geographic Magazine* sent their own team out to Kashgar that the arch's existence was finally confirmed, with their group becoming the first outsiders to visit it since Shipton.

A member of the diplomatic service, Eric Shipton arrived in the isolated outpost of Kashgar in 1940 to take up the role of British Consul. Perched on the margins of the mighty Taklamakan Desert, and at the doorstep of some of the world's highest mountains, Kashgar is the quintessential Silk Road town, permeated with two thousand years of history, and even today contains parts where time seems to have stood still, with houses made of mud and straw, and donkey carts regularly used as taxis.

During Shipton's tenure he launched myriad expeditions into the area's majestic surrounding mountains, and from time to time caught tantalizing glimpses of an intriguing peak hidden deep within a chaotic larger range that, bizarrely, had a gaping hole through the middle of it. His curiosity piqued, he made up his mind to find a route through the labyrinth of twisting conglomerate towers and narrow slot canyons to reach it. The extreme nature of the uncharted terrain made this no small undertaking, but if anyone had the credentials for the job, then it was Shipton.

In 1929, aged just twenty-two, he made the first recorded ascent of Mount Kenya's Nelion peak. By age twenty-four he and a group of five others were the first to scale India's Mount Kamet, which, at 25,447 feet, was the highest anyone had ever climbed at the time. And just two years later in 1933, he got within a thousand feet of Mount Everest's summit, and subsequently pioneered the route that in 1953 would see Tenzing Norgay and Sir Edmund Hillary finally make it to the top.

But despite such mountaineering prowess, Shipton's quest to reach the arch was foiled on three separate occasions by the terrain that stood in his way: a mindbogglingly complex maze of shoulder-width canyons and tortuous barricades of rock that soared thousands of feet into the air, and closed in so much as to obscure the sky to the point where he was forced to light a match to see. Shipton changed tactics. Abandoning the southerly approach from where he at least had a glimpse of the arch when setting off, he rounded the entire range and began investigating from the north. From here the arch was invisible and the landscape just as challenging, but eventually he and his team, consisting of wife Diana and faithful golden retriever, Sola, discovered what they were looking for. Writing of the experience in *The Mountains of Tartary*, Shipton recalls:

> At last, emerging from one of these clefts, we were confronted with a sight that made us gasp with surprise and excitement. The gorge widened into a valley which ended a quarter of a mile away in a grassy slope leading to a U-shaped col. Above and beyond the col stood a curtain of rock, pierced by a graceful arch.

Climbing the grassy slope, the Shiptons looked out through the elegant window of rock at a monumental panorama. Here the arch continued downwards, dropping abruptly into a sheer and dramatic gorge a thousand feet below, where several canyon walls rose up at angles beyond vertical, curling backwards like giant top-heavy waves about to break. Beyond lay "scores of bold pinnacles," the formations that had thwarted Shipton's previous attempts from the south; and further on, about a hundred miles away across a rippled ocean of desert, were the distant peaks of the Pamir Mountains, thrusting skyward over twenty-four thousand feet at the colliding junction of the Himalayas, Kunlun, Tian Shan, Karakoram, and Hindu Kush ranges.

It was a view I had previously savored with Emily. We reached it several years ago on a snowy day when the sun's back-lighting created a giant ethereal beam through the archway, highlighting gently falling snow that filtered through it.[157] It created a poetic scene, and one we had mostly to ourselves. We made our way there with a local Uyghur guide and an American gentleman we met the day before in a café in Kashgar, who, on hearing of our expedition, asked to tag along. However, both he and the guide headed back long before Emily and me, leaving us in the valley all alone. It was a special moment that I will never forget.

I was determined to visit this enigmatic wonder again and encouraged the audience in front of me at the hostel to come too. It wasn't a hard sell.

"We will join you at this place!" stated Etienne with excited eyes.

* * *

At a camping store I purchased something I should have bought a long time ago: a super thick goose-down jacket and thermal inner pants. They made a world of difference and filled me with a new-found confidence for the difficult Silk Road journey ahead.

Urumqi wasn't a bad sort of place to spend a couple of days. There were two main attractions within walking distance: the People's Park and the Xinjiang Museum. The park was a winter wonderland, the center piece a two-tiered pagoda with bright red columns and traditional tubular tile-roofing. It stood in the middle of a huge boating lake, accessible over a gray stone bridge lined with elegant arches. The water was frozen solid and covered with a thick layer of snow, with sections cleared to create circular ice-skating tracks. Elsewhere the park was a celebration of trees, dormant skeletons hibernating until spring, naked now but for a coating of snow, leaving them resembling great growths of coral. Despite the conditions, the park was alive with activity. Jugglers and string musicians practiced their skills in the hazy frozen air. On opposing ends of a seesaw sat an elderly couple, merrily swinging up and down while letting out whoops of delight with every rise and fall. A communal ballroom-dancing class was in progress, men and women waltzing together with big beaming smiles. The male to female ratio was out of kilter, but no problem, several guys spun around by themselves, grasping the hand and waist of an imaginary partner, holding the gaze of make-believe eyes with a smile that was all courtesy and respect. There was something so innocent about it all, that I almost wanted to grab a hold of my own fantasy partner and lead her onto the floor for a twirl.

In the early afternoon I wandered over to the Xinjiang Museum. It was a large blue-domed building in the center of the city, with a rounded façade of smoky glass and smooth white-stone-cladding that was very much in the communist style. Few of its exhibits had English explanations, but most were visual and self explanatory. I went first to a section related to the lives of Xinjiang's thirteen different ethnic groups: Uyghur, Han, Kazak, Kyrgyz, Mongolian, Uzbek, Daur, Russian, Tatar, Tajik, Xibe, Hui (Chinese Muslims) and Manchu. Collections included everything from traditional clothing to hunting and farming tools, as well as mock-ups of traditional yurt housing—the once common portable accommodation of Central Asia's nomads, and still a quintessential icon of the region.

Constructed around a circular willow frame swaddled in multiple layers of felt, the outermost one waterproofed with a sloppy application of sheep fat, yurts are the perfect answer to the region's extremes of weather. Of great importance to the yurt is the central hearth, both practically, for heat and cooking, and symbolically, with guests given pride of place at whichever spot is nearest to it yet farthest from the door. Belying their rather simple external appearance, yurts' interiors are often sumptuously decorated with colorful cushions, textiles, quilts, tassels, horse and camel bags, and beautifully carved doors—all reflective of the owner's status. Lightweight and taking only three hours to erect, they are also highly portable. Although somewhat rare today, yurts were once a common sight across Central Asia, stretching from the grassy plains of neighboring Mongolia through Xinjiang, Kyrgyzstan, Kazakhstan, Tajikistan, Uzbekistan and beyond.

Other exhibits were of an altogether more macabre nature. One of the museum's proudest collections is the preserved bodies of several men, women, and infants, discovered in Xinjiang's ancient tombs, whose center piece is the "Loulan Beauty," a 3,800-year-old woman with long fair hair. I can't say I've ever liked the idea of digging up the dead and sticking them inside sterile glass display cabinets to be gawked at, but I seem to be in a minority here, at least if my visit to the Xinjiang Museum, and indeed my last visit to the British Museum, is anything to go by, so I did now as I had then—had a quick cursory glance, then wandered on to examine something else. Pottery and bronze statues were the next to catch my eye, all coming from the great trading corridors so synonymous with Xinjiang and Central Asia as a whole: the Silk Road.

No matter which route you take through Central Asia, you will almost certainly be following a branch of the network of historic Silk Roads that weave across the region like great arteries, connecting the dots of a string of desert oases and high mountain passes, creating a way through what would otherwise be a landscape of impassable physical barriers. The genesis of the Silk Roads came around 105 BC when China and Parthia (the empire of the nomadic Parthians from the Iranian plateau) opened up corresponding embassies and initiated official bilateral trade along the Central Asian lands between their territories. For at least a century prior to this, the Parthians had been the largest consumers of the mysterious, shimmering Chinese fabric, for which the trading routes were subsequently named—a term that was actually coined in the nineteenth century by German geographer, Ferdinand Van Richthofen. The Romans were quick to follow the Parthians in their obsession with silk, and came up with several false conjectures on how it was made, such as being combed from leaves after a thorough soaking. To the Romans, China was Seres—The Country of Silk.

The journey across the Silk Road was a treacherous one, taking in some of the most challenging environments on the planet: mountain ranges so high they were known as the "Roof of the World" (the Pamirs), deserts so forbidding they acquired the sobriquet "Go in and you'll never come out" (The Taklamakan); sandstorms, blizzards, ferocious heat, horrendous cold, attack by bandits and wild animals—just some of the challenges facing those who negotiated the route. And right bang in the center of it all was Central Asia, the territorial nexus between the great civilizations of East and West, providing the service industry to the caravans of traveling merchants.

Cultural exchange swept in through the region like a sandstorm off the Gobi. Art, religion, technology, philosophy, music, dance and ideas were exchanged, often coalescing into new and improved hybrid forms.

In the eighth century the Silk Road took a hit. The Chinese lost their greatest industrial secrets in the aftermath of The Battle of Talas—the knowledge of how silk and paper were produced, both obtained from captured prisoners in the know. The victory of the opposing Arab forces over the Chinese in the Talas valley (modern day Kazakhstan and Kyrgyzstan), and their acquisition of this monumental industrial know-how, had several dramatic knock-on effects: Islam cemented itself as the dominant religion of Central Asia, the introduction of paper production in Europe served as a catalyst for a much wider technological revolution, the Arabs established their own silk makers, and Chinese expansion westward came to an end.

Considering the tensions today in Xinjiang between the Han Chinese and Uyghurs, it's ironic that it was the Uyghurs who came to the assistance of the Chinese after The Battle of Talas, coming down from their ancestral home on the Siberian and Mongolian borders in the north, as allies of the Tang dynasty. It was this political alliance that saw the Uyghurs settle in Xinjiang, doing so at oases along the Silk Road, making them the first of the Turkic peoples to abandon their traditional nomadic lifestyle. With geographical permanence sprang literacy—the original Uyghur writing system served as the underlying template of Mongolian script—and a flourishing Turkic culture renowned for its traditional medicine, which some credit with the invention of acupuncture.

Although tensions have existed between Uyghurs and Han Chinese for a long time, it was shortly after the establishment of the communist People's Republic of China in 1949, and the introduction of the official policy of "sinicisation"—where literally millions of Han Chinese settlers began flooding into the region—that relations between the two ethnicities really began to boil over. Such an influx of Han Chinese has led to them becoming the majority in Xinjiang's north, while Uyghurs still remain dominant in the south. In the nineties a wave of violence spread throughout the region, including bus bombings in Kashgar and Urumqi, pitched battles between the Chinese police and Uyghurs in the streets of Baren, and riots in Hotan and Yining. The Yining riots alone saw at least fifteen killed and over a hundred injured. Mass arrests, "re-education" programs, and executions followed—often carried out on the day of trial—which, in turn, led to more unrest, including the bombing of three buses in Urumqi that left at least nine people dead. Further trouble has flared in this century, some igniting just three months after I left Kashgar, with a series of incidents occurring in the town, leaving at least fifteen people dead and many more injured.

* * *

Danilo and I trudged through a fresh layer of snow that squeaked like polystyrene underfoot, as we made our way towards the consulate of Kyrgyzstan, a more humble governmental outpost I'd never seen. Located in an obscure area of the city near one of the main highways, from the outside it looked like a dingy travel agency rather than a nation's administrative center abroad. It was so nondescript it required several circuits of the area before we determined that we had the correct place, when Danilo noticed that one of its two front doors was now ajar. There's something about consulates and embassies that always has me on edge, perhaps because the bureaucratic gatekeepers there have so much power. They hold all the cards, and can, at a whim, deny you access to their country, even if on paper they should not. With this in mind, as I stepped through the door I snapped into professional mode, taking on the polite, self-aware manner of someone about to be interviewed for a job.

The male staff member manning reception was currently preoccupied with a woman in a thick fur-lined coat, so we took a seat on a comfy leather sofa beneath a giant picture of a stallion galloping across the wilds of Kyrgyzstan. If ever there was a seat made to kick-back and melt into, then this was it, but without prior consultation, Danilo and I both sat upright.

With us we had our passports, photocopies of their I.D. pages and Chinese visas, as well as individually written letters of intent. These were benign personal statements of our plans when in Kyrgyzstan: foment new revolution through cross border smuggling of armaments, clandestine visits to sensitive military sites and disputed border regions, and importation of Class A narcotics to corrupt and ruin youth of country—all your standard tourist fare.

When the woman left, Danilo approached reception.

Before getting the chance to open his mouth, the man pointed, with a sausage of an outstretched finger to a clock high on the wall.

"Consulate open twelve o'clock," he stated bluntly.

It was only 11:15 a.m.

He thrust some forms towards us and shooed us out the door.

We retired to a hotel down the road where we ferreted out a gloomy restaurant area in the hope of finding food. The place was empty, and none of its lights on, giving the impression it was closed.

"Might as well take a seat and fill our forms out," suggested Danilo.

Ten minutes later, just as we were finishing up the paperwork, a Russian-looking girl in a crisp white shirt and neat black skirt, came out from a kitchen area and, seeing us, threw a look our way that said, with mild alarm: "You're not supposed to be here."

"Err, Вопа?" stated Danilo in a lilting Russian accent, impressing me beyond measure with his linguistic gymnastics.

The girl gathered herself, nodded, then disappeared back into the kitchen.

"I asked for bread," said Danilo.

"I *am* impressed," I responded.

"Oh, it is nothing. In fact it's the only word I know in Russian."

"Well it's a damn sight more than I could have managed."

He laughed to himself on hearing this, as if some hidden subtext existed that I would soon become aware, then leaned in towards me in the manner of someone about to depart delicate information. "But I studied Russian for eight years."

Cue the sound of a needle scratching off a record.

"Eight years?!" I stated with a laugh of disbelief, my mind boggling before Danilo's very eyes. "And this is the sum total of your near decade of diligent study. One measly word: 'bread'? I am confident that never has such an inordinate amount of study amounted to less. You know this doesn't exactly fill me with confidence as to the merits of a German education."

I was expecting my good natured banter to illicit but a mild chuckle, but German humor being the enigma that it is—at least to the unaccustomed English mind—Danilo burst instead into fits of raucous laughter.

"I know, but the thing is," he said, struggling to compose himself through an onslaught of chortles, as if on the cusp of delivering a killer punchline, "Growing up in East Germany, we were all made to learn Russian in school but nobody really wanted to, and so I never paid much attention!"

More uncontrolled laughter followed, during which I mentally replayed Danilo's last utterance, scanning it for a hidden punchline. I didn't find one.

Minutes later the Russian girl returned and supplied one of her own, bringing to our table not bread but a metal teapot filled with hot water.

It was hard not to be impressed with that.

When we returned to the Kyrgyzstan consulate at twelve o'clock, Manon and Etienne were sitting on the comfy leather sofa, diligently filling out their forms.

Danilo and I proceeded to the counter.

"I'd like the express next-day visa, please," I stated politely, handing across my paperwork.

"No," replied the man matter-of-factly. "Five days for visa."

Danilo and I gasped in shock. This was an unexpected bombshell. Etienne and Manon sprang from their seats and joined us at the counter. We all planned to hit the road tomorrow and had read online that the consulate offered an "express service" for a small additional fee, which fast-tracked the normal waiting period.

"Is there no express service?" I asked.

"It is too expensive," stated the man with a dismissive shake of the head, as if in possession of my credit history and full net worth.

"How much is it?" I asked.

"Twelve hundred."

"Oooh," I said sucking through my teeth.

This was far more than I expected. Still, did I really want to stick around in Urumqi for the next five days? I wavered for a moment weighing up my options.

"I really do need an express visa but that *is* expensive," I pondered aloud. "Erm, I'm going to have to think about it," I added, almost apologetically, stalling for time while the cogs in my mind slowly began turning, totting up whether or not the extra cost of five days' worth of food and accommodation wiped out the financial gain acquired from sticking around for a cheaper visa.

He looked at me with a touch of sympathy. "Okay then, I do for seven hundred."

I was dumbstruck, lost for words; this was unheard of, a consulate where you could haggle on price.

"I'll take it," stated Etienne, quickly jumping in before I regained the ability to talk.

The rest of us followed suit, hastily reaching into our wallets for the fee.

I wondered what else I could have got thrown into the bargain with some additional negotiating, and laughed at the thought of someone trying to haggle at the U.K. or U.S. Embassy: "I tell you what, Mr. Ambassador, if you throw in the first night's accommodation then I'm willing to come up to fifty dollars for your visa. Can't say fairer than that. Have we got a deal?"— Spitting on palm and holding out an outstretched hand.

Twenty-four hours later and we were all back at the office picking up our passports, complete with fresh Kyrgyzstan visas. As we stood outside inspecting them in the snow, we said our goodbyes, for now at least. Manon, Etienne and Danilo were heading onto Turpan for a couple of days, before catching a bus to Kashgar where we all arranged to meet and travel onwards together to my beloved Shipton's Arch.

As for me, I was hitting the road.

CHAPTER TWENTY
Kashgar's Lost Arch

Two and a half days later, after pushing west along the fringes of the mighty Taklamakan desert, I arrived in the oasis town of Kashgar, the last major settlement in the west of China before the high mountain passes of the Tian Shan range, a giant frozen barricade of rock thrusting skyward to heights of 24,400 feet, beyond which lay the former Soviet republics.

A cool wind blew through the town's crowded streets, and a bright but tepid sun shone down at an oblique angle on the central square and its six-hundred-year-old Id Kah Mosque, bathing it with a holy crimson light and casting passing faces into portraits of distinction. When you're this far west in China you are nearer to Baghdad than Beijing, and it shows: a Uyghur heartland where the faces of Tajiks, Uzbeks, Kyrgyz and, increasingly, Han are also found. An intoxicating ethnic mixing bowl, whose very name conjures up the evocative romance of the Silk Road; a location where the southern and northern branches converge on either side of the Taklamakan before splintering again on their long and arduous journeys west and north.

I arrived in Kashgar in the late afternoon following an interesting, if somewhat tiring, hitch to get there. I had made slow progress the first day on the road out of Urumqi, reaching Korla, only two hundred miles away. The view there had been magnificent, the road weaving through a dramatic mountain gorge that was strangely bereft of snow, and rose almost vertically from the roadside in angry crusted fractals, fluctuating in hue between golden and scarlet depending on our vehicle's meandering angle of orientation. At one section a giant sand dune spilled down over the rocks, smothering them with a creaseless layer of silica several hundred feet in depth, betraying a wider ocean of sand out of sight beyond its craggy breaches.

I spent the final few hours of the first day with the same driver, an affluent-looking Han Chinese man in his mid-thirties wearing a canary-yellow golfing shirt who, once again, drove a white SUV. There was no chance of us verbally conversing, but we got on nonetheless and he proved the epitome of generosity when, after our arrival in Korla, he insisted on driving me from cheap hotel to cheap hotel, until we found one that permitted foreigners to stay—a process that ate up around forty-five minutes of his time, and ultimately proved a failure, with me settling on somewhere that wasn't really cheap at all purely to bring his inconvenience to an end.

At this establishment I learned a valuable life lesson: never pinch a towel from a hotel.

For some reason the room I was given came with a gargantuan abundance of drying cloths—seven towels in total, all graduated in size, every one soft and fluffy—and so, having used but a tiny flannel in place of a towel since setting off from Hobart, I thought it was high time for an upgrade. There wasn't much thought process beyond this, in fact it was something of an afterthought once I'd packed up and was ready to leave. If a pang of conscience did exist, then it was swiftly batted away by the counter-thought that the hotel was part of a large chain, and not a particularly cheap one, so hey, no one was going to miss it; right?

Wrong.

With hindsight I should have seen it coming. When checking in the previous night, the staff member on duty had only agreed to waive the hotel's substantial room deposit, the cash for which I did not possess, in exchange for my passport as security. So when I handed my room key across the reception desk the following morning, and asked the dead-behind-the-eyes female employee for my passport back, I shouldn't have been surprised, but of course was, when in unusually good English she announced, "First we need to check room."

My heart sank.

Picking up the reception phone, she punched in an internal extension and began barking orders at some hapless colleague, presumably instructing them to launch the inspection. As she hung up the phone I did my best to appear nonchalant. Casting a little smile her way, I rolled my eyes ironically, as if to say, "Protocol, hey, what a bore?"

She stared back at me without warmth, her face unchanged like she'd been paralyzed from an industrial syringing of Botox. Time passed agonizingly slowly but still her colleague had yet to ring back—and I bloody-well knew why too: she couldn't find one of the towels and was turning the room upside down to make absolutely sure of as much, before going out on a limb and pointing the finger at me.

Eventually the phone rang.

If it is possible to let out a deep internal sigh of foreboding while simultaneously maintaining a gormless casual veneer, then that is what I did. As the receptionist took the call she momentarily looked away before suddenly whipping her head back and fixing me with an accusatory glare.

I responded with an innocent inquisitive look that begged, "Is there a problem?"

There was. And her expression said it all: "You've nicked one of our towels!"

She hung up the phone.

"One of the towels is missing," she stated with the authoritarian air of an SS commandant.

"Really?" I replied. "How very odd. Are you sure?"

She didn't answer, but burned a hole in me with her cold eyes, while an uncomfortable silence lingered in the air between us.

I broke the deadlock. "Oh!" I responded from out of the blue, as if a cartoon lightbulb had pinged into existence above my head, alerting me to some previously overlooked nugget of information, "What color are *your* towels?"

"White," she spat through gritted teeth.

I tutted in a way that implied: "Oh, how could I have been so silly."

"So is *my* towel," I exclaimed. "I must have confused the two and picked up yours as well by mistake."

I could see what she was thinking: "Yeah, sure!"

She knew that I was lying, and what's more she knew that I knew as much, but I continued with the charade regardless—there was little other option now.

Unclipping my backpack I opened up its main compartment. Sitting there, as plain as day, right smack on top of the contents was a fluffy white towel complete with fetching corporate motif. I lifted it out and handed it over, receiving a dagger-like stare in response. Begrudgingly she reached down and retrieved my passport from beneath her desk. As I went to take it she grasped a hold of it for a second longer than necessary, requiring a little yank from me to free it from her claw-like grip. With a contrite little smile I slid it into my pocket, then turned and made a hasty beeline for the exit.

It was time to get on the road.

Clambering over a pile of rubble left from the collapse of a large wall blocking access to the highway, I stumbled onto its roadside heading west. I was on the far outskirts of Korla, and here picked up a ride in a clunker of an old people carrier. Two middle-aged Uyghur men sat up front, big and stocky with large rounded stomachs. Residing in the back among a sea of luggage and bags were two Uyghur women wearing dark brown headscarves. Verbal communication was non-existent, but from what I could gather, the men, Yusup and Karima, were brothers, and the women, whose names I didn't make a note of, were relatives but not their wives; sisters or cousins, perhaps.

Several hours of driving and we stopped at a café in a little dusty village lined with fastigiate poplar trees, where we settled down for lunch, this time traditional Uyghur cuisine of fresh seeded bread, pigeon soup, and kebabs made from succulent "fat-tailed" sheep. On finishing up, Yusup and Karima got their heads down for a brief nap in the vehicle. It was now that I encountered the most ridiculous, even comical, snoring I have ever come across—and I've come across plenty—with both of them releasing great fog horn grunts, staggered slightly so there was no respite from the noise. As soon as one great emission finished, the other would begin, providing a near constant groan. It was insanely loud, so bad that I got out of the vehicle and went for a stroll nearby, shaking my head in disbelief.

"Thank God," I thought, "I don't have to share a bed with them."

By dusk we rolled into Aksu, one of many oasis settlements dotted along the northern border of the Taklamakan desert. Much the same situation occurred as the night before, with all the reasonably priced hotels refusing to let a foreigner stay. One apologetic English-speaking owner summed up the situation: "If the authorities discover you have stayed here I will lose my license." It was a convincing argument. In the end the brothers invited me to crash at their place. After dropping the women off in Aksu, we headed out of town into the surrounding countryside, bumping our way along a gray and dusty potholed road until we reached a rustic little dwelling with blue window frames and faded whitewash plaster walls. Tagged onto its side was a collection of stable buildings constructed from mud and straw, where roughly twenty inquisitive-looking sheep mingled, penned off from the main area in front of the house. To the side of the stables stretched a small orchard of fruit trees, currently bare in the winter cold.

People erupted from the house on our arrival, pouring out to greet Yusup and Karima, who were mobbed by their extended families; eleven people in total, spanning three generations, all living together in the same little house. The brothers received a hero's welcome with hugs and back-pats flowing all round. I was introduced to wives and sons, aunties and uncles, their mother and father, all of whom accepted me unquestioningly into the fold. Several of the men wore traditional square turquoise Uyghur hats, decorated with bold white geometric patterns. All the women wore headscarves.

Yusup guided me indoors, through a small entrance hall that led to three equally small rooms, all with bare concrete floors. Most of the walls were similarly barren, save for a couple of posters displaying a picnic spread and a bunch of flowers, both laminated with wipe-clean plastic. Whether the house had electricity or not I don't know, but the only light inside while I was there came from an orange glowing central hearth in the kitchen area. But the real light that spread throughout the interior was from the atmosphere: laughter permeated the dwelling, filling it with love and tenderness, a womb of happiness and sanctuary for the departed brothers to return. In Western terms these people were poor; they had no central heating, no carpets, no iPhones, no internet, no McDonald's or Starbucks, but they were rich in spirit, so much richer than so many materially better off in the West. I cast my mind back to the misery of commuting on the London tube, of trains stuffed full with dead-faced corporate types, staring zombie-like into colorless voids of isolation; of carriages imbued with a collective cold depression, the sum total of all the desperate individual spirits poisoned by the virus of never-ending acquisition; of muffled spirits screaming silently to be somewhere else. I might not have been able to communicate verbally with the family, but through their acceptance and generosity we spoke a shared common language of the heart.

One of the women began cooking in a large cast-iron cauldron above the hearth, producing a delicious meaty stew, which we all ate sitting around a tiny wooden table, no more than a foot tall. Just like the traditional welcome for visitors to a Central Asian yurt, I was given pride of place nearest the hearth.

With nightfall's arrival, the household began preparations for bed. It quickly became apparent that the men slept in one room and the women in another, all lined up sardine fashion on floppy roll-out mattresses placed on top of the raised platforms. One of the women kindly prepared a bed for me right up next to another little hearth. Once lit, it transformed the men's bedroom from cold and uninviting into a haven of toasty warmth.

Being amid such hospitable surroundings, I really should have felt relaxed and at ease before I got my head down, but I felt nothing of the sort—for I knew what awaited me if I didn't get to sleep and fast: earth shattering snoring. It began all of a sudden, erupting from the grizzly-bear-like form of Yusup next to me, and moments later from the one prostrate next to him—snoring so loud and in such close proximity that I could actually feel its vibration. I had my wax ear plugs in but they were as good as useless against such a brutal onslaught of dissonance, and after about thirty minutes I admitted defeat. With a reluctant exhalation of breath, I said farewell to my comfy position by the fire and crept with my bedroll and sleeping bag, past multiple groaning bodies, to the cold concrete of the hallway instead. It wasn't the best of locations to bed down, and one that caused all manner of confusion come the morning when my former sleeping partners emerged from their room to find me here. I mimicked the sound of snoring. Everybody laughed.

After a hearty breakfast of leftovers from the night before, Yusup drove me to the main road for Kashgar. With a hand on my heart I thanked him for his generosity. Reaching into his pocket, he pulled out a wallet and retrieved his official Chinese photo I.D. card, which, bizarrely, he handed to me to take. At first I thought he wanted to give me this as a souvenir by which to remember him, but after a bit of miming it seemed that he was passing it on in the misguided belief that it would enable me to stay in budget hotels from now on—at least, that's what I interpreted his gestures to mean. Despite trying repeatedly to refuse this odd offering, he was adamant, so I accepted it.

Several car, truck, and SUV rides followed, including one from two young Uyghur guys who at one stage pulled over to smoke hash from a bong made out of an old plastic water bottle, and by the time the sun began to set I made it into Kashgar. Having arranged to meet Danilo, Manon, and Etienne at a hostel in the historic old town tomorrow, I made my way there first along twisting ancient streets of quiet decay that ran behind the town's iconic pastel yellow Id Kah Mosque. I knew the area well, having walked through its interconnecting labyrinth of alleyways lined with mud brick homes years earlier on my first visit to Kashgar.

I felt like I'd stepped into another century. Donkeys dragged carts laden with firewood along winding lanes past homes clad in timber scaffolding; cobblers demonstrated their skills by the roadside; butchers cut up great carcasses in the open air; shoeshine men hawked for business; wily carpet traders sat in their lairs piled high with Afghan and Persian rugs; Arabian music played out; women shopped in bright multi-colored silk headscarves; and old men in sheepskin hats sat watching the world go by from the comfort of tea houses. It felt great to be back in such an atmospheric place until, that is, I rounded the corner.

My heart sank at the sight that stretched before me. A vast block that had once consisted of a vibrant community, made of row upon row of mud and straw clad homes and businesses, hundreds of years old and dripping in character, was now nothing but a razed and empty lot of rubble—a literal hole in the heart of the district where no doubt another faceless Chinese tower or shopping precinct would soon emerge, planted like a flag of occupation. The official explanation for much of this comes under the guise of planning regulations, to make the region earthquake proof, to modernize, but a more sinister reality exists beneath the surface: the greater the destruction of Uyghur history, culture, and identity, and the greater the number of Han Chinese settlers that swamp the area, the more Uyghurs will be forced to assimilate into China proper, and forever give up the dream of independence. As if on cue, a platoon of Chinese soldiers marched past, batons swinging from their wrists, souring the atmosphere in an instant.

I located the hostel, which had escaped the destruction but was all locked up. As I stood pondering where to go instead, a Uyghur man approached me.

"My name is Elvis," he said in good English, flashing a beaming smile my way and holding out a hand to shake. "I am tour guide. They mention me in Lonely Planet book. I like to help the foreigners. Can I help you?"

He could indeed.

"Is there another hostel nearby?" I asked.

"No. But I will show you hotel off the main square."

"Does it let foreigners stay?"

"Yes. Yes. I will talk to them."

Together we ambled back past the Id Kah Mosque to a hotel on the corner of the square, where Elvis got me a room for ninety Yuan (about fourteen dollars). He wished me well, gave me his business card and promptly departed.

After dropping off my gear, I headed back to the locked up hostel, where, with some sticky tape borrowed from my hotel's reception, I stuck a message on the door addressed to Manon, Etienne, and "Germany's great linguist—eight years study!" letting them know where to find me.

* * *

By the time they arrived in Kashgar, arrangements had already been made to get them and me to Shipton's Arch. After visiting several tour operators, I selected one that seemed the most confident in providing an appropriate guide and four-wheel-drive to tackle the winter terrain we'd have to negotiate to get within hiking distance of the arch. This was imperative, since a fresh layer of snow had fallen the night before.

Danilo booked in at the same hotel as me, whereas Manon and Etienne selected a more interesting-sounding place on the other side of town—the former Russian consulate, now converted into a hotel. When last in Kashgar, I stayed in a hotel on the grounds of its one time rival establishment, the former British consulate, which in the late nineteenth and early twentieth centuries was a hub of espionage and intrigue when the political struggle known as the "Great Game" played out between imperial Britain and Russia.

For the players of this titanic game of strategic chess, the grand prize was the domination of Asia. Lying at the junction between these great powers was Xinjiang. Although ostensibly controlled by the Chinese, the region was no stranger to uprisings, subjugation and civil war, making the authority of a then impoverished China a tenuous one, and the ultimate future control of the territory an unknown outcome.

From the British consulate Eric Shipton had despatched his secret reports to India, the jewel in the British Empire, detailing movements of troops, uprisings, intrigues, and counter tactics of the Soviets—information often gleaned through his climbing and hunting expeditions around Kashgar's surrounding terrain. Following India's independence in 1947, the Great Game came to a close, with neither Britain nor Russia having achieved much of anything. Had the ebbing tide of fate and empire shifted away from stalemate, a very different reality would exist today for the unfortunate pawn of Xinjiang. If Russia had won and subjugated the region for its own ends, then with the collapse of the Soviet Union, the Independent Republic of Uyghuristan would have risen out of the smoldering ashes of empire, rich in black gold from the colossal oil reserves under the Taklamakan.

Danilo and I stepped out from our hotel into the cold half-light of a pre-dawn morning, and headed in the direction of the old British consulate. We made our way there through a section of the old town, where life was beginning to stir, and in the same manner that it had done for centuries. A horse-drawn cart ridden by an old man lurched from side to side along the bumpy lane while a butcher sat skewering meat outside his splinter-fronted shop. Further on we passed a bakery where the internal oven burned so greatly that the building itself looked ablaze, throwing raging smoke out over its blackened window frames and pumping a brilliant heat into the frigid air. Danilo took a photograph, beautifully capturing the drama of the scene. (Reproduced in this book.)

Waiting for us at the end of the lane, in front of a metallic green and silver SUV, exuding off-road confidence, were Manon and Etienne, conversing with our English speaking tour guide, Ali, and driver, Turghunjun. After saying hello we bundled in and got moving. I could barely contain my excitement at the thought of standing once again beneath Shipton's Arch and overlooking the jagged floor of the world below.

We made our way north through staggered oasis villages on the road leading to the border with Kyrgyzstan, a route I would have to hitchhike in the next few days. A craggy gorge ran to our right, rising from an ice-covered flood plain where meandering waters cut a swathe and rounded boulders tumbled in the frozen wastes. I recognized the spot. It seemed only yesterday that I had traveled this route with Emily.

For the last few minutes the driver, Turghunjun, had been speaking to Ali in agitated tones. Ali cast an unconvincing smile our way as if to reassure us nothing was wrong.

"This will be the most adventurous tour I have ever been on," Ali announced a moment later, flashing us the same smile.

"Have you not been to Shipton's Arch before?" asked Danilo.

"Once, but not this early in the year or with so much snow. I just hope we will be able to make it," he added in a manner that implied there was genuine doubt.

I didn't like the sound of this. It was like he was priming us for bad news around the corner. Was there something he knew that we didn't? When we had spoken the day before, Ali had been all confidence and enthusiasm about the trip. Had something changed? The last time I visited the arch it had been snowy, and although deeper today, it seemed likely that our chunky four-wheel-drive could more than cope with transporting us safely to the beginning of the hiking trail. So long as we could get there, I was confident all would be okay.

Suddenly, Turghunjun began slowing down, displaying a caution that was out of all proportion to the conditions, reducing his speed until we were moving at a pace that made no sense for someone behind the wheel of an off-roader—more so since we had yet to leave the road.

"Is everything okay?" asked Danilo.

"Yes. Yes," said Ali, masking over some undisclosed issue with the same smile.

A little hatchback overtook us.

"We've just been overtaken by a two-wheel-drive!" exclaimed Etienne.

"I think Turghunjun is concerned in the snow because he doesn't have a four-wheel-drive," said Ali.

"But this *is* a four-wheel-drive," I replied.

"No, I couldn't get a four-wheel-drive. This is a two-wheel-drive."

Cue again the sound of a needle scratching off a record.

For a moment I was dumbstruck. The vehicle supplied certainly looked the part, it had a good ground-clearance, chunky treads, nasty-looking bull-bars and a spare tire hanging off the rear, but if it was only two-wheel-drive, then its appropriateness ended there. It was all looks and no substance, the ultimate sheep in wolf's clothing. If there was one thing I had been clear about when booking the tour with Ali, it was the necessity of us having a four-wheel-drive. We had twenty miles of snow-covered off-road to cover before we reached the beginning of the hiking trail. Whether we would make it there now looked seriously in doubt.

"Is it front or rear-wheel-drive?" asked Etienne.

"Rear," replied Ali, missing the significance.

This was even worse. With our power coming from the rear we'd be sliding around all over the place with far less control than were it coming from the steering end. In forthright terms I let Ali know of my significant angst at his empty logistical promises. I could see my dream of reaching the arch evaporating before me, and since I'd been the one who'd arranged the tour and encouraged Danilo, Manon, and Etienne to join me, I felt responsible.

"Maybe it will all be okay," replied Ali in a blasé manner of groundless optimism.

It didn't seem likely, but as we rounded a corner to our left and approached a small sign announcing the beginnings of the off-road track, things perhaps didn't look quite so bleak. Snaking along the track were tire marks that had compacted the snow, making it easier for us to drive along. For the next couple of hours we crawled through open country at little more than walking speed, making scant progress. On this section Turghunjun demonstrated that despite living in a snowy environment, he knew next to nothing about driving in the snow, that or he simply didn't want to be here and so was doing everything he could to justify bringing the whole affair to an early end. It began to look like the latter.

Despite Ali revealing that there were snow chains in the rear of the vehicle, and our collective encouragement that these be fitted to the tires,

Turghunjun was extremely reluctant to invest the ten minutes required to do so—even after getting bogged in the snow several times, and the subsequent group digging and pushing required to get the vehicle free. After much badgering, he conceded.

"I don't think the driver wants to continue," Etienne confided as Turghunjun begrudgingly fitted the last of the chains.

"I think you are right," agreed Danilo.

The extra traction from the chains helped tremendously, but Turghunjun's driving soon compensated for any benefit, deteriorating even further.

"Could you tell him he needs to put it into second gear and not to rev it so hard," Etienne politely asked Ali, in his usual calm and gentlemanly manner.

Ali translated this sound advice, but did Turghunjun heed it? Instead he kept flooring his foot in first gear whenever a deep section of snow appeared or the tires began to lose grip, succeeding only in sending the wheels into a spinning frenzy and getting us stuck again. This process repeated itself several times, but eventually Turghunjun found the get-out excuse he'd been looking for.

Further along the track we came upon a small canvas-covered farming truck that had veered slightly off the track and was now stuck in the snow, keeling over at a precarious angle, partially blocking our path. A handful of shepherds stood around pondering how to get it free. We could have gone around it, but Turghunjun refused point blank to carry on. With a look that said, "This is as far as I go," he switched off the ignition, gave a little obstinate nod and folded his arms.

We got out to discuss the situation.

"I think it is over," said Etienne.

Danilo nodded his agreement.

Things didn't look good, and by now I was in a filthy temper. Damn it, I'd come a long way for this, and now it was being snatched from me because of incompetence. I thought back to all the hardships I had gone through to get here, distorting reality in my mind until it almost became the arch that I had set off to reach from Hobart, not England. It wasn't Turghunjun that I blamed, but Ali. Had he supplied the four-wheel-drive on which we'd agreed, then we would have been making our way through the slot canyons by now and approaching one of nature's finest wonders. I let rip at him, pointing out as much and more, while Danilo, Manon, and Etienne looked on uncomfortably at the heat of our conversation. In what, with hindsight, must have looked, and indeed was, a petulant display, I concluded our dialogue by throwing my coat, which I had been holding in my arms, on the ground.

Etienne guided me gently to one side.

"I think that was too much, Jamie," he said.

He was right, of course. I apologized to him and then with slightly less sincerity to Ali.

"How far is it to the start of the walking trail?" asked Manon, lightening the mood.

I didn't know exactly but knew it was a long way.

Ali asked the shepherds.

"They say eighteen kilometers but I think this is wrong," he said. "It is much less, maybe twelve."

"Can we hike it?" suggested Danilo, providing us with a glimmer of hope.

Etienne responded with trademark Gallic shrug.

Whatever the distance we would have to do it there and back. If it was the lower of the two estimates then it was doable, especially on the compacted track ahead, but I knew this driving section didn't go the entire way to the hiking trail. From memory, it petered out near some isolated shepherds' huts, beyond which you had to carve your own line through the landscape. Since no group had been to the arch yet this year, there would be no established vehicle tracks beyond the huts, only deep virgin snow to trudge through, something that on foot would make the journey incomparably harder.

Just as we were pondering this, Turghunjun began casually throwing trash out of the vehicle's window, littering the pristine snowy surroundings with old drink bottles, candy wrappers, cigarette packets, and the like. I picked them up and with a loud "No!" shoved them back into the rear of the vehicle. It was something I had encountered throughout Asia, but especially China, where the nonchalance for discarding trash from a car's windows was staggeringly common. Just about every driver who gave me a lift in China did this, as if it was the most normal and acceptable thing in the world. Back in Urumqi, a Spanish traveler at the hostel had regaled Manon, Etienne, Danilo and me with tales of a horrendous forty-eight-hour standing room only train ride he'd taken, where, at a small single platform station in the middle of the desert, everyone was made to disembark so that the mountains of accumulated trash could be swept straight out into the desert.

After our group council, we reached a decision: we would attempt to hike all the way to the arch, turning back at whatever point the sunlight dictated, in order to give us enough time to return to the vehicle before last light. This wasn't without risk. We were in the middle of nowhere and would soon plunge into some seriously mountainous terrain. Since Ali had no map of the route, we would have to rely on his and my memory to reach the arch—and neither of us had been there more than once. Were we driving there and got lost then our protection would have come from being in a shelter on wheels; should we lose our way on foot then it might mean digging a snow hole and crawling in for the night; and if one of us broke an ankle or leg, then it was either a long wait for assistance in hypothermic conditions or a painful limp/crawl out. Or death.

I grabbed my pack and labored forwards into a world of brilliant white, pushing hard through a glistening landscape of rounded hillsides and rugged cliffs. Every now and then a tuft of desiccated grass broke through the lower ground, dappling the snowy mantle with an occasional brown shock of vegetation. I set the pace, throwing myself into the task ahead and slipping into my own little world of exertion and resolve, my lungs heaving and heart racing in a frenzy, while clouds of vapor came billowing from my depths.

We pushed on for hours, but finally a handful of tiny mud and stone structures appeared in the distance: a pen for sheep, a stable for horses, a shepherd's home. Outside a little dwelling cocooned in snow, stood a proud head-scarfed woman wearing a chunky red sweater, thick brown skirt, and shiny black boots, which, oddly, she wore within a pair of sandals. Pottering about next to her was a toddler, wrapped up in a warm-looking pink jacket, woollen hat, leggings, and bright red boots. We nodded hello and stopped to get our bearings. The track ended here; from now on it was cross country the entire way.

From inside the stable building came a cheerful Kyrgyz shepherd who walked over and joined us. It was obvious where we were heading. Pointing at the horizon, he gestured to a chaotic mountain range visible through a veil of alpine haze. It looked a world away, but hidden somewhere in its midst was Shipton's Arch. In the snow the shepherd sketched our route, gesturing afterwards toward a valley we needed to aim for.

We thanked him and set off.

I pushed out in front again, squinting into the glaring light and wading through knee deep snow that made forward motion infinitely harder than on the track. It wasn't long before I burnt myself out. The long days on the road and diet of a single meal a day had taken its toll on me physically. I was exhausted, and we had barely even begun. My pack felt heavier with every step. I stopped for a breather, while the others caught up, soaked in the mesmerizing beauty of the range ahead. Jutting thousands of feet into the thin air was a surreal landscape of towers and gulleys, canyons, and pinnacles, all dusted with an icing of snow, highlighting the contours of the darker rock. A movement caught my eye above. Soaring effortlessly on an invisible column of air, surveying its domain in an ever-rising spiral, was a majestic bird of prey. I marveled at its beauty and wondered if it could glimpse the elusive arch from its vantage point.

Hours of drudgery came and went. My body became racked with an overwhelming fatigue, which I struggled to control, its extreme nature gnawing away at my purpose, tempting me with beguiling images of rest. I hadn't been this tired for years. I began to wonder whether it was a hopeless quest. Would we get to see the arch at all before daylight demanded our return? Eventually though, we reached the range, entering into a narrowing canyon, its meandering walls climbing steeply in snowy layers of stratum, as a wild chaos of towers gradually began closing in. Etienne and Manon were ahead of me, their long distance cycling endurance serving them well. Their progress propelled me forward by default: I sure as hell wasn't going to be the one to quit first. If they were going to make it to the arch, then so was I. I turned back to check on Danilo; he looked as battered as me. We shared eye contact and a nod but neither of us could muster a smile, it was too much effort right now. Far off behind him, now but a speck in the distance, was Ali. I turned back to the canyon ahead and plodded on.

After what seemed an eternity, Danilo and I reached the spot where, had Ali supplied us with the correct vehicle, we would have parked at hours ago and begun our hike. If only. From here the towers began to close in even more, flanking us tightly on either side until the canyon narrowed into a steeply rising series of clefts, only arm's width apart, tightly crowding out the now gray and ever-receding sky. Manon and Etienne had long disappeared from sight. I knew we were close, but couldn't quite remember how close; weakness had clouded my memory.

"Is it far now?" rasped Danilo.

"I think it's just around the next bend!"

It was a sentence I would utter around every twist and turn in the rock from now on with increasing desperation, until the words had long lost all potency.

We staggered forward into deep drifts. One cleft was so deep and compacted that it completely blocked our path, forcing us to jam ourselves between the crumbly canyon walls and shuffle our way up to the top layer. Between another narrow slot was a frozen waterfall. On my first visit to the arch we had used a removable bamboo ladder to scale this cleft, but things had evidently moved on; now a permanent metal ladder led the way.

We pushed on up through the twisting slot canyons, rounded a bend and emerged from a bottleneck into a snowy wonderland of such perfection that it stopped us dead in our tracks. On either side the cliffs swept back to form an expansive valley, sealed at the end by a gentle sloping hill, above which rose a colossal elegant window of rock, over twelve-hundred feet from top to bottom. We stood in silence for a moment, enchanted and humbled by the sight in front of us. I smiled to myself. I loved this place and had finally returned.

Suddenly, rapturous cries from above stole our attention.

"Woohoo!"

"Yeah! You made it!"

Etienne and Manon were partially up a nearby slope punching the air. We clambered up to join them at this vantage point. Ecstatic greetings and triumphant expressions of accomplishment flowed among us, before Etienne dropped a bomb shell.

"We will have to turn around soon if we're going to make it back before dark."

"How soon?" asked Danilo.

With a pained expression Etienne replied, "About five minutes."

I knew he was right. There was simply no time to press on and scale the slope leading to the arch, to stand beneath her and gaze out at one of nature's finest vistas, meditating on the enormity and timelessness of things. She was tantalizingly close, roughly a quarter of a mile away, but in these conditions, with the snow up to our waists, that could take us the best part of an hour to cover. I was more disappointed for them than for me. What we could see from here held our rapt attention, and was awe-inspiring enough, but to be under the arch, I knew, was something else. To get so close and be denied the final glory was a bitter pill to swallow. But we were burning daylight. And that was that.

I savored what time we had left and soaked in the splendor that lay ahead, reminiscing on the last time I was here with Emily. One noticeable difference between then and now was the merciful absence today of "buzzers"—rocks that detach themselves from peaks above and tear through the air with such speed as to create a heart-stopping "*vhzzzzz*," before smashing into the canyon with an almighty echoing clang. Back then one particular buzzer had ripped the air with such ferocity, and sounded so close, that I'd yelled, "Get down!" to Emily before diving on top of her. Today's heavy snow, it seemed, was holding them in place; and all was calm in the valley.

The placid mood didn't last for long. From out of nowhere, a wind began to moan and some clouds came in behind the arch, noticeably darkening the sky.

"We need to get moving," stated Etienne. "We could still die out here."

He was right on both counts. There was no time to linger.

As we turned and headed back, I glanced for a final time upon the arch before it disappeared from sight again behind the narrow walls of the slot canyons. I was sad to see her go, but I knew that one day I would return and stand beneath her again. Only next time, it would damn well be in summer. And with a 4 x 4.

CHAPTER TWENTY-ONE
Honey Trap

"Do you think this has meat in it, Jamie?" said vegetarian Danilo on picking up an ambiguous doughy offering from a food stall at Kashgar's colossal livestock market.

It was a phrase I had heard often from Danilo, and was not a question that I was entirely motivated to answer truthfully; after all, whenever he made an error and purchased a product that turned out to contain animal, he always passed it my way as a result.

"D'oh," he would tut in disappointment on biting into something and realizing his mistake. "You will have to eat it, Jamie."

"Well, if you insist," I would answer with fake reluctance.

He was always getting it wrong. But on the upside, I got to eat well around him.

Danilo and I had arrived at the renowned livestock market, the largest in all of Asia, by way of horse and cart, bumping our way along a muddy, churned-up lane lined with poplar trees, at the end of which appeared a throbbing sea of black in a huge open-air field. Here thousands upon thousands of men in black sheepskin hats and dark jackets haggled over fat-tailed sheep, yaks, goats, cows, dogs, and donkeys, most tethered together, facing each other head to head, in long tidy lines. Also on sale was the occasional Bactrian camel, amazing creatures that have evolved to cope with the region's extreme desert environments by having two sets of eyelids and eyelashes, and nostrils that they can completely seal.

The scale of the market was something else. Where there wasn't animal trading there was the associated industry: fast-fit shoe changing for horses and donkeys, sheep shearing with nothing but a pair of scissors, knife sharpening and knife sales, countless stalls selling animal collars, and of course food—for people.

In one spot near some tethered goats we found a man doing a roaring trade with a cut-throat razor; not dispatching the animals halal style, but, bizarrely, shaving the heads of locals, a tradition followed by many of the older men. It was an odd location for a hairdresser, plying his business from an old wooden chair next to a murky puddle, but Danilo and I took the opportunity while it presented itself and opted for a facial shave. If I was expecting something of an indulgent grooming session then was I in for a shock! First came a facial massage of such unimpeded vigour it felt like the bloke was trying to rip my checks clean off. Next came a lathering, although really it was nothing of the sort, with the bare minimum of suds applied to my now bruised face; and finally, a forthright hacking shave, much of it against the grain. It got the hair off all right, but I'd opt for a lubricated Gillette in front of the mirror any day.

We stuck around for a long time soaking in the sights, and on the way out came upon a corner where the market took on a medieval feel, with animals not only being traded but fought. Here two pit bulls tore each other apart in front of a circled crowd of spectators, several of whom were young boys. Danilo and I browsed at the dogs for sale instead, then headed back to the old town by way of horse and cart. Our driver was quite the character. Despite having what to us appeared a rickety old wooden platform on bicycle wheels, dragged along by an unkempt shaggy-maned horse, he obviously saw his "wheels" in an altogether different light. With a superior air and a disparaging point of the thumb, he gestured to one of his competitors trundling along nearby: "Donkey!" he exclaimed with a laugh, as if to say, "Look at that pleb, can't even afford a horse." It wasn't like he was driving a Range Rover himself. But then I guess to him, he was.

We spent the rest of the day wandering in another century, and in the evening met up with Manon and Etienne at a night market just off the main square, where such culinary treats as boiled sheep's head and feet were offered. We opted instead for a civilized hot chocolate at a nearby café.

I said my goodbyes here while I could. Tomorrow I would be setting off early.

* * *

"All Uyghurs want to be independent!" exclaimed the Uyghur passenger sitting next to me on the seat of a battered old farming truck that lurched from side to side along the potholed road to Kyrgyzstan.

His English was reasonable, the result of several years study in Europe, so I asked him about the political situation in Xinjiang. One of these he translated for the truck's driver. It didn't go down well. Jumping on the brakes, he brought us to a halt on the outskirts of an oasis village, and told me to get out.

"I am sorry," explained the passenger. "But he thinks your questions will make political problem for him."

There was no changing his mind. The ride lasted only minutes.

Other lifts came and went, taking me in staggered steps towards Kyrgyzstan.

I'd seen some dramatic scenery so far on my trip, but the journey to the border, known as the Irkeshtam Pass, was right up there with the best of it. Great gorges flanked by vertical cliffs appeared triumphantly then perished against the ranges. Veil-like clouds capped many of the highest peaks, rising from their snow-clad forms before dissipating into the sky like the holy departed drifting from an earthly plain up into heaven. The snow was undecided here: enveloping one moment, receding the next. At once a flaming rocky landscape would become exposed, saturating the foreground with sanguine hues of red, orange, and pink that mingled like glowing embers in a wider backdrop of browns and grays; and then the world was white again, all but for the clearest of deep blue skies, awash with light but bereft of any warmth. Horses and camels drifted in and out of picture. Meadows concealed beneath a drape of silken pearl rolled on towards the mighty Pamir mountains. China was fading out now, and a new frontier lay ahead. I pondered a saying attributed to a group of nomadic reindeer herders from Siberia, the Evenk: "The best thing in life is moving on to the next place." It was indeed. By the time I reached the border I was on a high.

There was a backlog of trucks but none seemed to be moving, so I said goodbye to the chain-smoking, old truck driver who brought me here and headed to the Chinese customs building on foot. During Soviet times the border with Xinjiang was all but closed, but today I slipped through without issue, and in good time too, taking minutes to clear the main checkpoint. A long walk of roughly three miles stretched ahead to reach the Kyrgyz side, but not a minute down the road, several ferocious guard dogs charged towards me from the scruffy yard of a run-down building that backed onto the road. I ran back in the direction of the customs post, praying the dogs would lose interest. They did, but their continued barks and snarls convinced me to wait for a vehicle. They clearly weren't accustomed to strangers passing by on foot.

As luck would have it, a scrap metal truck came through a minute later and responded to my gestures for a ride. I clambered in but no sooner had we cleared the dogs, than the truck broke down. With a reluctant wave I bade the driver farewell, and set off again on foot, marveling at the snowy mountain scenery as I went, which included a frozen river, bulging in form like a mini glacier. Eventually I reached a little booth on the far reaches of the Chinese side. Emblazoned on the hill opposite was a huge depiction of the map of China, with the country's red and yellow-starred flag in the center. An official here with his head buried in a book spotted me at the last minute, and waved me over with a grunt.

"Why have you come to China?" he barked in an obstinate manner.

"I haven't," I replied, correcting him with an element of challenge, "I'm leaving!"

The main border section had already given me an exit stamp so there was nothing I needed from him; he could, to put it bluntly, shove his sanctimonious attitude up his arse.

"Err, why have you *been* to China?" he grunted instead.

I had never been questioned like this on exit, so decided to mix things up a bit.

"To bring down the totalitarian state for its egregious atrocities against the subjugated Falun Gong," I replied.

He looked at me, perplexed.

"Tourist," I stated simply, as if in summation.

He waved me through.

I stepped into Kyrgyzstan.

From here the road took a steep downhill turn, twisting its way towards some official Kyrgyz buildings at the bottom. When approaching them it happened again: a handful of vicious wolf-like guard dogs came rushing out from the buildings' surroundings, charging along the road in a frenzy towards me. I scrambled up onto a crumbly hillside, sending a mini avalanche of rocks below, and began hurling stones and yelling abuse at my pursuers. It did the job and they remained below, but their furious barking alerted a uniformed military official to my presence—entering his country high up on the hill, shouting like a deranged mad man while throwing rocks all over the place, and only feet away from trampling disrespectfully over a map of Kyrgyzstan, which was emblazoned on the hillside. It wasn't the sort of first impression I would have chosen to make.

He ordered me down and rounded up the dogs, securing them inside the compound. Smoothing things over proved easier than expected, helped tremendously when the official discovered my nationality. He spoke no English but enthusiastically began dropping names of English soccer teams. We were mates now, and to show it he drove me down the road in his ultra square-lined, un-aerodynamic *Lada*—the sort of car a three-year-old might draw in 2D—to the battered little outpost of Irkeshtam. The place was a right hovel made up of rusting old trailer homes and a few weathered buildings with rickety tins roofs, surrounded by aged Russian scrap-metal trucks and decrepit-looking containers. The customs and passport control was a little better, but not much. Once again the process proved painless, and soon I was marching down the road again, skirting the edges of a vast and desolate valley.

A couple of miles of walking, during which time no vehicles passed, and I approached a little checkpoint on the road. Just beyond were three green military-style metal huts, each with a small chimney, the furthest issuing a wispy trail of white smoke into the air. I could almost sense the warmth emanating from them. By now it was late afternoon, and the temperature had dropped markedly, so when a squat young man in a puffy camouflage jacket stuck his head out from one and gestured for me to join him, I accepted without hesitation. Inside sat his older colleague, nursing a cup of tea at a little table covered with a kitschy cloth. He poured a cup for me from a flower-patterned teapot. Neither spoke any English, so I handed them a note I had acquired from a Kyrgyz couchsurfer, explaining what I was up to. They read it with intrigue and before I knew it had offered me the hut as accommodation for the night—for free. It was a tempting offer. Although tiny, the hut was super warm and cozy, with a glowing coal-burning stove and a comfy-looking bed that came in the form of a long bench with a roll-out mattress. If I didn't get a ride then it was the perfect place to crash. In fact, it was the perfect place to wait for a ride too. I could take it easy inside, remaining nice and warm, and only brave the cold when drivers came to a halt at the checkpoint. It took some doing, but after a bit of miming I managed to convey to them that I accepted their offer of accommodation for the night, but with the proviso that if I managed to get a ride, then I would push on further instead.

Kyrgyzstan was reportedly going to be a challenge. When I had first met Danilo, Manon, and Etienne in Urumqi, they had all expressed surprise bordering on concern when I told them that I planned to hitchhike through Kyrgyzstan. Not from a safety point of view—although the British Foreign Office was currently advising against all but essential travel to the country due to several violent uprisings—but from a feasibility standpoint. According to the transport section of their guidebooks, hitchhiking in Kyrgyzstan was impossible. It was, supposedly, a common sight to see people standing by the side of the road asking for a ride, but they were always expected to pay for the privilege.

I wasn't convinced.

Given that the note I'd handed to drivers through China had worked so well, I was confident a Kyrgyz one would do likewise. However, my responses from couchsurfers in Kyrgyzstan weren't that optimistic:

> . . . your plans are great but in Kyrgyzstan it's impossible. I am here since 6 years but never seen drivers help a stranger without money.

> Greetings from Kyrgyzstan, its soundz very exciting that u r travelling from Australia to London hitchin! Unfortunately . . . if there is a driver who interested in talking wt a foreigner, he would only do it for pay.

Despite these naysayers, I received several translations of my note both in Kyrgyz and Russian—apparently, people in rural areas knew primarily only Kyrgyz, whereas in urban areas Russian was the most widely understood. In addition to the translations, I received an offer of accommodation from a young American guy called Charlie who was currently living and working in the country's capital, Bishkek.

After forty-five minutes I got to put my note to the test. A medium-sized truck pulled up at the checkpoint. Sitting inside were two guys in their thirties. Handing the driver a note, I scanned his reactions as he read its contents, trying to work out his decision before he gave it. With a nod of approval he gestured me on board. I double-checked that he understood I was asking for a free ride, then clambered in, perching myself on the bed behind the two occupied front seats—so much for hitchhiking being impossible in Kyrgyzstan. With a heartfelt wave, I bade goodbye to the guys at the checkpoint and began my journey westward.

Neither of my new companions spoke any English but it was easy enough to ascertain their names, Benoit and Hamid, and where they were going: Osh, the country's second largest city, near the border with Uzbekistan. Being such a small country, there was no British Embassy in Kyrgyzstan, but the British Foreign Office website had some interesting travel advice on my next destination:

> We advise against all but essential travel to… Osh and Jalal-Abad. An evacuation of British nationals from Osh was completed on 15 June. Any British nationals remaining in these regions should exercise extreme caution and maintain close contact with the British Embassy Office in Almaty [in neighboring Kazakhstan] and the British Embassy in Astana [also in Kazakhstan].

I wasn't going to be bothering with any of that nonsense, and it certainly didn't seem reason enough to prevent me from hitchhiking to or from the place, but it did give me pause for thought. The Foreign Office assessment went on:

> Official reports suggest that nearly 300 people died during violence in Osh and Jalal-Abad Oblasts in June, but others put the figure at nearer to 2,000.

Other advice included: "Due to the recent violent unrest in Kyrgyzstan, British nationals in Kyrgyzstan should avoid flagging down taxis;" "Wherever possible you should use main roads when travelling… and continue to avoid large crowds even if in a vehicle;" "Taking photos of anything that could be perceived as being of military or security interest may result in problems with the authorities;" and my favorite, especially for a hitchhiker: "Be wary of any strangers offering assistance or being over-friendly."

We made our way along a twisting, high altitude, deteriorating mountain road, with large tracts consisting of snow-covered gravel. If the Kyrgyz landscape has one thing, it's mountains. Ninety-four percent of the country is mountainous, with an average elevation of slightly over nine thousand feet. Roughly forty percent is above ten thousand feet, and seventy-five percent of that, buried under a constant covering of snow and glaciers. The scenery of Kyrgyzstan is, to put it bluntly, bloody marvellous.

Soon a clear night sky replaced a raging sunset and the world turned black outside, broken only by the blazing stars and occasional orange-glowing windows of remote mountain villages. It was hard to categorize, but the houses looked distinctly different to those in China, more European perhaps, bestowing a sort of vague familiarity on the scene. I was a long way from home, but it made me feel on the home stretch for the very first time.

Around midnight we came to a halt at a tiny backcountry truck stop. As I stepped out of the truck and looked up into the cold clear sky, I was taken aback. The stars were magnificent, the best I'd seen since sailing out of Hobart; there was a depth and complexity to the sky that was so very inspiring and uplifting, and I stood for a while transfixed. I might have been tired from a long day on the road, but I was delighted to be exactly where I was at this moment.

Inside we settled down to a hearty meal—my first of the day—of thick pasta-like noodles served with meat and vegetables, and drank tea from dainty little porcelain cups, now coming with sugar. As we finished up, Benoit, the driver, called someone on his cell phone and handed it to me.

"My friend would like to gift you bed for the night. No charge," said the voice on the other end.

I accepted and asked him to pass on my thanks.

At 4 a.m. we arrived, pulling up outside a medium sized two-story house at the end of a dark, potholed, residential cul de sac in Osh. By now we had dropped Hamid off in another part of the city. Like cat burglars, we crept inside, making every effort to avoid waking the rest of the family as we climbed a flight of creaking stairs. Just off the landing was a small room with a roll-out mattress set up on the floor, complete with fluffy pillows and a thick duvet. Benoit waved goodnight and departed, closing the door behind him. No sooner had my head hit the pillow than I was out.

A nearby cockerel's crowing announced the arrival of the dawn, followed, soon after, by dusty shafts of light seeping into the room through gaps in the curtains. I desperately wanted more sleep but it wasn't to be. Benoit stuck his head in and gestured for me to follow him next door. Here, in a small, sparsely furnished sitting room, was the rest of the family: Benoit's wife, two young toddler sons, an elderly mother and, I think, sister. They all sat on a rug on the floor in front of a patterned tablecloth where breakfast was laid out. The old woman, or *babushka,* as they are known affectionately in Kyrgyzstan, indicated that I should join them. With a gracious nod and a hand on my heart I sat down to a meal of bread, thick-grained brown rice and preserved cherries with the pit still in them.

In what seemed like double-quick time, the meal was over and Benoit was indicating it was time for him to go out—possibly to drop the truck off. I thanked the family and bade them goodbye. Before jumping back in the truck, Benoit led me to a water tap in the garden where he began washing his face. I followed suit, the super-cold water jolting me to full alertness. We said our goodbyes on the edge of town by the single-lane road I would need to reach the country's capital, Bishkek. As this kind and hospitable man pulled off into the traffic, I raised a thumbs up sign to him in thanks. With a beaming smile Benoit returned the gesture in solidarity.

Looking rather unkempt and carrying a dirty great backpack, my presence here caused quite a stir. A woman drove past in a Lada and began gawking at me, diverting her attention from the road, causing her to crash into the car in front. The two got out and a heated verbal fight ensued that looked on the cusp of turning physical. I stood where I was and watched on, bemused. Although I'd managed to get a ride from the border yesterday, I wondered whether this had been due to the area's remote location rather than my written note. I was on the edge of a city now, so this would be the first real test of Kyrgyzstan's viability as a hitchhiking destination, and the success, or otherwise, of my Kyrgyz and Russian translations. After less than ten minutes an old-style Audi pulled up, whose driver, a rugged-looking guy, wagged his finger at me on approach. I didn't know quite what he was getting at, but after passing one of my notes through the window, he gestured for me to get in. And that was that. Hitchhiking was most definitely doable in Kyrgyzstan.

To be fair, this was a lucky first attempt, as I discovered thirty or so miles down the road when dropped in the town of Uzgen. From here I received four refusals in a row from drivers who, on reading my note and discovering I had no intention of paying, promptly drove off again. Not that this was really a problem, as it was more than balanced out by the sheer volume of vehicles that pulled over. With this being so high, it still made hitchhiking easy, since about a third of drivers were still willing to give me a lift for free. And so it went all the way to Bishkek, which I arrived at by mid-morning of the following day, after making my way there through mountain scenery of such spectacle and size that it convinced me to take up mountaineering when I finally made it back to Europe.

I was dropped just outside Bishkek by an old truck driver called Abdul, whom I had pushed on with from late afternoon until 3 a.m., and spent the night with in his cab as accommodation—me in the two front seats, him in a bed behind. My final ride into the city came from, of all people, a taxi driver, albeit an off-duty one, who dropped me by Bishkek's central square—a masterpiece of Soviet Brutalism, surrounded on all sides by communist era buildings, one of which, I learned later, was actually a massive façade, clad onto a former clothing factory to give it a grandiose appearance befitting the capital of a Soviet satellite state. Flanking the square's eastern and western sides were buildings made up of arches, from which hung giant colorful banners depicting traditional Kyrgyz life: men on horseback or training falcons; women outside yurts, all set to a backdrop of green hills and snowy mountains. At the northern end of the square was a museum dedicated, in large part, to Lenin, outside which stood a huge statue of a winged woman grasping onto a *tunduk*, the round central roof section of a yurt. Known as the Kyrgyz Statue of Liberty, it is a controversial symbol for a country where it is considered bad luck for a woman to hold a *tunduk*, and where superstition pervades to the extent that politicians slaughter sheep inside parliament to ward away evil. (Soon after I left the country, the statue was torn down—a victim of a widespread belief that it was cursed, and somehow responsible for the two revolutions and ethnic violence that befell Kyrgyzstan since its erection in 2004, when it replaced a statue of Lenin.)

Fluttering nearby was a massive Kyrgyz flag, deep red in color with a golden *tunduk* in the middle, issuing forth a ring of forty flames, each symbolic of Kyrgyzstan's different tribes. And at the square's southern end, tucked into one of the corners, was a burnt-out four-storey police station— torched during the recent unrest. I took a discreet photo, then went looking for an internet café, finding one a few minutes down the road.

After the I.D. restrictions in China, it was a delight to use a computer and the internet unobstructed. I pulled up couchsurfing.org and jotted down the telephone number of Charlie, the U.S. couchsurfer who'd offered me accommodation. With the phone booth in the internet café broken, and my cell phone long out of credit, I resorted to paying the guy who ran the place to borrow his.

"Hey, Jamie!" exclaimed an enthusiastic voice on the other end. "Where are you?"

Bishkek was a city of nearly a million people, so wherever Charlie was, it seemed unlikely that he was close, but to my delight he turned out to be no more than five minutes walk away.

I waited for him on a nearby street corner, hoping that I'd recognize him from his online profile picture. He spotted me and my cumbersome backpack first, evident when a guy in his twenties wearing a traditional Kyrgyz felt hat known as a Kalpak began waving in my direction.

"Welcome to Bishkek, Jamie!" he said with a wide smile and a firm handshake.

We walked to a gray, spirit-crushing Soviet-era apartment block, and climbed its dark and cold concrete stairwell to reach Charlie's apartment above. Inside was a cozy homage to the 1970s, with Day-Glo orange tablecloths and bright-red flowery curtains making up some of the more tasteful décor. Taped onto many of the walls were handwritten notes. "Washing machine" "To Wash" "In the washing machine," read one, next to the appropriate translations in Russian.

"Practising my language skills," explained Charlie.

Walking through a thin hallway lined with dark wooden cabinets with sliding glass doors, we emerged in a sitting room where another couchsurfer, Jason, a red-headed Brit in his thirties, sat writing up his diary notes. We all settled down for a chat.

Jason had been in Bishkek for the last few days and was heading to Kazakhstan next before flying on to India. He was in the early stages of a year long world tour and had been through some interesting places to get here, including the Kurdish section of northern Iraq, somewhere, apparently, much safer than the rest of the country. He had no shortage of funny tales from his journey so far, including an intriguing stay in Istanbul with a male couchsurfer who made him a novel pre-bedtime proposition: a massage to "help get to sleep." Jason politely declined, and wondered to himself whether this was some Turkish tradition he was unaware of, until, that is, a week or so later, he met another couchsurfer in a different part of the country who, without prompting, recalled for him a similar offer he'd received from a couchsurfer in Istanbul—albeit with an additional twist.

"I had to share a single bed with this one guy, who offered me a massage and a blow job."

"His name wasn't Serdar, by any chance?" asked Jason.

"Yes, that's him!" confirmed the unfortunate backpacker. "He told me, 'I'm not gay, I'm getting married soon, I just want to know what it's like to suck a dick. Go on, let me suck your dick. Please!'"

I laughed and then with mock sincerity turned to Charlie, "There's not going to be any of that sort of thing going on here is there?"

He laughed and gave me a little wink.

It was great to have some fluent English speaking company for a change, whom I could not only converse with but banter. We all chatted for some time, talking of our travels and getting to know each other better. Jason, I now discovered, was a doctor of mathematics who had worked in the nuclear industry; Charlie, a former microbiologist, who now worked in microfinance.

"That's a big career change," observed Jason.

"Well, I kept the small bit," responded Charlie with a laugh.

Jason had some work to do, so Charlie and I left him to it and went for a stroll. On the way, walking through streets made up of an increasing number of Caucasian Russian faces, I asked Charlie more about his travels. I was particularly interested to hear about his time in Israel and the occupied West Bank—something that had culminated in him being beaten, bound, blindfolded, and thrown into an Israeli dungeon.

"I'm Jew-*ish*," he told me, emphasising the last bit, which he accompanied with a twiddle of his downward facing palm, as if to say: a little. "I went there in 2009 as part of an organization called Birthright, which believes all Jews have a right to return to Israel."

Having taken a college course on the Israeli Palestinian conflict, Charlie had gone with a view to furthering his knowledge of this, to investigate the situation on the ground for himself, and with an open mind, but soon found himself alone among the group in that regard. Appalled at some of their attitudes and bigotry, he stormed out of a group discussion and not long after decided to venture out of the comfort zone that is Israeli, and into the occupied West Bank, to see the world from the Palestinian side. Having spent, in Charlie's words, his "entire life as an American Jew blindly supporting Israel," he was unprepared and appalled by the extent of the Palestinian tragedy that unfolded before him: a land under occupation, fragmented by illegal Israeli "settlements" and choked with Israeli military checkpoints manned by overtly racist soldiers; a place where heavily armed hilltop "settlers" would torment Palestinian villagers in the valley below, throwing stones, shining bright lights down at night, setting fire to crops, and chopping down olive groves; a place where land owned for generations by the same Palestinian family could be confiscated and their home bulldozed, and where the Israeli Army would then bill the family for the cost of demolishing their home, and if the victims raised their voices in non-violent protest they were silenced with deadly force.

If the oppression of the Palestinians was a revelation, then so too was their attitude towards Charlie, something that, as an American and a Jew, he had been afraid of before entering the West Bank. He needn't have worried. From the offset he was shown a humbling hospitality, where multiple

Palestinian families routinely welcomed him into their homes and lives, to the extent that whenever he walked the young boys of one family to the shops, he would have to promise several other families that he would visit them later in the day to drink traditional Arabic coffee.

His incarceration came after a spree of arrests in one village that saw Israeli soldiers bursting into homes in the middle of the night and dragging from their beds any males between the ages of twelve and twenty-five, who were then taken to an unidentified prison and interrogated about their involvement in weekly protests against the so called "security fence"—in reality a grotesque apartheid wall that seals in the West Bank's Palestinian population so their land and resources beyond can be stolen by Israel.

Charlie had joined a group of Palestinian, Israeli and international activists, patrolling the village streets at night, warning the population of approaching Israeli arrest squads and documenting any violence on video. One night at around 4 a.m. the alarm cry went out that Jeeps and soldiers had entered the village. Charlie found himself watching helplessly as a young man was dragged from his home and arrested. An Israeli solider violently struck Charlie in the chest with his rifle, while another began beating his Palestinian filmmaker friend nearby. As the fist and baton strikes rained in on the filmmaker, Charlie, acting on instinct, stepped in front of the Israeli soldier to try and prevent the attack, his hands held up to the sky in passive response. The next thing he knew, an arm had grabbed him around the neck and he was dragged onto the concrete floor where he was kicked. Suddenly, he was pulled up onto his feet again, but only so multiple soldiers could use him as a punching bag. They floored him once more, where he was zip-tied around his hands and feet, blindfolded, and had his pants torn off. Battered, bruised, and bloodied, Charlie was dragged by the soldiers to a nearby Jeep.

A six hour long interrogation followed, and he was given an ultimatum: sign a confession saying he attacked the soldiers and be deported immediately, or go to prison. He refused to sign and was sent to the horrendous Ramla Givon prison complex for fifteen grueling days—a break compared to what a Palestinian prisoner could expect, with Palestinians subject to arbitrary six month administrative detention, which can be renewed an indefinite number of times upon the order of a military judge. In court the judge asked him, "What would your mother think of you, a good Jewish boy, playing out there with those Palestinian monkeys?" Charlie's mother and father later learned of his arrest on their wedding anniversary via a news story that included pictures of him being beaten.

By all accounts, Charlie had balls the size of grapefruits, and was a man of conscience and conviction. I couldn't have asked for a more inspiring couchsurfing host to stay with.

"We can go for breakfast together in the morning, if you like," said Jason on our arrival back at the apartment. "There's a café nearby that's run by the honorary British consulate; apparently he's not very good at the job."

"Running a consulate or frying sausages?"

"Oh no, his sausages are first rate."

We spent the rest of the day hanging out, and when nighttime arrived it was with a sense of mild anticipation for the indulgent period of rest ahead. Having spent the previous night trying to sleep with an annoying gap around my mid section—from the space between the two front seats of Abdul's truck—tonight's arrangement was near luxury to me: a bed-roll on the floor, while Jason took the sofa.

As Jason settled in for the night, I turned off the light, throwing the room into darkness.

"Jason," I said in hushed tones as if about to venture a delicate question.

"Yeah."

"Would you like me to give you a massage to help you get to sleep?

"Fuck off!" he said with a laugh.

* * *

I received word that my old German buddy, Danilo, had made it to Bishkek and just booked into a hotel nearby. By now Jason had departed for Kazakhstan, Charlie had headed south on work, and two new couchsurfers had arrived, Caroline and Joris from Belgium, who were being hosted by Charlie's roommate Marcin, a strapping politics and security student from Poland with an easy smile and cheerful persona, who was studying at a local university.

Danilo and I met up at the main square in the evening, then jumped on a local bus with Marcin, Caroline, and Joris, to what Marcin described as "The Underground Bar," an interesting sounding establishment that was apparently hidden away behind metal bars in the basement of a dingy old building, located out the back of a parking lot. Here we planned to meet up with some of Marcin's other friends, two of whom I had met the night before: Alice, a Londoner working in Kyrgyzstan for UNICEF, and Laurence, a Swiss girl volunteering with the UN Development Program. On the bus ride there, Caroline suffered the misfortune and indignity of getting pick-pocketed, losing nearly one hundred and twenty Euros.

"Nearly everybody gets robbed on these buses once," confided Marcin to me later.

As we strolled into the car-lot, it looked a most unlikely place for a bar, with no apparent sign of its existence. All that was visible was a locked, barred door, where some unlit concrete steps led down below. The actual name of the place was "Eepjora" or "Bear's Nest,"—a Russian play on words that suggests a bear's nest with a beer—but to others it was simply "The Underground Bar" or "Anton's Place;" Anton being the owner, bartender, waiter, and bouncer, whose only staff member was his mother. He'd take the orders and pour the beers, she'd do the washing up and cook greasy food.

Marcin rang the door bell and moments later an orange light came on below, revealing an odd cage-like structure flanking the steps where a man appeared. He made his way up, giving us a suspicious "once-over" from behind the security gate, but then, on spotting Marcin, opened up. This, it seemed, was Anton.

Jason had mentioned to me trying to get in by himself a few nights earlier. He had rung the bell, and when Anton appeared asked to be admitted, only to be told he couldn't come in, and, what's more, there was no bar here anyway—despite piano playing and merriment emanating from its depths. Anton, it seemed was rather selective on who got access; and he had good reason. During the revolution, a group of ski masked soldiers had apparently raided the place, sticking AK-47s into people's faces, demanding to know why they were here drinking during the nighttime curfew—as good a motivation as any to install metal bars at the top of the steps.

Pushing through a rusting metal door, we entered into a wonderful little subterranean world, thick with the aroma and smoke of tobacco. A dilapidated basement had been transformed into an ultra-atmospheric little bar. It was more shabby than chic, but I loved the place. A roof clad in undulating white wooden beams hung low over a floor made up of bare concrete, the occasional section covered in loose off-cuts of carpet or lino. Dusty piping and random wires stuck out from multiple walls, and an exposed brick column—artificially created from what looked like the partial sledge-hammering of a non-supporting wall—stood in the main bar area, covered from waist height up in a thick coil of blue rope to protect customers from its jagged protruding bricks. Space inside was limited, but crammed in among the tables and chairs was an old piano, on top of which sat a trumpet, a bunch of aged plastic flowers and a framed photo of Anton with some unknown Kyrgyz celebrity. Hanging from the tiny bar were dried fish, and on the walls, ice axes, mounted antlers, and other curiosities.

We sat at an empty table just in time for a giant rat with a thick pink tail to scurry past on top of a dusty pipe sticking out from a nearby wall. It was enormous, the largest I'd ever seen and, if rumors were to be believed, was responsible for despatching one of Anton's cats.

As my parched lips touched the first of the evening's beers, served in huge Stein glass mugs, Danilo told me of a downright insane experience he'd had on his way here.

Having been unable to get a bus from Kashgar to Osh, he'd resorted to hitchhiking with a young Japanese guy he'd met after I left. They'd made it there okay and booked in together at a cheap boarding house, where all had seemed fine, until, that is, Danilo found himself being shaken awake in the middle of the night by his roommate.

"Men come in here with flashlights and machine guns for you. They point guns at your head and discuss whether to shoot you, and if you are terrorist," whimpered his Japanese friend in the dark.

"Don't worry. You've just had a bad dream," Danilo reassured him.

"No. It real," he protested. "They talk of killing you!"

"It's just a nightmare, everything is okay, I promise. Now go back to sleep," Danilo replied, closing his eyes and drifting off again.

In the morning when he had all but forgotten about his rude awakening, and while the Japanese guy was still asleep, he spotted that the door to their room was ajar. Having been convinced he'd locked it the night before, Danilo made his way out into the hallway to find the boarding house's owner. She spotted him first, and immediately came over.

"I'm so sorry about the soldiers last night," she said, "They were looking for a terrorist and I had to let them in."

Danilo looked at me now with a wry smile that belied the gravity of the situation.

"Bloody hell! Thank God you didn't wake up and panic, you could have been shot in the head."

Danilo gave me a knowing nod, then took a deep drag on his cigarette.

* * *

It was time, I decided, to ponder some of Kyrgyzstan's recent history. And so, in the morning I made my way to the State Historical Museum in the main square, where a superb exhibition-cum-shrine to Lenin was located. There were next to no English translations but it hardly mattered, not when the exhibits comprised towering, larger-than-life metallic sculptures of Lenin preaching to the masses, or heroic revolutionaries fighting the tsar's armies. On the ceilings murals depicted more of the same: workers breaking free from their chains of bondage; women, children, priests, and the disabled facing the charge of the tsar's sword wielding cavalry; proud Soviet couples holding the hammer and sickle triumphantly aloft.

When the Tsarist Russians arrived in what would later become Kyrgyzstan, they found its inhabitants splintered into multiple clans, with no concept of a collective nation state. Theirs was a country of family and kin, where identity was derived from oral histories passed down through the ages. Following treaties between Russia and China, Kyrgyzstan was ceded to Russia, and in 1876 officially became incorporated into their Empire. With more and more of their land handed over to Russian settlers, the Kyrgyz staged a major revolt in 1916, with disastrous consequences: 120,000 Kyrgyz were massacred by the Tsarist Russians out of a total population of only 768,000. Another 120,000 fled to China. Following the tsar's ousting by Lenin's Bolshevik Revolution, Kyrgyz lands became a part of the Turkestan Autonomous Soviet Socialist Republic (ASSR) in 1918, and then a separate province seven years later, the Kara-Kyrgyz Autonomous Oblast (oblast meaning province).

Following Lenin's death in 1924, a reconfiguring began to occur, with Russia now deciding that Kazaks and Kyrgyz were not only separate peoples but nationalities. Up until this time they had referred to Kazaks as "Kyrgyz" (to avoid confusion with "Cossacks"), and called the people who are now known as Kyrgyz, the "Kara-Kyrgyz" (Black Kyrgyz). Stalin drew Central Asia's new territorial boundaries, codified the people's languages and initiated a savage policy of "forced collectivization," whose primary aims were to eliminate the ownership of private property and bring an end to the wandering habits of the region's people: to catapult them from nomadic feudalism into a settler life of communism. Its consequences were catastrophic. Rather than give up their herds to the authorities, people simply slaughtered what animals they had and ate their fill. Subsequent famines set in, followed by rampant disease, their combined effects killing millions throughout Central Asia. Anyone who dissented was imprisoned or executed—as were those whom Stalin considered potential dissenters. Thousands upon thousands of Central Asians were "purged" this way, dragged from their homes in the middle of the night and murdered outright or locked up without charge. For the few who were charged, accusations of a hopelessly vague nature faced them: "having bourgeois-nationalist or Pan-Turkic attitudes." A sickening wave of mass executions and burials swept through the region, with entire sitting governments "cleansed" this way.

Despite the many horrendous aspects of Russian control on Kyrgyzstan and the wider region, it is not uncommon to hear people hark back to the good-old-days as part of a stable Soviet Union, something I experienced from a couple of people who gave me lifts on my way to Bishkek; their general reflections being that during Soviet times everybody had a job though no one was very rich, whereas now a few were rich and lots of people poor.

Through free health care and huge new construction and infrastructure projects, the Soviet era was responsible for substantially raising living standards across Central Asia, which saw farms, ranches, mines, factories, and other industries employing millions of people. Education made a huge impact and extended to all levels of society; literacy became practically universal, and in Kyrgyzstan the language was given an alphabet for the very first time. The sciences were encouraged, as was artistic expression—so long as it fell within the ideological parameters of communism—and distinctive national identities began to take shape.

After the fall of the Soviet Union, Kyrgyzstan and the other Central Asian republics suffered massively from the economic armageddon wrought upon Russia by "shock therapy"—the radical vision of U.S. economic advisers and political theorists which saw Russia become a laboratory for an extreme and catastrophic form of capitalism. In 1992 the U.S. government passed the Freedom Support Act, which, along with aid, saw a group of U.S. economic advisors arrive in Russia with the claimed aim of helping the country reconstruct itself. Led by Harvard economist Jeffrey Sachs, the advisers' economic prescriptions would wreak untold poverty on millions, see life expectancy nosedive and bring the country to its knees,[158] ushering in a unipolar world with the U.S. as the only superpower.

Having aligned themselves with fellow free-market disciples close to then Russian president, Boris Yeltsin, the U.S. economists drew up their proposals. The central tenet of their prescribed shock therapy was the instantaneous removal of all control by the Russian state over the economy, through the removal of price subsidies and the privatization of all state owned industries. The results were cataclysmic. As subsidies were done away with on day one of the plan, the cost of all goods sky-rocketed, to the extent that millions of ordinary people could no longer afford the most basic and essential items for their survival.[159] In desperation, and with no meaningful social safety net, millions took to the streets with their meager possessions, to sell whatever they could, and at any price, just so they could eat.[160] The currency became practically worthless, and instead of money, factory workers found themselves paid in the very products they produced, which they then had to hawk on the street. As privatization took effect, the state issued vouchers to all citizens so they could purchase stock in the former national assets. But being in such a perilous financial predicament, most people simply offloaded their shares to a few monied business men, for pennies on the dollar. And so rose up a new super rich elite, the oligarchs, in whose hands was concentrated the immense wealth of Russian industry, and the tremendous power that came with it. Further consolidation continued. In exchange for loans, President Yeltsin did the bidding of the oligarchs, handing over the remains of Russia's industry to them, at times for as little as two percent of its genuine worth.[161] Protesting deputies of the Russian parliament described shock therapy as "economic genocide." Violence erupted inside parliament with the protesting deputies occupying the building. Retribution was brutal; Yeltsin ordered the army to shell parliament, killing scores of people. The opposition was banned by Yeltsin, who announced that he would rule by decree.[162]

Interestingly, despite shock therapy having led to the collapse of infrastructure, plunging production, dire shortages, and extreme poverty on an almost unimaginable scale in Russia and beyond, the godfather of the plan, Jeffrey Sachs, now lauds himself as an expert on, wait for it . . . poverty reduction. Quite the canny rebranding exercise; and a rather successful one too, with useful idiot celebrities such as Bono and Angelina Jolie now singing Sachs' praises as, in Jolie's case, "The world's leading expert on extreme poverty;" but then, I guess if you've played a part in causing so much of it, you should be.

After gaining independence in the turbulent wake of the Soviet Union's collapse, Kyrgyzstan experienced bloody revolutions in 2005 and 2010, the latest erupted following the government's decision to raise communal charges for water and electricity. With huge swathes of the population struggling with crippling poverty and mass unemployment, this proved the spark that ignited the popular revolt. As one demonstrator put it: "I'm unemployed. There is no work and no factories. [President] Bakiyev stole everything. All that was left was the air we breathe."[163]

Trouble flared first in provincial cities where government buildings were torched, and quickly spread to the capital, escalating into an outright national uprising. As protesters attempted to storm the parliament building, snipers and police began shooting. Bodies and burnt-out cars littered the streets; shops were looted, state-run TV stations stormed; government buildings occupied, set alight or looted of everything from their drainpipes to ornamental shrubbery.[164] As thick black smoke poured from the carcasses of burning buildings in downtown Bishkek, President Bakiyev boarded his presidential plane and made a hasty exit. Inter-ethnic violence followed the revolution, particularly in the Osh provinces, where some four hundred thousand people were displaced.[165] With Bakiyev's departure, a transitional president was announced.

Bakiyev had himself swept to power in the "Tulip revolution" of 2005, but after failing to tackle the problems of widespread corruption, organized crime and the black market, and with the economy in dire straits, his support soon withered, and in 2009 he resorted to extensive vote fraud to retain power.[166] Having previously cozied up with the United States, and sanctioned, in the face of Russian opposition, the continuation of a U.S. military base near Bishkek—established in 2001 under the cover of "the war on terror"—Bakiyev dramatically increased tensions in the region between Russia, the U.S., and China. As a result Kyrgyzstan is now something of a geopolitical chess piece in a strategic game between the three, with the U.S. base at

Manas being the main bone of contention. Just one of approximately nine hundred acknowledged U.S. military facilities worldwide, which constitute a ridiculous 95 percent of all the world's military bases maintained by any nation on foreign soil,[167] the base at Manas is used as a supply post for the U.S. military's occupation of nearby Afghanistan, and serves as a handy launch pad for future U.S. military "interventions" across the region—"full spectrum dominance" in U.S. military parlance. Despite the interim government having promised, when in opposition, to send the U.S. packing, the Manas base remains open, and at the time of writing it is unclear which way the wind will eventually blow.

A long stint at the museum complete, and I headed off to explore Oak Park, a charming, century-old parkland in the heart of Bishkek. Next to the park was somewhere Marcin recommended I stop for a bite to eat: The Old Edgar, a little restaurant that was apparently superb, and, like Anton's Place, located in a basement, this time underneath the Russian Dramatic Theater. Shortly after it got dark I met up outside The Old Edgar with Danilo.

Making our way through an exposed brick entrance porch and down a small staircase, we entered a charming wooden-clad restaurant-cum-nautical shrine. From the restaurant's walls and ceiling hung model sailing boats, wooden helm wheels, bulging fishing nets and life-rings. Added to this seafaring theme were some strange, although not unwelcome, additions: antiquated typewriters and tape recorders, and, in one corner, a framed picture of none other than Stalin. It was certainly different.

We took a seat near "Old Joe" and surveyed the menu.

"Do you think this will have meat in it?" asked Danilo, pointing optimistically at some unknown meal description.

"If your eight years of concerted Russian study can't decipher it, then what hope have I?"

He decided to risk it. Minutes later a stern-looking waitress who could have doubled for a henchwoman in a Bond film, plonked in front of him a plate of spaghetti with a thick meaty sauce slopped in the middle. I received a tasty fish. As I tucked into my food in earnest, Danilo picked around the edges of his spaghetti with a look of stoic resignation. Finally, with a palpable sigh, he pushed the remains over to me, then made the best of things by filling up on beer instead.

While finishing the last of the food, we chatted about our next destinations. Mine was Kazakhstan (for which I had just obtained a visa), Danilo's, Uzbekistan.

And then something rather odd happened.

An attractive blonde woman sitting at a table nearby with an equally enticing brunette with long sparkly blue nails, got up and walked towards us, and then, without making any eye contact whatsoever, placed a paper napkin on our table, discreetly pushing it towards me. Turning around, she then walked off again.

Danilo and I shared a look of confusion.

I turned over the napkin, revealing a little note written in Biro pen:

> We are pressmen from Russia. Would like to know your opinion about KG after revolution 07.04.10. What do you know about this? Dont worry it is just a privet conversation. Sorry for our bad English. Would you like to talk?

Glancing their way, we received a discreet acknowledging nod from the blonde who'd proffered the note. It was all very "cloak and dagger."

"What do you think, Jamie?" asked Danilo.

"Sure, why not?"

We lifted our beers from the table and ambled over to join them.

After rather formal introductions, the blonde one got straight to the point.

"We hear rumors of another revolution, what is it that you know of this?"

It was news to us, and so we said as much; but why, I wondered, would they think two random Europeans would know anything about this? And so from the outset Danilo and I were both rather guarded, especially after Danilo's experiences in Osh.

Prying questions followed from the Russians—who were apparently in Kyrgyzstan on assignment from their Moscow newspaper—receiving coy or just plain untruthful answers from us in response, with me claiming to be a salesman not a writer when asked my profession, and Danilo stating he was going to China not Uzbekistan when asked where he was heading next. It was difficult to categorize, but there was just something about our inquisitors that didn't add up. Their napkin approach had been downright weird, as if they'd seen it on a bad spy show or something, and their subsequent questions weren't far off either. I began to question their motives and wondered if they were something other than journalists. When they asked us what our opinions were of the leaders of Kyrgyzstan's recent revolution, I decided to test my theory, at least partially, by turning the question around.

"Tell me first," I said, "What do you think of your own leader, do you like Putin?"

"Yes, of course," replied the blonde enthusiastically.

"But Putin is no friend of Russian journalists, when Litvinenko criticized him, Putin had him murdered."

(Russian exile Alexander Litvinenko had been assassinated in my home town, London, in a manner straight out of a Cold War spy thriller—by having his tea spiked with a rare radioactive isotope, Polonium 210. It took him three weeks to die, and from his deathbed he accused Putin of the plot, hatched in retaliation for Litvinenko's exposé of the Russian Secret Services' role in blowing up multiple Russian civilian apartment blocks in order to blame the atrocities on the Chechens, and so provide a pretext for a second Chechen war—classic "false flag" tactics of the Hegelian Dialectic: Problem-Reaction-Solution.)

"Oh, we are not interested in politics," said the blonde dismissively.

"But you are writing about politics," challenged Danilo.

An awkward silence lingered for a couple of seconds, broken by the brunette, whom until now had spent most of her time smoking long thin cigarettes, while silently regarding us.

"I have been to your country," she stated, staring a hole through me.

"Err, where have you been?"

"Buckingham Palace and Stonehenge."

"Did you like Britain?"

"No," she replied without warmth.

Danilo and I laughed at her marked absence of diplomacy. I didn't mind that she wasn't enamored by the place. Hell, I slagged it off enough myself. But was curious to discover why.

"Any reason?"

"The weather is terrible!"

It was a fair point, or at least it seemed one, until that is, we discovered, later in the conversation, which part of Russia she was from—northern Siberia no less!

"Listen love," I said on hearing this. "Our summers may be a bit drab, I grant you, but I don't think someone from Siberia, of all places, is in a position to criticize anywhere for want of its climate."

Despite there being zero chemistry at the table, with no shortage of awkward questions and uncomfortable silences, the women were insistent on meeting up with us the following night at the same time and location.

"We will see you here tomorrow, yes?" insisted the blonde as Danilo and I got up to leave.

"Yes, quite possibly," I replied.

Danilo echoed my fudging non-committal sentiment.

We said "good night" and headed for the door, stepping outside into a snowy night.

"Do you think they were really journalists?" asked Danilo.

I wasn't sure; but if they weren't, then what were they, and what was it all about? Was it somehow tied with Danilo's visit from the anti-terrorism squad in Osh? Could he be under surveillance, and the women a crude honey trap continuation of this to see if he possessed any information on a counter revolution? They'd arrived at the restaurant after us so it was possible he'd been followed there, and in a sense I wouldn't have blamed them, after all, there was definitely a dash of the villainous about Danilo; the old bugger would have made a fine extra on a pirate movie, that's for sure. But there was no way of knowing; although one thing was certain, we weren't meeting up with the Russian beauties again tomorrow evening.

Despite the women's rather strange approach and odd manner, we discounted it as paranoia. Regardless, as we made our way back to Charlie and Marcin's apartment, it was with a marked degree of furtive glances over our shoulders.

CHAPTER TWENTY-TWO

Raving with the Cops

Danilo stood before me, naked as the day he was born, sweating profusely in the darkened room, flagellating his torso with a soaked cluster of oak twigs, letting out little yelps with every stinging swipe, while a group of blubbery Kazakh men in a similar state of undress looked on bemused.

"What would your mother say if she could see you now?" I said shaking my head through laughter.

For our last day together we decided to experience the delights of a Russian banya, or sauna. It was an odd establishment, not wholly dissimilar to what I imagined, where nakedness was mandatory and flagellation optional. Split into two main isolated domed structures akin to giant igloos, were large gender-specific ice-cold swimming pools where, after emerging from a super-hot and darkened stone sauna room, you cooled down by either tipping a great pail of cold water over your head or plunging into the rigor mortis-inducing pool. Over the last couple of hours Danilo and I had fluctuated from sauna to pool—a process said to promote blood circulation through the rapid opening and closing of the capillaries under extremes of temperature—and by now were thoroughly exhausted, although not without a marked degree of satisfaction.

Several additional extras were on offer at the banya: large condensation-beaded bottles of beer, full body massages, and the sale of birch or oak twigs for use in self or group flagellation—something Danilo and I witnessed in the sauna where three men lashed the splayed and whimpering body of a third on the floor. Rather surprisingly, and for reasons I could not decipher, all of them wore a single item of clothing: knitted beanie hats. The massages available were from either professional-looking men in Soviet-style tracksuits who charged for the privilege and looked capable of ripping your arms off, or freebies from fellow naked banya users who operated on a sort of "you do me and I'll do you" basis, scrubbing each other up and down with soap suds and gusto, administering the fullest of full body massages that reached within a hairs breadth of the most sensitive areas. We skipped the massage but purchased some oak and birch branches, soaking them for several minutes in a bowl of warm water to liberate the tannins, which could then be imparted to the skin when struck against it, thus transferring some medicinal benefit.

After a marathon session at the banya we headed back to Marcin's place. While getting packed for my big push on into Kazakhstan in the morning, I received a tempting offer from Marcin's other couchsurfers, Caroline and Joris: to stick around a while longer and accompany them to a fascinating traditional sporting event called buzkashi. Often compared to polo, buzkashi's similarities to "the sport of kings" ends with the riding of horses. The literal translation of buzkashi is "grabbing the dead goat," and for good reason too, for instead of a ball, a headless goat carcass (or boz) is used. Slaughtered the day before, the goat is decapitated, has its lower legs hacked off, and entrails scooped out, before being soaked in water to toughen it up. The aim of the game is to grab a hold of the carcass and, amid a rugby-like frenzy of aggression from the other players on horseback, fight your way with it around a post at one end of the field, and drop it into a circular goal in the center. Believed to date back to the rule of Genghis Khan, the original version of buzkashi is said to have used not a goat's carcass, but a human's. It was a tempting offer to stick around and witness, but in the end the urge to push on won out.

Come the evening, Danilo and I shared a farewell meal at a Chinese restaurant, and said our final goodbyes, with promises to stay in touch and provide updates to the other on our travels. It had been great to spend time with him in China and Kyrgyzstan, and his humble, self-effacing company was going to be sorely missed.

"Don't get shot in Afghanistan, you hear me," I said on departure.

"I'll do my best," he replied with an optimistic smile.

* * *

I was on the road at dawn, making my way out of Bishkek with a wrestling coach called Adilet, who had an alien life-form of a "cauliflower ear" stuck to the side of his head—the tell-tale sign of a seasoned wrestler—and had stopped to give me a lift because I had, as he put it to me, "happy eyes."

Three more rides and I made it to the border. It was a rather undramatic affair with scant guards on either side and minimal infrastructure, making for a smooth and rather painless passage through to the other side where I stepped into the biggest of the Central Asian republics, the ninth largest country in the world, and the very largest landlocked nation of all—Kazakhstan. Trekking down the road from the border, it was hard not to think of spoof Kazakhstani reporter, Borat, and I wondered whether the country bore any semblance to its backward fictional portrayal. I would soon find out.

Although the film is obviously nonsense, albeit extremely funny nonsense, one aspect of it that I knew had a basis in reality—after reading up on it in Bishkek—was the scene where Borat tries to kidnap Pamela Anderson to be his bride. Amazingly, bride kidnapping, or *alyp qashu* is actually practiced in the region, and to a staggering extent. In Kyrgyzstan it is unfathomably common, with a third of all modern Kyrgyz brides entering marriage through a kidnap,[168] which, according to the country's former interim President, Roza Otunbayeva, amounts to 15,000 abducted women a year.[169] In Kazakhstan it is less common, but since the fall of the Soviet Union it has seen a resurgence, particularly in rural areas.

Sometimes brides are kidnapped by people they know, sometimes by complete strangers prowling the streets for a wife. Typically, a man enlists the assistance of friends or male relatives, who help bundle the woman into one of their cars or, if they don't have one, a taxi hired for the event. She is then taken, kicking and screaming, to the man's house, and held captive by his female relatives who apply psychological pressure on her to comply. This can be long and brutal, with the kidnapped woman often pinned down by force for many hours, while the older women threaten her with a curse if she does not submit to wearing a traditional white headscarf signifying her "acceptance" of the marriage. Often they simply tie the headscarf onto her while she is restrained. When the scarf goes on it's game over; an imam is summoned and the following morning the couple are wed.

Most are persuaded to stay for fear of scandal and resign themselves to their fate. With virginity greatly prized, if a woman ends up spending the night in a man's house then she is considered tainted, whether raped or not. If she leaves, then often her own family will not accept her back, leaving her with nowhere to go. Even if her family is unhappy with the marriage and the way it came about, they will often bow to traditional pressure and endorse it. Domestic violence, rape, and suicide are, unsurprisingly, not uncommon consequences of the practice.

The traditional roots of bride kidnapping are unclear, but it is thought to date back into the region's nomadic past. Some believe it originated with tribes who, when low on horses, sheep, and women, would simply ride into a village and take whatever and whoever they needed for their clan's survival. Others think its inception lies with couples who, because of class or clan differences, would have been unable to secure their parents' approval to tie the knot, and so staged kidnappings by mutual consent as a way of eloping; if the guy kidnapped and incarcerated the girl, then her family would consider her unclean and so agree to the marriage. Still others believe it originated as a way for the groom's family to avoid paying excessive traditional "bride wealth" fees to the family of the woman, or to sidestep the cost of an expensive ritualistic wedding.

Whatever its roots, since the collapse of Soviet rule, cases of bride kidnapping have sky-rocketed in the region, in part because many see it as a component of their national identity which was denied and outlawed by the Soviets. Today the practice is officially illegal in both Kazakhstan and Kyrgyzstan, and indeed outlawed by the dominant Islamic religion; but in a region where tradition trumps both religion and the law, it is rarely prosecuted, and as a result is unlikely to die out any time soon. And so for many women their lives will not be dictated by their own dreams and free will, but by whomever decides to thrust themselves upon them. If a woman is a student in the city with high hopes after graduation, and is kidnapped by a shepherd from the mountains, then a life of tending sheep, making bread, and producing babies awaits. (For more on this thoroughly baffling and shocking tradition see the excellent PBS documentary: Kyrgyzstan— The Kidnapped Bride: www.pbs.org/frontlineworld/stories/kyrgyzstan).

Rides came and went from the border, as did plenty of refusals from drivers who, on reading the new note I'd obtained for Kazakhstan, discovered I wasn't paying, and so drove off. An interesting feature of two of today's rides were bribes paid to policemen. The cops would flag the driver down, point out what appeared to be an arbitrary problem with their vehicle, and then the money would come out—it was something I would see repeatedly across the country, and brought to mind a remarkable article I had read a few weeks previous in the *Times of Central Asia*, which revealed the malleable and opportunistic nature of Kazakh officials, this time at the border:

> A study completed in 2008 for an international firm seeking to invest in Khorgos identified a glaring discrepancy. According to the Kazakh customs' statistics, 3,000 trucks passed through Khorgos from China to Kazakhstan in 2007. Yet, Chinese customs authorities put the figure at 36,000 trucks. The difference, the firm concluded, was rooted in black market activity.

The difference being a mind-boggling 33,000!

Soon the landscape transformed. A distant parallel spine of mountains stretched from east to west along the southern border with Kyrgyzstan, where the last remnants of the mighty Tian Shan range died against the flat grassland steppes that cover much of this huge country. Agricultural land dominated now; vast flat fields stretched northward, irrigated by run-off from the mountains. Villages with cozy-looking wooden-slatted homes passed by, their walls whitewashed, and window frames highlighted in various shades of blue—a popular Kazakh style.

By mid-afternoon I found myself riding in a large articulated truck with a cheerful middle-aged Russian called Dmitriy. Although Dmitriy spoke no English, I managed to ascertain where he was going—Aktau, my final destination, not of the day, but of the country. This was one hell of a long distance. By way of my map I conveyed that I was going there too, and continuing across the Caspian Sea (actually a lake) to Azerbaijan. He nodded enthusiastically, then pointed to himself, confirming that he was doing likewise.

"How long? Err, Monday, Tuesday, Wednesday . . ." I continued through the week, making progressive step-like motions with my hands, before switching to counting on my fingers.

He held up nine fingers—nine days of solid driving. This seemed incorrect. Surely, I reasoned, it wouldn't take that long. Kazakhstan is a huge country, for sure, but the point I entered it meant I'd cut out at least a third before I'd started. I asked for clarification. Dmitriy sketched out his route on my map with his finger. It bypassed the most direct line of travel to Aktau, taking a preposterously long detour north, right up to Kazakhstan's border with Russia, before heading all the way down south again to the Caspian Sea—a detour in the order of 1,300 miles.

I needed some convincing, and it took some doing by sign alone, but apparently the more direct road on my map was so bad as to be practically undrivable. Both this and Dmitriy's route went through a vast desert, but despite the added mileage from heading north, surface quality made all the difference, with the longer of the two being by far the quickest, and the only feasible option. Dmitriy offered me one of two comfy-looking bunk beds behind the cab, and clearly had no issue with me hanging around with him for the next nine days, but as tempting as this offer was, I couldn't quite justify sticking to only one lift across the whole of Kazakhstan. Being a long distance trucker, Dmitriy would no doubt be pushing on at pace, leaving me little chance to stop off at sites of interest along the way. And so, as we pulled up at a remote and deserted truck stop in the early evening where Dmitriy planned to spend the night, I decided to say goodbye and push on alone.

A biting wind followed me down the thin minor road as I walked to an appropriate spot. Standing here, staring at the empty road and then back towards Dmitriy's inviting-looking truck, I wondered if I had just made a very poor decision. Since Dmitriy was, like me, going across the Caspian,

I wondered too if he knew something about the schedule of a notoriously sporadic cargo ship that crossed this gargantuan lake, the largest land-locked body of water in the world. The Aktau cargo ship was the only way to get from Kazakhstan to Azerbaijan without flying, and was the big unknown of my sojourn through the country. According to Danilo's guidebook on the region, it was impossible to predict when the cargo ship arrived or departed, with waits of up to two weeks between crossings. This worried me. Should it take me fourteen or more days to reach Aktau, then I was at risk of my Kazakhstan visa expiring before the cargo ship arrived. Dmitriy's estimated time of arrival was nine days from now so this seemed a distinct possibility. I made up my mind to only briefly stop off when checking out sights on the way, to have a quick look around and then get moving again. If it was taking Dmitriy nine days, then that was what I had to aim for. I doubted I could match his pace, but I wanted to get close to it on the off chance he possessed some insider's knowledge of when the cargo ship left, and had planned his journey to coincide—something I had attempted to ask but failed miserably to convey.

There was, in fact, one further unknown, at least for tonight—whether I had accommodation awaiting me in the city of Shymkent. Being an oil nation, accommodation was apparently seriously expensive in Kazakhstan, and so, in an attempt to make my funds last through the country, I had messaged a couchsurfer the night before from Marcin and Charlie's apartment, asking for a place to crash. The recipient of my request was a twenty-four-year-old American girl, Sipra, who was stationed there in the Peace Corps, but with no access to the Internet in the back of beyond, I had no idea whether my request had been accepted. To find out, I would have to reach Shymkent and locate an Internet café.

To get moving again took about thirty minutes, achieved by way of a small farming truck that dropped me in a little settlement about fifty miles from Shymkent. By now the sun had disappeared, the temperature dropped further, and a howling wind arrived—a wind that induced shivering flashbacks of my freezing night in China. As darkness enveloped the world, my earlier optimism of reaching Shymkent tonight diminished. Getting a ride in the dark is always tricky, but out here, with no street lamps revealing my presence to approaching drivers, it was even harder. Had I accepted Dmitriy's offer, I would be stretching out in bed now, not standing in a cold and dark Kazakh backwater, scanning about for a place to throw a tent in case I failed to get a ride.

I waited on the opposite side of the road to a small dilapidated village store to maximize my visibility. Out came four local guys in their early to mid twenties, who, by the looks of things, were drunk. The odd sight of a backpack-carrying foreigner trying in vain to hail a ride served as a source of laughter and derision. I did my best to ignore them. It began as gawking my way while sniggering among themselves, but graduated to them calling at me, saying god-knows-what in Russian or Kazakh. A vehicle appeared and they were throwing out exaggerated hitchhiking gestures of their own to the approaching driver. They found this hilarious. After a couple of minutes, one of the group with a mouthful of gold-colored teeth and a face that looked like it had been set on fire and then extinguished by way of a beating from a cricket bat, stumbled over and began talking at me with a detectable air of disdain. I had no idea what he was saying but in an attempt to shut him up, thrust one of my hitchhiking notes into his hand.

"Kazakhstan, no free!" he said aggressively, pointing with a bony finger, presumably, at the bit stating I had no intention of paying for a ride.

Shouting across the road, he informed his buddies of his discovery. They continued yelling at me until one of then upped the ante. Reaching into the pocket of his jeans he dug out a wallet and began waving it in my face. I was tired, cold, and annoyed at myself for not sticking with the warm and comfy accommodation Dmitriy had offered me, and so was in no mood to deal with this sort of shit.

I wasn't really sure what to do, but thankfully he swaggered back to his mates. Another car approached, eliciting the same response from the group as before. That was it, I wasn't sticking around here. Turning on my heels, I continued down the road towards a gas station at the far end of the village, leaving the pricks behind.

I waited and waited, getting colder and more demoralized by the minute. On several occasions I considered bailing, finding a spot to throw my tent and crawling inside my sleeping bag to shiver out the night. But the thought that I might, just might, have a delightful couchsurfing bed awaiting me in Shymkent was motivation enough to push on. "One more car," I kept telling myself, and when it had passed

I'd say it again, repeating it like a mantra until finally one stopped. Euphorically I ran on over and handed the driver a note. He took one look at it and drove off again, leaving me in a cloud of dust, staring into the cold night air at the ever diminishing glow of his red tail lights.

Shit.

My spirits sank. To be only fifty miles away was a killer. I trudged off down the road, resigned now to an uncomfortable night outside, but then another car approached, a little white Lada, and so for the hell of it I threw out a hand. I didn't hold out much hope but it began to slow and then came to a halt right next to me. Inside were two guys about my age listening to dance music blaring from the stereo. The passenger wore a baggy gangster-style Puma hoodie, the driver, a full police uniform—by the looks of it making his way home from work in his civilian car. I handed him a note, accompanied by multiple gracious thank-yous in an attempt to avoid a repeat of last time.

"Get in!" said the passenger, waving me inside in a manner that also said, "What you waiting for?"

I did as instructed and was on the move once more, delighted beyond words to be heading away from this godforsaken dump, off into the night towards Shymkent.

"DJ Pilgrim, Uzbekistan!" said the driver enthusiastically, turning up the music.

The car became a disco. My new companions began bopping along, then laughing manically as the driver swerved to the beat, snaking along the road. I laughed too and joined in with the party, delighted at the instantaneous transformation of my situation, and so very happy to be on the move again, with two upbeat, friendly nutters, who introduced themselves as Gaxa and Pyctam.

We approached a police checkpoint on the outskirts of Shymkent. Quickly grabbing their seat belts, Gaxa and Pyctam pulled them across their chests, holding them in place to appear buckled-up.

"Fuck you, Pigs!" shouted policeman Gaxa, as we safely passed the cops, flicking the bird.

Pyctam and I laughed ourselves silly.

The next twenty minutes passed in a blur. Twisting our way through a surprisingly vibrant Soviet-era city, past flood-lit monuments and along leafy streets, we came to a halt by a small Internet café. Inside I discovered my luck held strong—Sipra was offering me a place to crash. Pyctam gave her a call on his cell, and before I knew it I was saying hello to a pretty, dark-haired American girl opposite a sprawling "Mega" mall, and bidding Gaxa and Pyctam farewell; and then, a few minutes later, stepping into Sipra's basic high-rise apartment and being introduced to her flatmate, Dina, a twenty-one-year-old Kazakh English teacher.

"Would you like something to eat or a beer?" asked Sipra, answering both of my prayers in a single utterance.

From the kitchen fridge came a brown bottle of renowned local brew, Shymkentskoe Pivo. Cracking it open, releasing an intoxicating heady aroma of nuts and malt, I took a methodical first sip, savoring the bubbles' waltz on my parched and wanting tongue. Life felt good; and it was. I thought back to the numbskulls I'd encountered at the village store and wished they could see me now, not the vagrant any more but in a world of satisfaction. But no matter how good the beer, I was even keener for sustenance. Instead of taking a hand out, I offered to cook. The girls accepted, but having already eaten requested something light. A swift inquisitive appraisal of available food and it was decided I'd rustle up one of my few culinary specialities—super thin crepe pancakes, served with lemon and sugar. They went down a treat, with Sipra and Dina having two a piece, and me doing what any self respecting guest would under the circumstances—helping to prevent wastage by devouring four.

Sadly, both the girls had to be up early in the morning, so after recommending places to visit along my route they turned in for the night. Tomorrow's suggestion: Turkistan, a Silk Road city home to Kazakhstan's greatest piece of historic architecture, Khoja Ahmat Yssawi Mausoleum.

Set up for me on the floor of the sitting room was a bed that was comfort itself: a good supportive mattress, downy pillows and a fluffy floral-patterned duvet—luxury that even Dmitriy's cab would have been unable to match. I was warm, had a full stomach and a first-rate place to sleep. I wanted for nothing and almost glowed with satisfaction. Things couldn't get much better—or so I thought. Before crashing out I decided to take Sipra up on her offer to use her laptop. I logged onto couchsurfing.org again, then afterwards checked my emails. A solitary message sat in my inbox, the sender's name jumping out at me as if written in great big neon letters:

OLIVER STONE

Bloody hell. This looked auspicious, and I had an inkling what it was about. Hovering the cursor over the name I clicked open. Inside, just as I hoped, was a gracious acceptance of an offer I had made to the Hollywood legend: to send him an advance reader copy of my book on Venezuela—a country that featured heavily in his recent documentary, *South of the Border*—with a view to him writing a short endorsement for the book, provided, of course, that he liked what he read and saw promise in it. I was delighted he'd agreed, and sat with a smile from ear to ear.

* * *

As the sun rose in a bright and clear blue sky, I set off for Turkistan, home to Kazakhstan's greatest historical building and its most significant site of Muslim pilgrimage, the Khoja Ahmat Yssawi Mausoleum. Built in the fourteenth century over the grave of renowned Turkic holy man and mystical poet, Khoja Ahmat Yssawi, the mausoleum was constructed by one of history's great tyrants, not Iraq butcher Tony Blair, but Tamerlane (also known as Timur), an interesting, if thoroughly ruthless, despot whose rampage of conquest killed seventeen million people and created an empire that stretched from Turkey to the frontiers of China, and from Russia to northern India. If anyone epitomizes the cruel and merciless despot then it is Tamerlane. Throughout Asia he constructed towering cemented pyramids of human skulls outside the cities he conquered, the structures' main ingredient coming from the heads of the men, women, and children who once resided there.

Unlike other empire builders, Tamerlane demonstrated little interest in actually governing the areas he sacked. Rather, his approach was that of a ram-raid looter, but with one key distinction; as well as stealing and then carting back to his place everything that took his fancy, he would often indulge himself in the wholesale slaughter of the city's inhabitants. In Northern India alone he put five million people to the sword. Such a total and utter just-for-the-hell-of-it overkill terrified inhabitants of other cities to the extent that often they would surrender without a fight. Were there an award for history's top malignant and vindictive bastard, then Tamerlane would certainly be one of the nominees. Legend has it that when he conquered Ottoman Turkey, rather than kill the Ottoman Sultan, he opted instead for unending humiliation for the unfortunate former ruler. Tamerlane is said to have kept him as a pet, shipping the Sultan back to his palace where he was forced to live out his days in a cage, looking on while his naked wives were made to serve Tamerlane and his guests.

But there was more to Tamerlane than vengeful spite alone. In a sense he was the ultimate James Bond villain of his time, a maniac set on world domination but with a strange fondness for the refined: culture and the arts, both of which he promoted. He surrounded himself with scholars and scientists—often captured during conquest—and would plunge into impassioned debate with them, even on campaign. His private library was packed with scholarly manuscripts, and his quest, it seemed, was sometimes as much for knowledge as power, with him displaying a passion, love even, for mathematics, medicine, architecture, and astronomy. On a giant 110 square board he would play a modified version of chess, known today as Tamerlane Chess, that included several new pieces: giraffes, elephants, war engines, camels.

His love of architecture saw the transformation of city Samarkand (in modern day Uzbekistan) into the greatest city of Central Asia, a monumental trophy to Tamerlane's ego and military prowess, a magnificent capital city that swelled in size with captured scholars, architects, artisans and craftsmen—the lucky ones, spared the grisly fate of so many of their fellow vanquished, thanks alone to their profession. To Tamerlane's court came foreign envoys, including the Spanish ambassador of King Henry III, Ruy González de Clavijo, who returned to Europe with tales of magnificence and brutality, fueling the West's imagination for the exotic and mysterious Samarkand, which under Timur's rule became a masterpiece of Islamic architecture, stuffed with fine works of art and literature, as did other cities of his near empire—an example being the one I made my way to now.

I arrived at Turkistan by mid-morning after an easy hitchhike from Shymkent that took me past several massive billboards plastered with magnanimous images of the country's iron-fisted dictator, President Nursultan Nazarbayev (whose regime, irony of ironies, has enlisted war criminal Tony Blair and his low-life former director of communications [minister for propaganda], Alastair Campbell, to help clean up his image),[170] and onwards through an ever flattening landscape of cotton fields, salt marshes and steppe, to the fringes of the Kyzylkum desert.

A wrinkly old truck driver dropped me off in the center of this modest Silk Road city of seventy-thousand people, opposite three clapped-out Russian buses parked outside the dusty grounds of Tamerlane's greatest Kazakh construction, the Khoja Ahmat Yssawi Mausoleum. Standing proudly behind a mud-brick fortress wall, dotted along its length with regularly spaced battlements, it was a building unlike any I had seen before. It looked part desert fortress, part mosque, part royal palace. Towering out of a brown and faded landscape, rose the giant structure, its front comprised of a sandy-colored brick façade with a cavernous arched entrance portal that rose into a V-shaped point, making up the tallest part of the mausoleum. Protruding from this archway, rising high up on its walls, were multiple twisted beams of wood—the purpose of which I have no idea. Two rounded battlement-topped bastion towers sandwiched the portal on either side; behind which the structure suddenly transitioned into something very different: more mosque than castle. Perching on its upper levels were a pair of glorious domes, one big, one small, both tiled in turquoise and gleaming in the light of a cloudless sky. Beneath the domes fell clean straight walls clad in exquisite light and dark blue tiles, laid out in repetitive geometric shapes and Arabic scripted calligraphy, their uniformity only broken by the occasional carved wooden door or delicate lattice window. And standing alone in front of the main structure was a smaller building in a corresponding style, its diminutive size serving as an exclamation mark, highlighting the majesty of the larger architectural wonder behind.

I strolled towards the mausoleum along a path of crazy-paving, thronging with hordes of Kazakh tourists and school groups. After mingling among the other sightseers examining the mausoleum's extremities, I passed through the arched entranceway and stepped into a cool and surprisingly plain interior. There were no grandiose embellishments here, only plain white walls and ordered gray floor tiles, creating a serene atmosphere. Several rooms were open to visitors, but none compared to the majesty of outside. With no placards for me to read in English, I quickly had a look around, then headed back outdoors where I spent the next hour marveling at the intricate detail of the structure's exterior.

* * *

I was long since used to my presence drawing plenty of attention in remote towns, and as I walked through Turkistan's bustling streets it was no different. Such atypical appearance served me well, with a lift quickly coming from the driver of a beat up Soviet-era car.

A curious-looking chap sat behind the wheel, sporting a tufty beard from his chin. Wrapped up in a thick leather jacket with big furry lapels and cuffs, he wore a brown skull cap on his balding head. I handed him a note. Considering it silently for a moment, he looked at me and smiled.

"I am Muzappar," he said "I take you to meet my wife."

Fair enough, I thought, let's see where this leads.

It led to a local school canteen.

The children must have been in class, or maybe off on an excursion, as the place was empty but for several teachers and catering staff, sitting at a row of plastic-covered tables eating cakes, breads, candies, and sipping at bowls of yogurt.

Muzappar introduced his wife, a plump old mother hen of a woman with a mouthful of gold teeth—a common sight in the region—and sat me down between her and an attractive, and rather buxom, young teacher, who among a mouthful of pearly whites flashed a single golden tooth my way as she smiled; something I found rather fetching.

"This celebration for Norouz," said Muzappar's wife. (Norouz being the imminent Persian New Year).

Neither she nor Muzappar spoke much English, and the young teacher none, so I did as often before: graciously smiled and nodded while getting stuck in to the food. On completion of the meal I received a surprisingly forward and unexpected offer from the delightful young lady next to me: would I like to stay at her house tonight? Muzappar's wife delivered the question, noting that, "she has own house and will guest you tonight." Muzappar was a world of none-too-subtle suggestive nods, whose meaning was clear.

The free accommodation was tempting, but this one seemed like a bad idea. I didn't fancy a repeat of the situation with Mandy, so I politely declined. Muzappar sighed, accompanying this with a slight shake of the head, and an expression that spoke of lost opportunities. Such was his disappointment it almost seemed as if he'd received the offer himself. In fact, I got the distinct impression that he not only fancied his wife's work colleague—an understandable reaction—but also the prospect of living vicariously thorough any potential escapades I could have got up to with her.

Minutes later and we were back on the road together, with Muzappar dropping me on the outskirts of town on the road heading north. Waiting here was a line of Kazakh hitchhikers, doing so in the Central Asian tradition, where money was changing hands. I didn't want to appear part of this group, so I hiked on up the dusty road into an expansive flat landscape of perfect uniformity; two simple halves, one of clear blue sky, the other scrubby grassland-steppe.

My next destination was Otrar, the ruins of a former Silk Road city where, a century before Tamerlane, the actions of the city's governor would change the course of human history, bringing down the mighty Khwarazmian Empire of Persia, and setting in motion the expansion of another far greater empire that, at its height, was eight times the size of Alexander the Great's, and four times the size of the Romans'; an empire built upon a simple natural resource, grass, that fed horses by the millions ridden by unstoppable waves of nomadic archers; an empire that would lead to the brutal death of millions and see its founder's name go down in legend, as both an evil and ruthless barbarian, and the most successful military commander the world has ever known—Genghis Khan and the Mongol Empire.

The story of Genghis Khan begins in the heart of the vast grassland plains of Central Asia, the steppes, where nomadic tribes roamed wild and free, characterized by their equestrian lifestyle of hunting on horseback (a Central Asian innovation) with distinctive and formidable bows made from a combination of wood and bone that were capable of a range of over 1,500 feet. Born to the name Temujin in a remote Mongolian yurt in 1162, the child who would go on to be called Genghis Khan was delivered clutching, so the legend goes, a coagulated blood-clot in his tiny hand, a sign from heaven that the infant was destined to be a mighty warlord. The young Temujin's upbringing was marred by the butchery and killing of inter-clan feuds that saw his father poisoned when he was nine years old. His father had been the head of his small clan, and so by tradition this role as leader would normally have passed to his eldest son, Temujin. But at such a young age, the rest of the clan refused to be led by him, and so

deserted Temujin and his immediate family, who were forced to roam the
remotest parts of the region's steppes and reduced to hunting small game
and digging for roots. It was during this time that Temujin, still in his
teens, murdered his half brother for refusing to share the spoils of a hunt
with the rest of the family.

As he grew older, Temujin realized that the only way his small band
of family members could survive was through forging links with other
clans, and the best way to do that was marriage. So he was wed, but soon
afterwards his wife was kidnapped by a rival tribe, a common practice in
the dog-eat-dog world of the steppes, where if you wanted something you
simply took it. Incensed, and with the assistance of his childhood friend,
Jamuka, Temujin gathered together a band of warriors to ride in and rescue
her, and then destroy the offending tribe. The mission was a success, and
at just twenty years old Temujin had successfully annihilated one of the
great tribes of Mongolia, a tribe that had feuded with his father. Despite
Temujin and Jamuka's collaboration and subsequent joint leadership of their
increasingly powerful tribe, tensions grew between the pair, centered around
a disagreement as to who was eligible to serve in the tribe's highest ranks. In
contrast to tribal tradition, Temujin believed it was simply a case of ability
and loyalty; whereas Jamuka, son of a nobleman, believed in the old way of
doing things, reserving the highest ranks for those of aristocratic birth. In the
end, Jamuka rode off in disgust, splitting the tribe and taking his supporters
with him. Two years passed before Jamuka and Temujin would meet again,
when Jamuka, who had now formed a coalition of tribes, ambushed Temujin
and his followers. Despite Temujin's forces suffering a crushing defeat, he
managed to flee with his life, regrouping, with his loyal survivors, to fight
another day. For his captured generals there would be no second chance:
Jamuka boiled them alive.

If this was meant to piss off the man who would become Genghis Khan
then it did the job. Temujin swore that never again would he be defeated
and he began building an army in earnest, uniting disparate tribes against
Jamuka. Casting aside the old tribal conflicts, he created a fighting force
based on merit where the spoils of war would be shared accordingly, and
instigated a system of training where even children were required to practice
the arts of horsemanship and archery. This was something they were trained
to do in conjunction, learning to fire arrows at the precise moment the

hooves of a galloping horse were simultaneously off the ground, providing the archer with stability and accuracy of shot.

As Temujin's forces rode out to confront Jamuka's, they employed the tactics of psychological warfare. When setting up camp at night within their enemy's territory, Temujin instructed his men to light five fires apiece. It had the desired effect, with Jamuka's scouts reporting that Temujin's army had more fires than there were stars in the sky. The next morning the two armies rode against each other in battle for control of Mongolia and the rule, for the first time ever, of all its tribes under one undisputed leader. It was a battle that Temujin won, and soundly, making him Genghis Khan: the supreme leader of all. Jamuka's fate was an appropriately grisly one. Despite having initially managed to make a run for it, he was soon betrayed by his own who handed him over. In what was supposedly an act of clemency, Jamuka was granted an honorable death—having his back broken, so as to avoid the spilling of blood.

With the unification of the once disparate and warring Mongol tribes, a powerful nation emerged, a nation that would next head south to take on the colossus of eastern civilization: China. Not that the Chinese emperor seemed fazed when he heard of their advance: "Our empire is as vast as the sea, yours is but a handful of sand, how can we fear you?" he stated in a dispatch. It was to prove a terrible underestimation of the Mongols. Genghis Khan ordered the "total annihilation" of Beijing, and he got it. A year after the Mongol hordes had raped, pillaged, burned, and slaughtered their way through the city, visiting foreign ambassadors reported that its streets were still "slippery with human fat."

Following the military stampede of Beijing, Genghis Khan's attention turned west, not for invasion's sake but trade's. In an effort to initiate commerce with his settler neighbors, he sent out a party of roughly four hundred and fifty merchants to Silk Road city, Otrar—part of the Khwarazmian Empire that stretched from Persia, across much of Central Asia, to the steppes of Kazakhstan—with a camel train laden down with gold, silver, Chinese silks and furs. The welcome they received from Otrar's governor was not one that was likely to win favor with Genghis: he accused the envoys of being spies, seized their booty, and locked them up. In what, considering Genghis' past form, can only be considered an altogether restrained response, he sent a message to the head of the Khwarazmian Empire in Persia, the Shah, demanding that the merchants be released and that Otrar's governor be handed over to him for punishment. Things didn't quite work out like that. The envoys were executed, and the decapitated head of Genghis Khan's messenger sent back to him in a box. It was a casus belli that the Shah would bitterly regret.

It was these actions by the Shah and Otrar's governor, Inalchik, that saw the Mongol army turn west. They arrived at Otrar the following year, in the autumn of 1219. The sight that greeted the city's inhabitants was one that quite possibly led to the greatest en masse pant-soiling in world history. Beneath Otrar's city walls, stretching as far as the eye could see across the vast barren planes, was a two hundred thousand strong horde of mounted Mongol warriors, itching for a fight, the air thick with their collective furious roars and the scream-like neighing of their horses and iron-armored mules. Picture the scene: you're surrounded, there is no hope of escape or place to hide across the plains, no chance of reinforcements arriving in time, no chance of your own forces repelling the attack, and no way of placating the hordes baying for blood; you may as well stick your head between your legs and kiss your arse goodbye; you are, in a word—fucked.

Having once attended a rock concert in a field with 125,000 people,[171] I can appreciate, at least in part, just how ridiculously big a group of people that is in one place. But a concentration of nearly twice that, and on horseback, and heavily armed, and with a reputation for barbarity, and intent on leveling your home, raping your wife, and butchering your children; it hardly bears thinking about. Otrar succumbed to the inevitable. The governor barricaded himself within the citadel with twenty thousand soldiers, but it was a futile effort. They soon ran out of arrows and in desperation began throwing roof tiles at the Mongols. It was a valiant, if hopeless, last stand that was hardly likely to intimidate an army who had faced down somewhat more effective airborne projectiles from the Chinese: a bombardment of catapulted bombs containing crude oil, chemicals, molten metal, and human faeces. For Inalchik, the governor who had so instigated the Mongol's wrath, there awaited a brutal fate. Into his ears and fear-dilated eyes was poured molten silver.

After their taste of blood at Otrar, the Mongols rode on in a whirlwind of brutal savagery, rampaging toward Persia, and smashing through every town and city in their path. While Mongol horses trampled the Koran under hoof, and soldiers smashed their way through the streets of Bukhara (in modern day Uzbekistan), Genghis entered the city's pre-eminent mosque and scaled the pulpit with a message for the congregation: "I am God's punishment for your sins!" he bellowed before razing their magnificent city to the ground. In the Mongol's wake lay a sea of carnage and burning ruins that stretched across the region and saw over a million people slaughtered, the Khwarazmian Empire brought to an end, and the Mongols push for the first time into parts of Eastern Europe.

Genghis died a peaceful death in 1227, and if he was remorseful for a life of slaughter then he didn't show it on his yurt deathbed. His last words to his followers and heirs: "I have conquered for you a large empire, but my life is too short to take the whole world, that I leave to you." For a man who believed his mission from God was to conquer the entire world, it made sense. Following his death, his sons and successors gave his last wish a pretty good stab, doubling the size of the Mongol empire, pushing as far into Europe as the borders of the Austrian capital, Vienna. What prevented them from taking Vienna, and in all likelihood the rest of Europe, was not the abilities of the Austrian army, but rather Mongol law. During the campaign the new Khan died, an eventuality that called for all chiefs to immediately return to Mongolia to elect the next ruler. They did, never returning to finish the job, with the Mongol empire eventually disintegrating a generation after Genghis Khan's death, in part because they inadvertently passed on to those they conquered the warring tactics that had made their subjugation possible in the first place. Horse warfare was adopted and adapted by the technologically superior settler states, and soon the Mongols got a taste of their own medicine. Interestingly, some historians believe that medieval European chivalry has its origins in Mongol horseback culture, which European knights then refined and imbued with a sense of gallantry.

Perhaps the biggest legacy that Genghis Khan forcefully stamped on the world was not the biggest land empire the world has ever known, or the tactics of mounted warfare, or serving as the inspiration for the Dothraki in *Game of Thrones*, but his DNA. Notorious for his multiple wives and of rape on an industrial scale, where he would have his way with the most desirable women among the vanquished, one thirteenth century Persian historian claimed that Khan was responsible for a lineage that amounted to over twenty thousand people within a century of his birth. Such a claim might sound preposterous, but recent genetic studies of Central Asian men have revealed that eight percent of the population, that is sixteen million men, have the same type of Y chromosome as Khan, and in men worldwide about 0.5 percent. This equates to roughly one in every two hundred males alive on the planet today who can trace their genetic lineage back to the mighty Mongol King.

Passed from father to son, the Y chromosome is normally inherited unchanged except for occasional random mutations. These mutations are referred to by geneticists as markers. Such markers can then be used to trace backwards through time to the point where they first emerged, and so provide a lineage back to a common ancestor. The study in question traced back these markers to roughly three generations before Genghis Khan's birth, so if the theory is true then this genetic marker was most likely passed onto Khan by his great-great-grandfather, before being spread far and wide across the empire by Khan's own sexual appetite and opportunity.

Such a hypothesis is, of course, guesswork, as no sample of Genghis' DNA exists today, nor is it ever likely to as he received a clandestine burial where great lengths were taken to conceal his tomb's location—the main precaution being the wholesale slaughter of all those who witnessed the funeral possession. A befitting parting gesture if ever there was one. But what can be known, is that for such a Y chromosome to be so prevalent, then it had either to be responsible for passing on some biological advantage— apparently unlikely, as it is little more than the switch responsible for turning an embryo into a male child—or, on the other hand, its possessor had some extreme social advantage. And Khan is the only feasible candidate. Lending further weight to the hypothesis is the geographical spread of the chromosome's possessors, which matches, almost exactly, the territory of the Mongol Empire.

Now here's something that I'm not particularly proud to mention, but it only seems right. I never got to visit the ruins of Otrar. I wanted to go to Otrar, I planned to go to Otrar, and what's more, damn it, I thought I had gone to Otrar, but by some inadvertent cock-up on my behalf I ended up going to the wrong deserted Silk Road city ruins; not the one where the governor's actions had sparked a wave of Mongol retribution that engulfed much of the ancient world, but one further down the road called Sauran Krepost, which served as the capital of the Mongol White Horde in the century following Genghis Khan's death. And here's the thing, this monumental blunder only became apparent to me a year after the event when writing up my experiences for this book.

While going through my notes, I decided to have a quick aerial look at the place via Google Maps. What I saw left me scratching my head in bewilderment. The website pinpointed Otrar as being far further off the main road than I recalled, and its representation from above bore no resemblance to my memory. Having detected the occasional error on Google Maps before, especially in remote regions, I initially put the anomaly down to website error, and so began scanning the desolate landscape closer to the main road, where I was confident I would find the site. But there was still no sign of it. After much zooming in and out, and plenty of confusion, I turned to my notes where I found several photocopied pages from the Kazakhstan section of a *Lonely Planet Central Asia*. For some reason on these I had circled the directions to both Otrar and Sauran Krepost. I can only deduce that through a combination of fatigue, inability to converse with locals, and downright carelessness, I followed the directions to the wrong ruin. Another factor that might have led to my mistake was that both sites were described in very similar terms: Otrar as a "large dusty mound" and Sauran Krepost as a "long, low mound," visible from the road, something I had been scanning the landscape for on approach, and disembarked on spotting.

A bamboozled truck driver dropped me off, in what I'm sure to him seemed the middle of nowhere, with the dusty mound about a mile away across the flat and barren steppe. I hiked towards the ruins, passing through a little tunnel leading beneath a train track that ran parallel to the road. The city's ancient walls were now a crumbling geriatric spine of crude mud-clad brick, resting on top of a vast circular grassy mound, stretching about a half mile in diameter. Looking back at my actions now I feel a bit of a plonker, for at the time I climbed high up onto the walls and gazed out across the steppe, recreating in my mind's eye the great Mongol attack, which, unbeknown to me, had occurred fifty miles to the south.

But no matter, I may have arrived at the wrong site and been oblivious to the fact, but it was marvellous, nonetheless. Stepping from the wall, I entered the citadel's abandoned grassy basin where the ancient remains of sandy-colored brick buildings stood, their gaping foundations reaching deep into the earth, exposed by past excavations. Shards of pottery lay strewn across the site, some heaped in great piles as if archaeologists had collected them up to study en masse, then just abandoned them where they were. I roamed through a collection of shiny glazed fragments, decorated in swirling patterns of blues, whites, and grays.

Every so often a soft breath of wind would stir, which along with the gentle chirping of birds created a soothing music for the soul. If there was one thing that struck me about the place it was its serenity, helped, I'm sure, by me having the entire deserted city to myself. I spent a good while ferreting about, trying to picture it in its heyday, and at one stage lay back in the center propped up against my pack, feet stretched out in front of me, soaking in the sunshine, which, for the first time in a long while, held a discernible and transferable warmth. I felt so at peace and yet so alive, as if a part of everything around me. Thoughts of people I hadn't seen for years drifted into my consciousness. I wondered what they were doing and if their days were filled with such adventure and exploration. A smile rested on my face as I pondered the wonder and insanity of the obvious: I had hitchhiked from Tasmania into the middle of an abandoned Silk Road city on the barren steppes of Kazakhstan. It was a realization that couldn't help but fill me with satisfaction.

CHAPTER TWENTY-THREE
Environmental Apocalypse

I rode with a Russian guy dressed in a blue-collar factory uniform, who picked me up in a comically square-formed Lada on the outskirts of once-thriving Soviet industrial city Kyzylorda, now marked with an array of rusting pylons, old decrepit factories and rice silos. His name was Feder, and together we traveled for about a hundred and fifty miles, a journey that saw what little color was left in the flat and barren landscape drain away, until the sandy desert plains turned a dull and lifeless grayish brown, lashed by localized sand storms that attacked the car's rattling windows. We were on the eastern fringe of the mighty Kyzylkum, or red sands, desert, the eleventh largest in the world. In the middle of this apocalyptic landscape was one of the world's remotest military installations—Baikonur, home of the Russian space program, the oldest space launch site on the planet.

The Baikonur Cosmodrome is still leased to Russia who use it for rocket launches, as is a nearby garrison town, but as we entered the area it became apparent that neither would be visible from the road. In 1988, Baikonur was the site of the maiden launch and landing of a fascinating, and largely unknown, spacecraft—the Soviet Union's space shuttle. Known as Buran, or Snowstorm, the shuttle's existence had been rumored for years and was confirmed just days before its launch by the Soviet newspaper *Pravda*, not splashed triumphantly across the front page as you might expect but revealed somewhat discreetly on the second page—a lovely bit of understatement if ever there was one, a sort of, "Oh yeah, by the way we've got one of those space shuttle things ourselves." Although it looked incredibly similar to the U.S. version, the Soviet media was at pains to point out that their version was a technologically superior craft; and by all accounts it seems that it was.

On a cold November's morning thick with snow clouds and the sort of erratic swirling winds that would have postponed the launch of any U.S. shuttle, Buran was powered off into space, thrust into orbit by its giant Energia rocket. For the next three hours it performed two orbits around the earth, then re-entered the atmosphere and glided, despite adverse wind conditions, with extreme precision to as perfect a landing as could be hoped—just nine feet from the center of Baikonur's runway. And what's more, it accomplished all this via remote control, not a single astronaut was on board—that, and it never made another flight.

A year after its maiden voyage, the Berlin Wall came down and the Soviet Union crumbled soon after. The Buran project was shelved, and the shuttle itself put into storage in Baikonur's hangar 112. As funds for maintenance of the hangar dried up, the building began to deteriorate, with water dripping from the roof forming into pools on the floor around the high-tech equipment. In an attempt to repair the roof, on May 12, 2002, an eight man team scaled the building. According to eyewitnesses, it began to shake violently as if struck by an earthquake. The roof collapsed, obliterating the shuttle and killing the maintenance team.

As Fedar drove through the area, I scanned the landscape, hoping upon hope, that maybe, just maybe, I'd be lucky and we'd pass by at the exact moment the Russians launched one of their conventional rockets into space. Nothing so exciting occurred, although I did spot several marmots: little prairie dog-like mammals that live in burrows and stand up on their hind legs to look around. Fedar and I parted by a side road that led further into the barren wastes where, at some point in the unseen distance, a hub of launch pads, satellite dishes, antennae and rockets was situated. I would have loved to have asked him about his role here, but it was beyond my linguistic ability. Before he drove off, Fedar handed me a brown paper bag. Inside was a mound of damp carrot shavings, some dried fish and fried bread. With thanks I wrapped it up for later and struck off, my head hunched down against the flailing sand, hoping that another vehicle would soon come by.

It did; and it was driven by a policeman.

He demanded my passport. I gave it to him along with one of my notes.

"This is closed area," he stated, burning a hole through me with a stare.

"What about the area ahead?" I asked in as courteous and conciliatory a manner as possible.

"Closed."

"And behind?"

"Closed."

Great. So I was smack bang in the middle of a restricted military zone.

"Can I continue walking?"

He shook his head. "I will take you up road," he stated in as emotionally flat a manner as is possible, rather Arnold Schwarzenegger in Terminator, neither friendly nor hostile, just extreme matter-of-fact.

By late afternoon I arrived at my final destination of the day, Aralsk. Once a thriving fishing port on the coast of the Aral Sea, it had lost that rather crucial commodity necessary to sustain a fishing industry—the sea where its fish once swam.

Of course you don't just lose a sea like you do a set of keys down the back of the sofa, it takes quite a bit more carelessness than that. You have to do something pretty drastic, and that's what the Soviets did to the Aral's precious tributaries, the Amudarya and the Syrdarya. These river systems funneled run-off from the distant Pamir and Tian Shan ranges into the Aral Sea—actually a lake, that in the 1960s was more than twice the size of Belgium—serving as a crucial counterbalance to water lost from evaporation in the glaring desert sun. But in order to irrigate the region's newly constructed cotton plantations, the inflow from these essential tributaries was channeled, pumped and diverted away from the Aral, reducing the water that reached the sea to barely a trickle. With next to nothing coming in from the mountains, it wasn't long before evaporation began sucking the sea up into the atmosphere. Not that the Soviet planners seemed particularly bothered, at first at least, with them anticipating that the Aral Sea *would* shrink. Such was their obsession with greater cotton yields that they even made plans to construct a giant canal stretching all the way to Siberia, not to channel water to refill the Aral but to further boost production. It all led to an ecological catastrophe of truly biblical proportions, often described as the worst environmental disaster caused by man, and one that is clearly visible from space.

The Aral Sea once boasted beautiful clear water, pristine beaches, varied and unique ecosystems supporting diverse flora and fauna, and abundant fish stocks; so much fish, in fact, that in 1960, forty thousand metric tons was harvested. The Aral was a paradise in the middle of the desert, an island sea, cut off and isolated by a surrounding ocean of sand, and one that provided mass employment at Aralsk's fish canning factory, the largest in the Soviet Union. In 1960 the sea stretched over 250 miles in length, was 173 miles wide, and covered 26,300 square miles, and had passenger ferries and fleets of fishing boats sailing across it. Not any more. Today it is a shadow of its former glory, a mere puddle by comparison, which by 2005 had leached sixty miles away from former coastal town Aralsk, and by 2010 had shrunk in size by more than 90 percent.

It was in the seventies that without warning the sea said goodbye to Aralsk, leaching away from its expansive harbor and disappearing into the desert, leaving nothing but a dry and dusty seabed in its wake, where landlocked fishing trawlers lay, never to set sail again. God knows what it must have been like for the locals, people who were as used to seeing the sea as they were the sky; and now it was gone, vanished as if someone had pulled the plug on a giant bath tub.

Making my way past a ubiquitous collection of white-washed houses, I booked into the only hotel in Aralsk, a decrepit four-floor establishment with plenty of boarded up windows, run by an old crone who practically growled at me as she handed me my room key. I went out immediately to look around. On the street outside, I passed three despondent-looking youths in their middle teens. One snarled and threw an empty cigarette package at me. It missed but landed at my feet. With an aggressive kick I hoofed it back towards him.

Jeez, what was it with people around here? And then I saw; their sea had gone.

At the end of the street lay a decorative blue gateway. Beyond stretched an apocalyptic scene of desolation, made all the more pronounced by a surrounding wharf with rusting cranes, a derelict fish-canning factory and several empty, broken-windowed port buildings. Here the ground dropped away into the deep banks of a vast harbor—containing scrubby wasteland rather than water. Past the harbor, stretching as far as the eye could see, was nothing but desert. A brown and white cow grazed nearby across the former seabed. Some old decaying fishing boats stood lined up on the sand, resting on plinths; a reminder of happier times, or perhaps a warning to future generations of what happens when nature isn't treated with respect.

As I looked out at the bed of what was once the fourth largest lake in the world, I shook my head in disbelief: there was no water here! Obvious, I know, and something I knew before arrival, but now here it was difficult to comprehend. To be honest, the place gave me the creeps; this one-time paradise was thoroughly defiled and ruined. Was this a glimpse into the sort of future that beckoned for mankind if we do not reverse our wanton destruction of the planet? I hoped not, but was hardly confident; the amount of people I had met on my trip who had casually tossed trash out their vehicle's windows was ridiculous, so common in fact that it only seems worth mentioning now collectively in retrospect. Which it to say nothing of the staggering industry and construction I had witnessed, slowly devouring the landscape along the way.

I thought back to a travel agency I had popped into in Kashgar, with a photo in its window of Shipton's Arch taken in the summertime. Lined up under it were about thirty people. While discussing with the agent the specifics of a trip to the arch, I had casually asked whether the increased numbers visiting the place had had much effect on the landscape, specifically whether there was any trash there now—something that on my trip with Danilo, Manon, and Etienne went unseen under the thick layer of snow.

"Of course!" he replied, "There is lots." This was said in such a way as to also imply a self evident, "Duh! What do you expect?" as if the only natural response for a human visiting such an area was to desecrate it.

A Native American saying thundered in my brain: "What mankind does not understand he fears, and what he fears he ultimately destroys."

It seems clear to me that society as a whole is too removed from the land to have any real connection with it, and without an emotional connection or bond with the land, people feel no loss or pain in destroying it—at least in the short term. But it pained me now as I gazed out at the destruction that lay before me. The Aral Sea, or lack of it, cast a wave of pessimism over me. A melancholy I found difficult to shift, for the disappearing waters were only part of a far darker tale.

As the waters receded, they exposed a layer of fine, highly salted sand, which was then churned up into the air by the region's howling winds, creating vast storms of salty, desiccated sediment that blanketed the immediate area. Since most cultivated plants have a very low tolerance for salt, the new saline rich cotton fields saw a dramatic plunge in the production of their precious fluffy fibers. The Soviet planners answer to the problem? Simple: pump the cotton fields of the Aral Basin full of more than ten times the average amount of herbicides, pesticides, and defoliants used in the Soviet Union, and between ten and fifteen times the average amount of fertilizer used in Russia.[172]

The results of this gargantuan influx of vile ingredients was catastrophic. Run off from the fields leached into the area's drinking water and locally grown food, and new super noxious storms took to the air: toxic cocktails of salt, sand, and dust, infused with the residues of agricultural chemicals. Communities around the Aral became plagued with diseases.[173] According to some reports, one of the defoliants, Butifos (classified as a deadly poison that affects the central nervous system, heart, liver, and kidneys),[174] which was used in the region until around 1990, was so toxic that it killed thousands.[175] In 2006 a UN report found that over the last forty years the Aral's shrinking shoreline and the area's subsequent pumping full of chemicals, had left behind an estimated 45 million metric tonnes of contaminated dust.[176] On average, Aralsk suffers a dust storm every week.

No surprise then that infant mortality rates around parts of the Aral's southern shores have reached levels of one in ten babies, or that birth defects and premature births are also common.[177] In 2002, the health ministry for the region of neighboring Uzbekistan that borders the Aral, found an 80 to 90 percent rate of anaemia among women and children,[178] which, according to the World Health Organization, is the highest rate anywhere.[179]

All this after the residents of the blighted towns around the Aral lost their livelihoods, and a large part of their staple diet. As the water receded, the Aral became far saltier—over twice as salty as a typical ocean[180]—causing most of the fish and smaller organisms to die out, including all of its 24 indigenous species.[181] Before its destruction, 173 species of animals lived around the Aral Sea, this is now thought to number in the thirties.[182] The once dense Toghay forests around the Aral's fringes have also diminished greatly, reducing in size by about four fifths.[183] And the climate has changed too; winters are colder and longer, summers hotter, and the air much drier. With drier air comes less rainfall, a shorter growing season, lower crop yield, and a higher probability of drought.

As if all that wasn't enough, an island within the Aral was formerly used by the Soviets as a biological warfare testing ground. Known as Vozrozhdeniya—the ironic Russian translation of which is "rebirth"—this secluded island base contained a secret town, Aralsk-7, where several thousand bio-warfare experts lived and worked, carrying out mass experimentation with the most deadly strains of bacteria and viruses known to man, "weaponized" versions of anthrax, plague, typhus, smallpox, Q-fever, botulinum and Venezuelan equine encephalitis, among other lethal nasties,[184] that were tested on a wide range of laboratory animals—and quite possibly wild ones too. Roughly half a million antelope mysteriously dropped dead on the northeastern side of the Aral over the course of a single hour in May 1988,[185] an event the authorities tried to palm off as the result of a spacecraft from Baikonur jettisoning its fuel on top of them.[186] Other incidents around the Aral saw entire flocks of sheep lose their wool, and the local human population experience outbreaks of the plague and smallpox.[187]

Once isolated and surrounded by water, Vozrozhdeniya island is now part of the mainland, a result of receding waters splitting the Aral Sea in two in 1987—creating a Little Aral in the north and a Big Aral in the south. In 2007 the Big Aral split again. The fear is that if weaponized micro-organisms have survived on Vozrozhdeniya, which was hastily abandoned after the break-up of the Soviet Union, then they could make their way overland to population centers, by way of fleas or rodents, or, in the case of biological agents like anthrax—whose spores can survive for centuries—simply blow there on the wind. Such an eventuality is all the more worrying as many of the strains of disease developed for the Kremlin at Aralsk-7 were specifically concocted to resist conventional antibiotics.

If there remains any action that can be taken to alleviate, at least in part, the nightmare of the Aral Sea, then it seems not in trying to reverse the clock by reinstating the whole colossal body of water, nor in saving what precious water is left, but rather in focusing on saving the northern Little Aral only, where salt-tolerant flounder have been introduced.[188] This section is fed exclusively by the Syrdarya, which, with less irrigation schemes than the Amudarya feeding the larger, hopelessly receding Big Aral, provides enough water to keep the Little Aral stable, so long as the two bodies of water are permanently blocked off. In 2005 a dam was constructed, sealing a thin channel that once connected the two, preventing the Little Aral from leaching away forever. Today, the waters of this limited section are slowly creeping back towards Aralsk, where it is hoped one day fishing can be reinstated.

It is, in truth, a mere glimmer of hope, a Band-aid solution to a gross environmental problem, whose success remains to be seen, but, ultimately, it's better than nothing. The real solution would be to end irrigation of the Syrdarya and Amudarya. If only it were that simple. At their upper reaches, these are held by Kyrgyzstan and Tajikistan; they then pass downstream through the giant irrigation systems of Kazakhstan, Uzbekistan and Turkmenistan. With cotton production making up a huge part of the industrial output of the downstream countries, any diversion or disruption of the water would require the complete restructuring of these economies. Were such a scenario forced upon a nation by an upstream neighbor, it would likely lead to regional conflict. So the choice is stark: industry or the living planet. To economists the environmental effects of industry are "externalities," incidentals along the endless road to greater productivity and profit. Industry will no doubt prove more resilient than the fragile ecosystem of the Aral. With the exception of the token Little Aral, the fate, it seems, of the far larger ecosystem is sealed as a blighted environmental nightmare. We are a society that kills our grandchildren to feed our children, and no doubt will continue to do so until there is bugger-all of anything left.

CHAPTER TWENTY-FOUR
Extreme Hitchhiking

It was too cold to remain stationary, so I began hiking off along the arrow-straight road into the desert's blank interior, periodically turning back to look behind me, checking for approaching vehicles. I was in as concerning a location as I've ever found myself—right in the middle of the flat and frozen desert, by the side of a stony track, where the truck driver who dropped me here had turned, disappearing in a cloud of dust, presumably to some distant mine. The road was deserted and stretched northwest across the desert for nearly four-hundred-miles before the next significant settlement, Aktobe. With sections of this thin road fluctuating between mud, loose gravel and tarmac, Aktobe was a full day's travel away. Should I fail to reach there, and get stuck outside tonight, then I could be in serious trouble, with temperatures plummeting perilously low. This seemed a genuine possibility. Today was Norouz, Persian New Year, a celebration that was likely to see the amount of traffic using this already sparsely driven road diminish further.

Over half an hour passed before I spotted a car on the horizon. It was so far off that nearly ten minutes expired before it reached me. I stretched out an arm, accompanying it with a trusty hand-on-heart gesture, asking, somewhat pleadingly, for a ride.

It drove straight past, the driver barely looking at me.

Turning back to face the wind I trekked onwards, sand and cold lashing at my frozen face, as I watched the car slowly melt into the wide open horizon.

Being out here all alone was worrying and exhilarating at the same time. It was as bleak a landscape as I had ever seen, and one that from a survival point of view concerned me. Often I find myself scanning a landscape trying to figure out where, if necessary, I could build a shelter, source water, and gather materials for a fire; but out here there was next to nothing on offer, just mile upon mile of flat and seemingly endless sand and scrub, with the occasional lonely ball of tumble weed adding a forlorn touch to the setting. It left me scratching my head for options. There were no trees to build a shelter, or material to make a fire, or discernible presence of water. In the sacred order of survival, your priorities are shelter, water, fire, food—in that order. Generally speaking you can go without water for four days, and food for forty, but hypothermia can set in within minutes—accounting for shelter's prime importance. If I was stranded out here tonight and it got seriously cold, then I'd be relying on my tent, sleeping bag, and jacket to keep me alive. I was hopeful that they could, although not entirely certain. The official comfort rating of my sleeping bag was -10 degrees Celsius, but it already felt close to that right now, and this was daylight; when darkness arrived it would become much colder. Through repeated use my sleeping bag had lost much of its loft—that all important quality that creates small pockets of dead-airspace to trap heat next to your body—meaning it was no longer as effective as its rating professed. What's more, the jacket I'd bought in China had been leaking feathers for the last couple of weeks; apparently not the high quality goose down that its label professed. If push came to shove, and I spent the night out here, then at the very least I was in for a thoroughly unpleasant experience.

Despite the remoteness of my crazy location, for the first time since setting off from Australia I felt seriously close to completing my long hitch home to London. After Kazakhstan, lay the tiny nations of Azerbaijan and Georgia—each hitchable in a single day—after that was a country I had hitchhiked through three times previously, Turkey; where Europe began at its far western reaches. From there, I knew from experience, I could push hard along super fast modern highways and be home, sleeping in my own bed, just three or four days later. Having traveled around Europe and Turkey many times before, I had no intention of stopping off along the way, so in essence I had just two countries to go, both very small ones. In some respects it was an encouraging thought, although a rather misrepresented perception of things. I was, after all, still in the middle of a Kazakhstani desert, nearly 5,500 miles along my chosen route from Britain. Were the journey reversed, and I was setting out from London to Kazakhstan, then I would no doubt have considered it a ridiculously long way to go, but having covered so much distance to get here, it no longer seemed so far.

I walked on and on, and after half an hour or so spotted a convoy of six mining trucks coming up behind me. My spirits dropped as first one, then two, three, four, and five trucks drove straight past. I'd given up hope that the last one would take pity on me but to my surprise and delight it did, not so much pulling over as stopping in the middle of the road. Such was my desperation to secure the ride that I dispensed with my normal prerequisite handing over of a translated note, and just gave a sort of "let's go" double nod to the driver—a middle aged man. Only once the huge tires began to turn did I hand one over. With the road so straight and empty he had no trouble reading it at the wheel, and raised no objection on discovering that I wouldn't be paying. Unlike my earlier lift in a mining truck, all six of these were carrying a full payload: a heaped mound of some sort of ground up rocks. This boded well; had the trucks been empty then it seemed likely they would be heading to another mine in the middle of nowhere to load up, whereas being full it seemed likely they were heading to civilization. After all, I surmised, they weren't going to dump their loads in the middle of the desert.

Wrong.

Don't ask me why, but an hour or so up the road and they did just that, pulling off onto a little side section where they began offloading their cargo via hydraulic tip-up units. With an almost apologetic expression, the driver indicated that he and the others were turning around now, heading back in the direction they had come. It was quite the disappointment, but as I bade him goodbye and climbed down onto the stony surface of this oddly located dumping ground—maybe situated here for use in road maintenance?—I noticed another truck, a lone vehicle beginning to depart; this time in the direction I needed.

I was gutted, a minute earlier and I might have got it. Despondent, I trudged back towards the main road, but then all of a sudden started running in a frenzy—a quarter of a mile away the truck had stopped. I couldn't believe it and powered forwards, desperate to make it there before it took off again. Suddenly the distant form of a driver climbed down onto the road, where he began inspecting something on the side of the truck. I pushed on, waving my arms about like a lunatic while shouting to get the driver's attention before he jumped back in. If he spotted me, then he gave no indication, continuing with whatever he was doing. By the time I reached the truck I was panting like a mad man, and hardly in the composed state of decorum required to initiate a pitch for a free ride. With an expectant smile I handed him a note. He didn't even look at it. With an annoyed glare, some aggravated Russian dictum, and a dismissive wave of the back of his hand, he sent me packing.

I trundled on a few hundred feet past the truck, grabbing my breath in the freezing cold while I waited for a different ride. Twenty minutes later, after raising and lowering the truck's hydraulic dumper section several times, the driver scaled his cab, pulled off along the road, and came to a halt exactly where I stood. The passenger door swung open, and the man whom minutes earlier had been the picture of annoyance, beckoned me in with a smile. I didn't need asking twice. By the looks of it, the old fella had experienced a pang of guilt for his earlier short-tempered reaction, and confirmed as much by pouring me a steaming cup of tea from his flask and insisting I try a few of his cookies.

I gladly accepted and saw a bit of myself in him, having once launched into a rather uncalled for outburst at a Turkish taxi driver who, instead of taking me to the Syrian Embassy as requested, had dropped me at the American Embassy instead. After letting myself down and yelling at the poor bloke, I had ended up feeling so bad that I handed him a tip several times the cost of the ride.

My new-found companion and I traveled together for several hours across a landscape of monotonous uniformity, broken only by the strange appearance of a giant isolated Muslim cemetery. I had seen plenty of these monumental graveyards randomly appear on the horizon in the wilds of

Kazakhstan, but never was I anything other than amazed at the sheer size of them, not in surface area covered, but in the scale of the grave markers. These were nearly always proper buildings the size of small houses, often far more elegant and intricately designed than dwellings of the nearest villages, where, presumably, the relatives of the deceased who funded their construction lived—an indication, perhaps, that more importance was placed on the next life than on this. Collectively, they made up little towns of mausoleums, isolated in the middle of nowhere among the swirling desert sands; literal ghost towns of the dead.

It was dark by the time I arrived in Aktobe, a surprisingly large city of some 250,000 people, the provincial capital of a region with the same name that sits upon huge reserves of oil and gas. Trudging through its crowded, slushy ice and snow-laden streets, I went in search of an Internet café. Having previously messaged some Aktobe couchsurfers, my priority was checking if any had responded to my request for a place to crash, but sourcing the internet proved difficult, and soon I was wandering, hopelessly lost, along rows of old Soviet-era tower blocks.

It was time to marshal a local to my cause.

Stopping a kindly-looking, mustachioed man in his middle years, I quickly mimed typing on a computer keyboard, accompanying it with an inquisitive, "Internet?" It did the job, and instead of just pointing me in the right direction, the man guided me well out of his way on a ten minute detour to my requested destination, where he joined me inside to converse with the staff.

I logged on and received bad news: no one had offered me accommodation. A hotel it would have to be. A further inquiry with my newfound buddy, whose name, if I'm interpreting the scribble he wrote down for me correctly, was Cokeh, and he took me to a run-of-the-mill hotel—only its price sure as hell didn't reflect this. The staff member working the dark and gloomy reception demanded an extortionate seventy dollars a night. Cokeh near choked on hearing this, and looked as disgusted as I was. He promptly walked me out again, and rightly too; it was way out of my league. And then occurred one of those wonderful bits of travel luck. This man, who had been a stranger just minutes before, offered me a place to stay with him—achieved by him miming sleeping, then washing his face, before finally pointing at himself, as if to say "my place."

I accepted immediately.

Cokeh and I made our way through an ever increasing downfall of snow, transformed by the glow of street lamps into lazy illuminated streaks in the blackened sky, arriving at a grimy inner-city apartment block. Curiously bypassing the main entrance, we headed around the back of the tower, trudging our way through deep snow to a little padlocked metal door that looked like some sort of janitor's store room. Furtively glancing around, after unlocking the padlock, Cokeh ushered me through a thick red drape of fabric hanging behind the door. Beyond lay a tiny windowless room, maybe eight foot by ten foot in size. A single exposed, low-watt lightbulb burned in the middle of this miniature squat, dangling from a cable in the cracked ceiling. Water and bathroom facilities came by way of bottles and a bucket.

Quickly closing up behind us, Cokeh gestured for me to take my backpack off and sit down in a worn sofa chair. Next to no space presented itself, so I dropped my pack on top of two innocuous but sturdy-looking U-shaped metal bars, resting, a couple of inches above the ground, on two bricks. With a panicked lunge, Cokeh grabbed my pack and lifted it clear of the bars, leaving them smeared in a covering of noxious-smelling melted plastic from my backpack. The metal bars, it quickly became apparent, were elements from a crude heater, left on to keep the place warm while Cokeh was out. With the exposed elements no more than a foot or so from the disintegrating sofa chair, the place was a crazy fire hazard. I apologized and surveyed the damage: both my pack and the cover of my externally attached sleeping bag were burnt straight through. I wasn't particularly bothered about the cover, but I'd had my trusty Berghaus backpack for thirteen years. It had served me well on every overseas trip I'd ever made, proving as tough as guts, but this was the end of the road for it now; some sewing would patch it up to get me home, but afterwards it would need decommissioning. (I would like to interject here that should the powers that be at Berghaus, care to reward my endorsement with either a backpack replacement or a nifty sponsorship deal, then I will happily accept.)

Cokeh flicked on a radio, filled up a kettle, and brewed a couple of teas, serving both with a mountain of sugar. I'd eaten nothing but a few cookies today and was really hungry, so when he offered me some of his loaf of bread I gladly accepted. Cokeh tore off and handed me a thick wedge. We couldn't verbally converse but much was said between us as we shared this simple meal. Gratitude and respect welled up inside me for this kind and generous man, whose warm-hearted hospitality was humbling. He didn't have much, but what little he had he shared. Experiences like this strip away all the bullshit of life, where your wants and needs are cut perfectly in two, separated so your genuine requirements are brought sharply into focus, and everything else simply fades away. I had a hot drink, something to eat, a roof above my head and great company. No matter how strange and dingy the surroundings, it was more than enough for me, and I wouldn't have swapped it for the sterile comfort of any hotel.

For sleeping arrangements I was given the chair, while Cokeh used a thin mattress in the corner. I slipped into a deep and dreamless sleep.

A sudden unexpected knock on the door jolted me to consciousness in the middle of the night. Turning on the light, Cokeh cast a worried look my way and placed a finger on his lips for quiet. We froze like dead men, our gazes going from each other to the door, staring in silent apprehension. A woman's voice called out from the other side. Letting out a sigh of relief, Cokeh called back and opened up. In came a portly lady in a big black puffer jacket, who, after taking off her coat, quickly clambered into bed with Cokeh. The light went off, and before I knew it I had drifted off once more to sleep.

* * *

A fresh layer of snow had fallen overnight, carpeting the world outside Cokeh's squat with white. I waved goodbye to him at the door, and set off for the city's outskirts. My problem lay in how to get there. Walking past faceless tower blocks and similar-looking snowy streets, it soon became apparent that I had no idea where to go. It was early morning with few people around, so when I saw two guys moving a broken down car along the road—one pushing, the other steering—I decided to assist the pusher in the hope he'd be able to point me in the right direction afterwards. He was appreciative, but, speaking no English, didn't have a clue what I was inquiring after. For the next half an hour I walked around trying to find people to ask for directions, producing the same disappointing result.

In the end a guide came to me without asking.

After making an unsuccessful inquiry with an old watery-eyed *babushka* hobbling along the sidewalk, a modern SUV pulled up opposite.

"Do you need help, mate?" yelled its driver, a big chunky guy in his twenties with a beaming self-satisfied grin, and warm rounded Kazakh features.

This was more like it. I headed over and introduced myself, telling him of my predicament.

"Jamie, I have friends getting married who I am picking up at the train station and taking to a wedding. I can take you to the road after."

That was good enough for me. I jumped in and off we set for the station. My new friend was Nurbek.

"How long you fucking been here, mate?" he asked, in an odd mixture of Kazakh and Australian twangs.

I told him and asked where he learned English.

"I work with fucking Aussies, mate," he replied.

Nurbek explained that he mingled with ex-pat Aussie contractors working alongside him in Kazakhstan's oil industry.

"Do you know what the Kazakh word for sugar is? The Aussies love it, mate," said Nurbek, laughing hard as we pulled up and parked outside the train station.

"No," I replied, intrigued.

"Cunt," he stated flatly.

"Cunt?"

"Yeah," he giggled, "It's spelt *kay aye enn tee*, but you say it 'cunt.'"

I laughed.

Nurbek gave me a cheeky smile, "Too much cunt can rot your teeth, mate!" Too true.

While we waited for his friends' train to arrive I got to know Nurbek better, whom, it's got to be said, had some, err, "interesting" philosophies.

"Have you been to Japan, Jamie?" he asked.

"No, not yet," I replied, "but I'd like to."

"I think the earthquake and tsunami is God's way of punishing the Japanese."

(The twin disasters had occurred about a week beforehand and were all over the news.)

"Err, why?"

"I look at all these Japanese websites and they're so fucked up, mate! People masturbating into socks and school uniforms; they're crazy!"

I was tempted to ask him what this said about those logging on to check them out in the first place.

Nurbek departed for the station building soon after to meet his friends, leaving me to wait in his SUV listening to some novel music—Fatboy Slim, mixed, apparently, with tribal Russian. He returned with the bride and groom, a nervous-looking young couple, neither of whom spoke English. They clambered into the back, and we were off again, this time for a house where they would get ready for the big event. Nurbek left them to themselves, and instead gave his sole enthusiastic attention to me.

"There will be five hundred guests tonight, and special Indian dancers hired from an Indian commercial fair. You want to come?"

It was an appealing offer, and one I wanted to accept, but uncertainty as to when the Caspian Sea cargo ship departed for Azerbaijan weighed on my mind. I thought back to Dmitriy, the trucker I met on my first day in Kazakhstan, who was heading to Azerbaijan by way of Aktau, a town on the coast of the Caspian Sea that he had said would take him nine days to reach. As things stood I was set to match his time frame, so if he had scheduled his arrival to coincide with the enigmatic cargo ship's departure, then a day lost at the wedding, coupled with any waiting around for an Azerbaijan visa, could make all the difference; and with disastrous consequences: my Kazakhstan visa could potentially expire before the arrival of another ship. It was a difficult decision, but in the end I declined.

Nurbek came to a stop in a residential area on the outskirts of Aktobe, made up of large, but rather run-down-looking houses, in various states of completion and upgrade, several with half-finished extensions tagged onto their sides. Standing outside one house was a small group of well wishers: men, women, young and old, all waiting for the arrival of the bride and groom. As they, and Nurbek and I, got out of the SUV, the crowd erupted into cheers, and a traditional guitarist struck up a tune and started singing.

"He is mentioning everybody's name, so guests will have to pay him for this respect," explained Nurbek.

Confetti, candies and, oddly, U.S. dollar bills were thrown over the couple as they made their way inside one of the homes. With their departure those gathered began collecting the candies and dollars off the floor. Nurbek picked up a bill for me and signed it as a memento.

Then we were off again.

Heading past tired infrastructure and grimy vodka factories, we made our way out to a single lane road leading west to the town of Uralsk, and the border with Russia just beyond. When there I would be closer to Vienna than Kazakhstan's former capital and largest city, Almaty, in the southeast, giving some indication as to just how big the country is. The realization was both encouraging and demoralizing at the same time. I had hitchhiked once from the English coastal town of Dover to Vienna in a day, so I felt seriously close to home knowing how near the Austrian capital was, but unfortunately I would not be taking the most direct route there through Russia. As a British passport holder, securing a Russian visa on the move outside of the U.K. is a seriously difficult undertaking, and something I had failed to do. So, despite wanting to continue north westerly at the border, I was forced instead to plunge south by over a thousand miles—clearing Kazakhstan, the Caspian, and the Caucasus—before I could start climbing north once more.

"Be careful near Caspian," said Nurbek as we approached our final drop off point. "It is more dangerous than here."

"In what way?" I asked.

"The people. Do not trust," he instructed.

"I won't," I replied, not really meaning it.

As we pulled over he turned to me with a look of despondence.

"Actually, I don't really want to go back to wedding, too many people, but I have to—" he said, pausing as if about to deliver a punchline, "—because I'm fucking hungry, mate!"

The food, Nurbek explained, would be superb and include a Kazakh favorite that I had yet to try—horse meat.

"It is a very sweet meat, but it *must* be boiled," he told me with a degree of insistence.

Before bidding Nurbek farewell, I decided to ask him about the film *Borat: Cultural Learnings of America for Make Benefit Glorious Nation of Kazakhstan*, and how it had gone down in his country, with its unflattering portrayal of the populace as backward Jew and gypsy hating racists, who sleep with their sisters, eat cheese made from breast milk, have a fondness for being scrubbed down by other men, and drink urine.

"It is stupid film," Nurbek told me in disgust. "They film in Romania and show Romanian mountains, but we have no mountains like that in Kazakhstan!"

And that, I thought, was priceless.

* * *

A day and a half on the road after leaving Aktobe, and I found myself riding in the back of an old Russian car between Atyrau and my final destination in Kazakhstan, Aktau. Although officially traveling along a "highway," it was, in reality, the worst road I have been on in my life; nothing more than a slushy strip of mud, cutting through another stretch of flat and empty desert, made all the more insipid by a dull and overcast gray sky. There were deep bumps, and no surface covering of any sort, forcing us to travel at a pathetic top speed of fifteen miles an hour.

I journeyed with two middle-aged Kazakh men, one of whom, the driver, spoke English. Although grateful for the ride, I can't say I warmed to him much; nor, it seemed, did he to me. Despite having picked me up, for some reason he took exception to me hitchhiking, as if this was somehow an inappropriate thing to do.

"But *why* do you travel in this way?" he demanded of me for the umpteenth time.

I did my best to explain the reason for my trip once more, but it fell on deaf ears.

"It is dangerous, you should not do!"

"So is driving without a seatbelt," I countered—not that it convinced him to buckle up.

On he went, lecturing me on my lack of a proper job, on not being married, on the whole concept of my trip really, and, oddly, on going to too many places—something he implied was overindulgent. It was disparagement after disparagement.

"And where will you sleep tonight?"

"I'll camp out here," I replied, gesturing to the desert.

"What about the wolves?" he stated. "They will eat you."

"I'll be okay," I said. "I'll be inside my tent."

"Oh, is it made of steel?" he laughed.

To be honest, I didn't have a response for that, and it made me pause for thought. Wolf pack attack was an eventuality I hadn't really considered, and was something I had no experience or knowledge of. Images flashed across my mind of being alone on the desert steppes, hundreds of miles from the nearest town, trapped inside my tent in the dead of night, while a pack of wolves howled outside, before ripping apart the tent's lightweight fabric. What the hell *would* I do? Not much beyond attempting to create enough noise to put them off an attack, or making a futile last stand with my knife before being devoured.

There were certainly wolves out here on the steppes, but whether the driver was trying to scaremonger me, or if wolf attack was a common real and present danger, I don't know. Would the scent of a human repel or entice them, I wondered? I had no idea, and just hoped to strike it lucky like I had the previous night, where, following the touching hospitality of Cokeh in Aktobe, I received more of the same from my final lift into Atyrau, when an affable fellow called Mysufaliev let me sleep in the laundry room of his white-washed wooden house. Such luck had seen me escape pitching my tent at all so far in Kazakhstan, but would it last? My current lift had already made clear he would drop me when he turned down a side track for a remote village, so it hardly looked promising.

A lone weathered building appeared in the distance, a solitary feature among a flat world of mud and dirty-colored scrub. It was no St. Paul's Cathedral, but a visual respite amid a landscape that required vigilance to extract interest from its overall monotony, usually by way of its minor details. Set well off from the "road," this remotest of road houses had two large articulated trucks parked out front that must have had a hell of a time negotiating the slush to get here. As we came to a halt next to one of these, and got out to venture inside the building, the most improbable sound greeted me.

"Jamie!" It was none other than my old buddy Dmitriy, the trucker heading for Azerbaijan whom I had met roughly two thousand miles away to the east. I couldn't believe it and was delighted to see him. Jumping from the cab of his truck, Dmitriy thrust his spare palm into mine. We hadn't been able to communicate much on our first encounter, but from his mannerisms now it was clear he was asking whether I wanted to jump ship, to continue with him instead—and all the way to Aktau. I dropped my current cantankerous chauffeur and was led away by Dmitriy to meet two of his trucker colleagues, who were servicing their vehicle parked up next to his.

They immediately stopped what they were doing, and welcomed me into the fold. An initiation began. A small off-cut square of carpet was produced, laid on the dusty floor and furnished with an offering: a tin of sardines, jar of gherkins, bag of bread rolls, several shot glasses, bottle of vodka and a soft drink made from birch sap. None of those gathered spoke English but it was irrelevant to us bonding; we were brothers of the road, comrades of the wild plains far beyond the familiarity of civilization. Vodka cemented our fellowship, sloshing into shot glasses and held aloft in unison. We drank as one, the liquid flushing us with warmth. Gherkins and sardines came next, robbing the vodka of its acrid taste, leaving only its blessed internal glow. Shot followed shot; afternoon slipped into evening and another truck driver joined our esprit de corps. Together we adjourned into the simple empty roadhouse. Sitting on the floor at a little table in the only room, illuminated by flickering candles, we settled in for the night. Meat, sautéed onions, and a soup served with pasta and a big dollop of cream arrived: holy sustenance after a day without food. I sat back and beamed with contentment. I was fully in the moment, the golden hour, the only place where life and true happiness can ever exist. Anything else is illusion. The road, its people, and moments like this, were becoming ingrained in my spirit, hard-wired into my soul. And I would cherish them forever.

CHAPTER TWENTY-FIVE
Dog Fights and Departure Gripes

I had seen it once from the northern shores of Iran, but the sheer scale of the Caspian still surprised me on my first glimpse of it from Kazakhstan. Larger than Germany, if I didn't know better I would have concluded that the colossal body of water in front of me was the ocean. Multiple giant oil tankers and container ships dotted the coast, while sea birds drifted idly by and a thick salty aroma clung to the air, mixed, in places, with the rank stench of sewage. The largest landlocked country in the world didn't look like one here.

Aktau is no architectural Florence; on its outskirts sat rusting pipelines, decommissioned nuclear power stations, industrial plants and tall-stack chimneys belching fumes into the air. On the coast, empty seaside resorts were left corroding in the salty air alongside abandoned apartment buildings, several with their roofs collapsed and beyond repair. In the town center, gray concrete towers made up the staple residential fare. It looked like a place whose best years were long behind it, and those years had never been particularly good in the first place.

Sandwiched between the Caspian and the desert, Aktau only survives as a town thanks to water derived from desalination, which from 1973 to 1999 was supplied by a plant powered by a nuclear-reactor, *BN-350*. Seriously cut off from the rest of the country, Aktau sprang into being in the 1960s after the discovery of nearby uranium deposits. This rather uninspiring raison d'etre is reflected in its grim utilitarian address system, where, instead of names, numbers are given to residential areas, streets and apartment buildings—so a typical Aktau address reads: 7, 4, 87 (district 7, building 4, apartment 87.) It might not have been the inspiration for U2's "Where the Streets Have No Name," but if anywhere matches that literal description, then it's Aktau.

A public holiday saw the Azerbaijan consulate closed and any hope of me picking up a visa dashed until it reopened in the next few days. It seemed my race to reach Aktau had been futile. If the cargo ship left before the consulate reopened then I would miss it. What was open today, and located just down the road, was the Azerbaijan Chamber of Commerce. It seemed a good place to make inquiries as to the consulate's opening times, and while there I used their computer to log onto couchsurfing.org to check the status of an accommodation request I had sent a local English-speaker, Timur. I received good news in response: he had a place for me to crash. Through a combination of luck and charm I managed to transform a simple inquiry on how to get to Timur's workplace into a free ride there in the back of one of the Chamber of Commerce's official shiny SUVs. Recently valeted and with a fresh-off-the-production-line aroma, its interior smell stood in contrast to my own honking scent—the consequence of not washing for four and a half days. Driving along the coast road to the center of town, we passed an old MIG fighter jet mounted on an angled plinth, making it look as if blasting off into the sky, and pulled up at an ugly gray tower block. The driver pointed me towards its metal door, where half-hanging off the wall, was a battered-looking intercom. Thanking him, I grabbed my pack and headed out. A quick double-check that I had the correct number, and I pressed the buzzer, setting off a brutal electronic retch. Moments later, an indecipherable Kazakh voice answered on the speaker.

"Hello, is that Timur?" I responded.

There was no reply but the door buzzed open and I was in, stepping inside a short dark entrance hallway. Standing in the doorway at its end was a generously proportioned Kazakh man in a gray sweater.

"Welcome to Aktau," said Timur. A quick handshake and he led me through to a little ground floor office with a single desk, two PCs, a filing cabinet, and leather sofa.

"I'm sorry, but I have some work to attend so can't spend today with you," apologized Timur. "I have an American staying with me as well who will be here in a minute, you can wait for him if you like or go straight to my home."

I decided to stick around, crashing on the sofa while Timur got down to business, picking up the phone and making several animated calls. Fifteen minutes later the American arrived. In walked a well-groomed, mustachioed young explorer, with Harry Potter-style spectacles and the sort of handsome good looks that made you sick. Dressed in a combination of modern Indiana Jones meets lord-of-the-manor attire, he was the epitome of a dashing gentleman adventurer—the sort of person you could equally imagine negotiating the Sahara on camel back in a Lawrence of Arabia-style Keffiyeh headscarf, or donning some fresh pressed whites to play a spot of gentlemanly lawn tennis at the *All England Club*.

"Hi, I'm Ethan," he said in a velvety-smooth east coast tone, reaching out his palm.

We shook, and, it's fair to say, hit it off from the start.

A New Hampshire native, Ethan had traveled to Kazakhstan overland by train, ship, and bus all the way from Korea—a place he'd spent two years teaching English—and was continuing overland to Europe, where he planned to take a boat back home across the Atlantic. Like me, Ethan was in need of a visa for Azerbaijan and would be catching the cargo ship across the Caspian.

"You'll need to put your name down for the ship, would you like me to show you where?" offered Ethan.

We headed out to a small travel agency around the corner that handled the bookings. The moment we walked through the door, the three attractive young women working there were swooning over Ethan and his debonair ways. Punctuating his charismatic discourse with tentative little nods and just the right amount of eye contact that lingered ever-so-slightly, he made the girls melt like ice cubes. I had to hand it to the bugger, he was a smooth operator and knew how to carry himself. I put my name down for the next departing cargo ship that carried only a handful of foot passengers, and asked when it was leaving. The girls were in the dark as much as we were, and could only advise us to check in with them several times a day—possibly so they could flutter their eyelids at Ethan, but apparently because the first they would hear of the ship's arrival was after it had actually docked. It would then be loaded with train carriages containing coal and depart again. If we left it too long before checking in again, then we would miss it. With up to two weeks between crossings, it looked like we'd be stuck in Aktau for a while.

We went in search of food, and found ourselves near the coast surrounded by rows of gray Soviet tower blocks, whose depressing uniformity was only broken by the total clash of "styling" to exteriors of individual apartments, particularly their built-in verandas. Standing nearby in a little park, in stark contrast to these eyesores, was a rather fetching mass of interconnected colored metal bars, jutting out all over the place to form a cross between an adventure playground and a cryptic work of modern sculpture, whose center piece was a large cylindrical metal tube that flared at the end like an oversized musical horn.

"It looks like a 1970s version of the future in steel," commented Ethan.

A bit more walking and we located a McDonald's rip-off called McBurger, where we ordered enormous burgers that were practically impossible to eat without a knife and fork, or in my case, without dropping the sloppy filling on my lap.

Over our food Ethan filled me in on his experiences in the country, including an interesting conversation he'd had the night before with a Dutch guy based in Aktau who worked with heavy lifting equipment in the oil industry.

"I went for a beer with him and Timur," said Ethan, somehow managing to eat while maintaining his decorum. "He used to live in a serviced apartment that was looked after by a local woman who always neatly folded his clothes and tidied his belongings, so after a while he bought her some flowers as a little thank you. Poor woman began crying buckets and told him no one had ever bought her flowers before. Anyway, he tells her that he's heading back to Holland for a while and asks if there's anything he can get her over there, and she says a pair of boots, and sketches out their design for him. When he returns he gives her the boots but refuses any money for them, and afterwards he always sees her wearing them at work, so he says to her, 'You must really like the boots, what does your husband think of them?' And she tells him that he doesn't know about them, that she keeps the boots at her sister's place and leaves her home every morning in her normal boots, walks to her sister's, then changes into the new boots to go to work, then goes back to her sister's afterwards to change into the old ones again before going home."

"Why?" I asked.

"Well, that's what the Dutch guy asked too, and she told him: 'If my husband knew about the boots he would kill me'—and she wasn't being metaphorical."

Lunch complete, we made our way back to Timur's home, located outside town at the end of a dirt track lined with cinder block walls. It was a simple single-story house with a gray rendered surface and a front yard full of sand and stones. Chained up to a post in the middle was a fearsome guard dog. The moment the yard's metal gates groaned open, the dog erupted into barks and growls, lurching forward until restrained by the limit of its chunky chain. Edging well outside its range towards the front door, we made our way through a yard strewn with old carpet, random bits of wood, a crude handmade kennel, and a discarded metal sink.

Unlike its exterior, the inside was surprisingly clean and up to date, with comfy sofas, decorative rugs, and a modern fitted kitchen. After dumping my pack and taking a long overdue shower, Ethan and I set off to visit Dmitriy and the other truckers. Despite plenty of cargo ships visible on the Caspian, there was only one that accepted paying passengers. Since this ship's cargo consisted of wagons from coal trains, it seemed likely that Dmitriy and Co. were waiting for a different ship, which, were we to travel with them in their cabs, might just permit us on board. If it was leaving soon then it might get us to Azerbaijan without any undue hanging around for the proper passenger one. We'd still have to secure visas first, but it seemed prudent to make some inquires, nonetheless.

We found their trucks parked up in the same spot that I'd arrived with them in Aktau at 3 a.m. this morning, on the side of the road just outside the town's gritty port with its towering rusty cranes, random industrial infrastructure and rows of cargo-train gas carriages backed up on the railway tracks outside. Two of the trucks were empty, and the third, Dmitriy's, had its black curtains drawn across its windows and windshield. Clambering up its outer steps I knocked on the door. Dmitriy pulled the curtains back and broke into a broad smile, welcoming us into a crowded cab. All four truckers were here, squeezed in on the seats and lower bunk bed, watching a film on a small portable television. It was a tight fit but we managed to join them. No sooner had I introduced Ethan than out came the vodka. My friends, it seemed, were here for the long haul. It took some doing, but Ethan and I established that they had no clear idea when their ship across the Caspian was arriving either, but when it did we were welcome to join them—giving us a second place to regularly rendezvous, in our quest out of the country.

We stuck around for a while, and after conveying to Dmitriy that I no longer needed to take him up on his earlier kind offer of accommodation, Ethan and I headed back to Aktau's town center, making our way there with a rather interesting taxi driver.

"I can lift you, but must stop at my house to collect dog and take to animal doctor."

"Sure, no problem," said Ethan. "What's wrong with him?"

"He get into fight with pit bull."

"Oh dear, I'm sorry," I said at the thought of the man's beloved pet getting mauled.

"No," he replied emphatically. "I win five hundred dollar!"

Thus began our introduction to the bizarre world of Kazakh dog fighting.

We came to a halt on the outskirts of town next to a scruffy little house on a sandy track, whose surface rose on the wind into swirling coffee-colored clouds. Out jumped the cabbie, making his way to a set of ornamental metal gates that seemed far too grand for the basic residence beyond. He returned with another man and the biggest dog I've ever seen in my life; it was like a bear, with vicious teeth and a powerful muscular frame. It was seriously scary, a look accentuated by a torn nose and a face covered in blood. With Ethan sitting comfortably in the front riding shotgun, there was only one place it was going to go, and that was crammed in the back with me. There was no way I was snuggling up close and personal with a bona fide fighting dog, so when the cabbie returned and stuck his head in the front door window, I waved my hands at him and exclaimed, "No room!" He shook his head as if I'd misunderstood the plan and, reaching beneath the dashboard, popped the trunk.

"In back," he said.

I hoped he wasn't referring to me.

Moments later he and his associate heaved the dog up and then into the trunk.

We were off.

"What sort of dog is it?" asked Ethan.

"It is Alabai and Caucasus cross. Alabai is only dog good enough to fight with wolf."

"You fight them with wolves?" I asked with a mixture of disgust and morbid curiosity.

"Yes. Of course."

"Where do you get the wolves from?" queried Ethan.

"We catch with motorbike. Traditionally we use horse, but now motorbike. If you ride behind wolf it will run with head turned around to look at you but will never get tired; it run all day. After much time, wolf's head will be fixed in place and cannot turn. When this happen another man on motorbike rides to wolf from side it cannot look and throws net on it."

"Do the wolves ever win the fights?" I asked.

"Yes. My father, who was real fighter man, had own wolf, and won many time, but it is not animal pet. It bite family members more than one time, when my brother taken to hospital, my father get very angry with it and take iron bar and break every one of its teeth before killing it."

"Jesus!" I exclaimed under my breath.

When Ethan and I stepped from the taxi on arrival in town, Ethan turned to me, and with a disbelieving shake of the head said, "The longer I'm in Kazakhstan, the longer I think that *Borat* might be true."

After a good stroll around, we popped in to check on Timur, who put the kettle on and brewed us up a couple of teas. Over these he confirmed for us the popularity of dog fighting, which was, he said, common, despite officially being illegal. When we mentioned the breed of the taxi driver's dog, he echoed the cabbie's comments.

"Other dogs, they smell the wolf and become scared but not Alabai. It is the only dog that can fight wolf. If you want to train other dog to fight wolf, you should nail wolf skin inside puppy house so it becomes used to smell, and later when it fights it will not be scared."

This he explained in a sort of blasé manner that betrayed some deeper familiarity.

"You wouldn't have ever fought your dog, would you, Timur?" asked Ethan.

"Oh, I try him out once after I buy him, but he was not very good."

Ethan and I shared a subtle "bloody hell" glance of surprise.

When we finished our teas Ethan and I left Timur to his work and stepped outside.

"If you buy a sports car in America," discerned Ethan, "you take it up to a hundred-and-twenty-five once or twice, just to try it out. You buy a dog in Kazakhstan, hell, you throw it in a fight."

* * *

Aktau is not the sort of place you want to get stranded. After seven long days waiting for the arrival of the cargo ship, Ethan and I were going stir crazy, itching to sail off across the Caspian's choppy waters to new and uncharted territory. With no attractions beyond the beach, we spent an inordinate amount of time in Aktau just wandering and observing, trying to wring what little interest from the place we could to pass the time. We snuck into a huge tower block under construction and climbed onto its roof to check out the view. We purchased Borat-style Kazakhstan t-shirts and shorts, and through near tears of laughter took spoof "Blue Steel" modeling photos of ourselves against a gritty industrial Soviet backdrop. We attended a very strange pop concert in honor of the country's dictator, starring a one-legged vocalist who performed in front of a huge stage filled with a banner depicting the president's face, and was attended by audience members wearing t-shirts with the English slogan "I love President." We sat on the beach watching army recruits being put through their paces in a section cordoned off with razor wire. We attended a local kickboxing and kung-fu tournament (as spectators); and we visited the country's largest and only yacht club, home to no more than twenty vessels, not a single one in the water, or indeed, not resting on wheels or a makeshift plinth of bricks—somewhat dashing our hopes of hitchhiking a ride with one to Azerbaijan. Just when we were beginning to think we would be stuck in this godforsaken town forever, Ethan's cell phone rang.

It was the girls from the travel agency, and with good news: the cargo ship had arrived; if we could get to the port in the next couple of hours, then Kazakhstan would soon be but a memory. Having finally acquired our visas this very morning, the timing couldn't have been better. With no food facilities on board the ship, we quickly stocked up on bread, cheese, meat, and beer, then, after thanking Timur for his hospitality, headed for the port. Still waiting outside, stuck in their trucks, were Dmitriy and friends. They must have been bored out of their minds; and it showed. Despite it being mid-day, Dmitriy was wasted on vodka and had a permanent cheesy grin plastered across his face. We said our goodbyes, then entered the port's waiting room.

To wait.

And wait.

And wait.

An hour here or there we kind of expected, but forty-two hours later? Let me state that again through gritted teeth, FORTY-TWO HOURS LATER!

The reason for this gargantuan hiatus? Some fog on the Caspian was proving too vexing for the ship's antiquated navigational equipment. If we'd known it was going to be so long, we would have headed back to sleep at Timur's, but with officials popping in periodically to tell us that all would soon be well, we were damned if we were going to take the risk of going away and literally missing the boat.

"Any longer here and we'll develop Stockholm Syndrome and will start latching onto that woman in customs," said Ethan, after thrashing me at the umpteenth game of chess.

When the glorious moment finally arrived, and an official waved us through to customs, I almost didn't believe it.

"You go on without me, Ethan," I joked, "This is my life now. I've been here so long I've become institutionalized. The thought of stepping out into the wider world is just too daunting a prospect. But you go ahead and lead your life. Please explain to my family and friends; I hope they'll understand."

* * *

Standing on the deck of the cargo ship as the shore of Kazakhstan slowly receded in the distance, we cracked a celebratory beer, toasting our departure. Soon not a speck of land was in sight; water stretched to every horizon, and I could feel the allure of moving on, of imminent new adventure.

The ship was dated and empty. With only three non crew members on board, us and an Azeri man named Shakvalad, its long barren corridors, empty seating areas and abandoned upper deck, bestowed an eerie quiet—almost that of a ghost ship. Ethan and I shared a cabin, a basic but homely little space containing bunk beds with 1970s-style bright orange blankets, chintzy curtains, a tatty old porthole, and chipped and peeling laminate wood walling. Compared to the waiting room in Aktau, it was heaven.

"You want see eagle?" asked a crew member we came across changing the Kazakh flag to an Azerbaijani one on the upper deck.

"Err, sure," replied Ethan.

We shared a look of intrigue and followed him down a dark and empty corridor.

"Must be quiet," said the crew member softly as we stopped outside a particular cabin.

Opening up, he led us in, where, perched on top of the bed, looking longingly out of the porthole window, was a young bird of prey. Taking off his beanie, the man cast it on top of the bird's head to temporarily blind it, then quickly grasped its talons and picked it up to show us.

"We call Shaheen," he said.

He was a magnificent creature with wild piercing eyes and a beautiful plumage, of orange, brown, gray, black, and white. Eventually the man released his grip. Flapping back to the window, he sat once more, staring forlornly at sea birds drifting merrily by on the breeze outside. Every so often he would flap his wings and attempt to push through the transparent surface that stood between him and the life he longed for. What a cruel fate, so against the natural order of things. Hundreds of thousands of years of evolution had created him for such a different life, and every fiber in his being knew it. I felt so very sorry for that bird, and empathized deeply with his predicament. I knew what it felt like to be confined, to be trapped somewhere that I desperately wanted to break free from but could not, yet there was nothing I could do to help him. At this moment I was free and he was trapped. It was as simple as that. With a pained smile I said a little internal goodbye to the bird, promising that I would carry him in my heart and honor his memory by taking every opportunity to feel the wind in my hair, the sun on my face and to soar wild and free in spirit.

CHAPTER TWENTY-SIX
Tank Graveyard

A day and a night on board, and the rain-lashed skyline of Azerbaijan's capital, Baku, came into sight. Cutting-edge modern architecture mingled with stately old European-style buildings that wouldn't have looked out of place on the opulent streets of Paris. Not that it was all grandiose or avant-garde. Mixed in were the usual drab towers you'd expect from a former Soviet republic, along with plenty of port infrastructure; but even from a long distance, it was clear that this was no Aktau that lay ahead.

Dominating the scene was the most out of proportion flag I've ever seen, a ridiculously oversized national banner, quivering in the breeze atop a colossal pole. I later learned the pole measured 531 feet, making it, at the time of its erection in 2009, the tallest unsupported flagpole in the world. With the ensign stretching 98 feet by 229 feet, and weighing in at nearly half a ton, it had petroleum-funded delusions of grandeur written all over it.

Having selected the cheaper transit visa option instead of a tourist one, my stay in Azerbaijan was limited to a fleeting five days; but given that this tiny country could fit into Kazakhstan thirty-one times, it seemed more than adequate for my purposes. I had arranged for Ethan and me to stay in Baku with an Azeri friend of mine, Jamil, a couchsurfer who had previously crashed at my place in London. He agreed to meet us on the main road outside Baku's port, where a deluge of BMWs, Mercedes-Benzes, and other luxury cars drove past, making clear, along with billboards for swanky top-end fashion brands, how awash with oil money the city was.

It had all begun in 1872 with the deregulation in Baku of commercial oil extraction, leading to one of the world's great oil rushes that saw entrepreneurs and workers flocking there from every corner of the Russian Empire, and further beyond. In under thirty years Baku's population sky-rocketed by 1,200 percent, and by 1905 the city was producing an amazing 50 percent of the world's petroleum, creating gargantuan fortunes for a select few. Although nowhere near responsible for such a lofty figure today, a new pipeline stretching from Baku, through Georgia and Turkey, to the Mediterranean Sea a thousand miles away, has seen the boom time return. Since going online in 2005, rents, property prices, and hotel costs have hit the roof, making it a huge stroke of luck that I knew a local: accommodation would have cost us a small fortune.

"You know what, if Jamil arrives in anything other than a Benz, I think I'm gonna feel disappointed now," I joked to Ethan as another one tore past.

Fifteen minutes later he arrived in a shiny—Benz.

It had been a while since I'd last seen him, but he looked the same as ever, with a shaggy mop of jet-black hair, tufty goatee beard and a geeky pair of glasses that made him look every bit the computer expert and IT consultant he was.

"Jamie!" he cried through the car's window. "Welcome to Baku!"

We bundled in and soon arrived at Jamil's charming apartment in a nice leafy district of the city. Here Ethan took a turn for the worse, the color draining from his face and his normal joie de vivre departing.

"I think it's the flu," he groaned. "Been feeling ill all morning."

I could tell he wanted to crash-out, but when an offer came from Jamil to take us to see Baku's central Fountain Square, he dug deep and tagged along.

It was a nice enough little spot with decorative, scalloped-pattern paving, plenty of benches and, of course, a fountain. But Baku's real attraction, at least for me, was its historic, fortress-walled Old City. With Ethan in no state to go traipsing around, I arranged to meet him and Jamil later, and went solo to this nearby twelfth century UNESCO World Heritage Site, where atmospheric back-alleys and lanes twisted their way past traditional carpet sellers, mosques, art galleries, museums, an old sand-stone palace complex, and the country's most iconic historic building: Maiden's Tower. According to legend, this ninety-five foot stone tower had been constructed by a wealthy king who fell in love with his own daughter, and then asked the poor girl to marry him. Repulsed, but in no position to deny the King, she requested that before she gave him an answer he build her a tower from where she could observe his whole domain. When finished she climbed up to the top and leapt off to her death.

* * *

The following morning Ethan looked like death warmed up, but he soldiered-on for another outing, this time a road-trip heading south along the road towards Iran. Joining us now were Jamil's auburn-haired Lithuanian girlfriend, Ieva, and their photojournalist friend, Vladic.

Soon Baku's generally pleasant inner center gave way, on its southern outskirts, to an industrial nightmare of nodding-donkey oil pumps that stretched along a color-drained sandy corridor to the distant shores of a gloomy Caspian. It was horrendous; and today's miserable gray weather just added to the look.

"Have you seen the James Bond film, *The World Is Not Enough?*" asked Jamil.

"Sure."

"This is where they filmed the opening scene. We call it the James Bond oil field."

It didn't get much better further along the road. Scruffy beaches, rusting pipelines and hideous petro-chemical plants, made up most of the view across a post-apocalyptic landscape.

"I've never seen it, but apparently there's a giant statue of Lenin's head out here near the Azerbaijan Methanol Company," said Vladic.

Flicking through his copy of Mark Elliott's *Azerbaijan* travel guide, Vladic found the appropriate page and handed it to me. Sketched out was a hand-drawn map depicting a gas station, some chemical works and a small boxed section labeled, "Lenin still stands in grounds of factory."

Locating the gas station, we traipsed across barren fields with rusting pipelines emanating from the huge industrial complex, the Azerbaijan Methanol Company, where the statue was said to reside. Being Sunday there were few workers about with whom to make inquiries, but we found a couple of bemused guards who told us Lenin had been removed and was now in storage. Not that this spelt the end of our jaunt out here.

"Fancy trying to find an old tank cemetery instead?" asked Vladic, pointing out the details in his book.

There were two, one marked with, "Now a closed military zone – Keep Away!" that contained mostly parts, the other, also off limits, contained mostly tank chassis. Traipsing in the direction of the chassis cemetery, we came across a battered old factory with a rusting metal frame and huge vacant gaps in the sheet-metal paneling of its walls. Out the back was what we were looking for: two huge padlocked metal gates. Beyond stretched the decaying serried ranks of a brigade's worth of gutted and oxidized tanks and armoured vehicles. Gaining access was easy. Although locked together, the gates sagged so much on their hinges that we simply squeezed through, entering a bizarre decaying world of coiled tracks, chunky axles, spiked drive sprockets, old unidentifiable engine parts, and the skeletons of the tanks themselves.

Climbing among an amassed mountain of parts spilling out between these old mechanical war horses, we clambered inside multiple vehicles. With arms spread out tightrope walker-style, we took turns shuffling along the tanks' main guns, perching on their ends to pose for photos. Many were practically stripped bare, missing turrets and almost everything else that would have once identified them as tanks, others relatively intact and lined up in battle-ready formation as if poised for a final big push that never came.

On our way out, we happened upon a nearby factory worker who explained the tank cemetery for us. After the fall of the Soviet Union the tanks had been brought here on the executive orders of the President. Those with salvageable components were stripped and the parts used in a nearby factory that produced shiny modern tanks, whose munitions were tested on the hills opposite—a good reason not to go strolling that way in search of the second graveyard. We made our way back to the car instead.

* * *

With Ethan still ill and planning to spend the next couple of days recuperating before catching the train to Georgia, I said goodbye to him and Jamil at first light—for now anyway, as both were soon planning separate trips to London—and got myself to the outskirts of Baku via local bus and the city's swanky subway system, lavishly decorated in sections with fetching mosaics.

Hitchhiking in Azerbaijan proved far easier than Kazakhstan. Despite having acquired a note explaining what I was doing, I didn't really need it; far more people spoke English, and the rides came frequently, if at times for short durations. By the afternoon I had cleared half of the country, and found myself traveling in an SUV along a rural road that cut through a green and hilly landscape, with charming little villages and farms, so very different from the urban sprawl of Baku.

My new chauffeur was Adil, a senior operations officer at a mine clearance organization.

"Some years ago we lose a little territory to Armenia," he told me. "Our army soldiers take a little bit back; but a lot of these areas are heavily mined. The region is fertile soil: gold and agriculture and wine factories, and it is very beautiful, but it cannot be used for agriculture now. Each year there are many civilian casualties so we do mine awareness as well as clearance."

"How many mines are left?"

"Thousands, but the Armenians leave no records."

He was on his way to the organization's regional training base just outside the city of Goygol, about two hours drive from the border with Georgia, and asked if I'd like to have a look around the place. I wanted to arrive in Tbilisi, the Georgian capital, before dark, but with it being only an hour or so beyond the border, this left plenty of time for a side trip.

Several billboards on the road depicted Azerbaijan's former leader and KGB man, Heydar Aliyev, who ran the country during much of its Soviet period as chairman of the Azerbaijan Communist Party, and was the first and only Azeri to become a member of the U.S.S.R.'s executive committee, the Politburo. After independence, Aliyev performed something of a political about-face, becoming President, but now as an endorser of the "free-market." The sight of these billboards led to an interesting discussion with Adil, who I queried about the differences between Azerbaijan under communism compared with today.

"In Soviet times it was much better," he told me. "Some things were very bad but most things very good. The people were more generous, happy and sharing. But now everyone is chasing money and worrying for tomorrow. In Soviet times you absolutely knew tomorrow would be better than today. We had good school, free university, lots of jobs, good apartments, and stability. Money was enough for food and saving, and to get a car; it was sufficient to have a good life. There was no criminal, no Mafia. When we get independence, a few people get a lot of money, but most people nothing! If this is democracy, I don't want it!"

We arrived at The Azerbaijan National Agency For Mine Action through big green gates, and made our way along a dirt track lined with cypress trees to the front of the complex, a modest school-size building, mostly hidden from the outside world behind a large screening wall. Out the front, fluttering in the breeze, were the flags of Azerbaijan, Georgia, and NATO. Leading me inside, Adil took me past a large map depicting the locations of landmined areas, and a fascinating life size 3D wall display, featuring all the different sorts of landmines, grenades, cluster bombs, projectiles, rockets, and munitions they might come across.

"Are you hungry?" he asked as we entered a staffroom full of uniformed personnel.

"A little," I responded, not wanting to appear presumptuous at scoring a free feed, even through the truthful answer was "very."

Adil introduced me around and, because he had some work to attend to, got one of his subordinates, Firkret, to take me to the staff canteen. Firkret did the ordering, getting me meatballs and noodles in a steaming bowl of soup, served with a bag of bread, and a bowl of bright pink cabbage-like vegetables.

"What is this?" I asked Firkret, pointing at the Day-Glo contents of the bowl.

"It is something to make delicious," he replied.

And indeed it was.

We chatted about his work and my trip, and when Firkret discovered that I wrote books, he was insistent to impress upon me one important point: "Please tell the world that Muslims are not terrorists. This is very important for us."

I promised him I would.

A generous extra lift from Adil got me to a good nearby hitchhiking spot, from where I plowed on through a surprising amount of rain to the Azeri/Georgia border. I reached it in four rides and set off on foot, leaving the truck driver who got me to the crossing behind in a vast backlog of vehicles. Skirting alongside a meandering river, I made my way along a road that stretched through no man's land. Some sections were properly surfaced, others reduced to mud and slush in the increasing rain. To my left rose a green and scrubby hillside; to my right, spanning the river, was an irregularly arched seventeenth century red brick bridge, for which the border crossing was named: Krasny Most or Red Bridge.

As a British passport holder, entering Georgia was a breeze. There was no need for a visa, and my nationality permitted me to remain in the country for a full year without additional documentation. From now until London I needed only one more visa, and that was for neighboring Turkey, which I could purchase on arrival. It gave me an instant sense of freedom.

Before leaving Baku, Jamil's girlfriend, Ieva, had kindly arranged for me to stay in the Georgian capital, Tbilisi, with an Estonian couchsurfer friend of hers, Madis. It was a big help, and as I hitched my way there, through increasingly green and hilly scenery, it was with an overwhelming feeling of calm. I would get there long before nightfall and everything would be arranged and awaiting me on arrival.

The driver of a clean and modern Volkswagen dropped me roughly twenty miles from Tbilisi, in the shadow of a treeless range of hills. A lone shepherd and his flock roamed nearby, making their way towards a distant peak where a towering metal-framed crucifix stood, proudly announcing Georgia's dominant religion. Nestled in the lee of the hills was quite possibly the ugliest town I've ever seen: Rustavi; a Soviet nightmare of town planning that looked designed for collective anxiety. A sickly forest of neglected gray towers rose from the lower plains in such a depressing and extensive sprawl that it made me feel like popping some Prozac.

Picking up a ride here with a couple of bearded old-timers on their way to Tbilisi in an SUV, I reclined in leather-seated comfort and soaked in the view. The outskirts of the capital were nothing to look at, but the center was phenomenal. Surrounded on three sides by the Southern Caucasus Mountains, this ancient city branched around, and perched on top of, a haphazard collection of hills, ridges, gorges and cliffs, making for a stupendous setting. Majestic churches with semi-conical, segmented domes commanded the best positions. Ancient fortress walls, proud statues, grandiose public buildings, tree-lined avenues, and an abundance of attractive and historic housing created a feast for the eyes. It had an instantly uplifting effect.

The odd thing about couchsurfing is that after you've done a bit of it, you no longer feel strange rocking up at the door of a complete stranger and settling into their home for the night, often receiving complimentary food and drink, even your own set of keys. And so it was with Madis, who handed me a collection of keys to his place. And what a lovely place it was to spend the night. Large and spacious, if minimally lit and furnished, this once grand building with high ceilings, ornate arched entranceway, wooden floors, and an old piano, was now a charming, student-style abode. The house had communal living areas partitioned by way of curtains and a wall made out of cardboard boxes, and empty beer bottles doing their best to serve as decorative adornments.

Madis shared the place with a collection of Estonians and Poles, and introduced me around his rabble of house mates, most showing the sort of polite disinterest characteristic of people accustomed to random guests. Madis led me through to his room, decorated with impressionistic Soviet-era tourist-board representations of the Caspian and Black Sea, and an "artistic" image of a woman's naked torso. Set up in here was a spare bed with fresh white linen, comfy-looking pillows and a fluffy duvet.

"I know how much I appreciate a properly made bed when I'm staying with others, so hopefully this will help you sleep well tonight," said Mandis.

Having crashed on Jamil's floor in Baku, Timur's floor in Aktau, Dmitriy's truck when on the road, in a laundry room in Aktobe, and a chair in Atyrau, this would be my first proper bed since the hotel at the Aral Sea. I was delighted and touched at his thoughtfulness.

Sadly, Madis had some work to complete, so there was little chance to get to know him or score a guided tour of the city. I left him at his desk and set off to explore by myself, catching a subway train to the outskirts of Tbilisi's Old Town, where I wandered long after dark without plan or destination, taking in the major flood-lit architectural wonders on the larger thoroughfares, and discovering some hidden gems along its twisting cobbled alleyways: crooked houses, secluded courtyards, naturally heated sulphur baths. It was a city that deserved far more than a fleeting inquisitive browse, but I felt an overwhelming, if completely illogical, urge to move on, as if some invisible force was propelling me to abandon this gorgeous capital come the morning. I'd experienced compelling urges when traveling many times before, and knew from experience that to deny them only ever brought me misery or pain. It might have made no rational sense, but I knew without question I would obey.

* * *

"It is like something out of *Lord of the Rings*," said my second ride of the morning, gushing enthusiasm for the place.

"You will never forget Vardzia caves," added his passenger. "It is special place; a whole town carved into a mountainside."

It sounded fantastic, a twelfth century monastic complex with over three thousand caves that, according to a tourist pamphlet I had picked up from Madis, included churches, libraries, barns, living quarters, wine cellars, stables, even antiquated drug stores—all carved out of the rock and encompassing thirteen stories. Located near Georgia's southern border with Turkey, it was slightly off my intended route but I was confident that I could hitch to it, and still make it out of the country, all in one day.

There were three others in the car with me, all guys in their twenties, who had picked me up on a highway turn-off just beyond the beautiful riverside city of Mtskheta, the country's former capital that was nestled among lush green mountains and dominated by a towering cathedral visible from the road. They were on their way to Khashuri, about an hour's drive to the west, to visit what they described as a "fun reel."

"A fun reel?" I asked.

"Yes, a fun reel," replied the driver.

"I'm sorry, I don't know what that is?"

"You know, a fun reel."

"Is it like a fun park?"

"No a fun reel; when someone's died."

"Ah, funeral!" I exclaimed at the sudden realization, perhaps with a little too much enthusiasm given the circumstances.

A lush and green rural landscape passed by as we headed towards Khashuri that contained a very encouraging sign: the occasional tree teetering on the edge of spring, its buds swelled, although not yet burst, in preparation for the new season. After Georgia I would continue south into Turkey, where, with the lower latitude, it seemed likely spring had already arrived. Having encountered my fair share of biting cold in Central Asia, savoring the glow of the sun on my face once more was going to be bliss.

Just north of the road we traveled on, at some stages only a couple of miles away, was South Ossetia, a small breakaway region of Georgia that, due to the actions of Georgia's President, Mikheil Saakashvili, saw it become, in 2008, the center of the greatest crisis in East–West relations since the Cold War, amazingly, even raising the spectre of nuclear confrontation.[189]

Having come to power in a George Soros funded "revolution," the so called "Rose Revolution" of 2003,[190] American-educated Mikheil Saakashvili quickly demonstrated his willingness to be a U.S. stooge president of an order that would make even Tony Blair blush. Despite having a population of just 4.6 million people, Georgia's deployment of troops to Iraq stood, at the time of their withdrawal in 2008, as the largest contribution to the invasion force outside that of the U.S. or U.K.[191] Such craven obsequiousness to Washington, soon led to Saakashvili becoming the darling of U.S. neoconservatives and their Israeli allies. High-tech arms, intelligence agents, military advisers and money flowed into Georgia from the U.S. and Israel, with the C.I.A. and Mossad (Israel's secret intelligence service) running stations out of the Georgian capital, Tbilisi.[192]

With membership to NATO on the cards, and the backing of powerful allies, Saakashvili decided to pick himself a fight with South Ossetia, located on Georgia's northern border with Russia. Formerly part of Russia, it was Stalin who first assimilated South Ossetia into his home province Georgia, where it became an autonomous protectorate. When the Soviet Union fell apart, Georgia gained independence and abolished South Ossetian autonomy; but with the majority of South Ossetians being Russian citizens, who have a different history and ethnicity from Georgians, and speak a different language, it is hardly surprising that the overwhelming majority wanted to reunite with Russia. In 2006 a referendum was held in South Ossetia, with residents asked if they supported independence from Georgia. In a ballot that was monitored and approved by thirty-four international observers, ninety-nine percent responded that they did.[193]

On the night of August 7, 2008, the Georgian military unleashed a ferocious and indiscriminate barrage of artillery on South Ossetia, shelling apartment buildings, firing on civilians and razing buildings to the ground.[194] With the Georgian army having received training and equipment from the U.S. and Israel—to the extent that these countries' military advisors were stationed with Georgian forces all the way down to battalion level[195]—it is inconceivable that the U.S. was unaware before the event, or that Saakashvili launched the assault without the green light from his foreign benefactors.

Alongside hundreds of civilian deaths were those of Russian peace-keeper soldiers, who had been stationed there legally under international agreement for the last sixteen years. As Georgian tanks rolled into the streets of South Ossetia, the invaders began celebrating their occupation. It was to prove short lived; the mighty Russia bear was about to respond. Scrambling to get organized, it took the Russians two days before their main body of forces arrived, and when they did they swatted the Georgians like flies, liberating the grateful populace, many of whom had been holed up in basements to escape the Georgian onslaught. Briefly rolling on into surrounding parts of Georgia, Russia could have easily taken control of the whole country, but, in a sign of remarkable restraint, or perhaps mindful of not getting sucked into a wider protracted conflict, withdrew.

Not that you'll have heard much of the above from reports at the time in the Western corporate media, who—surprise, surprise—responded to Georgia's aggression and humiliating defeat, by portraying the Russian army as instigators, casting the truth that Georgia invaded first down the memory hole.[196] U.S. President at the time, George W. Bush, even had the gall to castigate Russia by commenting, without the merest hint of irony, that, "Bullying and intimidation are not acceptable ways to conduct foreign policy in the 21st century;"[197] and 2008 presidential hopeful, John McCain, getting in on the action by announcing, "I'm interested in good relations between the United States and Russia, but in the 21st century, nations don't invade other nations."[198] This coming from the hawkish advocate of the invasions of Iraq and Afghanistan, and one of the major cheerleaders for an invasion of Iran.

With U.S. Secretary of State Condoleezza Rice proclaiming that the U.S. would "fight" for Georgia, it is extremely fortunate that Georgia's membership to NATO was rejected by European members of the military alliance. Had Georgia been allowed to join NATO, as was reportedly promised to Saakashvili by Washington before his invasion of South Ossetia (in contravention of U.S. agreements with Russia not to expand NATO's influence into areas of the former U.S.S.R.), then a state of war would have existed between Russia and the U.S., as well as its other NATO allies. In an attempt to foment as much, when Russia sent troops to defend South Ossetia against Georgia's attack, Saakashvili announced, "This is not about Georgia any more. This is about … American values, that we always ourselves believed in. This is about … [the] future of the world order."[199] But faced with a well-armed and capable adversary, the U.S. huffed and puffed but did nothing; Putin had drawn a line in the sand: ethnic cleansing of Russians in South Ossetia would not be tolerated. South Ossetia became a protectorate of Russia, along with Georgia's other breakaway region Abkhazia, and the two recognized by the Kremlin as independent states.

I stood at the beginning of an empty road, deep in a mountainous valley cut by the mighty Mtkvari River, a watercourse I had meandered alongside for the last few hours through an astonishing array of beautiful canyons, spanned, every so often, by a precarious rope bridge lurching in the wind above icy waters and rounded slippery boulders. Splashed with patches of green and brown, the walls of these precipitous valleys rose up in a chaos of stone, punctuated by fairy-tale castles, ancient ruins and exquisite churches with distinctive semi-conical segmented domes that nestled among the rock, blending in as if part of the mountains themselves.

Despite several reasonable rides, and a hell of a lot of hard trekking in-between, by late afternoon I had still not reached the Vardzia Caves, and found myself teetering on the edge of giving up, turning back and heading for the Turkish border. I was exhausted and famished, but my main concern was whether enough daylight remained to reach the caves. As I stood contemplating my options, dark clouds formed behind the mountains, enveloping the area with a ghastly gray light. Trees lining the river began to creak wearily in the increasing wind, as waves spread across the water, and a cold slashing rain descended from above, mocking my flesh and testing my resolve to continue.

Although only ten miles as the crow flies from where I stood, I was reluctant to set off for the caves on foot. Seriously twisting and undulating terrain lay ahead, making the real distance far greater. The minor back road that led out to the caves diverged from a larger one that I had hitchhiked along to get here, so if I stayed put then at least I had the option of turning back along the larger road. It didn't possess much traffic, but there seemed enough to offer me a reasonable chance of making it to the border. Were I to continue on foot along the minor road, but fail to pick up a ride on it, then I would, in all likelihood, be spending the night in the middle of nowhere, neither having reached the caves nor being in any position to get back to the larger road until dawn.

With this in mind, I decided to only accept lifts going all the way to the caves; anything else would be too risky. But then, despite such reasoned logic, after forty minutes of waiting in the rain a semi-full taxi van pulled up, whose driver took pity on my dejected-looking, rain-drenched form, and offered me a ride to the next village—for free. Maybe it was the thought of temporary warmth and comfort, maybe the novelty of scoring a free ride from a vehicle surrounded by others who had paid for the privilege, but it overrode all sense and reason.

Oh, what the hell, I thought, and got in.

I traveled with the villagers through more dramatic rainy scenery, deeper into the gorge until I was dropped at the turning for the village of Nakalakevi, just down the road from an old stone enclosure that had once been a slave market. The van disappeared along the side road, leaving me almost exactly halfway to the caves. I was now fully committed to pressing on. No sooner had I begun than my lungs were heaving and heart pounding like an engine revving into the red zone; my legs went numb and feet felt like I was walking barefoot on hot coals. Twisting cruelly up and then down, the road undulated its way along the rocky hillside, faithfully following the snaking route of a ribbon of icy water, tumbling over rocks in the belly of the valley below.

By itself the hike would have been manageable, but after miles of earlier hiking and next to no sustenance, I was toasted, and began the walk from an existing position of exhaustion. Then there was my backpack. I had no idea how much the thing weighed, but when I got home I intended to throw it on the scales to find out. After lugging it around for months and sleeping in so many awkward locations, my back was in serious need of a chiropractor.

I dug deep and labored on, dragging myself forward through a landscape reminiscent of the rugged beauty of the Scottish Highlands, past ancient ruins and a majestic thousand-year-old hilltop castle, the Tmogvi Fortress, until finally the first caves came into view, not the Vardzia complex, but a smaller one, the Vani Caves, visible high above on a craggy mountainside. Among the grottoes hewn out of the sandstone was a small domed church, wedged into a deep fissure in the rock. Unfortunately, there wasn't the daylight left to climb up, not if I wanted to reach the larger Vardzia Caves down the road.

Downhill for most of the way now, I picked up the pace, and soon the area's star attraction appeared before me. Rising up on the other side of the river was an enchanting and arresting sight: a mist-capped mountain, with an almost sheer exposed rock face half way up—a giant step, honeycombed across its surface with hundreds of man made caves, carved over multiple levels; dwellings that would once have housed thousands of monks. Some were embellished with arched entranceways, others with pillars and external stone staircases, a few with flamboyant recessed verandas.

Out of *Lord of the Rings* it most certainly was.

Reaching the caves required continuing past them upstream on the opposite bank, where a small bridge spanned the river, connecting with a path that led back towards the site, where it traversed its way up the distant mountainside. The place looked deserted, but as I hiked along the track towards the mountain, a small inconspicuous door in the rock next to the path flung open, revealing a tiny but cozy-looking gray-walled cave, decked out with a wall-mounted cupboard, electrical light, and a wooden table, where three men sat sharing a crusty loaf of white bread and a bottle of red wine. The man who had opened up gestured me inside.

None spoke much English, but it seemed they were some sort of custodians of the caves, who, in the absence of other visitors, were whiling away the evening with a good bottle of red. They poured some into a little tumbler and tore a hunk off the loaf, passing both to me. I was all for staying in here out of the rain making merry with them, but I was running out of daylight. If I didn't take an excessive amount of time exploring the caves, and managed to get a lift back to the main road before dark, then I might still reach Turkey tonight.

The wine was sweet, full-bodied and delicious, but I guzzled their kind offering in as quick a manner as was possible without appearing hasty or uncouth, then struck off for the caves, bread in hand, having left my backpack behind with my new-found friends. The absence of its weight was bliss, and I bounced up the track like a mountain goat, climbing higher, until I was halfway up and looking down on the greater canyon below, where a fertile tree-lined floodplain stretched from the grassy scree slopes to the banks of the river.

Straddling the track in front of me was a square keep-like building crafted out of stone, with arched entranceways. Beyond it, I knew from my earlier sightings across the river, lay the caves proper. I stood still for a second at the entrance to the building, savoring the anticipation while I got my breath back. When the sound of my heartbeat died down below the soft chirping of nearby birds, I decided I was ready. Stepping through the archway into the building's cool interior, I gazed up in the fading light at its beautifully carved ceiling, its once-white rock now stained black from the grimy residue of centuries of candle smoke. Passing through to the other side, an enchanting city of rock emerged. External paths and stairways skirted along a tiered rock face, going to and from the hundreds of cave dwellings of this otherworldly former monastery, climbing from one level to another.

Making my way along one of the paths, I went into the grand ruin of a cave, its walls covered with the scars of picks, still clear to see eight hundred years after their original wielding. Inside was a mountain womb, a cozy shelter with alcoves in the wall for books and candles, a high ceiling, raised sleeping platform, and an internal corridor leading to another room; and then another; and another after that. Internal staircases, tunnels, and secret passages criss-crossed the entire site, interlinking many of the chambers over its thirteen levels, in a bewildering maze of complexity where you could enter at one spot and then pop out, blinking into the daylight, at another. It was a phenomenal site, like an abandoned mystical hobbit city, which I proceeded to explore, ducking in and out of it like a rabbit in a warren.

In the center of Vardzia was its beating heart, the Church of the Assumption, a twelfth century chapel announced by way of a double-arched façade, with exquisite biblically-themed frescos. While marveling at their detail and beauty, I pondered what it would be like to reside here permanently, cloistered from the outside world, living a life of contemplation and asceticism. I reached the startling conclusion that retreating from society for a couple of years as a monk—so long as I could be stationed in a place like this—held a surprising amount of appeal.

Distracting me from further thought of an ecclesiastic career change was the sight of three great bells hanging from the arches of the church's façade. With the mighty canyon directly below, I wondered what the echo would be like. I gave it a tentative tug. Echoes resonated far and wide, producing an eerie ghost-like response in the misty canyon, and a wholly unexpected consequence closer to hand. Suddenly a nearby door in the rock swung open, and there before me appeared a fully cloaked, long-bearded monk, screwing up his ugly mug, looking anything but the picture of inner peace I'd imagined moments earlier, and the source of his torment was me. I had no idea the place was still inhabited, even by a solitary contemplative. His holiness wasted no time in berating me in Georgian for ringing his precious bell, giving me a right old roasting over my indiscretion, a forthright blast of Christian charity delivered by the end of a jabbing finger. In an act of hasty contrition, I apologized for my sins, and concluded that a monk's life wasn't for me after all.

It seemed a good time to hit the road.

Several lucky lifts, including one with a priest, this time a cheery old soul, who bopped along to dull-as-dishwater British/Georgian singer Katie Melua on his stereo, saved me from being marooned in the dark. Just before the last of the day's light faded away, I scored a ride across the border: another modern SUV, this time with a young couple, Nizam and Ia, who were heading to the Turkish town of Ardaham, seventy miles away.

It proved a quick and easy transit on into Turkey, where we soon found ourselves twisting up mountain roads, climbing in elevation until the altitude brought with it a thick blanket of snow. Another language barrier endured, so I reclined in the back in silence, savoring the warmth and comfort of the interior, secure in the knowledge that I was being taken to a destination where I intended to spend the night. There would be no more hiking along or standing by the side of the road for me today. It was a reassuring thought, and soon my weary eyes became heavy, and I drifted off to sleep.

My serenity shattered in an instant.

From out of nowhere an extreme centrifugal force threw me hard against the door, jolting me awake, as the vehicle pitched violently to one side, spinning out of control off the road. Ia let out a piercing scream, and for a second I thought my number was up. Instinctively I braced myself, ready for a crushing impact. It never came. With an abrupt lurch we came to a skidding halt in a snowy ditch, having spun almost 360 degrees. The emotional dust took longer to settle. Ia was in near hysterics. Doing his best to calm her down, Nizam employed a softly-softly approach, then, when it became clear this wasn't working, resorted to the verbal equivalent of a slap across the face.

"Kadin sakin ol!"

It did the job and she sat in a more manageable stunned and submissive silence.

Stepping outside into knee-deep snow, Nizam and I surveyed the situation. We were in the middle of nowhere, on top of an unlit, wind and snow-lashed mountain plateau, with terrible visibility and no sign of civilization or any other vehicles. There had been plenty of perilous drops next to the roadside earlier on, visible in the hazy illumination of the headlights; if there had been one here, then we would all be dead; no question about it. On the surface of it the SUV looked undamaged, but the snow was jammed up to the bumpers and wheel arches, holding her firmly in place. Having pulled herself together, Ia began pointing back the way we'd come. She seemed to be telling Nizam they had passed a dwelling of some sort just beyond the near horizon. If so, then we might be able to source a shovel. Visibility was terrible in the flurry of falling snow flakes, but our tire tracks were still clear enough, so Nizam and I set off in the building's supposed direction, leaving Ia wrapped up in a blanket in the SUV.

She soon faded from sight behind us, and the snow and darkness became our world, broken, eventually, by the warm enticing glow of illuminated windows in the distance. A large house appeared to the left of the road, its forefront strewn with heavy duty mechanical machinery. Knocking on the door, a surprised old man appeared who immediately beckoned us inside his cozy-looking home. No doubt mindful of Ia, Nizam politely turned him down, explaining the situation and our need for a digging implement. A quick shout behind him, and the old man summoned a younger male who came outside with us and retrieved the perfect tool: a long-handled shovel with a tapered head. With this in hand we thanked the man and made our way back to the SUV. After a world of digging, Nizam jumped in the driver's seat, firing up the engine. Fumes billowed from the exhaust, illuminated in the dark by the red glow of the tail lights. The SUV wailed in effort, rocking back and forth as it struggled for traction, wheels flailing around in a wild frenzy, until finally it lurched forwards. We were free.

Whatever arrangements had been made for the return of the shovel, I don't know; but Nizam made no attempt to take it back. He put it in the trunk and we were off. Any euphoria at being back on the move again quickly subsided, replaced by a cautious and somber respect for the dangers of the road ahead, a silent and subdued realization that things could have easily worked out very differently, and with dire consequences.

CHAPTER TWENTY-SEVEN
The Home Stretch

When I closed my eyes at night I saw road, a seemingly everlasting tract with no final destination. Did England really exist at the end of one of them? Actually, no, not if you consider the English Channel. But that wasn't the point. The point was that by now I was good and ready for home, to forget about thumbing a ride altogether, to stay put for a while with no intention of dragging myself off for the next place shortly after arrival. The sheer cumulative effect of the last few months had taken its toll: the distance covered and the number of rides, over eight hundred and counting, that by now had blurred into one never ending stretch of road to nowhere. The thought of catching a train and chugging my way merrily back to England was extraordinarily tempting, but I hadn't come this far to cheat on the home stretch.

Despite promising myself that once I got to Turkey I would simply push on west without undue hanging around or sightseeing, after the delights of Georgia's Vardzia cave city, I couldn't quite resist stopping off at a similar location in central Turkey that I had visited twice before: Cappadocia, a sprawling geological wonderland renowned for its canyons lined with bizarre phallic rock formations known as fairy chimneys, where ancient underground cities and Christian churches were carved out of the stone. I spent a couple of days hiking through the region this time, where spring was no longer teetering on the edge of arrival but bursting fully into life, with fluffy pink offerings of blossom covering the region's almond trees, and fields erupting into golden blankets of sunny wild flowers.

I departed Cappadocia at dawn, leaving for Turkey's largest city, Istanbul, amid a fiery orange sunrise that seemed to set the stratosphere ablaze. My late night arrival in the western half of the city signaled a momentous geographical transition. Crossing a giant suspension bridge with cables dripping in bulbs like baubles hanging from a Christmas tree, my home continent appeared across the famous waters of the Bosphorus Strait. On the distant banks appeared a vibrant modern city with an ancient heart: a twinkling metropolis full of light and optimistic promise, where palatial apartments rose from the water's edge alongside spear-like spires of minarets, where the rampart walls of a floodlit stone fortress dazzled golden like an ethereal palace, while skyscrapers loomed large over the city in the distance, paying homage to the false gods of industry and commerce. I was back in Europe again, and it felt fantastic.

After a day relaxing in this spectacular city of 13.5 million people, I stuck to my plan of pushing on home unabated, clearing tiny neighboring Bulgaria and then Serbia in a day a piece, finding myself, on the morning of the third day, a stone's throw from Croatia.

I awoke with a jolt in the cab of the truck I had spent the night in at a roadside truck stop, prodded into sudden consciousness by the sound of a vehicle driving past in the pitch-black outside. Suddenly the realization hit me: people were moving towards the border. It was 4:30 a.m., but time was of the essence, I needed to get moving. Emily had inadvertently set the time frame, with an email mentioning she would be away from London for a couple of nights to play a gig with her string quartet, Indigo Strings, at an Elgar festival on the Isle of White. With Emily departing for her gig in three days' time, I was dammed if I was going to take more than that to get back to London. Having traveled such a crazy distance from Australia, pushing myself under what were, at times, very trying conditions, it just felt wrong to arrive home to an empty apartment. Not that Emily was aware of my plans; I intended my arrival to be a surprise.

I had reached the border the evening before with a Turkish truck driver who had picked me up in Bulgaria. He was on his way to Holland, a very nice distance of roughly 1,500 miles. Problem was, he was driving it at a leisurely pace, with an ETA just after Emily's departure. Having encountered a monumental backlog of trucks at the Croatian border, he had given up and parked at a truck stop while the backlog cleared. And so, I decided to say farewell and to go solo instead, shifting from one ride to another, when traffic started using the road again in the morning. Not only was it logically the right thing to do, but, more importantly, it felt right, with another powerful internal urge imploring me to jump ship.

With a sense of urgency I scrambled from my bunk in the pre dawn darkness, grabbing my gear and clambering outside the truck onto the wet gravel below, having passed on my thanks and said my goodbyes to the driver the night before. There was no time to properly pack my sleeping bag; every truck that passed could be the one that got me home. Slinging my sleeping bag around my neck, I stumbled through the slashing rain to the deserted road. With no idea how long I'd be stuck here, I undid my pack, tearing through its contents for my waterproof jacket, retrieving it in the nick of time: just as two powerful headlights appeared in the distance, slicing through the darkness. If I didn't pack away my sleeping bag soon it would become soaked, but the approaching truck was my priority.

Standing upright with my backpack prominently displayed beside me, I stuck out a thumb. In the darkness I couldn't really see into the cab, but when it was close enough for the driver to get a clear shot of me, I hit him with the "Maslin move," hand on heart, imploring him for a ride. He carried on past, but then, in what must have been a last minute change of heart, violently jumped on the brakes.

With my backpack half open and sleeping bag still out, I did my best to cradle them in my arms, hobbling down the road towards the truck. It was a cumbersome weight and my back paid the price. An electric shock-like pain raced through my left hand side. I winced, but it was more than worth the discomfort; one of the most fascinating rides I've ever had was about to commence.

Greeting me in the cab was a dark haired Caucasian guy of about thirty with a beaming smile and warm kind eyes, dressed in a black sweater and blue jeans.

"Thank you so much!" I said, heaving myself inside.

"You are welcome," he replied. "I need company."

He introduced himself as Miodrag, a Serbian long distance truck driver heading from his home country on a delivery to northern Italy.

Only minutes into the drive and we reached the Croatian border, where my passport caused quite a stir with the female official manning the drive-through booth. The problem was my mug shot. After months of roughing it, this now bore little resemblance to the long haired, unkempt and malnourished reality in front of her. Looking from the fuller-faced, clean shaven I.D. photo to my hideous reality, she recoiled as if staring into the face of the elephant man. In desperation she called a colleague, and then a second, their eyes flicking back and forth from the photo to me, desperately trying to reconcile the two.

"Come on guys. It's me," I said, pulling a silly smiley face, as if this would somehow assist in their marrying the picture with my ugly mug.

I tried a fatigued drawn face instead, then began counting on my fingers, while listing the countries I had been through, trying to induce the conclusion: *Goodness me, all those places, no wonder he looks such a state.*

They checked my passport stamps to verify I was telling the truth. A nod of the head was shared between them. They handed it back and waved me through.

I wasn't the only one with problems. For some reason Miodrag's paperwork for his cargo left something to be desired, and so to rectify the problem he had to pay a bribe.

"It is so corrupt here," he said in disgust as we pulled away. "Not as bad as Hungary but still bad. Hungary is worst in Europe. I have friend who stop for a madam, which was police woman dressed up. He had to pay 1,500 Euros."

"And he didn't even get laid!" I added.

"No," laughed Miodrag. "Fuck is twenty euro, blow job ten, so he could have fucked for a year!"

The further we drove and chatted, the more Miodrag opened up to me, telling me about his past and how he got into long distance truck driving.

"I am former teacher but I need travel like you," he told me.

"How long were you a teacher?" I asked.

"Five years."

"What did you teach?"

Miodrag laughed.

"I am hairdressing teacher, practical and theory. I love art, my father make sculpture: wood and stone. He is professional. My uncle is professional painter. I learn first by practicing on younger brother. I work one shift in school, one shift in my salon. I was really good at my job but I can't stay in one place."

His aversion to staying put had led Miodrag to do plenty of hitching before becoming a truck driver, and was one of the reasons he said he always tried to stop for people hitchhiking, or as he called it "autostop."

"I picked this guy up on highway in Portugal. I was tired and needed company. He autostop like you. But in cab he sweat and scratch and ill. 'Are you okay?' I ask, and he tell me 'I have problem, I need heroin.' 'Oh, no!' I think and say 'I not have any!' but I look at him and feel bad. I see he is good man but does have problem so I say, 'Where can I buy heroin?'"

Miodrag laughed and shook his head.

"He call friend at next town and I give forty euros to buy heroin."

"Did he inject or smoke it?" I asked

"No, he, err," Miodrag struggled with the words, then mimed snorting. "He say, 'At Lyon I give you money,' I think 'Oh yeah' but at Lyon he call friend and give me fifty euro! After that I try to tell him if he need he can keep. I was so surprised."

We chatted for a while about the drug problem in Serbia.

"We have big problem in my country with drugs. The police sell the drugs. You can sell but only if you work for police. We have officer in my town drive around in new Mercedes S Class. How this on 500 euros?"

The further we drove together the more we talked, and after a while, when we were skirting about a mile north of Bosnia and Herzegovina, I decided to ask Miodrag about the Yugoslav Wars of the nineties, and whether he was involved. We began with generalities of the conflicts, with Miodrag quick to stress that atrocities were carried out on all sides, including NATO, and then moved onto his personal involvement.

"I was youngest solider in the Serbian army—thirteen years old. I have pictures of me in newspaper. I was youngest and I was sniper. One man from special forces showed me how be sniper. I was three years; no, two years and couple of months fighting. When sniper you have complete control, sometimes waiting two or three days."

"Did you see much action?"

"Yes. When I shoot man first time I was like this—" He mimed looking through a gun-sight, then cringing and looking away before pulling the trigger. "I look through optic after and no smile, only dead. After I was not good for couple of days, very sad. But after time it like shooting signs. You lose human feeling for another."

He rolled up the legs of his jeans, and showed me two bullet wounds, then lifted his shirt and showed me wounds from a mine and another bullet on his stomach. Miodrag went on to describe many of his experiences during the war, but the most poignant and remarkable was his time in Sarajevo. Here he had been given the task of going from house to house in a district where just about everyone was dead to make sure there were no enemy forces. During this process he came upon two small children alone in a house whose parents had been killed. His concern was immediate. Directly outside was another soldier—also clearing houses—with a notorious reputation for unjustified killings, who, if he saw the children, would have executed them. Terrified for their safety, Miodrag implored the children to be quiet, hiding them in the basement. The solider outside asked him if the house was clear. "Yes," replied Miodrag, but moments later a clanging noise from inside alerted the soldier to their presence. In he went, dragging out the children, drawing his knife ready to slit their throats.

"They are just kids," protested Miodrag.

"No. They are Muslims," scoffed the solider, about to kill the first one, only stopping when Miodrag, who was just fifteen at the time, drew his pistol and threatened to shoot him if he didn't let them go.

A stand-off followed, but eventually the children were let go, who ran and clung to Miodrag for dear life.

"This isn't over!" stated the other soldier, but he died of natural causes soon after—well, in warfare a bullet in the head is pretty natural.

The children stayed with Miodrag for the next twenty days, even sleeping with him in the same bed as if they were, as he put it to me, "my own kids," before the UN came and took them away to safety. Both he and they were inconsolable to be separated. In fact, this big tough guy was nearly in tears recalling this and I wasn't far off too.

"After this twenty days I be very sad," he told me. "I don't know, I can't explain feeling. These kids only shine point of war for me during robbery, shooting, kill. They like angels."

Despite trying to locate them since, Miodrag has sadly never seen or heard of them.

It is a very long shot, but I told Miodrag that I was writing a book, and offered to recall his story, including details of the children's names and location that he last saw them, in the hope that someone reading it might know where they are, or is in a position to go through the relevant records to find out. And so, on the off chance that someone can assist in a very special reunion: the boy's name was Amir, the girl's name was Azra. Miodrag found them in Sarajevo in 1992, and they were collected by the UN in Vlasenica. Although far from certain, Miodrag thinks they were taken to Tuzla. Miodrag's army unit was the A.O.D. If anyone can help, please contact me through my publisher.

I said goodbye to this brave and humble individual at the border with Slovenia, where, once again, Miodrag encountered paperwork issues, only this time ones that he seemed certain would take him hours to resolve.

I pushed hard for the rest of the day, hitching and trekking through Slovenia, with its glorious alpine scenery of snow-capped peaks, bejeweled around their lower reaches by the bright new growth of birches and the more reserved evergreen hues of pines. Picturesque villages came and went, sprinkling the scene with traditional farm houses, quaint little white churches, and old barns with giant piles of wood out front. By late afternoon I entered Austria, twisting my way through thickly forested terrain towards the floor of a great valley, where I picked up a busy autobahn. Soon I was heading north towards Germany with excellent ride after excellent ride that deposited me at gas and service areas along the way. By the time I passed into Germany it was dark, but I pushed on, watching as the miles rushed by in a blur on the country's beautifully maintained multi-lane autobahn system. I secured my final ride of the night with four Romanian men on their way into a service station restaurant near Munich, who, on seeing me, came over and offered me a lift, but only once they had bought me a meal. After a large platter of sausage and chips, we headed off into an endless stream of head and tail lights, snaking their way across the country in endless illuminated processions, producing a trance-like effect on my tired and travel-weary eyes.

At 4 a.m. they dropped me at a service station near Karlsruhe, less than ten miles from the French border. Battered with fatigue, I made my way to an adjoining field and threw my nifty ex-army bivvy bag onto the ground. I put my sleeping bag inside it and crawled on in, bedding down to the constant drone of unrelenting traffic. Two hours later and I was up again, determined beyond determined to make the night just gone my final one away from home: come this evening I would sleep in my own bed.

I entered France near the north eastern town of Forbach, in a car driven by a Polish man carting a mountain of toys back to Paris for his nieces and nephews. Flat agricultural fields dominated the landscape now, on a sunny springtime day that had me bursting with excitement. The Pole and I said goodbye outside the city of Reims, where he dropped me within walking distance of the highway heading north. It would be my final stretch of continental road. Having a toll section to wait at, it was the perfect place to pick up a ride, and as I bounced my way towards it I noticed a most welcome destination on its overhead road sign: Calais. People swam the channel between England and Calais. Calais was as good as home!

"Home." I said it aloud and smiled, a smile that held a deep and hard fought satisfaction.

"Woohoo!" I cried into the air, and began clicking my fingers in frantic excitement as I ran towards the toll.

As I waited on the other side I spotted cars with U.K. number plates. Could I get a lift all the way back, I wondered?

A French car was the first to stop, pulling up way beyond where I stood, forcing me to run towards it. When I was a few feet away it pulled off, its occupants flicking me the finger and bursting into fits of laughter. It was the first time on my entire trip that it had happened. But no Frenchman was going to dampen my spirits today. I was on my way to England.

It didn't take long before a camper van with kayaks on the roof stopped. It was another French registered vehicle, so naturally I was wary it would pull off, but the middle-aged couple up front did the decent thing, staying put until I arrived, and giving me a lift to a service station three-quarters of the way to Calais. By now it was late afternoon, and as I waited for another ride

I hoped I hadn't missed the last ferry. Twenty minutes later a car driven by a smart-looking man wearing suit trousers and an unbuttoned white work shirt pulled up.

"Where are you going?" he asked through the window.

"Calais."

"Me too, get in."

And with that, I knew I'd done it.

The driver was François, and on our way there I told him of my trip and excitement at surprising Emily when I returned.

"You think it is a good idea to arrive without telling her?"

"Sure, why not?"

"Maybe she is with another man."

Ah, the French.

François took me all the way to the ferry terminal, and after thanking him and posing for a quick photo together, I made my way inside where I bought a foot passenger ticket for, as luck would have it, a ferry that was leaving in the next ten minutes. Approaching the U.K. border control section, I handed over my passport to the British official.

"Just been across for a day trip, Sir?" asked the border guard, looking from my passport to me.

"Hardly," I replied with a smile.

Compared to the Indonesian ferry with its cockroach infested dormitories, and the Kazakh coal train-lugging cargo ship, the ferry to Dover seemed like a luxury cruise, with bars, restaurants, duty free shops, and cafés. I took full advantage of the latter, indulging, as any self-respecting Englishman would, in a delightful cream tea. (For readers from foreign shores, that's a pot of tea, served with scones, strawberry jam, and lashings of clotted cream.)

Lovely.

When I'm in England I'm all too often finding ways and means of leaving the place, but having traveled so far to reach her, I was feeling rather nostalgic for good old "Blighty." Sitting back with my feast by a window seat at the front of the ship, I put some Noel Gallagher magic on my MP3 player, and took it easy, thinking back over my journey which was now very nearly at a close.

It had been an amazing trip, a once in a lifetime hitchhike across three continents and nineteen countries, encompassing four gradually morphing seasons. Summer had been in full glorious swing on departure in Australia, autumn had arrived in southern China, winter in northern China, and spring in Europe. A seemingly endless stretch of road had taken me through barren desert, tropical jungle, towering mountains, vast agricultural lands, and gentle temperate greenery. Wonders man-made and natural had come and gone, but the real highlight of the journey was undoubtedly the people who had drifted in and out of my life on the road. Several times on my long hitch home I had bonded with the strangers who picked me up to such an extent that by the time they dropped me off they parted with the same message: "Jamie, do not forget me." Some I never would, but, after over eight hundred rides, many more had inevitably blurred in my mind, intermingling into a happy collective outpouring of itinerant goodwill. I might not be able to remember them all individually, but I would never forget the gift of having met so many wonderful people from such different backgrounds and with such varied lives, whose generosity in sharing their bike, car, truck, SUV, yacht, food, drink, and home was a blessing I would carry with me always. Culture, nationality, and ethnicity might have changed often and dramatically en route, but a common generosity of spirit and a shared humanity linked so many of the people I had met. Mine, I concluded, was a pretty charmed sort of life, thanks in no small part to the accident of my birth that gave me a British passport. Having traveled through so many poor regions to make it back to Europe, it really hit home just how fortunate I was at having been born in a wealthy part of the world. So many of those I met along the way would never have the opportunity to do what I had just done, which in a sense made it all the more important for me to continue doing such things, to make the most of the opportunities I had been given, and to fight for a life of intensity and rapture.

Hitchhiking is a funny old business really, a dying art in the industrialized West, but one with so much to offer. I'm amazed more people, especially those in monotonous jobs, don't just grab a pack and hit the road. My first foray into hitchhiking came out of financial necessity, a need to get from A to B with little funds to do so. However, I soon discovered that it was, in so many respects, the ultimate way to travel. You might not get first class luxury, but there is no other means of travel that I know of where you do so not only for free, but as a matter of course get to meet and spend time with locals, often experiencing their lifestyle and culture in a real and intimate way—something people seem more and more willing to pay good money to attempt to do on contrived "cultural tourism experiences." With over a billion vehicles in the world, a giant, continuously shifting circuit of adventure and opportunity stretches across the planet that as a hitchhiker you can plug into at any time.

Thirty minutes into the ninety minute ferry ride to England, and I struck up a conversation with two Dutch brothers, Gerrit and Richard, sitting at the table next to mine, who were heading to a funeral in Reading, just outside of London. When I told them about my trip and that I planned to hitch from Dover to London, they offered to take me in their car. With that, my hitchhiking journey was over. Soon after I got my first glimpse of the famous white cliffs of Dover, rising above a gray seascape of the English Channel. By the time we docked and rolled off the ferry it was dusk, pulling off onto the left hand side of the road for the first time since Thailand. God, it felt good to be back. *Classic FM* welcomed me home on the car's stereo as we drove towards London. To reach Reading, Gerrit and Richard needed to skirt around the capital on the M25, but so long as they could leave me near a tube or bus route, then it was good enough for me. Much head scratching followed as to where the best place to leave me was, but in the end it became clear that the only feasible option was Heathrow Airport. So I arrived back in London at the same spot as if I had flown home. Not that I minded; in fact, I rather liked the irony.

Darkness had long since arrived by the time we pulled up outside Heathrow, and as I stepped out of Gerrit and Richard's car onto British soil for the first time in months, I was tired but over the moon to be back: within the hour I would be in my apartment. A quick walk through the bustling airport terminal and I jumped on the tube, riding it to Chalk Farm station, where I checked the balance on my account at an ATM to work out how much the last three and a half months of traveling had cost me: $1,900—food, accommodation, visas, everything.

Not bad, I mused.

I walked the last bit slowly, savoring the spring time blossom hanging from the cherry, pear, and apple trees of my street that I knew so well, breathing in their sweet aromas as a smile stretched across my face. My timing was perfect, Emily would be out at her weekly Salsa class, giving me time to shower, shave and make myself respectable for her return. As I unlocked the door to my apartment a strange realization hit me: I didn't have to go anywhere tomorrow; I could potter around all day, and then do exactly the same thing the following day, and, if I chose, the one after that as well. There would be no struggle to the city's outskirts or the long road ahead; I had finally made it. My nomadic lifestyle would be on hold for a while.

And it was exactly what I needed.

As the water from a steaming shower rained down on my tired body, a deep fatigue washed over me. The two hours of sleep I had grabbed since Serbia was not nearly enough. Bed was calling my name, and it wouldn't be denied. Before crawling beneath its familiar covers, I retrieved a Kazakhstan baseball cap from my pack that I had purchased in Aktau, and placed it outside the bedroom door.

As soon as my head hit the pillow I was out, drifting off into a blissful sleep, broken an hour later by the sound of keys unlocking the front door. I stayed where I was listening as the door was opened, followed by a gasp and then silence.

It was Emily, and she had spotted the hat.

"Are you home?" she asked excitedly through the empty sitting room to our bedroom beyond.

I was. And felt it now.

Notes and References

1. *Iranian Rappers & Persian Porn*. Available in all good book stores, and now in paperback and audio book.
2. Having researched my family tree of late, I know of a fellow Maslin who actually pleaded with a judge for transportation to Australia, as an act of commutation for the only other option available for his crime; a story that according to *The Times* of 17 August, 1838, had a rather sad, although somewhat amusing ending: *George Maslin was indicted for maliciously shooting Mr. Bryan Rumboll with intent to murder him . . . [the judge] Mr. Baron Parke, having put on the black cap, thus addressed the prisoner: "George Maslin, the crime of which you have been found guilty, and justly found guilty—for your own conscience tells you that you have committed it—upon a patient investigation of your case, in which there are so many circumstances against you, that no reasonable doubt can be entertained that it is one of so deep a moral dye, and shows as much disregard to your religious duties as if you were guilty of the crime of murder itself . . . " The awful sentence of death was then pronounced upon him... The prisoner was taken from the bar apparently unmoved, but the learned judge cried bitterly.* See *The Times* (17 August, 1838) for initial report, and *The Times* (27 August, 1838) for follow up in which George Maslin appeals to have his death sentence commuted to transportation to the colonies—without success.
3. Figure cited in *Time Magazine*, McCarthy, Terry, (02 October, 2011): www.time.com/time/magazine/article/0,9171,998067-1,00.html

4. Ibid

5. *Bringing Them Home: Report of the National Inquiry into the Separation of Aboriginal and Torres Strait Islander Children from Their Families,* April 1997: www.humanrights.gov.au/social_justice/bth_report/report/index.html

6. *Time Magazine,* McCarthy, Terry, (02 October, 2011): www.time.com/time/magazine/article/0,9171,998067-1,00.html

   Disgustingly, the mass theft of Aboriginal children is not a crime confined to history but one that continues today, often under the guise of welfare issues related to poverty and inequality. As John Pilger reports: In 2012 the co-ordinator general of remote services for the Northern Territory, Olga Havnen, was sacked when she revealed that almost A$80m (£44m) was spent on the surveillance and removal of Aboriginal children compared with only A$500,000 (£275,000) on supporting the same impoverished families. For more on this repugnant story see: www.informationclearinghouse.info/article38034.htm; and the film Utopia by John Pilger. Watch this film. It will shock you.

7. Figure cited in *The New Statesman,* Pilger, John, (12 May, 2011): www.newstatesman.com/australasia/2011/05/pilger-australia-rights

8. Ibid.

9. Ibid.

10. Yes, that's right. I do mean that Germany, France, Spain, Portugal, Italy, The United Kingdom, Ireland, Switzerland, The Netherlands, The Czech Republic, Austria, Belgium, Croatia, Cyprus, Andorra, Poland, Slovakia, Hungary, Slovenia, Bosnia & Herzegovina, Serbia, Albania, Greece, Macedonia, Bulgaria, Romania, Ukraine, Belarus, Lithuania, Latvia, Luxembourg, Lichtenstein, Monaco, Estonia, Finland, Sweden, Norway, Iceland, Denmark, Moldova, the Vatican City, Montenegro, San Marino and Malta, as well as the small section of Turkey that falls within continental Europe would all fit in with ample leftovers. I have included Cyprus and Iceland to the list above although they are not, in a purely geographical sense, within Europe. Strictly speaking, small sections of Kazakhstan, Georgia, and Azerbaijan are also classed as falling within the European continent. I have left these off the above list as they are generally considered Asian countries. However, it would make no difference if these small sections were included, they would still all fit into Australia with the other countries listed. Figures for land area in square miles taken from *Encyclopedia Britannica.*

11. Figures cited in *Financial Times* for market values and prices at 30 March, 2012: www.media.ft.com/cms/a81f853e-ca80-11e1-89f8-00144feabdc0.pdf.

12. Based on profit figures of $31 billion cited in *The Guardian,* Goodley, Simon, (24 August, 2011): www.guardian.co.uk/business/2011/aug/24/bhp-makes-big-profits-but-sound-a-warning , compared to data for other countries taken from *IMF World Economic Outlook Database*: http://goo.gl/acz4K

13. If the information I found out online about the man who ripped me off is anything to go by, then I'm far from his only victim.
See: www.vendingmachinesaustralia.blogspot.co.uk/2009/03/new-business-vending-machines.html; www.naturalvending-machinesaustralia.blogspot.co.uk/2010/03/paul-davies-and-adam-boman.html; www.fumingmad.blogspot.co.uk/2011/06/magazine-vending-headache.html; www.scam.com/blog.php?b=9004& goto=prev (among other sites).

14. A *Secret Country, The Coup*, Pilger, John (1992), London Vintage.

15. See report, *Senate Select Committee on a Certain Maritime Incident*: http://goo.gl/y1rk6 ; and *Report of Independent Assessor to Senate Select Committee on a Certain Maritime Incident: http://goo.gl/Crp9q*

16. Ibid.

17. Ibid.

18. See Australian Broadcasting Corporation article: www.abc.net.au/news/2011-07-07/former-sas-commander-breaks-silence-on-tampa/2785164

19. See Australian Broadcasting Corporation documentary film, *Leaky Boat*: www.youtube.com/watch?v=3c_phJsx1NE&feature=related

20. www.canismajor.de/reports/rep047.html

21. It is interesting to note that despite the widespread hysteria in Australia surrounding asylum seekers entering the country by boat—and the massive political capital gained from being seen to take a hard line stance against them—they actually comprise less than 2% of Australia's annual immigration. Figure cited in *The Guardian*, Rourke Alison, (15 December 2010): www.guardian.co.uk/world/2010/dec/15/asylum-australia-christmas-island

22. *Inside Indonesia*, Warren, Carol, (Edition 54 April-June 1998): www.insideindonesia.org/feature-editions/whose-tourism-balinese-fight-back. See also *The Politics of Environment in Southeast Asia*, Hirsch, Philip, (1998), New York, Routledge, reference 26, page 257

23. *The Politics of Environment in Southeast Asia*, Hirsch, Philip, (1998), New York, Routledge, page 246

24. *Danish Journal of Geography 2005, Community mapping, local planning and alternative land use strategies in Bali*, Warren, Carol, (2005), page 31. See also: *Bali Post*, 22/11/04.

25. Ibid.

26. *The Politics of Environment in Southeast Asia*, Hirsch, Philip, (1998), New York, Routledge, page 244.

27. *Inside Indonesia*, Warren, Carol, (Edition 54 April-June 1998): www.insideindonesia.org/feature-editions/whose-tourism-balinese-fight-back

28. Central intelligence Agency, Directorate of Intelligence, *Intelligence Report*: *Indonesia 1965, The Coup That Backfired*, Langley: CIA, 1968. See also *San Francisco Examiner*, May 20, 1990; *Washington Post*, May 21, 1990.

29. *The New Rulers of the World*, Pilger, John, (2002), London, Verso, page 36.

30. *The Disappearing Fear of Neutralism*, Hagen, Bernhard, (2007), Norderstedt, GRIN Verlag, page 5.

31. *Portrait of a Cold Warrior*, Smith, Joseph Burkholder, (1976), New York, G.P. Putnam's Sons, page 205.

32. Comments of F. Tomlinson of the British Foreign Office, cited in *Unpeople*, Curtis, Mark, (2004) London, Vintage, page 191. Foreign Office document: FO371/135849 (11 March 1958).

33. *The Ambiguities of Power: British Foreign Policy since 1945*, Curtis, Mark, (1995) London, Zed Books, page 57.

34. *The Invisible Government*, Wise, Denis, and Ross, Thomas, (1965) New York, RandomHouse, page 148.

35. *The Army and Politics in Indonesia*, Crouch, Harold, (1997) Ithaca, Cornell University Press, page 155 and 351.

36. *Portrait of a Cold Warrior*, Smith, Joseph Burkholder, (1976), New York, G.P. Putnam's Sons, page 228-9.

37. Mentioned in a memo from Allen Dulles to the White House, which briefly summarizes main points of the U.S. intervention, (7 April 1961), *Declassified Documents Reference System*, Arlington, released 18 December 1974.

38. *Killing Hope: U.S. Military & C.I.A. Interventions since World War II*, Blum, William, (2004) London, Zed Books, page 102.

39. *Unpeople*, Curtis, Mark, (2004) London, Vintage, page 194.

40. Comments of D. MacDermot, cited in *Unpeople*, Curtis, Mark, (2004) London, Vintage, page 191. Foreign Office document: *Annual report for the year 1958*, 12 January 1959, FO371/144065.

41. Comments of Sir Robert Scott to Foreign Office, cited in *Unpeople*, Curtis, Mark, (2004) London, Vintage, page 192. Foreign Office document, 12 December 1957, FO371/129531

42. *Killing Hope: U.S. Military & C.I.A. Interventions since World War II*, Blum, William, (2004) London, Zed Books, page 102.

43. Ibid.

44. *Unpeople*, Curtis, Mark, (2004) London, Vintage, page 194.

45. *Feet to the Fire, CIA Covert Operations, 1957-1958*, Conboy, Kenneth J, and Morrison, James, (1999) Annapolis, Naval Institute Press, page 115.

46. *Unpeople*, Curtis, Mark, (2004), London, Vintage, page 194.

47. *Legacy of Ashes: The History of the CIA*, Weiner, Tim, (2008), London, Penguin, page 175.

48. *Unpeople*, Curtis, Mark, (2004) London, Vintage, page 194.

49. *Subversion as Foreign Policy: The Secret Eisenhower and Dulles Debacle in Indonesia*, Kahin, Audrey R, and Kahin, George McT, (1997), New York, New

Press, page 134,148. See also *President's Secret Wars*, Prados, John, (1996) Chicago, Ivan R Dee, page 144.

50. *Killing Hope: U.S. Military & C.I.A. Interventions since World War II*, Blum, William, (2004) London, Zed Books, page 103.

51. *The Invisible Government*, Wise, David, and Ross, Thomas, (1965) New York, Random House, page 145.

52. *Legacy of Ashes: The History of the CIA*, Weiner, Tim, (2008), London, Penguin, page 175 and 177.

53. *The Times*, (August 8, 1986); cited in *Britain's Secret Propaganda War 1948-1977*, Lashmar, Paul, and Oliver, James, (1998), London, Sutton, page 4.

54. *Killing Hope: U.S. Military & C.I.A. Interventions since World War II*, Blum, William, (2004) London, Zed Books, page 197. Full quote cited is by Neville Maxwell, Senior Research Officer, Institute of Commonwealth Studies, Oxford: "A few years ago I was researching in Pakistan into the diplomatic background of the 1965 Indo-Pakistan conflict, and in foreign ministry papers to which I had been given access came across a letter to the then foreign minister, Mr. Bhutto, from one of his ambassadors in Europe (I believe Mr. J.A. Rahim, in Paris) reporting a conversation with a Dutch intelligence officer with NATO. According to my note of that letter, the officer had remarked to the Pakistani diplomat that Indonesia was 'ready to fall into the Western lap like a rotten apple'. Western intelligence agencies, he said, would organize a 'premature communist coup . . . [which would be] foredoomed to fail, providing a legitimate and welcome opportunity to the army to crush the communists and make Sukarno a prisoner of the army's goodwill'. The ambassador's report was dated December 1964." Blum notes in *Killing Hope*: "It should be remembered that Indonesia had been a colony of the Netherlands, and the Dutch still had some special links to the country."

55. *Remaking Asia: Essays on the American Uses of Power*, Selden, Mark, (1974), New York, Pantheon, page 47 and 48.

56. *Confronting the Third World*, Kolko, Gabriel, (1998), New York, Pantheon, page 181.

57. Figure cited in Unpeople, Curtis, Mark, (2004), London, Vintage, page 313 and 362. See also *Killing Hope: U.S. Military & C.I.A. Interventions since World War II*, Blum, William, (2004) London, Zed Books, page 193 and 420, which cites "various Amnesty International reports on Indonesia published in the 1970s."

58. *San Francisco Examiner*, Kadane, Kathy, (May 20, 1990): www.namebase.org/kadane.html. See also *Washington Post*, (May 21, 1990).

59. Ibid.

60. Ibid.

61. *New York Times*, (July 19, 1966); cited in *The New Rulers of the World*, Pilger, John, (2002), London, Verso, page 35.

62. U.S. National Archives, RG 59 Records of Department of State: cable no. 868, ref: Embtel 852, October 5, 1965; cited in *The New Rulers of the World*, Pilger, John, (2002), London, Verso, page 33.

63. Letter from Andrew Gilchrist to EH Peck, head of the South-East Asia Division at the Foreign Office, October 5, 1965; cited in *The New Rulers of the World*, Pilger, John, (2002), London, Verso, page 33/34.

64. *The New Rulers of the World*, Pilger, John, (2002), London, Verso, page 41. For more on the conference see *Power in Motion: Capital Mobility and the Indonesian State*, Winters, Jeffrey Alan, (1996), New York, Cornell University Press.

65. *Ramparts, The Berkeley Mafia and the Indonesian Massacre*, Ranson, David, (4 October 1970), Volume 9, Number 4.

66. World Bank, Confidential Assessment Corrupted Bank Funds: Summary of RSI staff views regarding the problem of 'leakage' from World Bank project budgets, Jakarta, August 1997.

67. Jubilee Debt Campaign: www.jubileedebtcampaign.org.uk/Indonesia+2792. twl

68. *A debt for Development Swap with Indonesia*, A policy paper by Jubilee Australia April, (2007), page 6.

69. Figure cited in *The New Rulers of the World*, Pilger, John, (2002), London, Verso, page 17.

70. *A debt for Development Swap with Indonesia*, A policy paper by Jubilee Australia April, (2007), page 6.

71. Ibid, page 5. Paper states: Indonesia spent 7.9% of GDP on debt repayments as compared to 1.1% on health and 0.9% education. Human Development Indicators, 2006 Human Development Report.

72. Ibid, page 5 and page 6.

73. *Los Angeles Times*, (15 June 1991), page 10. Figure cited from Amnesty International, who, by 1989, estimated that Indonesian troops had killed 200,000 people out of a population of between 600,000 and 700,000.

74. *Distant Voices*, Pilger, John, (1992), London, Vintage, page 233.

75. Ibid, page 267. Interview conducted by Pilger with wife of murdered reporter Greg Shackleton: "Shirley Shackleton has also spoken to eye-witnesses. 'What happened', she said, 'was that most of them were strung up by their feet, their sexual organs were removed and stuffed into their mouths, and they were stabbed with the short throwing knives that the Indonesian soldiers carry. Nobody knows for sure whether they choked to death or whether they choked on their own blood, or whether they just died from their wounds or whether they bled to death.'"

76. *The Guardian*, Pilger, John, (Tuesday 21 September 1999): www.guardian.co.uk/world/1999/sep/21/easttimor.unitednations

77. *Distant Voices*, Pilger, John, (1992), London, Vintage, page 253

78. Ibid, page 68.

79. Interview with the *Australian Broadcasting Corporation*, (February 9, 1991), cited by *Indonesian News*, (February 1991), Volume 19, No. 2.

80. *The Guardian*, (Monday 25 January 1999): www.guardian.co.uk/theguardian/1999/jan/25/features11.g29

81. *Indonesia's Forgotten War: The Hidden History of East Timor*, Taylor, John G., (1991)London, Zed Books, page 64.

82. Interview in documentary film, *The Trials of Henry Kissinger*: www.youtube.com/watch?v=2bFOhAAYfqk

83. Ibid. See also *If You Leave Us Here We Will Die*, Robinson, Geoffrey, (2009), New Jersey, Princeton University Press, page 59 and page 60.

84. *The Nation*, Hitchens, Christopher, (18 February, 2002): www.thenation.com/article/kissingers-green-light-suharto

85. Remember that British understatement a moment ago?

86. Not a euphemism.

87. Figure cited in *The Guardian*, Chambers, Andrew, (6 July 2012): www.guardian.co.uk/global-development/poverty-matters/2012/jul/06/landmines-toll-civilians-laos-bombs. See also National Regulatory Authority report, *National Survey of UXO Victims and Accidents*, Boddington, Michael AB, and Chanthavongsa, Bountao, (2010): http://goo.gl/XO0T8

88. Congressional Record, (18 July 1973), page 24520-22.

89. *Killing Hope: U.S. Military & C.I.A. Interventions since World War II*, Blum, William, (2004) London, Zed Books, page 144.

90. National Regulatory Authority report, *National Survey of UXO Victims and Accidents*, Boddington, Michael AB, and Chanthavongsa, Bountao, (2010): http://goo.gl/XO0T8

91. *New York Times*, (18 May 1958), IV, page 7. Cited in *Killing Hope: U.S. Military & C.I.A. Interventions since World War II*, Blum, William, (2004) London, Zed Books, page 411.

92. *Manufacturing Consent: The Political Economy of the Mass Media*, Chomsky, Noam, and Herman, Edward S, (1994), London, Vintage, page 254.

93. Testimony before the House Subcommittee on Foreign Operations and Monetary Affairs, Committee on Government Operations, Hearing on US Aid Operations in Laos, (May-June 1959); see also *New York Times*, (20 January 1961), page 2, and *Washington Post*, (10 April 1966) for statements of Laotian Prime Minister Souvanna Phouma re U.S. opposition to a coalition or neutralist government; cited in *Killing Hope: U.S. Military & C.I.A. Interventions since World War II*, Blum, William, (2004) London, Zed Books, page 411. See also *Manufacturing Consent: The Political Economy of the Mass*

Media, Chomsky, Noam, and Herman, Edward S, (1994), London, Vintage, page 253.

94. From congressional hearings cited in *Manufacturing Consent: The Political Economy of the Mass Media,* Chomsky, Noam, and Herman, Edward S, (1994), London, Vintage, page 254. See also *The Pentagon Papers and U.S. involvement in Laos,* in *Pentagon Papers, Senator Gravel edition,* Haney, Walter (1972) Boston, Beacon Press, vol. 5.

95. *To Move a Nation,* Hilsman, Roger, (1967), New York, Delta, page 111, and page 112.

96. *New York Times,* (20 January 1961) page 2. See also *Washington Post,* (10 April 1966).

97. *Killing Hope: U.S. Military & C.I.A. Interventions since World War II,* Blum, William, (2004) London, Zed Books, page 141.

98. *A Thousand Days: John F. Kennedy in the White House,* Schlesinger, Arthur, (1965), Boston, Mariner Books, page 326.

99. *Manufacturing Consent: The Political Economy of the Mass Media,* Chomsky, Noam, and Herman, Edward S, (1994), London, Vintage, page 254.

100. *A Thousand Days: John F. Kennedy in the White House,* Schlesinger, Arthur, (1965), Boston, Mariner Books, page 325.

101. *New York Times,* (25 January 1958), page 6; *New York Times* (25 February), page 6; cited in *Killing Hope: U.S. Military & C.I.A. Interventions since World War II,* Blum, William, (2004) London, Zed Books, page 141.

102. *Killing Hope: U.S. Military & C.I.A. Interventions since World War II,* Blum, William, (2004) London, Zed Books, page 141.

103. *Voices from the Plain of Jars,* Branfman, Fred, (1972), New York, Harper Colophon Books, page 15.

104. *Manufacturing Consent: The Political Economy of the Mass Media,* Chomsky, Noam, and Herman, Edward S, (1994), London, Vintage, page 254.

105. Ibid.

106. *Killing Hope: U.S. Military & C.I.A. Interventions since World War II,* Blum, William, (2004) London, Zed Books, page 142; cited references: *The Politics of Heroin in Southeast Asia,* McCoy, Alfred W, (1972), New York, Harper & Row; *The Politics of Heroin: CIA Complicity in the Global Drug Trade,* McCoy, Alfred W, (1991), New York, Lawrence Hill Books; *The Great Heroin Coup: Drugs, Intelligence,* and *International Fascism,* Krugar, Henrik, (1981), Montreal, Black Rose Books; *Air America,* Robbins, Christopher, (1979), New York, Avon Books; Testimony of Daniel Oleksiw, USIA, before U.S. Senate committee on Foreign Relations, *Hearing on US Security Agreements and Commitments Abroad: Kingdom of Laos,* October 1969, page 586, and page 587.

107. Ibid.

108. Ibid.

109. Ibid. See also, *New York Times,* (26 October 1969) page 1; documentary Film, *The Most Secret Place on Earth: The C.I.A.'s Covert War on Laos*, Eberle, Marc, (2008): www.marceberle.com/the-most-secret-place-on-earth/

110. San Francisco Chronicle, (25 July 1973).

111. *Air America*, Robbins, Christopher, (1979), New York, Avon Books, chapters 5 and 8.

112. Branfman, Fred, from *The C.I.A. File,* Borosage, Robert L, Marks, John D, (1976), New York, Grossman Publishers.

113. *Killing Hope: U.S. Military & C.I.A. Interventions since World War II,* Blum, William, (2004) London, Zed Books, page 142.

114. *Manufacturing Consent: The Political Economy of the Mass Media,* Chomsky, Noam, and Herman, Edward S, (1994), London, Vintage, page 254.

115. *A Thousand Days: John F. Kennedy in the White House,* Schlesinger, Arthur, (1965), Boston, Mariner Books, page 329. See also *Confronting Vietnam: Soviet Policy Towards the Indochina Conflict, 1954-1963,* Gaiduk, Ilya, (2003), Stanford University Press, page 148.

116. *New York Times,* (3 May 1964), page 1; *New York Times,* (7 May 1964), page 7; *New York Times* (14 May), page 11. Cited in *Killing Hope: U.S. Military & C.I.A. Interventions since World War II,* Blum, William, (2004) London, Zed Books, page 144.

117. BBC News: www.news.bbc.co.uk/1/hi/1100842.stm

118. See documentary Film, *The Most Secret Place on Earth: The C.I.A.'s Covert War on Laos*, Eberle, Marc, (2008): www.marceberle.com/the-most-secret-place-on-earth/

119. *Manufacturing Consent: The Political Economy of the Mass Media,* Chomsky, Noam, and Herman, Edward S, (1994), London, Vintage, page 254.

120. Ibid, and page 255.

121. *Voices from the Plain of Jars,* Branfman, Fred, (1972), New York, Harper Colophon Books, page 5.

122. See documentary Film, *The Most Secret Place on Earth: The C.I.A.'s Covert War on Laos*, Eberle, Marc, (2008): www.marceberle.com/the-most-secret-place-on-earth/

123. Cited in *Manufacturing Consent: The Political Economy of the Mass Media,* Chomsky, Noam, and Herman, Edward S, (1994), London, Vintage, page 255.

124. Ibid.

125. Ibid, page 257. See also *At War With Asia: Essays on Indochina,* Chomsky, Noam, (2004), Oakland, Aka Press, page 70.

126. *Far Eastern Economic Review,* (16 April 1970), page 73.

127. *Rogue States: The Rule of Force in World Affairs,* Chomsky, Noam, (2000), Cambridge, South End Press, page 42.

128. The cave of Tham Piu, cited in documentary Film, *The Most Secret Place on Earth: The C.I.A.'s Covert War on Laos*, Eberle, Marc, (2008): www.marceberle.com/the-most-secret-place-on-earth/

129. *The Guardian* (14 October 1971), page 4.

130. See documentary Film, *The Most Secret Place on Earth: The C.I.A.'s Covert War on Laos*, Eberle, Marc, (2008): www.marceberle.com/the-most-secret-place-on-earth/

131. *Refugee And Civilian War Casualty Problems in Indochina*, Staff Report for the Subcommittee on Refugees and Escapees, U.S. Senate, (28 September, 1970).

132. *New York Times*, (24 August, 1975). Cited in *Manufacturing Consent: The Political Economy of the Mass Media*, Chomsky, Noam, and Herman, Edward S, (1994), London, Vintage, page 382.

133. *The Guardian*, (Friday 10 December 2010): www.guardian.co.uk/media/2010/dec/10/war-media-propaganda-iraq-lies

134. Interview with Elizabeth Omara-Otunna: www.advance.uconn.edu/2004/041108/04110803.htm

135. Cited in *The Backroom Boys*, Chomsky, Noam, (1973), London, Fontanna, page 23.

136. Salon, Goose, Steve, and Docherty, Bonnie, (June 8, 2012): www.salon.com/2012/06/08/white_phosphorous_the_new_napalm/

137. *The New Rulers of the World*, Pilger, John, (2002), London, Verso, page 104. See also, *Heroes*, Pilger, John, (1987), London, Pan, page 234, and page 235.

138. Ibid.

139. Mines Advisory Group: www.maginternational.org/

140. Ibid.

141. *The Guardian*, Chambers, Andrew, (Friday 6 July 2012): www.guardian.co.uk/global-development/poverty-matters/2012/jul/06/landmines-toll-civilians-laos-bombs

142. Landmine and Cluster Munition Monitor: www.the-monitor.org/index.php/cp/display/region_profiles/theme/1935

143. Handicap International: www.handicap-international.org.uk/what_we_do/landmines_cluster_munitions/

144. The New Statesman, (09 April, 1999): www.newstatesman.com/node/134515

145. *New York Times*, (23 February 1973), page 1.

146. Election results from *New York Times*, (18 May 1958), page 7. See also *Killing Hope: U.S. Military & C.I.A. Interventions since World War II*, Blum, William, (2004) London, ZedBooks, page 140.

147. Figure cited in documentary film, *The Trials of Henry Kissinger*: www.youtube.com/watch?v=2bFOhAAYfqk . Figure of 600,000 cited in *Lying For Empire: How to Commit War Crimes With a Straight Face*, Model, David, (2005),

Monroe, Common Courage Press, page 140. Figure of up to 500,000 cited by PBS's *Frontline World*.

148. On 2 May, 1973, the C.I.A Directorate of Operations reported: "They [the Khmer Rouge] are using damage caused by B52 strikes as the main theme of their propaganda ... This approach has resulted in the successful recruitment of ... young men ... Residents ... say that the propaganda campaign has been effective with refugees in areas ... that have been subject to B52 strikes." Cited in *The Pol Pot Regime: Race, Power and Genocide in Cambodia under the Khmer Rouge, 1975-1979*, Kiernan, Ben, (2008), Yale University Press, page 22. See also *The New Statesman, How Thatcher Gave Pol Pot a Hand*, (17 April 2000): www.newstatesman.com/node/137397

149. *The New Statesman, How Thatcher Gave Pol Pot a Hand*," (17 April 2000): www.newstatesman.com/node/137397 . See also, *Heroes*, Pilger, John, (1987), London, Pan, Chapters 34, 35 and 36; *Distant Voices*, Pilger, John, (1992), London, Vintage, Chapter 9; documentary film *Cambodia Year Ten:* www.johnpilger.com/videos/cambodia-year-ten, documentary film *Cambodia Year Ten (update):* www.johnpilger.com/videos/cambodia-year-ten-update-, documentary film *Cambodia the Betrayal:* www.johnpilger.com/videos/cambodia-the-betrayal; documentary film *Return to year Zero:* www.johnpilger.com/videos/cambodia-return-to-year-zero. For more on Cambodia in general see *Year Zero: The Silent Death of Cambodia*: www.johnpilger.com/videos/year-zero-the-silent-death-of-cambodia, *Cambodia: Year One:* www.johnpilger.com/videos/cambodia-year-one

150. Ibid.

151. Ibid.

152. Testimony before the U.S. Senate Armed Services Committee, *Hearings on Fiscal Year 1972 Authoritarians*, (22 July 1971), page 4289.

153. Interview in Film, *The Most Secret Place on Earth: The C.I.A.'s Covert War on Laos*,Eberle, Marc, (2008): www.marceberle.com/the-most-secret-place-on-earth/

154. U.S. Congress, *The United States Security Agreements and Commitments Abroad: Kingdom of Laos*, page 484. See also, *Information Clearinghouse, The Executive Branch of the U.S. Government. Worlds Most Evil and Lawless Institution?* (28 June 2013): www.informationclearinghouse.info/article35432.htm; *Voices from the Plain of Jars: Life Under An Air War* (2nd expanded edition), Branfman, Fred, (2013); University of Wisconsin Press, page 36.

155. *New York Times*, 23 February 1973, page. 1. Cited in *Killing Hope: U.S. Military & C.I.A. Interventions since World War II*, Blum, William, (2004) London, Zed Books, page 145.

156. Subject to certain contractual stipulations;-)

157. www.youtube.com/watch?v=yBDL9jlUzFM

158. *The Russia You Never Met,* Bivens, Matt, and Bernstein, Jonas, informally circulated English version; Russian version was published in Demokratizatziya (1999), English version available online: http://goo.gl/UDRLC. See also BBC documentary film *The Trap: We Will Force You To Be Free,* (2007) www.youtube.com/watch?v=LFjCJFsbS0U (36minutes in). For general explanation and study of "Shock Therapy" globally see *The Shock Doctrine,* Klein, Naomi, (2007), New York, Metropolitan Books.

159. Ibid.

160. Ibid.

161. Ibid.

162. Ibid.

163. *The Guardian,* Harding, Luke, (8 April 2010): www.guardian.co.uk/world/2010/apr/08/kyrgyzstan-revolt-over-kurmanbek-bakiyev

164. Ibid.

165. BBC News, (17 June, 2010): www.bbc.co.uk/news/10341348

166. The *Organization for Security and Co-operation in Europe* diplomatically condemned the election as "falling short of key standards."

167. See U.S. Department of Defense Base structure report: www.defense.gov/pubs/BSR_2007_Baseline.pdf & *Base Politics: Democratic Change and the U.S. military Overseas,* Cooley, Alexander, (2008), Ithaca, Cornell University Press.

168. The Guardian, Mathews, Jackie Dewe, (27 March, 2010): www.guardian.co.uk/world/2010/mar/27/kyrgyzstan-kidnapped-brides-photo-essay

169. *The Telegraph,* Kilner, James, (29 Nov, 2011): www.telegraph.co.uk/news/worldnews/asia/kyrgyzstan/8922962/Kyrgyzstan-starts-anti-bride-kidnapping-campaign.html

170. *The Telegraph,* Lewis, Jason, (19 Oct, 2011): www.telegraph.co.uk/news/politics/tony-blair/8857689/Oil-rich-dictator-of-Kazakhstan-recruits-Tony-Blair-to-help-win-Nobel-peace-prize.html

171. Oasis at Knebworth, and very good it was too.

172. *Extremes Along the Silk Road,* Middleton, Nick, (2005), London, John Murray, page 243.

173. These include cancers, gastritis, typhoid, hepatitis, dysentery, paratyphoid, anaemia, heart disease and respiratory conditions such as tuberculosis. See Ibid, page 173. See also *Dying and Dead Seas: Climatic Verses Anthropic Causes,* Nihoul, Jacques C. J., Zavialov, Peter O., Micklin Philip P., (2004) Dordrecht, Kluwer Academic Publishers, page 107.

174. See report by United Nations Environmental Programme: www.unep.or.jp/ietc/publications/techpublications/TechPub-4/izumi2-5.asp

175. *Central Asia Lonely Planet,* Mayhew, Bradley, Plunkett, Richard, and Richmond, Simon, (1996), London, Lonely Planet Publications, page 41.

176. See report by UN Office for the Coordination of Humanitarian Affairs: www.irinnews.org/InDepthMain.aspx?InDepthId=13&ReportId=60534

177. *Central Asia Lonely Planet*, Mayhew, Bradley, Plunkett, Richard, and Richmond, Simon, (1996), London, Lonely Planet Publications, page 41. See also BBC News: www.news.bbc.co.uk/1/hi/world/asia-pacific/678898. stm

178. See report by UN Office for the Coordination of Humanitarian Affairs: www.irinnews.org/printreport.aspx?reportid=17839

179. See report by UN Office for the Coordination of Humanitarian Affairs: www.irinnews.org/printreport.aspx?reportid=17839

180. *Scientific American*, Micklin, Philip, and Aladin Nikolay V., (17 March, 2008): www.scientificamerican.com/article.cfm?id=reclaiming-the-aral-sea. For full article see: www.cis.uchicago.edu/outreach/summerinstitute/2010/documents/sti2010-micklin-reclaiming-the-aral-sea.pdf

181. *National Geographic*, Walters, Pat, (2 April, 2010): www.news.nationalgeographic.co.uk/news/2010/04/100402-aral-sea-story/

182. *Central Asia Lonely Planet*, Mayhew, Bradley, Plunkett, Richard, and Richmond, Simon, (1996), London, Lonely Planet Publications, page 41.

183. Ibid, page 42

184. *Extremes Along the Silk Road*, Middleton, Nick, (2005), London, John Murray, page 232. See also *Dying and Dead Seas: Climatic Verses Anthropic Causes*, Nihoul, Jacques C. J., Zavialov, Peter O., Micklin Philip P., (2004) Dordrecht, Kluwer Academic Publishers, page107.

185. *The Economist*, (8 July 1999): www.economist.com/node/220659

186. *Extremes Along the Silk Road*, Middleton, Nick, (2005), London, John Murray, page 259.

187. Ibid, page 258, and page 259.

188. *Dying and Dead Seas: Climatic Verses Anthropic Causes*, Nihoul, Jacques C. J., Zavialov, Peter O., Micklin Philip P., (2004) Dordrecht, Kluwer Academic Publishers, page 104.

189. Interview between Amy Goodman and Col. Sam Gardiner, discussing Russia's threat to respond with tactical nuclear weapons to any United States use of precision conventional weapons against Russian troops: www.informationclearinghouse.info/article20492.htm

190. *Forbes*, Miniter, Richard, (9 Sept, 2011): www.forbes.com/sites/richardminiter/2011/09/09/should-george-soros-be-allowed-to-buy-u-s-foreign-policy/

191. *Anti Empire Report*, Blum, William (5 Sept 2008): www.killinghope.org/bblum6/aer61.htm

192. Information Clearing House, Margolis, Eric, (19 Aug, 2008): www.informationclearinghouse.info/article20556.htm

193. *The Guardian*, (13 November 2006): www.guardian.co.uk/world/2006/nov/13/russia.georgia

194. Although the vast majority of mainstream media reports at the time of the Georgian invasion focused instead on Russia's response, this BBC piece, broadcast, nearly three months afterwards, makes clear who attacked first and investigates allegations that Georgia committed war crimes: www.news.bbc.co.uk/1/hi/programmes/newsnight/review/7695956.stm

195. Information Clearing House, Margolis, Eric, (19 Aug, 2008): www.informationclearinghouse.info/article20556.htm

196. A nice example of this (as cited by William Blum) is the *Chicago Tribune* (28 Aug 2008), who referred to "Russia's invasion of Georgia," and "Russia's invasion of South Ossetia" without a single mention that it was Georgia who invaded South Ossetia. See also *Washington Post* (31 Aug, 2008) for more of the same.

197. National Public Radio, (15 Aug, 2008).

198. *Anti Empire Report,* Blum, William (5 Sept 2008): www.killinghope.org/bblum6/aer61.htm

199. Interview on CNN with Wolf Blitzer (10 August 2008).